Crusader Castle

Crusader Castle

The Desert Fortress of Kerak

Michael S. Fulton

Pen & Sword
MILITARY

First published in Great Britain in 2024 by
Pen & Sword Military
An imprint of Pen & Sword Books Limited
Yorkshire – Philadelphia

Copyright © Michael S. Fulton 2024

ISBN 978 1 39909 126 8

A CIP catalogue record for this book is
available from the British Library.

Typeset by Mac Style
Printed in the UK by CPI Group (UK) Ltd, Croydon, CR0 4YY.

Pen & Sword Books Limited incorporates the imprints of After
the Battle, Atlas, Archaeology, Aviation, Discovery, Family History,
Fiction, History, Maritime, Military, Military Classics, Politics,
Select, Transport, True Crime, Air World, Frontline Publishing, Leo
Cooper, Remember When, Seaforth Publishing, The Praetorian Press,
Wharncliffe Local History, Wharncliffe Transport, Wharncliffe True
Crime and White Owl.

For a complete list of Pen & Sword titles please contact

PEN & SWORD BOOKS LIMITED
47 Church Street, Barnsley, South Yorkshire, S70 2AS, England
E-mail: enquiries@pen-and-sword.co.uk
Website: www.pen-and-sword.co.uk
or
PEN AND SWORD BOOKS
1950 Lawrence Rd, Havertown, PA 19083, USA
E-mail: Uspen-and-sword@casematepublishers.com
Website: www.penandswordbooks.com

For

Lucas, Alexander and Nathan
Charli and Tessa

Contents

Preface

Kerak is a castle that has impressed visitors for centuries. Whether it is the first castle you explore or simply the most recent one, its size and state of preservation tend to leave an impression. The aim of this book is to provide a bit of something for everyone, from those with a casual interest in castles, the crusades or the medieval Near East, to established scholars who are fortunate enough to make a career out of studying such things.

A few words on names seems appropriate as this study spans a millennium of history and incorporates a diverse range of actors. In most instances, the personal names of Latin Europeans have been anglicized (e.g. 'John of Tiberias'). Muslim names have been transliterated using a common Arabic form; however, the names of many figures from the Ottoman period have been provided according to their common English spelling (e.g. 'Faisal ibn Hussein', rather than 'Faysal ibn Husayn'). Likewise, the title of 'sheik' has been spelled as such it applies to late Ottoman figures, but not in those instances where earlier Mamluk individuals took this as part of their name (e.g. 'Sheik Yusuf al-Majaly' and 'Shaykh al-Mahmudi'). The spelling of 'Kerak', rather than 'Karak', has similarly been chosen due to the popularity of the former in general scholarship.

Geographical terms also warrant some clarification. In most instances, 'Syria' refers to Bilad al-Sham or 'greater Syria'. This region is bound by the borders of Egypt and the Arabian Desert to the south, Anatolia to the north, the Mediterranean Sea to the west, and the Euphrates River to the east. 'Palestine' denotes the area west of the Great Rift (in this region this consists of the Jordan Valley, the Dead Sea and Wadi 'Araba) between the Lebanon to the north and the Sinai Desert to the south. 'Transjordan' identifies the area east of the Great Rift between 'Aqaba in the south and the Zarqa River in the north, fading into the desert to the east.

Finally, thanks and acknowledgements are in order. My first trip to the castle, in 2010, was made possible by Marla MacKinnon, Rachel Rabey, Fraser Reed and Victoria Wijnbergen, my weekend travel companions and fellow excavators that summer. In the years since, Robin Brown and Marcus Milwright have both been extremely kind in offering me some very helpful advice, without which this project may have never left the ground. Denys Pringle, whose guidance over the years has been transformative, and Steve Tibble, a great friend and colleague, have each reviewed large parts of the manuscript, which is much improved thanks to their suggestions and corrections. Micaela Sinibaldi has also been gracious enough to provide some targeted feedback in light of her own research. Heather Crowley's very generous help, which has taken innumerable forms over the past decade, has also been invaluable. The fabulous aerial photographs of the castle come from the Aerial Photographic Archive for Archaeology in the Middle East (APAAME). My thanks to David Kennedy, Bob Bewley and the rest of their team for allowing me to share these. Finally, I owe a great debt of gratitude to my family for their ongoing and seemingly limitless support. It is my hope that my nieces and nephews, to whom this book is dedicated, are able to pursue their passions in life as I have mine.

M.S.F.
Toronto, Canada
Christmas 2022

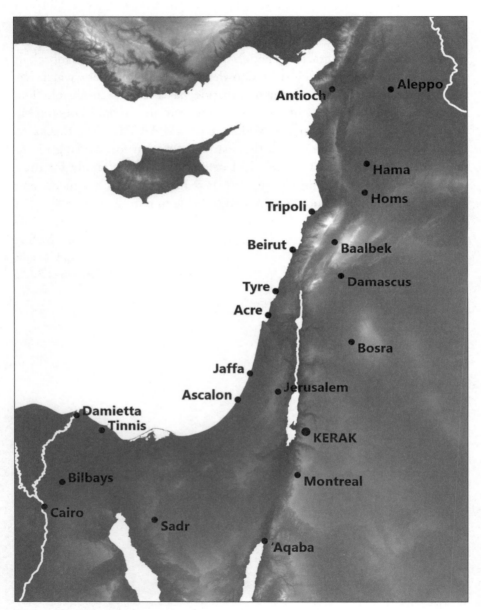

Map 1. The Near East.

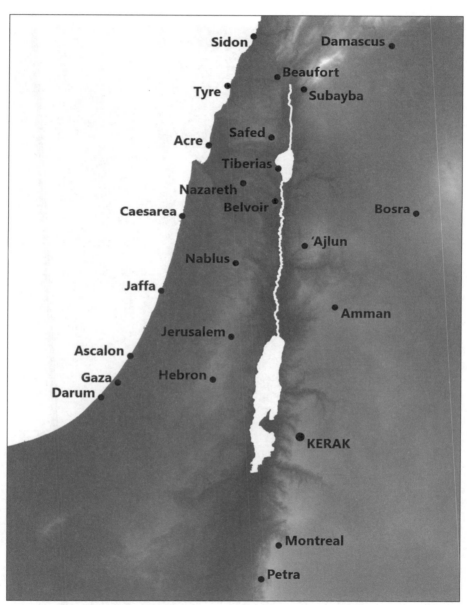

Map 2. Palestine and northern Transjordan.

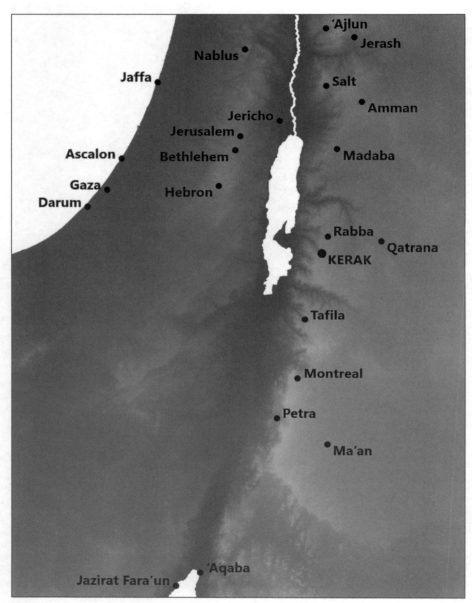

Map 3. Transjordan and southern Palestine.

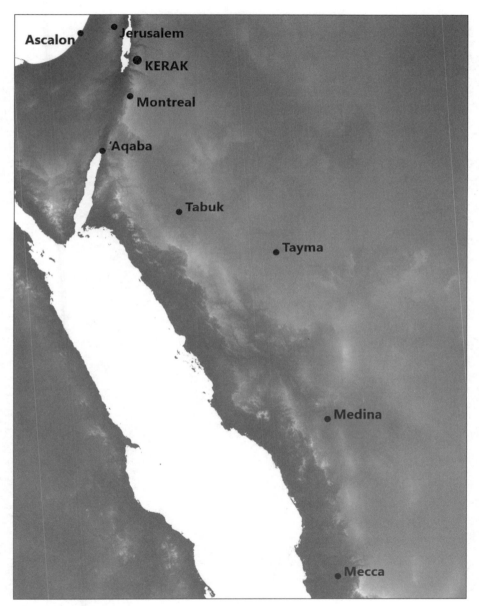

Map 4. The Hijaz.

Introduction

In the southern part of Syria, that depending particularly on Jerusalem, very few castles have been preserved. Later occupation is responsible for the destruction of most, but there are some, beyond the Dead Sea, still standing tolerably perfect, but quite undescribed. Rey has published a plan and description of Kerak in the Desert, but neither is his own work: indeed Kerak has never been studied by a medievalist. It has been hailed by Rey, and Professor Oman following him, as an untouched example of Latin military architecture. This claim seems a little dangerous, when it is remembered that Kerak was a Byzantine fortress before it became Crusader, and that after this it was the seat of a powerful Arab principality, and that finally Beibars's presence is shown by his name on one of the towers. It may well be that the share of Payn of Nablous in the building of it is infinitesimal. At least, until there is better material to work upon, elaborate deductions from it as to the state of Latin military architecture in 1140 are quite out of place.[1]

T.E. Lawrence (of Arabia) (undergraduate thesis, 1910)

A half-decade before the outbreak of the First World War and the Arab Revolt that followed, T.E. Lawrence travelled through the Levant as an intrepid undergraduate in 1909, visiting many of the great castles of Syria. He had undertaken the trip in support of a thesis that compared European fortifications with those built in the Near East during the period of the crusades. In a fitting example of the Levant's long history of conflict, and the importance of Transjordan in the broader region, Lawrence was prevented from visiting Kerak thanks to the disruptive efforts of some Bedouin, who had torn up a section of the Hijaz Railway near Amman. Although our understanding of the castle has improved since Lawrence composed his thesis, his words nevertheless continue to ring true; many scholars and countless tourists have visited Kerak over the past century, yet the great stronghold still awaits comprehensive study and excavation.

The mighty castle that dominates the town of Kerak (*al-Karak*) is the largest in the modern state of Jordan. In a region that has been occupied and contested for millennia, the castle is a fairly new addition to the landscape, dating back close to 900 years. It was commissioned around 1142 by a Latin noble, Pagan the Butler, and would continue to develop under Frankish rule over the following decades. From the time it was built, Kerak became the seat of power of the largest crusader lordship in the region, a lordship that would grow to become one of the kingdom of Jerusalem's most important and prestigious by the late twelfth century. Frankish dominance over much of southern Syria ended following Saladin's great victory at the Battle of Hattin in July 1187. The garrison of Kerak surrendered the following year, ending the first chapter of the castle's history, and less than fifty years of Frankish rule.

Saladin died in 1193 and his realm was divided between members of his family, the Ayyubids. Kerak remained the regional seat of power in Transjordan. Although never more than a secondary power centre, the castle's rulers were able to exert relative independence at times, exploiting rifts between the more powerful figures who controlled Cairo and Damascus. Ayyubid authority eventually gave way to that of the Mamluks, who rose to power in Egypt in the 1250s and extended their influence across Syria in the wake of the brief Mongol incursion into the Levant in 1260. Kerak, one of the last outposts of independent Ayyubid authority, fell to the Mamluks in 1263.

Although Kerak continued to thrive as a regional power centre under early Mamluk rule, its significance had peaked by the early fourteenth century, and the political importance and economic prosperity of Transjordan declined thereafter. The process of marginalization continued with the Ottoman conquest of Syria in 1516 and Egypt the following year. Under Ottoman rule, Transjordan became a distant frontier from Constantinople, allowing local tribal groups to dominate the region's affairs. The Ottomans firmly reasserted their authority in Transjordan in the 1890s, stationing a garrison and local official in Kerak, but this era of renewed interest was short-lived, ending with the collapse of Ottoman power during the First World War. Along with the rest of modern Jordan, Kerak subsequently passed under the authority of the Hashemites, in whose name the nation continues to be governed.

Sources

Thanks to the importance that Kerak held at various times, it was often mentioned by historical commentators. William of Tyre (d. c.1184), archbishop of Tyre and chancellor of the kingdom of Jerusalem, began composing a history of the Latin principalities during the reign of King Amalric. Although William is the best source from a Frankish perspective, his entries relating to actions in Transjordan are often generic and seem confused in places. It is unfortunate that William appears not to have visited the region, unlike Fulcher of Chartres (d. c.1130), chaplain to King Baldwin I and author of a history of the First Crusade and the early Frankish presence in the Levant. To

William's narrative history can be added a number of contemporary charters, which document the presence and grants of the Frankish lords of Kerak and other figures associated with the lordship.

Following Saladin's rise to power in Egypt in 1169, and his subsequent domination of Muslim Syria from 1174, his campaigns against Kerak were documented by his celebratory biographers, 'Imad al-Din al-Isfahani (d. 1201) and Baha' al-Din ibn Shaddad (d. 1324), both of whom enjoyed prominent positions in Saladin's administration. To these Arabic accounts can be added the letters composed by Saladin's chief administrator in Egypt, al-Qadi al-Fadil (d. 1200) and the comprehensive history penned by Ibn al-Athir (d. 1233). The latter, who was based in Mosul and served the Zankid dynasty, a branch of which Saladin overthrew in Syria, owed no loyalty to Saladin. Ibn al-Athir's account extends into the early Ayyubid period, as does the composite history assembled by Abu Shama (d. 1267) and certain Old French continuations of William of Tyre's history. Ibn Wasil (d. 1298) was another important man of letters in the thirteenth century. His higher education included a brief residency at Kerak in the mid-1230s, following which he enjoyed a career travelling around the Near East in the highest Ayyubid and later Mamluk circles. Some noteworthy details are also to be found in a couple of important Coptic sources, namely the *History of the Patriarchs* and the narrative history composed by al-Makin ibn al-Adim (d. 1273).

The rise of the Mamluks ushered in a new generation of contemporary historians. Ibn 'Abd al-Zahir (d. 1293) served in the Mamluk chancery and wrote influential biographies of Sultans Baybars and Qalawun. These works pair well with those authored by two Mamluk emirs, Baybars al-Mansuri (d. 1325), a mamluk of Qalawun and governor of Kerak from 1286 to 1291, and Abu'l-Fida' (d. 1331), who held Hama from 1310 and passed through Kerak on a number of occasions. Further details and insights into later events surrounding Kerak can be found in the celebrated works of figures such as Ibn al-Furat (d. 1405), al-Maqrizi (d. 1442) and Ibn Taghribirdi (d. 1470), to name only a few. In addition to these narratives, the accounts of certain pilgrims provide snapshots of Kerak as they passed by the castle. These include the German pilgrim Thietmar, who ventured through Transjordan on his way to Sinai in 1218, and the famed Maghribi traveller Ibn Battuta, who passed along the *hajj* route from Damascus while making his way to Mecca in 1326.

As the importance of Kerak waned from the end of the Mamluk period, it appears less frequently in written records. Early Ottoman references to the castle are rare, limited mostly to census data gathered during the sixteenth century, before such efforts ceased. Not until the nineteenth century were more descriptive accounts of the castle published. These were composed by Western visitors, among the first in centuries, who were drawn by the mysteries and ancient history of the region. The modern, or Western, study of Kerak can be traced back to this collection of nineteenth-century adventurers, geographers and antiquarians.

Ulrich Jasper Seetzen, a German explorer, travelled from Damascus to Acre during the winter and spring of 1806, passing through the Balqa' and south of the Dead Sea. His route brought him to Kerak, where he stayed from 24 March until 2 April. The next reported visitor, John Lewis Burckhardt, was a Swiss traveller who undertook a journey from Aleppo to Cairo on behalf of the English African Association. Burckhardt, who travelled incognito like Seetzen, spent twenty days at Kerak, longer than he would have liked, from the middle of July 1812. Six years later, Royal Navy officers Charles Leonard Irby and James Mangles spent a week in Kerak in May 1818, near the end of an extensive tour of Egypt and Syria that had begun two years earlier. Prior to their visit, they were joined by William MacMichael, who accompanied their party from Jerusalem to Kerak and onwards to Petra, the site all were most interested in. Sir Henry Layard, an Englishman, arrived in early 1840, having ventured northwards from Petra with intentions of continuing onwards to Jerash. William F. Lynch, leading an American expedition to explore the Dead Sea from the water, made a brief visit to Kerak in May 1848, staying less than twenty-four hours. Similarly interested in the region around the Dead Sea, Félicien de Saulcy, a French antiquarian, spent two nights in Kerak in January 1851.

The first expedition with the primary objective of examining the castle of Kerak was undertaken in 1866 by architect Christophe Mauss and diplomat Henry Sauvaire. They spent a fortnight in the town in April before heading onwards to inspect the castle of Montreal to the south. This venture was part of a broader investigative effort in the Levant initiated by Honoré Théodoric d'Albert, duc de Luynes, whose visit to Kerak two years earlier had impressed on him the value of sending others to conduct a closer examination of the castle and fortified town. In August 1868, Frederick Klein passed through Kerak on his first trip east of the Dead Sea. Klein was a missionary and biblical explorer who had for a long time been a resident of Palestine. Four years later, he returned as a member of a party that also included well-travelled English cleric and naturalist Henry Baker Tristram. In November 1876, Charles Doughty, an English writer and adventurer, accompanied the *hajj* pilgrimage south from Damascus and visited Kerak for an apparent second time along the way. A pause of sorts followed until March 1890, when it was confirmed to John Gray Hill and his wife, Caroline, that they were the first European travellers to pass through Kerak since Doughty. The Hills, also from England, had settled on a visit to Kerak and Madaba as a consolation when their plan to visit Petra was interrupted by a local conflict around Wadi Musa – their visit to Kerak would not be an enjoyable one.

In 1865, a year after Luynes had started his investigations, the Palestine Exploration Fund (PEF) was established in London. The PEF would coordinate a number of expeditions over the following years, though the first east of the Dead Sea was not undertaken until 1881–82. This was led by British officer Claude Reignier Conder, who famously surveyed Palestine with Herbert (later Lord) Kitchener in the 1870s. Conder made his way through the region north of Kerak until he was forced to cut short his efforts, without having visited the castle.

The imposition of direct Ottoman rule throughout Transjordan, and the stability that accompanied this, saw a surge of visitors to Kerak thereafter. Frederick Jones Bliss, a Lebanese-born American archaeologist with the PEF, spent four nights there in March 1895. The Hills, still hoping to get to Petra, returned to Kerak only weeks later; they were frustrated to learn that the road south was still firmly closed to travellers, but it was not long until the route opened. Six months later, Charles Alexander Hornstein, a native of Jerusalem, born to parents who had emigrated from Europe, spent about five days at Kerak and took a number of photographs before proceeding south to Petra. Theodore Edward Dowling, an Anglican priest and historian of the Eastern Churches, visited the following year. Hill, Hornstein and Dowling, like Klein before them, all published their experiences with the PEF. In August 1896, Czech-born Alois Musil made his first trip to Kerak, in the early part of what would be an extensive career studying and travelling throughout the Arab world.

Marie-Joseph Lagrange, a Dominican priest originally from France but based in Jerusalem, reached Kerak in October 1896. So many Westerners had published accounts of their visits to the castle by this time that Lagrange felt it unnecessary to recount his own journey. Like many others at that time, he passed through Kerak on his way to Petra, where he would record more valuable observations. The first visit to Palestine by Lucien Gautier, a Swiss theologian, corresponded with Ottoman efforts to impose direct rule over Transjordan in 1893–94, leading to a ban on travel to Kerak and the frustration of Gautier's hopes of journeying around the Dead Sea. Six years later, Gautier was able to realize his dream and found his way to Kerak in March 1899, where the local *mutasarrif* was surprised to learn that he planned to go north, rather than make the trip south to Petra like most others. By the time William Libbey and Franklin E. Hoskins arrived in early 1902, Kerak had become something of a tourist attraction for scholars and antiquarians based in Jerusalem, and a regular stop on one of the routes to Petra, where most scholarly attention in Transjordan remained. Not until the arrival of the eminent French medievalist Paul Deschamps in 1929 would Kerak receive the kind of devoted attention that it had been afforded by Mauss and Sauvaire more than six decades earlier.[2]

Academic Scholarship

While increasing numbers of European travellers were visiting Kerak, a parallel group of scholars was beginning to take a closer look at the historical material relating to the castle. E.G. Rey's *Étude sur les monuments de l'architecture militaire des croisés* (1871) is perhaps the first modern study of medieval fortifications in the Levant. Although Rey did not visit Kerak, he had access to the notes made by Mauss, as well as Mauss's plan of the site. Looking beyond just the narrative accounts, Rey attempted to use charter evidence to identify locations associated with the broader Frankish lordship administered from the castle. His later 'Seigneurs de Mont-Réal' (1898) provides a brief history of the lords of Transjordan, which was not included in his earlier discussion of the castle. By the time this appeared, however, a similar study, *Seigneurs du Crac de Montréal* (1883), had already been published by the distinguished medievalist Louis de Mas Latrie.

Deschamps, assisted by architect François Anus, was the first to bring together the history of Kerak and a first-hand appreciation of the site. His study of Kerak, including a survey, appears in the second volume, *La défense du Royaume de Jérusalem*, of his magnum opus, *Les Château des Croisés en Terre-Sainte* (1939), which is dedicated to the strongholds located in what was once the Latin kingdom of Jerusalem. Although much of Deschamps' work has been developed and improved upon over the decades, no scholar, before or since, has yet equalled the contribution he made to advancing a scholarly understanding of the castle. The influence of his study is readily apparent in many popular and influential works on so-called crusader castles, including Wolfgang Müller-Wiener's *Burgen der Kreuzritter* (*Castles of the Crusaders*) (1966) and Hugh Kennedy's *Crusader Castles* (1994).

The first archaeological excavations in the castle were carried out by Robin Brown in 1987. Although these efforts were limited to a probe dug in the southern palatial complex, the results, published in 1989 and revised in 2013, have established an important benchmark. Prior to Brown's excavations, Denys Pringle had conducted investigations in 1981 and 1983. Pringle was most interested in the castle's church and those found in the town, which he surveyed, publishing his findings in the first volume of his exemplary *Churches of the Crusader Kingdom of Jerusalem* (1993). Since Deschamps published his study, the only attempt to provide comprehensive original architectural observations of the castle was carried out by Thomas Biller, Daniel Burger and Hans-Heinrich Häffner in 1998. Although they did not have enough time to take detailed measurements, and their investigations were limited to the upper ward of the castle, the results they published, 'Neues zu den Burgen' (1999), provide a valuable update and encourage further study. Beyond the walls of the castle, the efforts of other archaeologists, such as Jeremy Johns and Bethany Walker, have led to considerable advances in our appreciation of the broader region, including changes in settlement and consumption patterns.

Kerak has also continued to attract the interest of historians. In *Monarchy and Lordships* (1989), Steve Tibble was one of the first to look beyond the rather simple histories of the lordship of Transjordan put forward by Mas Latrie and Rey. By far the most detailed study of the lordship, however, was published a year later by Hans Eberhard Mayer, the pre-eminent historian of twelfth-century Latin charter evidence. Mayer's *Die Kreuzfahrerherrschaft Montréal* (1990) complements a series of studies he produced examining the principal lordships of the kingdom of Jerusalem. Although most work on Kerak continues to focus on the period when the castle was under Frankish control, efforts by figures like Joseph Drory have helped shed increasing light on its history over the following century.

The declining importance of Kerak during the late Mamluk and most of the Ottoman period saw the castle receive less notice by contemporary commentators, and modern historians as a result. Renewed scholarly interest accompanies the reappearance of source material from the nineteenth century. Peter Gubser devoted his doctoral research, which included a trip to Kerak in 1968, to an examination of the town in the period following its reappearance in records of the later Ottoman era, subsequently published as *Politics and Change in al-Karak, Jordan* (1973). A generation later, Eugene Rogan's *Frontiers of the State in the Late Ottoman Empire* (1999), which similarly built on his PhD dissertation, has helped to fit Kerak into the broader fabric of Transjordan in the late nineteenth and early twentieth centuries.

The most comprehensive study of Kerak currently available is Marcus Milwright's *Fortress of the Raven* (2014). The ultimate result of his PhD work, Milwright provides a history of the castle, showing a clear effort to represent the different phases of occupation evenly, as the backdrop for his original examination of ceramic evidence from the site. This has helped to better situate the stronghold in the context of the surrounding landscape, particularly during the Ayyubid and Mamluk periods. Micaela Sinibaldi's ongoing analysis of twelfth-century pottery discovered in the broader region, similarly building on her PhD studies, promises to provide an invaluable complement, while her initial contextualization of the Frankish lordship, in 'The Crusader Lordship of Transjordan' (2022), pushes back against the still prevalent notion that Frankish Transjordan was a remote frontier. Since the 1980s, a group of Italian scholars, led by Guido Vannini, has investigated the Frankish outpost of al-Wu'ayra, near Petra, and has more recently conducted excavations at the castle of Montreal, between Petra and Kerak. The first notable study focusing on Kerak to come out of this broader project has been published by Lorenzo Fragai. Building on Brown's work, his 'Mamluk Qa'a at Kerak Castle' (2019) has explored certain notable internal structures, contributing to a better appreciation of the development of the castle during the Ayyubid and Mamluk periods.

Although Kerak has attracted the interest of visitors and scholars for centuries, the stronghold continues to withhold many secrets. What follows is an attempt to collate and present what is known about the castle, particularly its history. As it is assumed most readers will be interested primarily in the Frankish period, a conspicuous emphasis has been placed on the twelfth century. Looking forward, it is hoped that this book will be the first part of a larger project, with the ultimate goal of helping us better understand this magnificent structure. With an eye to this, certain foundations will be provided for: better appreciating the political and social significance that the castle has held at different times; more accurately understanding the development of the standing architecture; and discerning what life may have been like for those who lived in and around this great fortress over the centuries.

Chapter 1

Transjordan before the Crusades

The burden of Moab. Because in the night Ar of Moab is laid waste, and brought
to silence; because in the night Kir of Moab is laid waste, and brought to silence;
Isaiah 15:1 (KJV)

Kerak, like innumerable other places in the Near East, has been a site of
human congregation and interaction for thousands of years. Although
large enough to warrant mention in the Old Testament of the Bible, it
was not until the Middle Ages that Kerak became the dominant community
in the area. Only with the arrival of the Franks and the construction of the
great castle, however, does the town appear with any regularity in historical
records.

Situated about 1,000m above sea level, Kerak is positioned roughly midway
along the western side of a limestone plateau, Ard al-Karak. To the north and
south, the plateau is defined by Wadi al-Mujib and Wadi al-Hasa respectively.
These valleys cleave the landscape, dividing up Transjordan and separating
what was once the centre of Moab from the Balqa' to the north and ancient
Edom to the south. To the west of the Kerak plateau, the ground falls away to
the salty shores of the Dead Sea, more than 400m below sea level, and Wadi
'Araba (the portion of the Great Rift between the Gulf of 'Aqaba and the Dead
Sea). To the east, the ground slopes gradually into the Syrian Desert. Along the
western side of the plateau, which receives the most annual rainfall, the soil is
rich but shallow. The karst landscape provides a number of springs, which flow
out into the wadis (valleys) from between the limestone layers of the bedrock.
Traditionally, the region's people also relied heavily on cisterns to collect water
during the limited winter rains for use in the dry summer months.[1]

The old town of Kerak is surrounded by wadis that cut into the landscape
as it begins to break apart and fall away to the Dead Sea. These valleys collect
to the west of the town, forming Wadi al-Karak, which provides a natural
path down to Wadi 'Araba. The rise on which the town sits is the northern
extension of a spur, the remainder, a height called Umm al-Thalj ('mother of
snow'), overlooks the town from beyond a dip in the landscape to the south.

Looking northwest from the site of the castle, at the southern end of the town, the southern part of the Dead Sea can be seen through Wadi al-Karak, with Jerusalem visible in the distance on a clear day.[2]

Today, the dry landscape around Kerak appears almost barren to most who visit the castle in the hot summer months. Earlier in the year, however, following the winter rains, things are much greener, and particularly fertile parts of the wadi hint at the region's former productivity. In the early fourteenth century, Abu'l-Fida', the scholarly prince of Hama, described the valley below Kerak as having 'a *hammam*, and many gardens with excellent fruits, such as apricots, pears, pomegranates, and others'.[3] John Lewis Burckhardt, who visited the region in the early nineteenth century, remarked that the district to the north of the town was quite fertile and large tracts of it were cultivated by the people of Kerak. Much as Abu'l-Fida' had five centuries earlier, Burckhardt observed that a number of springs sprouted in the wadis to the north and west of the town; these facilitated the cultivation of some vegetables and many olive trees.[4] When Charles Leonard Irby and James Mangles reached Kerak a few years later, in May 1818, approaching the town from the valley to the west, they encountered fields of grain with grazing cattle. As they neared the foot of the town hill, they found that a stream still flowed into the valley, and along its bank was a strip of garden, 'in which we observed olives, pomegranates, and figs, with some vegetables'. Gardens containing olive, pomegranate and fig trees, as well as vines, were similarly noted by subsequent nineteenth-century travellers.[5] Some springs can still be found today, betrayed by the often green vegetation around them, which stands out in what is otherwise a fairly dry landscape in the summer.

References to Kerak are rare before the 1140s, when the Franks began work on the great castle that now dominates the town, but there is plenty of evidence of earlier human settlement. Pottery remains indicate the presence of people stretching back to the chalcolithic period, around 4000 BC; however, this does not mean that the site was occupied continuously throughout the year.[6] Gubser has suggested that it was during the early Iron Age, around 1000 BC, when the region was part of the kingdom of Moab, that Kerak was first permanently settled.[7] The town's name appears to come from the Moabite *qir*, and Aramaic *karkha*, both referring to a fortified town.[8] In the second century BC, the region was dominated by the Nabataeans, who ruled a great mercantile kingdom from their capital of Petra. Kerak would have benefitted from the north–south flow of Nabataean trade east of the Great Rift, along what was known as the King's Highway. The Romans began exerting their influence in the region from the first century BC, and formally annexed Transjordan near the start of the second century AD, during the reign of

Trajan. The Romans further developed the main north–south road, renaming it the *via nova Traiana*, in honour of the emperor.

As the western half of the Roman Empire collapsed in the fifth century, Kerak remained a part of the eastern, more Greek component – what historians have come to call the Byzantine Empire. Following the legalization of Christianity in the early fourth century, the empire was formally divided into diocese. In the mid-fifth century, the bishop of Jerusalem was elevated to the standing of a patriarch, to whom reported the archbishops of Caesarea, Scythopolis (Bethsan) and Petra (Wadi Musa). Kerak, known then as Χαραχμωαβ ('Charachmoab'), became a part of Palaestina Tertia, the metropolitan of which was the archbishop of Petra. A bishop of Kerak appears to have become the seat of a diocese by 536, when a bishop of Charachmoba is noted to have attended the synod held in Jerusalem that year.[9]

In the Church of St George in Madaba, the town, identified as '[Char]achmob[a]' (or Karak of Moab), is found on the famous sixth-century mosaic Madaba Map. It appears as a walled town, though it is debatable to what degree this might represent an actual depiction of the settlement at that time versus a more general stylistic representation. Kerak is also one of the seven cities of Transjordan depicted in the eighth-century mosaics of the church of St Stephen in Umm al-Rasas. It is labelled 'Charach Moba', and is again presented as a walled town.[10] Although the evidence is far from conclusive, these representations of Kerak suggest that the town was walled in the late Byzantine period; likewise, its inclusion in these church decorations indicate that it was of noticeable size, some regional importance, and that it almost certainly had a considerable Christian population.

In 629, the Battle of Mu'ta, part of the Muslim wars of expansion, was fought about 10km south of Kerak. Although this was a reversal for the Muslims, Arab forces nevertheless overwhelmed the Byzantine Levant in the years that followed, bringing Kerak under Muslim rule. There is little to indicate a change in Kerak's significance around this time, though the town would have benefited as the *hajj* (the annual pilgrimage to Mecca) became institutionalized: Muslim pilgrims from Syria would pass through Thaniyya, just east of Kerak, on their way to the holy cities of the Hijaz. Trade, meanwhile, continued to flow along the Roman road, still commonly called the King's Highway, which connected Damascus and Syria to the north with 'Aqaba (Bib. Elath, Rom. Ayala) and Egypt and Arabia beyond. Kerak remained a waypoint along this thoroughfare, while a secondary route broke off to the west, descending into Wadi 'Araba. This connected Kerak with the communities around the south end of the Dead Sea and trade routes that led onwards to Hebron, Jerusalem and Gaza.[11]

There are few mentions of Kerak dating to the early Islamic period. Among the exceptions to the general silence is the moment when the town was captured by the Fatimids. Having conquered Egypt from their base in North Africa in 969, the Fatimids continued their push eastward into Syria, occupying Kerak in 982–83.[12] Over the following century, various parties vied for control of the southern Levant. In addition to the Fatimids, these included local Arab groups, the Abbasids of the Middle East, the Seljuk Turks, following their subjugation of the Abbasids in the eleventh century, and even the wishful Byzantines, who would at times reoccupy parts of Syria, though never Transjordan. Ibn Shaddad, the thirteenth-century geographer and historian, struggled to find references to Kerak dating to this period:

> I myself found no mention of the place in the books of history that I have studied which were written in the early days of Islam, nor in works of geography. I continued my search until I was told by a reliable authority that Kerak had been a Christian monastery. The bedouin had been in the habit of abducting the monks who lived there; but the monks built it up and fortified it, and they went on doing this, expanding and fortifying the place until it became a fortress.[13]

This account of the origins of the castle is uncorroborated, as no evidence has yet been found of a monastery dating to this period; however, it speaks to the later strength of the site and the town's significant Christian population during the early Islamic period. Regardless of what Kerak looked like at the time, it would have been shaken by the earthquake felt across Palestine in 1068.[14]

Archaeologically, the early Islamic period has typically been cast as one of decline in the southern Levant. Surveys of the Kerak Plateau, beginning with that of Jeremy Johns, have shown a dramatic drop in the number of occupied sites following the shift to Muslim rule, from around seventy identified sites associated with Byzantine settlement to just six in the early Islamic period (five of these being associated with the pilgrim route). Issues reconciling this decline in the material culture, which does not suggest any significant recovery until the Ayyubid period (from the late twelfth century), with the historical evidence, has led many archaeologists to express caution and urge further investigation into the methodology of these surveys and the diagnostic criteria used to date the ceramics.[15] Aside from these general trends, the relative importance of Kerak in the region appears to have increased as power dynamics changed in the tenth and eleventh centuries, leading to the decline of certain traditional centres of authority, such as Rabba to the northeast.[16]

While Kerak became the main population centre of its plateau, there appears to have been little to distinguish it from other sites of a similar size in the broader region. The town probably owed its relative size and significance to its position along the main north–south trade route east of Wadi 'Araba, at the node where this was joined by those routes leading south of the Dead Sea to southern Palestine. It was not until the Franks arrived, however, that Kerak would be elevated from a local power centre to a regional one.

Chapter 2

Frankish Period

A certain nobleman, named Pagan – who had been the king's butler and later held Transjordan [the land across the Jordan] after Roman of Puy and his son, Ralph, as rewards for their sins, were disinherited and alienated from it – constructed a castle in the frontier of Arabia Secunda, which was named Kerak. It was strongly fortified by both the nature of the place and the work of hands.[1]

William of Tyre (d. c.1184)

In 1096, armed contingents from various parts of Latin Europe set out for the Near East in a movement now known as the First Crusade. The main group congregated at Constantinople before crossing into Anatolia in the spring of 1097. Following a series of surprising victories, due in large part to existing divisions between the various Muslim rulers of the region, the surviving core of this force reached Palestine and captured Jerusalem after a month-long siege in the summer of 1099. The holy city would become the capital of the crusader kingdom of Jerusalem; to the north, participants of the First Crusade had already established the foundations of two other principalities: the county of Edessa and principality of Antioch. A few years later, a fourth would emerge: the county of Tripoli. The Latin-Catholic Europeans who settled in the Levant were known to their Muslim neighbours as Franks, a term that was embraced to at least some degree by the ethnically European population.

The earliest recorded Frankish foray east of the Jordan River, which runs through the Great Rift north of the Dead Sea, took place during the short reign of Jerusalem's first Latin ruler, Godfrey of Bouillon. According to Albert of Aachen, a contemporary European historian of the First Crusade and the initial two decades of Frankish rule in the Levant, Godfrey joined Tancred, the first lord of Galilee, and together they led a raiding party into the territory of Damascus. Following this expedition, Tancred undertook regular raids east of the Jordan from his base at Tiberias, on the western shore of the Sea of Galilee. When the Damascenes sought a peace agreement, Tancred is said to have demanded the surrender of Damascus in exchange – the degree to which this anecdote is accurate is debatable, but Damascus would not at this time, nor ever, fall under Frankish rule. Regardless, Tancred quickly attempted to exert his hegemony east of the Jordan and by 1101 was formally laying claim to some of these lands.[2]

Godfrey died in the summer of 1100, and was ultimately succeeded by Baldwin I, his younger brother. Baldwin had established the county of Edessa, which he bestowed on one of his cousins in order to take the throne of Jerusalem. Following his arrival in Palestine, Baldwin wasted little time before probing the southern frontiers of his new kingdom. These actions were recorded in the history composed by Fulcher of Chartres, Baldwin's chaplain, who accompanied the king on this expedition.

At the head of a small force, Baldwin first travelled towards the coastal town of Ascalon. Finding this to be a prosperous region, the Franks raided those areas under Muslim control. During these activities, the king and his party are said to have held conversations with certain locals, from whom they learned about the broader cultivated and desert regions. This persuaded the Franks to go to Arabia – this is Arabia in the Roman sense, those areas south and east of Palestine. Baldwin and his party moved through the Judean hills, passing Hebron, and came to the Dead Sea, where most of the local Muslims fled ahead of them. They made their way around the south end of the Dead Sea, where Fulcher notes that delicious dates were found but little else, before ascending the hills on the eastern side. The villages they came across in Transjordan were abandoned before their arrival. It seems the Franks were exploring south of Wadi al-Hasa, and thus did not encounter Kerak as they continued southward. Fulcher claims they eventually reached Wadi Musa, where Moses had struck the rock producing a fountain (Numbers 20:1–11). He describes this as a productive place and notes that the lush stream powered mills. Finding only desert beyond the valley, the Franks ventured no further. After three days of rest in Wadi Musa, the king and his party began their return trip, via the south end of the Dead Sea and Bethlehem. The Franks reached Jerusalem on the winter solstice, and Baldwin's coronation took place a few days later back in Bethlehem, on Christmas day.[3]

Over the following years, the military resources of the kingdom of Jerusalem were directed to gaining control of the ports along the Palestinian coast and strengthening the Franks' position vis-à-vis Damascus to the northeast. Contemporary Frankish sources emphasize that the kingdom's fighting capacity was limited at this time: Ralph of Caen noted that barely 200 knights had remained in Palestine after the First Crusade; Fulcher of Chartres placed the number of knights at 300 in 1101, complemented by a similar number of foot soldiers.[4] In this context, Transjordan was not an immediate military priority; instead, it was a region of potential, which the king may have considered exploiting at a later date. As Schick has quite accurately highlighted,

Baldwin's expedition in 1100 confirmed to the Franks that neither Damascus nor Cairo had a recognizable military presence in the region.[5] For the moment, however, Baldwin directed his attention and resources elsewhere.

Baldwin I was drawn back to Transjordan in February 1107, from which point he took a greater interest in the region. According to the contemporary Damascene historian Ibn al-Qalanisi, Tughtakin, the ruler of Damascus, had granted Transjordan, consisting of Wadi Musa, al-Sharat, Moab, al-Jibal and the Balqa', to a certain Turkmen emir named Isfahbad. Albert of Aachen noted the force that subsequently moved into Transjordan numbered 3,000, and that their aim was to establish a stronghold in Wadi Musa and inhibit the actions of subjects of the Frankish king. Both sources provide vague suggestions that Frankish influence had by this point reached Wadi Musa. Rather than a settlement or military presence, for which there are no indications, this early influence appears to have been primarily economic – the Franks might have been attempting to tax these people, while the change of regime in Jerusalem may have provided a new market for goods produced as far south as Petra. To prevent a potential Muslim military presence in the region, Baldwin, having been informed of the movement of the Turkmen force by a Syrian Christian, led a reported force of 500 men to intercept it. Whereas the Muslims were assisted by some Arabs of the region, presumably Bedouin, the Franks enjoyed the support of the local Christians and their priest, who acted as their guide to the Muslim camp. The Franks took the Muslim army by surprise, putting it to flight. The Arabs who had supported the Turkmen force similarly scattered; some of those who attempted to hide in caves were smoked out. The retribution dealt out against the local Muslims was most likely meant to strengthen the resident Christian community; nevertheless, around sixty of these Syrian Christians are said to have returned to Palestine with the Franks for fear of reprisals by their Muslim neighbours.[6]

When recounting the return of the Frankish expedition, Albert of Aachen described the sharing of the booty that had been collected, which he notes took place once Baldwin and his party reached the Jordan; following this, the king went up to Jerusalem two days later. The wording may suggest that the Franks had travelled through Transjordan on their return, to the east of the Dead Sea and around its northern end, rather than follow the route that had been taken to the south and west in 1100. Although he was quite well informed of events in the Levant, Albert is perhaps not the most reliable source for such specifics, considering he was in Europe at this time. If, however, such an eastern route was taken, it is quite likely that the Franks would have followed the King's Highway, past Kerak.

Transjordan was very much a wilderness for European Christians at this time. Daniel the Abbot, a Russian pilgrim who visited the Holy Land around 1107, echoed many of the descriptive remarks provided by Fulcher of Chartres and Albert of Aachen. He noted the dangers of the road from Jerusalem down to Jericho and the Jordan, as well as those for travellers through the Judean hills to the south of Jerusalem.[7] Southern Palestine, let alone Transjordan, was not yet a safe place for Frankish travellers, due to what can be classified as local brigandage. Baldwin I, however, appears to have become increasingly interested in the affairs of the region. In August 1108, while besieging the coastal town of Sidon, the king sent a force to attack a caravan moving through Transjordan. This party, which reportedly consisted of 200 cavalry and 500 infantry, was led by William, the illegitimate son of Duke Robert of Normandy. From a Frankish perspective, this foray was successful, as considerable loot was seized and it was said that the few who escaped were captured by local Bedouin.[8]

The increasing power and influence of the Franks is evident in a peace that was concluded between Damascus and Jerusalem in 1109. The agreement outlined the sharing of certain districts east of the Jordan, notably the Sawad, east of the Sea of Galilee and the upper section of the Jordan, and Jabal 'Awf, the mountainous region east of the lower Jordan between the Yarmuk and Zarqa Rivers, north of the Balqa'. The accord was renewed in 1111 and al-Jabaniyya was added to the shared regions, while Frankish authority over the lands of the Banu al-Jarra was also recognized.[9] Transjordan, to the south of the Zarqa, was not included in any of these agreements, leaving it unclear to what degree the region fell under the influence of Jerusalem or Damascus.

In the spring of 1112, having just given up an unsuccessful attempt to take Tyre, Baldwin headed to Transjordan once more. Having learned that a wealthy caravan was heading from Syria to Egypt, he assembled a small force, reportedly 200 cavalry and 100 infantry, and successfully intercepted the caravan. As Milwright and others have observed, the wealth that Baldwin was seizing from these caravans must have been one of the principal elements pulling his attention increasingly towards Transjordan.[10]

The addition of two more regions in 1111 to the original peace agreement of 1109 appears to reflect the expansion of Frankish hegemony. In a later document, issued in 1166 by King Amalric to confirm the possessions and privileges of the Templum Domini, it is noted that the canons claimed 1,000 bezants per year from the tithes of Arabia, which had previously been granted by the Patriarchs Gibelin and Arnulf, with the consent of King Baldwin I. Mayer has argued that the original grant must have been made between late 1109 and April 1112, while Gibelin was patriarch of Jerusalem, following which the agreement was confirmed by his successor, Arnulf. With this in mind, Mayer proposes that Baldwin, who was beginning to oversee the allocation of the region's resources, was seriously considering expanding royal authority over the area south of the territories jointly administered with Damascus. This may also indicate that ecclesiastical administration of the area was entrusted to the Templum Domini from this time.[11] Regardless of whether or not the Franks had begun attempting to collect tithes from certain parts of Transjordan, the value of the initial grants seems to reflect a growing appreciation of the region's wealth.

Montreal

Baldwin I returned to Transjordan in 1115. On this occasion, he chose to make a long-term investment in establishing Frankish authority over the region by building a castle at al-Shawbak. This is often seen as the moment from which the Frankish lordship of Transjordan began to take shape. In the words of Fulcher of Chartres:

> King Baldwin went into Arabia and built a castle strongly situated on a small mountain. It is not far from the Red Sea, about three days' journey, and about four from Jerusalem. He placed a garrison in it to dominate the country in the interest of the Christians. He decided to name this castle Montreal in honour of himself because he built it in a short time with a few men with great boldness.[12]

Half a century later, William of Tyre composed a similar account:

> At this time, the Christians had no fortress in the country beyond the river Jordan. Accordingly, the king, desiring to extend the boundaries of the realm in that locality, proposed with the help of God to build a fortress in Arabia Tertia, which is called Syria Sobal. The garrison in this place would be able to protect the fields lying below it, which were tributary to the kingdom, from the inroads of the enemy. In pursuance of his plan, he levied the forces of his kingdom and led them across the Dead Sea. He passed through Arabia Secunda, whose metropolis is Petra, and came to Arabia Tertia. There, in an elevated spot well suited to his purpose, he built a fortress strongly defended both by its natural site and by artificial means. When the work was finished, he placed a garrison of both cavalry and infantry forces there and granted them extensive possessions. The place was fortified with walls, towers, forewalls, and a moat and was well equipped with arms, food, and machines. Since a king was its founder, he

gave it a name derived from the royal prestige and called it Montreal. The spot has the advantage of fertile soil, which produces abundant supplies of grain, wine, and oil. Moreover, it is especially noted for its healthful and delightful location. This fortress dominated the entire district adjacent to it.[13]

William is quite clear that the Franks possessed no strongholds in the region prior to the construction of Montreal. Tibble, however, has highlighted William's claim that the region was already a royal tributary.[14] While Fulcher notes that Montreal extended royal authority, and William emphasizes the fertility of the surrounding region, Albert of Aachen chose to stress the commercial benefits that Baldwin stood to gain. The king built the castle, in Albert's words,

so that in this way he might more powerfully subdue the land of the Arabians, and passage to and fro would no longer be available for merchants except by the king's favour and licence, nor would any ambushes or enemy forces suddenly appear, but would quickly be apparent to the king's faithful stationed in the citadel, and in this way the royal citadel would be a hindrance to them.[15]

When read together, the sources suggest there were a number of attractive reasons to establish a permanent Frankish presence in the region. Once there, the Franks may have been surprised by the quantity of traffic that passed through the area. The volume of trade moving through the region may also have increased after 1099, as some merchants travelling between Egypt and Syria sought to skirt Frankish Palestine. In addition to merchant caravans of varying sizes, there was the annual Muslim pilgrimage (the *hajj*) to the Hijaz, which made its way south along the King's Highway. The Bedouin had and would continue to enjoy a sort of protection racket when it came to permitting these travellers to pass through the region unharmed; the Franks would come to play a similar part.[16]

Baldwin's decision to establish a Frankish outpost in Transjordan at this time, a decade and a half after his first visit to the area, was partly a result of his evolving regional strategy – with the exceptions of Ascalon and Tyre, he now controlled the ports of the Palestinian coast. The king must also have had an awareness that the region east of Wadi 'Araba was essentially uncontested. Although a Muslim force had attempted to establish itself somewhere near Wadi Musa in 1107, it was Frankish armies that were to be found marching into the region more often between 1100 and 1115, where they found themselves virtually unopposed. It was probably this lack of opposition from Damascus that finally persuaded Baldwin to make an investment in the region – he had to be sure that if he committed himself to building a castle so far from his base of power that it was not likely to be threatened by a sizable army. He had twice attempted to establish similar strongholds in the Sawad: construction on the first was interrupted by Damascene forces; the second, built shortly afterwards, was captured while the army of Jerusalem was occupied besieging Tyre and unable to relieve the beleaguered garrison.[17] Montreal, by comparison, was considerably further away. Although quite a distance from Jerusalem, Tughtakin had shown no real interest in contesting control of Transjordan since the Franks arrived in the Levant a decade and a half earlier.

Prawer's argument that the Franks attempted to push the kingdom's frontier to the edge of the desert, 'preventing the concentration of Moslem troops on the eastern flank', is hard to support.[18] The desert was hardly an obstacle to travel and both Muslim and Frankish powers tended to concentrate their armies well within their own borders – there was no centre that could support the logistical challenges of a mustering in Transjordan. It was rather a desire to control this region, rather than deny it to Tughtakin, that persuaded Baldwin to establish a military presence there in 1115. The similar suggestion that Montreal, and the subsequent lordship of Transjordan by extension, was founded to sever the link between Egypt and Syria is a product of circumstances that followed decades later. Neither Egyptian nor Damascene armies had moved into Transjordan since the Franks arrived in Palestine, with the exception of the Turkmen expedition approved by Tughtakin in 1107. Although Transjordan would later act as a wedge between Syria and Egypt, the lordship's importance in this respect would not emerge until the second half of the twelfth century, and can hardly have been a motive behind the construction of Montreal in 1115.

Baldwin I returned to Transjordan in 1116, taking with him a force of close to 200 knights. He visited Montreal, then pushed on as far as the Red Sea. When the king and his party reached 'Aqaba, they found the inhabitants had fled in boats ahead of their arrival. From 'Aqaba, Baldwin had the option of moving west across Sinai to Egypt or south into the Hijaz; instead, he opted to return to Jerusalem via Montreal. Fulcher of Chartres, who had accompanied Baldwin to Transjordan in 1100 and taken considerable interest in the qualities of the Dead Sea, was evidently not part of this expedition in 1116, as he was forced to learn about the Red Sea from others who had accompanied the king.

More than half a century later, William of Tyre wrote that Baldwin 'crossed the Jordan' when setting out. Mayer has read this literally, suggesting that Baldwin's party moved north around the Dead Sea and then south to the east of it, potentially taking them past Kerak; however, it seems at least as likely that William used this as a turn of phrase.[19] Albert of Aachen, who combined the expeditions of 1115 and 1116, casting Baldwin's construction of Montreal and his trip to 'Aqaba as part of the same enterprise, noted that the Franks returned via Hebron. According to Albert, before turning back, Baldwin set out towards Mount Sinai, hoping to make a pilgrimage to the prestigious monastery of St Catherine and speak with those whom he found there. Messengers sent by the monks, however, urged him not to come, as they feared this might rouse Fatimid hostility and result in their expulsion.[20] Although there is nothing to corroborate this anecdote, which is noticeably absent from Fulcher's account, it is hard to definitively rule out the possibility that the king may have considered taking the opportunity to visit Sinai. Baldwin was certainly an adventurous figure; when he died two years later, he was in Egypt, having travelled along the Mediterranean coast to get there, rather than through Transjordan and across Sinai.

Baldwin I of Jerusalem was succeeded by Baldwin II, his cousin and earlier replacement as count of Edessa. Baldwin II's initial forays across the Great Rift were north of the Dead Sea, as the struggle for dominance over the region east of the Jordan continued. In July 1121, having launched a reprisal raid into Damascene territory, the Franks captured and destroyed a stronghold that Tughtakin had commissioned in the ruins of ancient Jerash. With the Franks exerting increasing influence east of Palestine, the outpost at Jerash appears to have been part of an effort to strengthen Damascene authority north of the Balqa'. Two years later, a Frankish raid struck across the Jordan south of the Sea of Galilee, returning with plunder and captives to Tiberias, and a more threatening invasion was directed towards Damascus in 1126. Not until the late summer of 1127 does Baldwin II appear to have visited Transjordan. According to Ibn al-Qalanisi, the king travelled to Wadi Musa, where the Frankish party reportedly captured those who were not able to escape, presumably local Muslim inhabitants. This episode does not appear in the Latin accounts, and it may be that this force was led by someone other than the king, perhaps even his deputy based at Montreal.[21]

While the Franks and Damascenes vied for control of the region east of the Jordan, power was contested less obviously further south. Despite the lack of opposition, it took time for the Franks to establish their authority in this area. More than a decade after a permanent presence was founded at Montreal, the show of force exhibited at Wadi Musa in 1127 speaks to the practical limits of the Franks' authority, but also their commitment to dominating the region.

Roman of Puy and Pagan the Butler

Following its account of the founding of Montreal, William of Tyre's history relates how Baldwin I encouraged local Christians from Transjordan to relocate to Jerusalem, where the population had still not recovered from the massacre that had accompanied the city's capture during the First Crusade.[22] This information is not found in those sources composed closer to events, and William appears to have inserted these remarks along with a few others between the expeditions of 1115 and 1116. Regardless of where William sourced this information, its reliability, and when he added it to his history, scholars have pondered the matter of where these people might have come from.

The most likely region appears to have been the area north of Montreal, which was not yet under direct Frankish rule.[23] Textual sources leave no doubt that Montreal was commissioned by Baldwin I, and they offer no hints that it was granted to a lord immediately thereafter. This implies that the castle remained a royal possession and that the surrounding area was incorporated into the royal demesne, rendering the king the most influential figure in the region. This would have facilitated any efforts undertaken by the monarchy to move local Christians from Transjordan to the city of Jerusalem, another royal possession.

Montreal's initial retention by the king appears to be confirmed by the only known Latin epigraphic evidence found at the castle. When Irby and Mangles visited Montreal in 1818, they discovered a Latin inscription in the architrave of the main door of what had once been the large castle church. This would seem to be the same inscription noticed by Lagrange almost eight decades later, which he describes as damaged and only legible at the ends. He could make out UGO VICE...QVI...MCXVIII, and the letters LES following were discerned a few years later by Brünnow and Domaszewski. This appears to refer to a certain Hugh, who, as viscount (*vicecomes*) of Montreal, would have administered the region on behalf of the king. The final three letters of the inscription may correspond with *ECCLESIA*, in which case this inscription probably refers to the construction of the church, which was overseen by Hugh in 1118.[24] It is quite sensible that the construction of a church would accompany the founding of the castle; sadly, we know little more about the provisions for the Latin Church in the region prior to the construction of Kerak. The viscount, Hugh, is unknown beyond this inscription, but his title seems to confirm that Montreal was still a royal possession in 1118.

The point at which the castle passed out of royal control is unclear. Although there is no direct mention of Baldwin I granting Montreal to one of his followers, popular belief since the late nineteenth century has held that the king gave the castle to Roman of Puy, and with it created the lordship of Transjordan.[25] The earliest mention of Roman in the historical records dates to 1110, where he appears as a benefactor in a royal confirmation issued to the Hospital of St John of Jerusalem. He can be found twice more among the witnesses to charters before the death of Baldwin I.[26] If indeed the king gave Montreal to Roman, this must have taken place in the first quarter of 1118, after Hugh the viscount had finished overseeing work on the church that bears his name, but before Baldwin set out for Egypt, where he would die.

Roman of Puy's link with Transjordan is similarly established in the charter evidence, where it is recorded that he, along with his wife, donated lands in the Balqa' to the Abby of St Mary of the Valley of Jehoshaphat. Although the original charter is lost, the agreement has been preserved in a confirmation issued by Baldwin II in 1130. Roman evidently held lands in Transjordan from the reign of Baldwin I; however, this does not prove that he was lord of Montreal and all of Transjordan, in the same way that the lands he also possessed around Nablus did not make him lord of all Samaria. Roman witnessed another three royal charters during the reign of Baldwin II, but at no point is he referred to as lord of Montreal or Transjordan, or indeed anything other than Roman of Puy (*Romanus de Podio*).[27] William of Tyre, writing a number of decades later, seems to have been the only figure to suggest that Roman might have held a greater title, calling him 'lord of that region which is beyond the Jordan' (*dominus regionis illius que est trans Iordanem*). By comparison, Pagan, the former royal butler, a position that he took as his surname, was clearly lord of Montreal by January 1126, when he appears in the official record as 'Pagan of Montreal' (*Paganus Montis Regalis*). Following Pagan, subsequent lords would similarly distinguish themselves in this way, or even more obviously as 'lord of Montreal' (*Montis Regalis dominus*).[28]

Pagan the Butler first appears in royal records in the spring of 1120, when he, along with Roman of Puy, was among the witnesses to a charter issued by Baldwin II remitting customs duties into Jerusalem. Pagan then appears as 'Pagan of Montreal' on the document dated to 1126 noted above, before he is found once more as 'Pagan the Butler' (*Paganus pincerna*) on a charter issued in March 1129. Roman was also a witness to the grant made in 1129, but whereas Roman had taken primacy of position in 1120, Pagan's name precedes Roman's this time, quite likely reflecting Pagan's rise in status following his reception of Montreal a few years earlier.[29]

In a later list that William of Tyre provided of the nobles who attended a council near Acre in 1148, during the Second Crusade, Pagan is found sixth, behind many of the principal supporters of Queen Melisende. Here, Pagan is identified as 'lord of the region which is beyond the Jordan'. This again speaks to the level of influence that Pagan came to hold, while the title that William gave him is almost the same as that which he had previously given to Roman. William evidently believed that Roman and Pagan had held the same position, or at least a very similar one. This connection is stated explicitly when William, discussing the construction of Kerak, wrote that Pagan had replaced Roman as lord of Transjordan following an act of treachery on the part of the latter.[30]

The matter remains of when Pagan became lord of Montreal, and how this relates to the possible disinheriting of Roman, who was clearly alive and well and still holding lands around Nablus following Pagan's rise to power in Transjordan. William of Tyre's history mentions only one baronial revolt in the kingdom of Jerusalem in the early twelfth century – this was led by Hugh of Jaffa, probably in 1134, and Roman of Puy is the only other figure implicated.[31] This, however, was eight years after Pagan the Butler is first identified in surviving records as lord of Montreal. Historians have put forward a number of possible scenarios in their attempts to explain this. Mayer and Murray have suggested that Roman, who initially held Montreal, actually revolted twice, first under Baldwin II, leading to his replacement in Transjordan by Pagan, and then later, alongside Hugh of Jaffa, in 1134. Both scholars have examined how each new king of Jerusalem elevated a body of supporters following his succession, leading to factional conflicts between the established baronage and those favoured by the new king. Pagan's elevation to the position of royal butler from otherwise obscurity indicates that he was a close supporter of Baldwin II. Roman, by comparison, had apparently enjoyed more favour under Baldwin I. Murray has even proposed that during Baldwin II's captivity, in 1123–24, some of those barons who had lost favour following his accession may have plotted to replace the king. Had Roman been one of the conspirators, it might explain his loss of Montreal to Pagan sometime before March 1129.[32]

Tibble has pushed back against the idea of a first rebellion, ahead of Hugh of Jaffa's revolt, and with this the very notion that Roman held Montreal before Pagan. Why, he has asked, is there no explicit mention of a first uprising in any of the historical accounts? And if there were one, why would Roman have been stripped of Transjordan but left with the remainder of his lands, leaving him in a position to revolt again in 1134? Beyond this, he highlights that the later grant of Transjordan to Philip of Milly, in 1161, defines the principal lands of the region as those once held by Pagan the Butler, clearly implying that Pagan, rather than Roman, was the archetypical lord of the region. No lord of Transjordan, from Pagan onwards, would ever mention Roman in the line of his predecessors. Tibble quite sensibly suggests that Roman held lands 'beyond the Jordan', including those lands he evidently held in the Balqa', but these should not be associated with Montreal or the region acquired by Pagan. Although this requires overlooking the similar wording that William of Tyre employed to identify the lands held by Roman and Pagan, and the implication that Pagan received Montreal after it was stripped from Roman, it removes any requirement to explain how or why the former came to replace the latter, because Roman never held Montreal. This eliminates any need for there to have been an otherwise unmentioned first revolt; instead, Roman revolted only once, in 1134, following which his lands were confiscated.[33]

When considering the evidence, Tibble's arguments are convincing. The contemporary historical sources are quite clear that Montreal was established as a royal castle, and the epigraphic evidence would appear to confirm that it remained as such to at least 1118. It seems very unlikely that Roman would have been in open revolt sometime before January 1126, when Pagan is known to have been lord of Montreal, if for no other reason than Fulcher of Chartres makes no mention of an uprising or any dispossessions that might be associated with one. Fulcher, whose account continues through 1126, was living in Jerusalem at this time, making him the closest source to these events. Although Murray has suggested that Roman's offences may have been less than open revolt, Tibble appears justified in questioning why Baldwin II would further frustrate an already unhappy vassal, by seizing Montreal, while leaving him strong enough to revolt again in 1134. Instead, it seems more likely that Montreal remained a royal possession until Baldwin II granted it to Pagan. As Murray has identified, Pagan was probably a close supporter of the king, to whom he owed his elevation to the position of royal butler, and then possession of what seems to have been a quite lucrative as well as distant lordship, in a region where the monarchy wanted to retain a measure of influence.

William of Tyre, who did not begin writing his history of events until the 1160s, and would continue to compose and revise his work into the early 1180s, never shied away from employing grand language. As will become apparent below, 'the lordship of Transjordan' is perhaps a label that can only be accurately used from 1161, when a number of smaller lordships were consolidated. William's impression of the lordship and the terminology he used to describe it were probably informed by his own period, hence his reference to Pagan, and even Roman, as 'lord of the region beyond the Jordan'. This might more accurately have been expressed as the less impressive sounding 'lord of some lands beyond the Jordan'. Although the lands held by neither man were equivalent to the lordship familiar to William, it seems that it was Pagan who was first entrusted with the core of this later, grander lordship, which initially centred on Montreal.

Roman of Puy, who quite likely continued to hold his lands in the Balqa' and elsewhere following Pagan's investiture with Montreal, was a party to the uprising led by Hugh of Jaffa in 1134. This opposition was directed against Fulk, the husband of Baldwin II's daughter and heir, Melisende, and king of Jerusalem from 1131. The episode began following an accusation of treason launched against Hugh by his own stepson, Walter Grenier. Rather than present himself for a trial by combat, Hugh sought the support of the local Muslim ruler of Ascalon. This provoked Fulk to move against Jaffa in force. Hugh eventually submitted to the king, agreeing to a three-year exile, though he was killed in Italy before he had the opportunity to return to the Levant and reclaim his lands. Mayer and Murray agree that factional tensions lay behind this episode; Hugh, along with Roman and the others whom we can imagine supported him, represented an established group of barons who saw their fortunes attached to Melisende. This led them to support her right to rule jointly with Fulk, who displayed efforts to rule without his wife's input following the death of her father, Baldwin II.[34]

Roman's fate is unknown, though it would seem he was exiled along with Hugh, as he does not reappear in the records of the kingdom. This fits with William of Tyre's remark that the lands of Roman and his son Ralph, of whom we know nothing more, were confiscated.[35] William states that Pagan held 'Transjordan' after Roman had been dispossessed; however, if William was slightly confused, and Pagan already held Montreal, it may have been that Roman's lands were simply added to those possessed by Pagan. This would seem a natural decision when considering that Pagan was already the main figure in the region. Pagan is also conspicuously absent from William's account of the events surrounding Hugh of Jaffa's revolt, suggesting Pagan may have been on the side of the king, or at least remained aloof from the conflict. This would further justify the royal support he received if indeed he was given Roman's lands in the Balqa', and any others the disgraced figure may have held in Transjordan.

Responsibility for transforming Montreal into the seat of a lordship seems to rest with Baldwin II. This had evidently happened by 1126, when Pagan the Butler is identified as *Paganus Montis Regalis*, without any suggestion that he was serving as a viscount. While most historians who disagree with this interpretation favour Baldwin I as the creator of the lordship, and Roman of Puy as the first lord of Montreal, others have proposed that it was Fulk, or even Baldwin III, who created what would become known as the Lordship of Transjordan.[36]

Construction of Kerak

Construction of the great castle at Kerak began under Pagan the Butler. The only indication of when building efforts commenced comes from William of Tyre, who dates this to John Komnenos's second visit to Syria, in 1142. When describing the castle's founding, and throughout his history, William demonstrates an inexact knowledge of the region, suggesting he never ventured there himself. In his words:

> It was situated near an ancient city, formerly called Rabba, the metropolis of this same Arabia. It was at the siege of this place, as we read, that by command of David, though at the hand of Joab, the innocent Uriah was killed. Later it was called Petra of the Desert; whence Arabia Secunda is now called Arabia of Petra.[37]

William associates the site of Kerak with the nearby community of Rabba (Rabbath-Moab, classical Areopolis), which hosted the biblical siege where Uriah the Hittite was killed by Joab (2 Samuel 11–12); however, he also mistakenly associates Rabba with the former metropolitan city of Rabbath-Ammon (classical Philadelphia, mod. Amman). William elaborates on his final remark in a second description of the castle when giving an account of Saladin's siege of the stronghold in 1183.

> Here upon a very high mountain surrounded by deep valleys, the city of Petra had once been located. For a long time, however, it had lain in ruin, utterly desolate. Finally, during the reign of Fulk, the third king of the Latins in the Orient, one Paganus, surnamed the butler, lord of a domain lying beyond the Jordan, built a citadel on this site. It was placed upon the same mountain where the city had once lain, but on a less precipitous slope which ran down to the plain below. The successors of Paganus, namely Maurice, his nephew, and Philip of Nablus, had added a moat and towers to render the place still more unassailable.[38]

By William's day, Kerak (or *Crac*) was also referred to as Petra of the Desert (*Petra Deserti*). The latter linked the main Frankish centre in the region with the earlier Nabataean capital city of Petra, 100km to the south, where the Roman archbishop of the region had initially been based. William is utterly mistaken when associating the two sites, but there is little reason to doubt that Pagan initiated building efforts. Likewise, there is every reason to believe that work to develop the stronghold continued under Pagan's successors, his nephew Maurice and then Philip of Milly. It seems unwise, however, to attribute the construction of particular elements of the castle to any figures based on William's testimony alone, considering his reliance on hearsay and such clear mistakes as placing the castle to the east of the town.[39] We are left to wonder how much better our understanding of the castle and its development might have been if William had the same sense of adventure exhibited by Fulcher of Chartres.

Although it was not founded among the ruins of ancient Petra, there were probably structures on the site of the castle prior to its construction. Like Montreal, Kerak was established in a location with an existing Christian population – the Franks considered Syrian Christians to be more trustworthy than local Muslims. According to Ibn Shaddad, an eminent geographer and historian of the thirteenth century, the castle had originally been the site of a Christian monastery, which had been fortified by its monks against the hostility of local Bedouin raiders. These monks later invited the Franks to settle among them, leading to the further development of the site's defences.[40] Ibn Shaddad demonstrates an excellent appreciation of Kerak's history from the 1170s, when it became intrinsic to the objectives of local Muslim figures, but no archaeological evidence has yet been uncovered to support his suggestion that there had been an earlier monastery on the site.[41] Although it is certainly possible that Kerak had previously accommodated a monastic community, there is no explicit reference to a monastery in or around the town during the Frankish period.

Regardless of what existed before Pagan commissioned the present castle, this became his new seat of power. He had been the principal lord in the region for at least sixteen years and his construction of Kerak appears to reveal his ambition as well as his wealth. It was twenty-seven years since Montreal had been founded, more than 70km to the south, and Frankish authority in the region had not been challenged since that point. Kerak, positioned halfway between Wadi al-Mujib and Wadi al-Hasa, was ideally suited to dominate this more northern plateau, while Wadi Karak provided access to the southern end of the Dead Sea, with Hebron, Jerusalem and the rest of southern Palestine beyond. Economically, the castle was ideally situated to extend Pagan's influence and dominate both the agricultural landscape of Moab and the movement of people and commerce through the region.

Maurice

Not much is known about Kerak in the decades immediately following the castle's construction, and similarly little is known about its early lords. Although William of Tyre claims Pagan adopted his title of royal butler as his surname, he is last referred to in the surviving charter evidence by this name in 1136. No other royal butler is named until 1145, leaving it unclear whether Pagan was replaced when Fulk came to the throne in 1131, and *pincerna* did indeed become his surname, or a new butler was appointed sometime after this. It is tempting to suggest that Pagan became a close ally of Fulk, and continued to serve as royal butler until the king's death in 1143. However, despite appearing second among the witnesses to the grant Fulk made to the Hospitallers at Nablus in 1136, this is the only one of Fulk's surviving charters that Pagan witnessed, though it should be noted that relatively few royal charters have survived from Fulk's reign.[42] Pagan himself lived until at least 1148, when he attended the great council near Acre during the Second Crusade. He had evidently died by 1152, when Maurice, his nephew and successor, issued a charter as lord of Montreal. Maurice is then found at the siege of Ascalon in 1153, but little else is known about him.[43]

The grant issued by Maurice to the Hospitallers in 1152 provides a rare, if still limited, window into the affairs of the lordship in the mid-twelfth century. Maurice granted the order: a village called Benisalem, in the region of Montreal; the revenues of a Syrian Christian and his family; a house between his own and that of the viscount of Nablus; some land for the planting of vines, between the vineyard of Seguin and the land of William the Ass (*Asinus*); a portion of the value of all goods and plunder taken from the Muslims, regardless of whether the order had a truce in place with them, after the church of St Mary had what it was due; a village called Cansil, in the region of Kerak; a tower in Kerak, which was on the left side as one passed through the gate of the castle, and a barbican, from the tower they were granted to the tower of St Mary; the right to cross the Dead Sea in a boat, free of any taxes or fees, except if they chose to take millstones or chains; and land beside the vineyard of John the castellan, alongside the main road and the vineyard of Maurice.[44]

The charter was drawn up by Maurice's chaplain, Reynard, with eleven witnesses, only one of whom, a brother of the Templum Domini, is identified as a cleric. Among the witnesses were John, the castellan of Kerak mentioned in the charter, and Seguin, listed first and second respectively. The fifth and sixth were Ayrald, the castellan of Montreal, and Martin the viscount, presumably also of Montreal. It is unclear whether the seventh witness, John of Tiberias, whose name reveals that he came from northern Palestine, was attached to the lordship or simply a visiting knight. John's presence, and the property held by the viscount of Nablus at Montreal, seem to speak to the continuation of links between Transjordan and rather distant regions of central and northern Palestine that can be traced back to the days of Roman of Puy. The variety of names mentioned in the charter may indicate that the lordship had become home to an eclectic group of men, who traced their lineages back to different areas of Europe. As for the castle, it evidently boasted a number of towers by this time, though identifying where those mentioned were located is difficult. What is more obvious is the presence of two lines of walls in one area – a 'barbican', in the context of the Latin East, refers to the space between such walls, regardless of their proximity to a gateway. Although Kerak was evidently developing rapidly, Maurice and his successors would continue to draw their title from the older castle of Montreal, even though Kerak probably became the main baronial residence in the lordship.

Another charter, from about 1160, records the gift of the village of Hara, near Wadi Musa, to the Hospitallers. The donation was made by the brothers Joseph and John; their father, Saba, whose name suggests he was a local Christian, had originally received the village from Baldwin II, perhaps around the same time that the lordship of Montreal was created.[45] The lands held by the brothers were apparently among a number of smaller fiefs that remained in the broader region of Transjordan, independent of what continued to be called the lordship of Montreal.

When all of the surviving textual evidence is considered, there are relatively few references to the lords of Transjordan in the two central decades of the twelfth century. Much as Pagan the Butler does not appear among the events associated with the revolt of Hugh of Jaffa, neither he nor Maurice are mentioned in the historical records associated with the power struggle between Baldwin III and his mother Melisende in the early 1150s.[46] Shortly after the conclusion of this conflict, William of Tyre mentions Maurice among those who had assembled at the start of the siege of Ascalon in 1153, but nothing more is heard of him. Also present at this siege were Philip of Milly, who would ultimately receive Transjordan seven years later, and Reynald of Châtillon, who would himself go on to acquire the lordship in 1176, following his marriage to one of Philip's daughters.[47]

From the mid-1150s, activity along the frontier between Egypt and the kingdom of Jerusalem increased. In 1155, the Fatimid vizier, 'Abbas, was compelled to flee Cairo with his son and entourage. While heading for Syria, this party was intercepted by a force of Franks. 'Abbas was among those killed and his son, Nasr, was taken captive, later to be sold to the new regime in Cairo. The emir and author Usama ibn Munqidh, who had fled Egypt alongside the deposed vizier, was among the lucky few who reached Syria. William of Tyre's implication of the Templars in this ambush might indicate that it took place near Gaza, which the order had received from Baldwin III a few years earlier; however, the description of the landscape points instead to Transjordan as the location of the encounter, possibly revealing that the Templars had established a noteworthy presence in the region by that time. Aside from the Templars, who received the largest share of the plunder, no specific Frankish figures are named.[48]

Back in Cairo, 'Abbas was replaced by Tala'i' ibn Ruzzik, who initially favoured peaceful relations with the Franks. This policy was unpopular with leading Fatimid emirs, who successfully advocated a more aggressive posture, leading to a number of military actions. Among the recorded campaigns is an invasion into Transjordan in the summer of 1156, which resulted in attacks against Montreal and Tafila. Two years later, another Fatimid force moved against Wadi Musa, where al-Wu'ayra was besieged for eight days; the Egyptians then continued northward, attacking Montreal before raiding southern Palestine.[49] These Fatimid incursions do not appear to have reached as far north as Kerak.

Philip of Milly

Following William of Tyre's notice of Maurice at Ascalon in 1153, no source composed in the Latin East mentions a lord of Transjordan until 1161, when Baldwin III bestowed the lordship, and others in the region, on Philip of Milly, leaving it unclear when Maurice died. Mayer has identified a reference to Maurice's death at the siege of Ascalon in the slightly later *Annales of Egmond*, composed in Holland. The *Annales*, which present Maurice in a negative light, accusing him of treachery, wrongly name him as the son-in-law of Philip of Milly.[50] This is not the only example where a source attempts to draw a family connection between Philip and the previous lords of Kerak. The *Lignages d'Outremer*, a work of the thirteenth century that examines the great Frankish baronial dynasties, suggests that Pagan the Butler was the maternal uncle of Philip of Milly and his predecessor as lord of Nablus, making no mention of Maurice at all. A number of historians have pointed out that there is no evidence to corroborate a family link between Pagan and Philip, let alone Maurice and Philip. Likewise, there is nothing else to suggest that Pagan was lord of Nablus; even Philip, who came to hold considerable lands around Nablus, was never properly 'lord of Nablus'.[51]

What can be asserted with relative certainty is that Maurice, having succeeded his uncle, Pagan, by 1152, was at the siege of Ascalon the following year, where he may have died. Who took over immediately after Maurice is unclear. When considering that William of Tyre names Pagan the Butler's successors as Maurice and then Philip of Milly, it seems Maurice died without an heir, leading the lordship to revert back to the crown, which explains why Baldwin III is found granting the lordship to Philip of Milly in 1161. If

Maurice died in 1153, a royal official was presumably installed in Kerak to administer things on the king's behalf until the castle passed to Philip, though there is no surviving record of such a figure. It is possible that this individual spent most of his time in Transjordan, perhaps responding to the increase in Fatimid raiding activities, which would explain why he seems not to have witnessed any charters. Likewise, he was apparently unknown to William of Tyre, who was himself in Europe at this time pursuing his education. Alternatively, Maurice may have survived the siege of Ascalon only to die at some point during the following eight years. In this scenario, there may have been little opportunity for an interim royal agent to appear in the historical records, or such an appointment may have been unnecessary if Baldwin granted Transjordan to Philip of Milly shortly after Maurice's death, perhaps having planned this in advance.

Barber has concluded that Philip of Milly most likely hailed from a Norman or Picard family. His father, Guy, who is first noted in the Holy Land in 1108, came to hold lands around both Nablus and Jerusalem. Philip's mother was Stephanie 'the Fleming', and he had two documented brothers, Guy *Francigena* and Henry the Buffalo. When the elder Guy died, his lands appear to have been divided among his sons, with Philip receiving those in the region of Nablus. Philip's mother was subsequently remarried to Baldwin of Ramla, with whom she had a daughter, Helvis. This made Philip the stepbrother of Renier, lord of Ramla. Helvis, Philip's half-sister, would marry Balian the elder, progenitor of the influential Ibelin family; her daughter, Ermengarde, Philip's niece, went on to marry Elinard of Tiberias. This web of connections linked Philip with some of the most powerful families of the kingdom of Jerusalem. By 1153, Philip had three children of his own with his wife Isabella: Renier, Helena and Stephanie (named after her grandmother).[52]

Philip of Milly first appears in the documentary evidence in 1138, and he is referred to as 'Philip of Nablus' for the first time in 1144. Although Philip seems not to have been 'lord of Nablus', as Queen Melisende retained the town until her death in 1161, Mayer seems justified qualifying Philip as lord in all but name. Philip was a loyal and influential supporter of Melisende during the conflict of the early 1150s. Following the death of Fulk in 1143, his wife, Melisende, the daughter of Baldwin II, had ruled as queen on behalf of their young son, Baldwin III. Even after Baldwin came of age, he continued to rule jointly with his mother for a number of years before eventually resolving to rule alone, leading to a brief civil war. The queen mother lost out and was forced to content herself with her dower lands of Nablus. Barber has argued that Philip continued to hold his considerable lands in the region around Nablus from Melisende, rather than the king. Although Philip had been on the losing side of this civil conflict, and he remained a loyal supporter of the queen mother, he was quickly reconciled with Baldwin III, reappearing in royal charters from 1152 and taking part in the king's siege of Ascalon the following year. While Philip's name is found on a number of Baldwin III's charters dating to the 1150s, so too did he witness a number issued by Melisende and her younger son, Amalric, revealing that he maintained close ties with both sides of the royal family.[53]

Melisende suffered from an extended period of illness leading up to her death in September 1161. Less than a month and a half before she died, Baldwin III arranged to acquire Philip of Milly's lands, which were second only to Melisende's in Samaria. As compensation, the king offered Philip Transjordan. When his mother died, and her lands reverted to the crown, Baldwin III thus became master of Samaria. Mayer suggests that Philip was less than enthusiastic about this forced exchange, which seems likely, considering how the lordship was restructured and Philip's eventual abdication.[54]

Although the timing and circumstances of Maurice's death remain unclear, he was certainly dead by the end of July 1161, when Baldwin III granted Transjordan to Philip of Milly. It is possible that Philip was related to Pagan the Butler, leaving him Maurice's closest male relative; however, the king's ability to insist that Philip give up his lands around Nablus before receiving Transjordan instead suggests that Maurice died without an heir, rendering the lordship of Montreal a crown possession. The timing of events is also suggestive, as the health of Melisende, Philip's patron, was evidently failing by this time. When the broader situation is considered, Baldwin may have seen this as an opportunity to test Philip's loyalty, while also setting himself up to acquire all of Samaria and strengthen royal authority in central Palestine. In compensation for his patrimony, the king could offer Philip Transjordan. For Baldwin, this had the added benefit of placing a man of demonstrated experience and ability in a region that had suffered recent Fatimid invasions. Even if it had been Philip who appealed to the king to grant him Transjordan, for which there is no evidence, it would still have been necessary for Baldwin III to strip Philip of his possessions in Samaria. Allowing Philip to gain Transjordan while also holding considerable lands in central Palestine would have left him too powerful and a potential threat to royal authority.

A New Lordship of Transjordan

Whatever may have led to Philip of Milly's acquisition of Transjordan in 1161, the charter detailing the transfer reveals that the lordship became larger and more cohesive at this time.[55] The principal power centres of the existing lordship were Kerak and Montreal, as well as Amman, the first apparent reference to the town in Frankish sources. The broader region is identified as those lands once ruled by Pagan the Butler, specified as stretching from the Red Sea in the south to the Zarqa River in the north. Given the apparent implication that Pagan had held Amman, it is possible that it was among the lands once held by Roman of Puy in the Balqa', before these were forfeited and given to Pagan following Roman's decision to support Hugh of Jaffa in 1134. If the Balqa', or a large portion of it, was granted to Pagan in the 1130s, a desire to link these lands with his powerbase to the south might have contributed to Pagan's decision to build a new seat of power at Kerak, roughly halfway between Montreal and Amman.

It was from the time that the lordship of Montreal, as it continued to be called, was granted to Philip that it came to include effectively all of Transjordan – everything beyond the Jordan, by which was meant those lands east of the Great Rift, as far north as the Zarqa River. This involved adding a number of smaller fiefs to the lands once held by Pagan the Butler. Those listed in the grant include Wadi Musa, which may have remained a royal possession until this point, and the Syrian and Saracen (Eastern Christian and Muslim) villages on both sides of the Jordan held by Baldwin, the son of Viscount Ulrich of Nablus, excluding only those villages that this Baldwin had himself established. Philip also gained the fief and service of John Gothman, another crown vassal in the region, who was to stay in place. Excluded from Philip's authority were the Bedouin who were born outside his new lordship. These nomads, as well as the caravans that passed through Transjordan, were to answer directly to the king, as they had presumably done prior to this.

The charter also lists the lands that Philip gave up at this time. These included most of those he had acquired from Rohard (presumably Rohard of Nablus, viscount of Jerusalem, who had also been a close supporter of Melisende and held lands around Nablus) and his wife Gisela. It has been proposed that these were the parents of Philip's wife, Isabella, which would explain why Philip held these fiefs (they were his wife's dower lands), a suggestion strengthened by the close political alignment of Philip and Rohard of Nablus. Philip also relinquished: those lands that had once belonged to his father; a fiefdom that his brother, Guy, had held of Rohard and then Philip; the fief of his other brother, Henry the Buffalo; that of Geoffrey Le Tor; as well as those lands Philip held in the rugged region of the upper Galilee (identified as the mountains of Tyre and Toron). The lands and their lords, who had previously owed service to Philip, would owe the king service according to the same terms. Among the many prominent figures to witness this agreement were two men who were, or would become, Philip's son-in-laws: Walter of Beirut and Humphrey [III] of Toron.

Little is known of Philip's actions at Kerak. Affairs in Egypt consumed considerable attention in the 1160s, as the Fatimid Caliphate imploded. Taking advantage of the situation, Nur al-Din, the powerful ruler of Aleppo and Damascus, attempted to extend his influence in Egypt from 1164; Amalric, the younger brother and successor of Baldwin III, tried to prevent this, leading Frankish and Syrian armies to clash along the Nile.[56] Leading up to this, Philip was still with Baldwin III at Jerusalem in November 1161, following which he may have travelled to his new lordship, as he then disappears from the charter records for a few years. During this lacuna, Philip may have overseen the completion of certain works at Kerak, as William of Tyre asserts that under Maurice and Philip a moat and towers were added to the castle. When Philip reappears in April 1164, he is found with Amalric, and then in July with the royal army at Ascalon, shortly before it set out for Egypt.[57]

In the contest for Egypt that was to play out through the remainder of the 1160s, Transjordan gained new importance, with Kerak the sharpened edge of the Frankish wedge between Syria and Egypt. In late 1163, the ongoing struggle for power in Fatimid Cairo saw the ousted vizier, Shawar, seek the support of Nur al-Din in Damascus. This led his rival, Dirgham, the new vizier, to appeal similarly to Nur al-Din in an attempt to dissuade the Syrian ruler from helping his opponent. A letter was carried by 'Alam al-Din ibn al-Nahhas, who was given a reply by Nur al-Din and sent back to Egypt. While making his way south, the messenger and his party were reportedly intercepted by Philip of Milly (known to Muslim historians as Qarib/Filib al-Rafiq)[58] as they passed Kerak. Although 'Alam al-Din lost his belongings, he managed to escape through the Negev and make his way back to Egypt. Al-Idrisi, a contemporary, claims that his uncle, al-Sharif al-Muhannak, was also, or perhaps alternatively, sent by Dirgham to turn Nur al-Din against Shawar. The envoy and his party were similarly ambushed, and al-Sharif Muhannak was briefly taken to Ascalon, though he managed to escape and reach Nur al-Din. Al-Idrisi claims to have himself been in Damascus with his uncle at this time, suggesting he may have been among those to escape the Frankish ambush.[59] The strategic value of Kerak, and the ability of its garrison to disrupt communication between Cairo and Damascus, was becoming obvious to everyone by this time.

Philip's tenure as lord of Transjordan ended after only four and a half years, when he resigned his great lordship to join the Templars. On 17 January 1166, Amalric confirmed a grant that Philip had made to the order as a gift ahead of his entry. This included Amman and half of the territory that he had held in the Balqa'. Transjordan was held by Philip's daughters thereafter, though practical power would be exercised by their husbands. Philip, meanwhile, would rise to become master of the Templars in 1169. For reasons not yet understood, he left the Templars, stepping down as master before setting out ahead of the king on a diplomatic mission to Constantinople in early 1171. Philip is not mentioned again in the historical records, suggesting he died while away.[60]

The reason for Philip's resignation of Transjordan and entry into the Templars is unknown. Did he resent this distant post, which had been pushed on him by Baldwin III? Alternatively, did he simply work out a more desirable arrangement with Amalric, Baldwin III's younger brother and successor? During the civil conflict of the early 1150s, Philip and Amalric had been close supporters of the latter's mother, Melisende; rather conspicuously, Philip appears much more regularly on royal charters from the start of Amalric's reign in 1163. The two men may have hatched a plan to see Philip become the next master of the Templars, a plan that ultimately came to fruition in 1169. Or, as Barber has proposed, might Philip's decision to join the order have been for more personal reasons, perhaps triggered by the death of his wife, Isabella, of whom we know little beyond the appearance of her name on a charter in 1155? Similarly, could this have been a reaction to the death of Renier, his son? Like his mother, Renier appears only once in the historical record, on the same charter. Another possible explanation, and perhaps one of the most likely, is that Philip of Milly sought to secure the inheritance of his daughters before he followed his son and wife to the grave. Philip of Novara, a thirteenth-century historian and author of a treatise on Frankish law, noted that entering a religious order was a way that a man could pass his estate on to his heirs in his lifetime. In the absence of more evidence, we can do little more than speculate.[61]

Helena, Beatrice and Walter of Beirut

Philip of Milly's only recorded son, Renier, was evidently dead by 1166; when Philip joined the Templars that year, Transjordan passed to his eldest daughter, Helena, and her husband, Walter Brisebarre. Until recently, Walter's family had held the lordship of Beirut, which they had received from King Baldwin I following the city's capture in 1110. In 1164, Walter, then lord of Beirut, along with his brothers, Guy and Bernard, were among the many prominent Franks captured by Nur al-Din near Antioch at the Battle of Harim. Walter's mother, Mary, appears to have stepped in to administer Beirut before taking her sons' place as Nur al-Din's captive, allowing her boys to raise an agreed ransom. According to the *Lignages*, Walter sold Beirut to the crown, which secured the necessary funds to free his mother, though she died shortly thereafter.

Although the *Lignages* is not the most reliable source, Beirut was evidently a crown possession by 1167, when Amalric gave it to Andronikos Komnenos, and a charter issued that November confirms that Walter had relinquished Beirut to the king, having received in return a money fief in the region of Acre.[62]

The evidence strongly suggests that Walter was compelled to sell his lordship in order to ransom himself and his brothers, while Amalric compensated this once great baron of the kingdom with a minor royal fief. It remains a possibility, however, that it was not financial desperation that saw Walter give up Beirut, but rather the king was able to force Walter to do so before approving his right to rule Transjordan. This would have been similar to the way that Baldwin III had compelled Philip of Milly to exchange his holdings around Nablus. Unlike Philip, though, Walter appears to have had a clear right to inherit Transjordan, through his wife, and as lord of Beirut he was already one of the most senior barons of the kingdom of Jerusalem, giving considerable weight to the idea that factors beyond a simple exchange pushed him to give up his patrimony. The reality of the situation, however, may have been more nuanced. If Walter had married Helena prior to the Battle of Harim, and her brother had died by this time, the prospect of selling Beirut to the crown to secure his freedom, and that of his brothers, would have been far less ominous, considering that he stood to gain another great lordship through his wife. The money fief Walter received from Amalric when he sold Beirut may have been a way to ensure Walter remained a respectable lord with a modest income until he gained Transjordan upon the death of Philip of Milly. This might also help explain Philip's abdication: he may have been eager to see his daughter and son-in-law restored to the highest ranks of the kingdom's nobility. Whatever the circumstances, Walter had given up Beirut and become lord-regent of Transjordan by 1166.[63]

Little is known of the marriage between Walter and Helena. She is mentioned in the charter of 1155, where her mother and brother are also found, and in another dating to 1167, by which point she had died.[64] Although it seems more likely that the couple were married before 1164, it is not inconceivable that their wedding took place after Walter's release from captivity and the sale of Beirut. This would have made Walter a man of status but no lands, and their marriage would have allowed him to climb back up into the top circles of power. Alternatively, if their marriage, and the death of young Renier, took place before 1164, Amalric's eagerness to acquire Beirut before Walter could lay claim to Transjordan is understandable.

Meanwhile, Frankish and Syrian forces continued to clash along the Nile during the second half of the 1160s. In 1167, Shirkuh, one of Nur al-Din's senior emirs, led an army into Egypt with hopes of conquering the region, compelling Amalric to intervene at the head of his own force to preserve Fatimid independence. Both armies withdrew about six months later. In late 1168, roles reversed: following a Frankish invasion of Egypt, Shirkuh intervened on behalf of the Fatimids. On this occasion, Amalric withdrew but Shirkuh remained and quickly assumed the position of vizier, extending Nur al-Din's nominal authority across Egypt. Unfortunately for Shirkuh, he died not long after, in March 1169. The role of commander of Nur al-Din's Syrian forces in Egypt, along with the position of Fatimid vizier, fell to Shirkuh's nephew, Saladin.[65]

Around the same time that Egypt became a part of the Zankid realm, an alliance was concluded between Jerusalem and Constantinople. Leading up to this, Amalric appears to have preferred preserving Fatimid independence; rather than try to conquer and then administer Egypt, as Shirkuh had been attempting since 1164, the king's priority was simply to prevent the region from falling to Nur al-Din, while collecting large tribute payments from the Fatimids for his troubles. The alliance with the Byzantines changed things. The terms of the partnership were based on a plan to conquer and divide Egypt, and its provisions were ratified by the emperor while Amalric invaded Egypt in 1168, suggesting this was one last effort to extract a large tribute from the Fatimids. The following year, a joint Frankish-Byzantine invasion force attacked Damietta, but the siege of the city would ultimately fail. When the Christians withdrew in December 1169, Egypt was left in the hands of Saladin, who continued to rule in the name of Nur al-Din.[66]

With the nominal, if not effective, union of Egypt and Syria, Nur al-Din became a much greater threat to the Franks. The strategic importance of Transjordan, the wedge between these two power bases, likewise rose considerably. Baldwin III's interest in claiming authority over the caravans that moved through the lordship when it was given to Philip of Milly in 1161 speaks to the capabilities of the lords of Transjordan to influence or otherwise interfere with traffic moving between Damascus and Cairo. While Kerak came to pose a significant obstacle to the free movement of men and materials between Egypt and Syria, so too did the castle face a far greater threat as the corridor that it dominated became much more valuable to Nur al-Din.

In early 1170, Nur al-Din invaded Transjordan and besieged Kerak. This campaign appears to have had the double purpose of attacking this potential obstacle to free communication between Cairo and Damascus, while also shielding the movement of a large party of merchants, soldiers and others, including Saladin's father, who were keen to exploit potential opportunities in newly Zankid Egypt. The siege lasted only a few days before a Frankish relief force approached. William of Tyre, whose dating of events is somewhat confused, reports that the Frankish response was organized by the constable of the kingdom, Humphrey II of Toron – the king was in northern Syria assisting Bohemond III of Antioch at this time. According to Ibn al-Athir, the vanguard of the Frankish force was led by Philip of Milly, who had been appointed master of the Templars the previous year, and his son-in-law, Humphrey [III] of Toron, son of the constable and husband of Stephanie of Milly. The approach of the Frankish army compelled Nur al-Din to lift his siege, but the Franks declined to offer battle. Nur al-Din proceeded to raid Frankish lands before making camp at 'Ashtara.[67] While Nur al-Din was still at 'Ashtara, a devastating earthquake shook the Levant on the morning of 29 June 1170, with aftershocks that followed. The epicentre of the earthquake was in northern Syria. Although the tremors caused destruction as far away as Tyre, and the ground was felt to move in distant Iraq, no damage was reported at Kerak.[68]

In December 1170, Saladin launched his first invasion of Frankish Palestine from Egypt, attacking the southern strongholds of Darum and Gaza. The Franks rallied under Amalric and some skirmishing followed before Saladin withdrew. Shortly after his return to Cairo, Saladin set out across Sinai for 'Aqaba, where he joined a force that had been dispatched to capture the Frankish castle there. 'Aqaba was clearly a part of the enhanced lordship of Transjordan, as defined by the charter to Philip of Milly in 1161. The significance and influence of the Frankish outpost, however, appear to have been minimal: there is no record of its construction or the installing of a garrison, and no material evidence of Frankish occupation has yet been identified. Nevertheless, Saladin's propagandists would celebrate this victory, casting it as part of a broader effort to remove potential Frankish interference on the route from Egypt to Syria and the Hijaz.[69]

In September 1171, two and a half years after coming to power in Egypt, Saladin suppressed the Fatimid caliphate. He then launched a campaign against the Franks, invading Transjordan and attacking Montreal. This was the first siege that Montreal had been subjected to, but William of Tyre's account presents a fairly positive picture of the situation, emphasizing the castle's strength and its lofty position. William also drew attention to the stronghold's plentiful supplies of arms and provisions, and noted that the local population consisted entirely of Syrian Christians, making them reasonably trustworthy in his mind. The account of Ibn al-Athir, in sharp contrast, suggests the garrison was brought to the verge of capitulation, being compelled to ask for a delay of ten days, after which the defenders would surrender if no help had arrived. Saladin, however, withdrew before this period expired. The reason for Saladin's departure was not the strength of the castle, but rather news that Nur al-Din had set out to support him. Saladin feared Nur al-Din would use the occasion of a meeting to replace him as his deputy in Egypt. When considering these and other sources, it appears as though Ibn al-Athir stretched the truth, embellishing the desperation of the garrison in order to highlight the rift that would subsequently develop between Nur al-Din and Saladin. It was this, he wanted his readers to appreciate, that was the underlying reason why Montreal was not captured from the Franks at this time.[70]

Two years later, Saladin again invaded Transjordan, though the sources provide a variety of conflicting details. Ibn al-Athir, who dated things to the month of Shawwal (May–June) presented this as the events of 1171 playing out all over again, with Kerak as the target rather than Montreal: Saladin arrived first and initiated siege efforts, but withdrew and returned to Egypt once Nur al-Din approached. Problematically, Nur al-Din was campaigning in eastern Anatolia in the summer of 1173. 'Imad al-Din's account also bears similarities to the one he composed for the incursion two years earlier. Although he served Nur al-Din at this point in time, 'Imad al-Din would go on to become one of Saladin's closest officials, giving him no incentive to play up any tension between the two men when he later composed his history. He instead presented the Bedouin of Transjordan as the main target of Saladin's campaign; the expedition was an effort to punish them for their willingness to help the Franks and an attempt to turn them back to the side of Islam. This religiously charged rhetoric smacks of Saladin's chancery, which had already begun to cast Saladin as a defender of Sunni orthodoxy. Baha' al-Din provided a short and rather vague entry relating to this episode, asserting that the campaign had been intended to open the route between Egypt and Syria. Often the most direct of these contemporary Muslim sources, the brevity of Baha' al-Din's remarks may reflect his distrust of the various explanations in circulation and his own lack of certainty. From a Frankish perspective, William of Tyre alleged that Amalric assembled his forces and marched south in response to Saladin's invasion. The Franks once more declined to offer battle, allowing Saladin to raid the lordship but denying him the opportunity to engage the army or lay siege to a Frankish stronghold. William noted that the campaign lasted from July to September. Although the details of Saladin's incursion into Transjordan in 1173 are hard to discern, it was probably primarily a raid, which may have reached as far north as Kerak. If Saladin had more ambitious plans, he was forced to abandon these when he received distressing news from Egypt. His father, Ayyub, had fallen from his horse, and would succumb to his injuries on 9 August.[71]

Adding an extra facet of mystery is the question of who was lord of Transjordan during these events. On 18 November 1167, during a visit by Amalric to Kerak, Walter of Beirut pledged an annual gift of 40 bezants to the order of St Lazarus. The funds were to be drawn from the money fief that he had received from the king in exchange for Beirut. The gift was made to benefit the soul of his wife, confirming Helena's death by this time, and it was offered with the approval of Guy and Beatrice, his brother and daughter respectively. Walter was thus still lord-regent of Transjordan, but he now served on behalf of his daughter, who had succeeded her mother as heiress. This is the only mention of Beatrice, who was evidently dead by February 1174, when Walter was no longer lord of Transjordan. When exactly Beatrice died, and thus when Walter's governance of Transjordan ended, is unknown.[72]

In February 1174, when Amalric confirmed the gift made in 1167, Walter is identified as 'Walter of Beirut, lord of Blanchegarde'. The confirmation was issued in Acre and among the ten recorded witnesses are the archbishops of Petra and Hebron, as well as the man who may already have succeeded Walter as lord of Kerak, Miles of Plancy. The *Lignages* states that Walter received Blanchegarde when he gave up Beirut; however, there is nothing to corroborate his possession of the small lordship before this confirmation was issued, leaving it possible that the king may have granted Blanchegarde to Walter out of pity following his daughter's death. Even though Walter is clearly identified as the lord of Blanchegarde from this time, a certain Arnulf appears as castellan of Blanchegarde between 1165 and 1178, suggesting that although Amalric gave the lordship to Walter, the king retained control of the castle.[73] Despite no longer holding Transjordan, or any other sizable lordship, Walter remained a person of some standing in the kingdom. He witnessed royal charters into the late 1170s, continuing to style himself as 'Walter of Beirut', after his original patrimony, despite having relinquished that lordship more than a decade earlier.[74]

The Archbishopric of Petra

In about 1167, during the tenure of Walter of Beirut as lord of Transjordan, a new Latin archbishop was appointed to Kerak. Centuries earlier, during the early Byzantine period, Petra (Wadi Musa) was one of three metropolitan bishoprics subject to the patriarch of Jerusalem; the archbishop of Petra had twelve suffragans of his own. In the middle of the seventh century, around the time of the Muslim conquest of the region, the seat of metropolitan authority was moved to Rabbath (Rabba, mod. Amman), though little is heard of a bishop at Rabbath or Wadi Musa thereafter. By the 1160s, Frankish authority and perhaps even settlement in Transjordan had become sufficient to justify restoring the diocese of Petra. Kerak, the main centre of Frankish power in the region, was chosen as the site for the episcopal seat and a Latin archbishop was appointed.[75]

The figure chosen to serve as the first Latin archbishop was Guerric, a canon of the *Templum Domini*; this is perhaps unsurprising given the order's prominent and longstanding presence in the region. A formal agreement concluded in 1181 between Archbishop Guerric and the Hospitallers, regarding the tithe owed by the latter, provides a small glimpse into the structure and personnel of the diocese, or at least the cathedral church. The charter was witnessed by seven canons of Kerak: a dean, archdeacon, cantor, three priests, and a subdeacon. Guerric was the only Latin archbishop of Petra to serve in Kerak. He survived Saladin's conquest of Transjordan but died in 1190, probably of disease, at the protracted siege of Acre, during what is now known as the Third Crusade.[76]

The Latin archbishop of Petra had a single suffragan, the Greek bishop of Pharan. The see of Pharan, an oasis in the Sinai, had been transferred to Mount Sinai in the ninth century, and by the twelfth century the abbot of St Catherine's Monastery also served as bishop. As late as 1166, a diptych produced for the monastery reveals that the monks recognized the authority of the Greek Church, offering prayers in the name of the Orthodox patriarch of Jerusalem, as well as the patriarchs of Constantinople, Alexandria and Antioch – not to the Latin patriarch of Jerusalem nor the pope in Rome. It is unclear if or to what degree the Orthodox abbot acknowledged the presumed authority of the new Latin archbishop at Kerak in the years that followed, but as there were apparently no Latin churches that might have fallen under this distant Orthodox bishop, there is no evidence of any jurisdictional issues.[77]

Stephanie and Miles of Plancy

With the death of Beatrice, the lordship of Transjordan passed to her aunt, Stephanie, the daughter of Philip of Milly and younger sister of Helena. Stephanie's first husband was Humphrey [III] of Toron, son of the apparently unanimously respected Humphrey II, lord of Toron and constable of the kingdom of Jerusalem. The two were probably wed around the time that her father became lord of Transjordan. Stephanie and Humphrey had two children: a son, Humphrey [IV], who became the heir apparent of his parents, and a daughter, Isabella. Humphrey [III] predeceased his famous father, and was thus never lord of Toron in his own right, though he is still typically designated as Humphrey 'III' or 'the younger' for the sake of clarity. Humphrey the younger is last found as a witness to a charter that was drawn up in August 1168, more than ten years before his father's death. As he is referred to simply as the son of Humphrey the constable, it is very unlikely that he had become lord of Transjordan by this time. It is unclear when exactly he died, but William of Tyre suggests that it was not long before Amalric arranged for Stephanie to remarry, choosing as her new husband one of his favourites, Miles of Plancy.[78]

Miles was originally from the Champagne region, and a distant relative of King Amalric. He first appears in the kingdom of Jerusalem in the charter issued by Amalric confirming the grant made by Philip of Milly to the Templars in January 1166. The first mention of Miles in William of Tyre's history is found during the Frankish expedition to Egypt in 1167, when Miles led a secondary action around Cairo during the opening phase of the campaign. William of Tyre, who had no affection for Miles, cast him as having considerable influence over the king during the Frankish invasion of Egypt the following year. Amalric had elevated Miles to the position of seneschal by May 1168, and that October he appears as 'Lord Miles of Plancy' among the witnesses to a grant made by the king to the Hospitallers. This latter designation seems to refer to Miles' rising rank in a general sense; the charter was issued only two months after the last mention of Humphrey the younger, which does not allow for a sufficient mourning period for Miles to have married Stephanie and become 'lord' of Transjordan. Miles is found on a number of subsequent charters, where he is listed as 'Miles the seneschal' or simply 'Miles of Plancy'. Not until April 1174 does he first appear as 'Miles, lord of Montreal' (*Milo Montis Regalis domnus*). When exactly Miles came to hold Kerak is thus unclear.[79]

Walter of Beirut lost control of Transjordan with the death of his daughter sometime between November 1167 and February 1174, during which period Humphrey the younger also died. It is not inconceivable that Beatrice predeceased Humphrey, which would have made Humphrey the lord-regent of Transjordan for a brief period, though nowhere is he documented as ever having assumed this position. Considering Miles' active and influential role in Egypt, William of Tyre would most likely have mentioned that he had become lord of Transjordan had this happened by the end of 1168. It is not unlikely that Beatrice lived until 1172 or 1173, quite possibly outliving Humphrey. This would justify contemporary suggestions that Miles married Stephanie, thanks to Amalric, and in so doing gained Transjordan, the implication being that she was heiress at the time of their marriage, which could only have taken place after an appropriate period of mourning for her first husband. The lack of any reference to Humphrey's death may suggest that it was less than sensational, perhaps after an extended period of illness, which would explain his absence from the charter evidence if he were still alive in the years following 1168.[80]

Miles, who probably did not become lord-regent of Transjordan until 1173 at the earliest, was not lord for long. His meteoric rise in the kingdom had been thanks to his close relationship with the king. Amalric died in July 1174, leaving behind a minor, Baldwin IV, as his heir. Amalric had not designated a regent for his son before his death, so temporary control of the kingdom, apart from the army, fell to Miles in his capacity as seneschal. Raymond III of Tripoli, Amalric's cousin, demanded to be named regent as the young king's closest male relative on his father's side, but Miles refused to agree to this before a meeting of the high court could be convened to formally address the matter. The standoff between Miles and Raymond came to an end later in 1174 when Miles was stabbed to death in the streets of Acre. William of Tyre provides no indications of who might have been responsible for Miles' murder. The later *Brevis historia*, however, implicates 'the lords of Beirut'. Significantly, there was no lord of Beirut at this time. Aside from its brief possession by Andronikos Komnenos, the lordship had remained under royal control since it had been given up by Walter in the 1160s.[81]

As Bernard Hamilton has argued, it is not inconceivable that Walter still harboured deep resentment that Beirut had not been returned to him when he lost control of Transjordan. Walter may have believed that Miles, as seneschal and temporary administrative regent, had the power to satisfy him but chose not to – though neither did Raymond of Tripoli when he became regent. If Raymond had a more direct part in Miles' death, William of Tyre was unlikely to mention this. It was Raymond, during his brief period as regent for Baldwin IV, from the autumn of 1174 to the summer of 1176, who was responsible for elevating William to two of the highest clerical offices, first archbishop of Tyre and then royal chancellor.[82]

Whereas it is unclear when exactly Walter stopped serving as lord-regent of Transjordan, and from what point Miles stepped into this role, Miles' death in 1174 marks a clear transition point. What is perhaps strange is that Stephanie did not immediately remarry once her year of mourning had run out.[83] It was not until late 1176 at the earliest that she took her third husband, Reynald of Châtillon. It was within the power of the monarch, or his regent, to pressure an important heiress to take a husband, and no heiress was as important as Stephanie at this time. Not until Baldwin IV had come of age would she remarry, and the husband she chose had only just returned to the kingdom. Arabic sources later give Stephanie quite a bit of agency when negotiating the release of her son, Humphrey [IV], after the Battle of Hattin, so it is not inconceivable that she was quite prepared to rule reasonably independently until a suitor appeared who satisfied both her interests and those of the king. Reynald would quickly prove himself a staunch supporter of young Baldwin IV, far from the domineering figure that Raymond III may have become.

What makes Stephanie's delayed remarriage all the more interesting is that the fief of Transjordan had never been as important as it became around the time of Miles' death. Nur al-Din had died in May 1174, two months before Amalric. Saladin, who still commanded Egypt, was the most powerful of Nur al-Din's former emirs, and it was not long until he set about expanding his influence and authority into Syria. In October, Saladin took control of Damascus. Continuing northward, he extended his authority across most of northern Syria by year's end. Although Aleppo would evade his grasp until 1183, Saladin's realm enveloped the Frankish principalities; never before had they faced a neighbour with such resources at his disposal.[84] Whereas Saladin may have initially enjoyed the Frankish presence in Transjordan, which formed a buffer between himself and Nur al-Din, as master of both Cairo and Damascus it was now very clearly in his interest to remove any obstacle to the free movement of merchants, pilgrims and troops between his two bases of power.

Stephanie and Reynald of Châtillon

Reynald of Châtillon is without doubt the most famous Frankish lord of Transjordan. He first appears in the records of the Latin East as a prominent knight who served Baldwin III for pay during the siege of Ascalon in 1153. Quickly thereafter, Reynald married Constance of Antioch, which elevated him to the position of prince-regent of Antioch on behalf of his young stepson, Bohemond III. Most information about Reynald comes from the account of William of Tyre; however, Reynald, not unlike Miles of Plancy before him, would find himself one of Raymond III of Tripoli's leading opponents, and thus on the opposite side of the political divide from William. The marriage of Constance and Reynald was criticized by William, who believed Reynald's station was well below that of his new wife. Despite this, the historian apparently thought Reynald of sufficient rank, or at least later importance, to name him among the nine leading secular figures who accompanied the king at the start of the siege of Ascalon. Some of the other eight names will at this point be familiar: Hugh of Ibelin, Philip of Milly, Humphrey (II) of Toron, Simon of Tiberias, Gerard of Sidon, Guy of Beirut, Maurice of Montreal, and Walter of St Omer, who served the king for pay, like Reynald.[85]

Reynald was energetic and headstrong. Although sometimes portrayed as a fanatic, he was rather opportunistic and forceful, if also rather impetuous in his younger years. The marriage of Constance and Reynald did not please the patriarch of Antioch, who became an opponent of the new prince. Their feud reached a pinnacle around 1154 when Reynald had the patriarch taken up to the citadel of Antioch, where the cleric was made to sit in the summer sun with honey covering his head to attract flies.[86] The following year, Reynald lashed out against the Byzantines.

The Byzantine emperors had maintained a claim to Antioch since the time of the First Crusade, when emperor Alexios Komnenos had insisted that the crusade's leaders agree to return any territory captured from the Muslims that had once been part of the Byzantine empire. When Alexios's son and successor, John, visited Syria in 1137–38, he was finally able to receive the submission of the Frankish principality, which was at that time ruled by Constance's first husband, Raymond of Poitiers. Almost two decades later, John's son, Manuel Komnenos, using his position of superiority, asked Reynald to deal with a rebellious figure in Cilicia. Reynald, who was promised support and a considerable reward, dutifully complied, but afterwards felt that the emperor had not lived up to his pledge to compensate him. This led Reynald to turn against the empire and raid Byzantine Cyprus, which was inhabited by Orthodox Christians, in 1156. Reynald was forced into a very public show of submission when Manuel opted to personally lead an army into Cilicia and then northern Syria in 1158–59.[87]

Despite his occasional recklessness, Reynald provided Antioch with almost a decade of strong and stable leadership. This came to an end in 1161, when he was captured while leading a raid into what had once been the county of Edessa.[88] Although Baldwin III of Jerusalem was called north to settle affairs, it was not long before Bohemond III came of age and could rule in his own name. A few years later, Reynald gained some company in the dungeons of Aleppo.

In 1164, while Amalric led Frankish forces in Egypt, countering the Damascene army sent there under Shirkuh, Nur al-Din scored a major victory in northern Syria. In August, not far from Harim, a combined army of Franks, Byzantines and Armenians was decisively defeated and most of its leaders taken prisoner.[89] To avoid provoking the Byzantines, Nur al-Din quickly ransomed those prisoners linked to the empire, including Bohemond III, whose principality was recognized to be a nominal part of the Byzantine realm. Other captives included Count Raymond III of Tripoli, Joscelin [III] of Courtenay, titular count of Edessa, and numerous others, including Walter of Beirut and his brothers. According to William of Tyre, Raymond of Tripoli was released after eight years, for a sum of 80,000 gold coins, presumably dinars. A few years later, in the second year of Baldwin IV's reign (July 1175 to

July 1176), Joscelin of Courtenay and Reynald of Châtillon were also set free. This took place after Nur al-Din's death in May 1174, and was symptomatic of the power struggle that had emerged in Muslim Syria. With Saladin actively campaigning to extend his authority, those ruling Aleppo on behalf of Nur al-Din's young son, al-Salih Isma'il, played the cards at their disposal, cashing in on ransoms as they looked to raise money and secure peace with their Frankish neighbours in the face of this greater threat to their autonomy. Michael the Syrian, who confirms the figure paid to secure the release of Raymond III, notes that Joscelin's ransom was set at 50,000 dinars, while Reynald's liberation cost a staggering 120,000 dinars.[90]

Reynald's ransom is exceptional. It was 50 per cent greater than that of Raymond of Tripoli, one of the four independent Latin princes of the Levant and a first cousin of Baldwin III and Amalric, and more than twice as much paid to free Joscelin of Courtenay, the maternal uncle and closest male relative of King Baldwin IV. Both Raymond and Joscelin were influential figures from ruling families, Reynald was not. During his captivity, Constance had died and Bohemond III had come of age, leaving Reynald with neither lands nor significant family connections. Although William of Tyre claims that Reynald's ransom was paid 'by his friends', it is possible that a large part was provided by the Byzantine emperor.

Manuel Komnenos was not only Reynald's former overlord, but he had married Maria of Antioch, Reynald's stepdaughter. Maria was older than her brother Bohemond III, making her a teenager when Reynald was captured, shortly before her imperial marriage in December 1161. Reynald's own daughter with Constance, Agnes, had followed her half-sister to Constantinople at a later date, where Manuel arranged for her to marry Béla III of Hungary. Reynald's son, Baldwin, accompanied his sister and entered Byzantine service, where he died commanding the right flank of the Byzantine army at the great Battle of Myriokephalon on 17 September 1176. The favour shown to Reynald's children would appear to confirm that the emperor had forgiven the prince for his actions on Cyprus in 1156. Hamilton has also identified Reynald himself at Constantinople shortly after his release.[91] If Reynald's ransom was paid by Manuel, it is possible that he travelled first to Constantinople, where he would have been able to see his son and stepdaughter, before proceeding to Jerusalem. Hamilton, however, proposes that Reynald was instead sent to Constantinople from Jerusalem, leading a delegation dispatched by Baldwin IV to renew his father's peace with the Byzantines, in which case Reynald would have arrived after his son's death. Regardless of when Reynald visited the imperial court, if his ransom was indeed paid by Manuel, he was a natural figure to serve as an envoy to Constantinople, or a more subtle advocate of Byzantine friendship at the Frankish court in Jerusalem – if the emperor bought Reynald's freedom, he presumably also secured his good will.

The timing of Reynald's visit to Constantinople hinges on a charter issued in the summer of 1176, which places Reynald in Jerusalem at that time. In recognition of his former position, he appears first among the listed witnesses, followed by his one-time fellow captive, Joscelin of Courtenay.[92] Reynald continued to receive the title of 'prince', an honorific in recognition of his former position that he would continue to employ throughout the remainder of his life. Despite holding no lands, Reynald enjoyed considerable prestige following his release, evidenced not only by his title but by his second marriage.

Rise to Prominence

Baldwin IV came of age in 1176, two years after his father's death. The young king, who had seen Miles of Plancy and Raymond of Tripoli contest the regency, and then the latter dominate the kingdom's affairs following Miles' death, may have looked for allies as he asserted his direct authority for the first time. Fortunately for the young king, this was precisely when Joscelin and Reynald returned to the scene. Both were men of high rank, Joscelin by birth and Reynald by marriage. Baldwin, or more likely his mother, Agnes of Courtenay, recognized that both men were of the highest standing but entirely reliant on royal favour. They would become the core of a new royalist faction, which would help ensure the king, a sickly adolescent, would not be dominated by his baronage.

Joscelin was appointed royal seneschal and given a considerable lordship in western Galilee. As Baldwin IV's maternal uncle, he was the king's closest male relative, yet had no claim to the throne, so posed no threat. Reynald had held an even more prestigious position, as prince of Antioch, and his marriage to Constance had brought him into the extended royal family. The king quickly agreed to Reynald's marriage to Stephanie of Milly; twice widowed, she was still heiress of Transjordan.[93] More than two decades after becoming prince-regent of Antioch, Reynald had again gained control of a large and influential lordship, though Transjordan was somewhat less prestigious. As with his earlier marriage to Constance, his new wife brought to their union the children she had with her first husband.

Reynald's return coincided with an increasing sense of uncertainty and insecurity in the kingdom of Jerusalem, due in part to Saladin's conquests, but also lingering dynastic issues. Baldwin III had been succeeded by his younger brother, Amalric, in 1163, but the baronage refused to approve Amalric's accession until he dissolved his marriage to his first wife, Agnes of Courtenay, the daughter of Joscelin II of Edessa and thus Amalric's cousin in the fourth degree. Amalric agreed to this, but their children, Sibylla and Baldwin (IV), were recognized to be legitimate. Amalric subsequently married Maria Komnene, the grandniece of Byzantine Emperor Manuel Komnenos, with whom he had another daughter, Isabella. Following Amalric's death in 1174, Baldwin IV became king. It was quickly acknowledged, however, that the young king suffered from leprosy and would father no children, leading the line of succession to focus on his older sister. Sibylla's first husband was William of Montferrat, whom she married in 1176. William died the following year, leaving Sibylla pregnant with a son, the future Baldwin V. The posthumous child complicated matters and made the search for another husband for Sibylla more difficult – just as Reynald had twice married widows with sons by their first marriage, Sibylla's next husband would rule in her name only until his stepson came of age.[94]

Baldwin IV's illness left him unable to command the kingdom's army at times, a role that would be expected to pass to Sibylla's husband, as guardian of her young son, the king's nephew and heir. With William of Montferrat's death, shortly after Reynald's return, this responsibility fell to Reynald: he had the rank and experience as both former prince of Antioch and current lord of Transjordan; and his first marriage provided a loose personal connection to the royal family. When Philip of Flanders arrived on crusade in the summer of 1177, Reynald quickly relinquished his position of authority in favour of the count, who was also a cousin of the king. When Philip refused the honour, it returned to Reynald.[95] It was at the hands of Reynald, as commander of the army of Jerusalem, that Saladin would suffer the greatest military defeat of his life.

Following his marriage to Stephanie of Milly, Reynald became the figure who stood to threaten communication between Saladin's two centres of power. Although he would prove a great menace to Saladin operating from Transjordan, the first engagement between the two men took place in southern Palestine. In the summer of 1177, Saladin had been preparing for a Frankish invasion of Egypt, and indeed a Byzantine fleet, responding to the renewed alliance between Jerusalem and Constantinople, reached Palestine to undertake a cooperative campaign. The planned action against Egypt, however, was sabotaged by Count Philip of Flanders, who arrived in the Levant around the same time. Through objection and delay, the count manoeuvred to arrange the postponement of the Frankish-Byzantine invasion until the following year. This freed Philip to campaign to the north in the autumn, fulfilling his crusading vow, and leave the Levant before any action against Egypt could take place. While the count was away to the north, accompanied by certain nobles of the kingdom, Saladin opted to go on the offensive. In the autumn of 1177, he led his army out of Egypt, taking the coastal road via al-'Arish. Finding what Frankish forces remained in the kingdom mustered at Ascalon, but showing no willingness to offer battle, Saladin and his army continued northward. As the Muslims began to spread out, raiding and pillaging the evacuated settlements around Ramla, the Frankish army moved against them. Still disorganized when the Franks arrived, Saladin's forces suffered a crushing defeat near Montgisard. William of Tyre placed the army of Jerusalem under the leadership of Baldwin IV, but Ernoul and Baha' al-Din would subsequently note that it was Reynald, rather than the sickly king, who commanded the triumphant Franks.[96] William, it seems, was reluctant to attribute the glory of this victory to Reynald, an emerging political opponent.

Reynald remained one of the most influential figures in the kingdom over the following few years. In 1181, he accompanied the patriarch of Jerusalem, as well as the masters of the Templars and Hospitallers, and Raymond III of Tripoli, to resolve a conflict that had developed to the north between Bohemond III, Reynald's stepson, and the Patriarch of Antioch. Back in Palestine, he commanded sufficient authority to moderate a dispute between the monastery of St Mary of the Valley of Jehoshaphat and the convent of St Mary the Great. Thanks to the king's favour, Reynald also negotiated advantageous marriages for his younger stepchildren. Stephanie's son, Humphrey [IV], was betrothed to the king's 8-year-old half-sister, Isabella, daughter of Amalric and Maria Komnene, in the autumn of 1181. For Humphrey's sister, Isabella, Reynald may have leaned on the connections and reputation he had forged in the north two decades earlier to arrange her marriage to Prince Roupen III of Armenia. When considering his influence at the time, Reynald most likely had a hand in approving, or at least endorsing, the marriage of the king's older sister, Sibylla, to Guy of Lusignan in 1180. Guy came from a family with a proud crusading history, but he himself was not of impressive rank. Guy's older brother, Aimery, had preceded him to the Holy Land, and became constable sometime following the death of his predecessor, Humphrey II of Toron, in 1179. Reynald probably also supported the candidacy of Heraclius, archbishop of Caesarea, following the death of Amalric of Nesle, the patriarch of Jerusalem, in 1180. The other patriarchal candidate, who lost the job to Heraclius, was none other than the historian William, archbishop of Tyre, who continued to serve as royal chancellor. Collectively, Reynald of Châtillon, Agnes and Joscelin of Courtenay, Guy and Aimery of Lusignan, and Heraclius, the patriarch, dominated the affairs of the kingdom during the early reign of Baldwin IV.[97]

Opposition to these figures, many of whom owed their influence to royal favour and advantageous marriages, mounted among the more established baronage, who came to rally behind Raymond III of Tripoli. Tensions only increased following Guy's marriage to Sibylla, from which point he, as stepfather of the king's heir, became the natural figure to lead the kingdom's army when Baldwin IV was unable to do so. Raymond, as Guy's main opponent, was the natural alternative when the king found his brother-in-law's conduct displeasing. Meanwhile, Reynald remained a prominent figure. When witnessing royal charters, and those issued by Guy and Sibylla, Reynald's name appears first among all secular figures during this period, except on one dated to 6 February 1182, when Reynald appears second to Guy, showing deference to the guardian of the royal heir.[98]

The Arabian Campaigns

When Guy of Lusignan married Sibylla in 1180, he replaced Reynald as the king's leading deputy. Having lost his position of prominence in Jerusalem, Reynald appears to have spent more time in Transjordan from around 1181. During Saladin's invasion of Palestine in 1177, Reynald had been the architect of the Frankish victory; operating out of Kerak, Reynald took the fight to his Muslim neighbours, preying on the lucrative caravan trade that moved between Cairo and Damascus. Free from duties associated with the regency, Reynald began to implement the type of aggressive foreign policy in Transjordan that had brought him renown in Antioch.

In early 1182, Reynald led a daring raid into the Hijaz, the prosperous western region of Arabia. The timing of the action is not entirely clear, as the raid is said to have followed the winter rains, which inundated 'Aqaba in December–January, but before Saladin left Egypt for Syria in May. Charters place Reynald in Acre throughout the month of February, and in Jerusalem in late April, leaving it possible that the raid took place in either January or March. Reynald led his party to 'Aqaba, where he left a detachment to guard his rear, before pushing on towards the pilgrimage town of Tabuk. Letters from the local official at 'Aqaba, who was fearing such a raid in the months leading up to this, confirms that it was the greater than average rains that year that allowed the Frankish cavalry to graze further south than would otherwise have been possible. The raiders may have made it as far as Tayma, a prosperous oasis town halfway between 'Aqaba and Medina. The Franks are said to have been compelled to turn back when they learned that Farrukhshah, Saladin's nephew and deputy in Syria, had invaded Transjordan, implying Reynald feared losses there and perhaps even the prospect of being pinned in northern Arabia. Although this is the first recorded Frankish raid into Arabia, there is no dramatic account of these events from a Latin perspective. William of Tyre rather ambiguously recorded that there were reports that Reynald had seized some people during a period of truce, which led Saladin to break the peace in order to take revenge, associating this with the sultan's subsequent march into Syria that spring. William, like 'Imad al-Din, was more concerned with what followed.[99]

Saladin's departure from Egypt for Syria in May 1182 had more to do with broader political developments than Reynald's raid into the northern Hijaz. Aleppo remained beyond his control, but al-Salih Isma'il had died in December 1181, providing Saladin an opportunity to renew efforts against the city. Upon reaching 'Aqaba, Saladin learned that the army of Jerusalem had assembled and moved into Transjordan. According to 'Imad al-Din, the Franks took up a position at Kerak, but this did not deter Saladin. The sultan continued northward with a group of elite forces, raiding Frankish territory as they followed the main road towards Kerak. Taj al-Muluk Buri, one of Saladin's brothers, led the remainder of the army along the eastern desert road, re-joining Saladin at al-Azraq, 85km east of Amman. William of Tyre similarly noted that Saladin approached Montreal, sending out raiders to scout the region and locate the Frankish army, which Baldwin IV had led to Kerak. Both William and 'Imad al-Din observed that the concentration of Frankish forces at Kerak in the south allowed Farrukhshah to send a large party of raiders from Damascus into northern Palestine. On its return, this force captured the cave fortress of al-Habis Jaldak, which was cut into the canyon wall above the Yarmuk River, east of the Sea of Galilee.[100]

In the background to these events, court politics in the kingdom of Jerusalem were becoming increasingly divisive. When it became known that Saladin was on the move, it was Reynald's allies at court who persuaded Baldwin IV to take the army of Jerusalem to Transjordan. Reynald, who appears to have been at Kerak to receive the king, had evidently set out ahead of the army around the end of April, probably anticipating Saladin's return to Syria. Thanks to the presence of the Frankish army at Kerak, Saladin was prevented from inflicting any meaningful retribution against Reynald following his raid into Arabia. Raymond III of Tripoli accompanied the king to Kerak, but he had led the opposition to this move, and it was his lands, which he held through his wife, Eschiva Bures, heiress of the principality of Galilee, that were plundered by the raiders dispatched by Farrukhshah when the army of Jerusalem went south.

Reynald's raid into the Hijaz was unprecedented, and perceptions of its significance varied. Aside from the letters that attest to Reynald passing 'Aqaba in early 1182, each account was written with a degree of hindsight and clear biases. William of Tyre was either uninterested, uninformed, or consciously downplayed the significance of the exploits of a political rival, while Baha' al-Din omitted any mention of the incident, passing over this blow to Saladin's reputation. The more dramatic accounts provided by figures like Ibn al-Athir, by contrast, appear to reflect a sensational version of events published by Saladin's chancery, perhaps at a later date. According to this tradition, Reynald had planned to raid as far as the holy city of Medina. Such exaggerations were used to advance Saladin's image as a *mujahid*, emphasizing the threats that he faced and was able to defeat, and at the same time to condemn those Muslim neighbours who resisted his suzerainty and prevented him from devoting all of his attention to fighting the Franks. Despite attempts to spin Reynald's raid to Saladin's advantage, it was nevertheless damaging to the sultan's image. It was around this time, however, that Reynald's influence also suffered a setback.

At some point following Reynald's departure from Acre in February 1182, Raymond III of Tripoli became the king's pre-eminent deputy. Starting that April, Raymond's name appears first among the witnesses of royal charters, preceding that of Guy, stepfather of the king's heir, while Reynald's name fell behind Joscelin of Courtenay's. Hamilton has suggested that Reynald's reversal of fortunes was a direct result of his raid, because it violated a peace that had been concluded between Saladin and Baldwin IV. Although plausible, evidence of such an explicit link is found nowhere in the sources.[101] Raymond of Tripoli would continue to serve as the de facto regent and commander of the army when necessary until Baldwin IV's health declined significantly in the summer of 1183, and then again until the king's death in March 1185. With the succession of Baldwin V, stepson of Guy of Lusignan, Reynald's name once more gains primacy in the lists of witnesses to charters issued by the young king's mother and stepfather.[102]

Even though his position had slid slightly during the intermittent years, Reynald was still clearly a figure of paramount standing and importance in the kingdom, and when considering that Raymond was promoted at the expense of Guy, Reynald's own demotion may simply reflect the reality that he was Guy's closest ally; Joscelin of Courtney, as the king's uncle, enjoyed greater political insulation. Reynald's raid into northern Arabia in early 1182 had been daring, but this was quickly overshadowed by a much more elaborate expedition the next year.

Following Saladin's return to Syria in the spring of 1182, he led actions into Galilee and then against Beirut later in the year. He then turned his attention beyond the Euphrates, undertaking an extended campaign that would establish his authority across the Jazira as far as the outskirts of Mosul. Intriguingly, Saladin concluded no peace agreements with the Franks before heading east, almost challenging them to move against him while he was away. Baldwin IV led a raid into the Hawran in the autumn, moving towards Bosra and then up towards Damascus, recapturing al-Habis Jaldak before returning west of the

Jordan. In December, with Saladin still away, plans were approved for another raid towards Bosra. William of Tyre noted that the king accompanied this expedition, but that it was led by Raymond III of Tripoli because it was his lands that bordered the region to be raided. This may have been a convenient justification or explanation for why command was not given to Guy. Although Guy is not mentioned during these actions, Patriarch Heraclius took part and presumably so too did Guy's brother, Aimery of Lusignan, in his capacity as the kingdom's constable. Reynald was not with the army during these actions; instead, he was in Transjordan preparing for an extraordinary enterprise.[103]

Reynald had been in Acre in late August 1182, but appears to have returned to Transjordan around the same time that Saladin headed for the Jazira. Far from waiting idly by, he oversaw the construction of boats at Kerak. With the help of the local Bedouin, who appear to have regularly supported Reynald's raiding activities, these boats were carried in sections on the backs of camels to the shores of the Gulf of 'Aqaba. The boat components were then assembled and this small fleet, which Ernoul claims numbered five vessels, was put to sea. Two boats were said to have blockaded the small offshore stronghold that Saladin had captured a decade earlier, while the rest proceeded southward. This is the first and only occasion where a Frankish force is noted to have embarked on the Red Sea. Indicative of his politics, William of Tyre fails to make any mention of the expedition, though it is noted by Ernoul, who was closely associated with the Ibelin family and thus belonged to the same baronial court faction as William. The purpose of the expedition, according to Ernoul, was exploration, a not unreasonable suggestion considering Reynald's move deep into northern Arabia the previous year.[104]

The group of vessels that pushed onwards from 'Aqaba crossed to the western side of the Red Sea, making for 'Aydhab, then sailed to the western coast of Arabia. Saladin was at this time in the region of Mosul, the furthest he would ever be from Kerak, so the task of dealing with this group of Franks fell to his brother, al-'Adil, whom he had left as his deputy in Egypt. Al-'Adil dispatched Husam al-Din Lu'lu', who brought boats to the shores of the Red Sea and there set about hunting down the Franks. The vessels that had stayed behind to blockade the island castle near 'Aqaba were dealt with first; Lu'lu' then pursued the rest, following them to 'Aydhab before catching up with them along the Arabian coast. The Franks eventually ran their ships aground and attempted to escape into Arabia, though they were overtaken by their pursuers. Those who survived to be taken captive were distributed through Saladin's realm for execution. In Alexandria, the traveller Ibn Jubayr came across a group of these Frankish prisoners. Ernoul confirms that those who had set out from 'Aqaba were never heard from again.[105]

Reynald, who planned the Red Sea expedition, did not personally take part. Although a group of Franks presumably led this campaign, the crews of these vessels almost certainly included a number of local Christians from Transjordan, who would have been relied on to do most of the sailing. Some of these Syrians may have left 'Aqaba when it fell back under Muslim rule in 1170, and would have been familiar with the waters of the Red Sea; others might have made their living on the Dead Sea and took part for pay or the prospect of plunder. Local Bedouin had been relied on to help move the boats from Kerak down to 'Aqaba. The involvement of some of these local nomads is not surprising given their implicit involvement in Reynald's raid into northern Arabia the previous year, where their knowledge of the region made them indispensable guides. When considering 'Imad al-Din's claims that Saladin's campaigns in Transjordan in 1171 and 1173 had been directed against the Bedouin of the region, it seems there was already a working relationship between the Franks and certain Bedouin groups. Saladin's increasing hostility may have pushed some into even closer cooperation with Reynald.

Following his return from the Jazira, Saladin finally captured Aleppo in June 1183. When he subsequently travelled to Damascus, the army of Jerusalem was assembled in anticipation of another invasion of the kingdom. While the Frankish army waited, Baldwin IV fell ill at Nazareth. Rather than having been simply overexerted or otherwise weak, it seems the king was not expected to recover on this occasion. In recognition of the line of succession, Guy of Lusignan, rather than Raymond of Tripoli, was appointed regent and commander of the army. Reynald, who had returned to Palestine shortly after the Red Sea expedition, and is found in Acre in mid-March, was also with the army at this time. Saladin crossed into Galilee in late September. A party under 'Izz al-Din Jurdik moved out ahead of the main army to scout the region and locate the Franks. This detachment encountered a force from Kerak and Montreal that was marching north to join the Frankish army; a hundred of these Franks were reportedly taken prisoner. When Saladin brought his main force forward, the Frankish army, under Guy's leadership, shadowed the invaders but refused to be drawn into a pitched battle. So long as the Frankish army was in the region, Saladin was unable to besiege a significant stronghold and gain any lasting advantage, forcing him to content himself with pillaging the towns that were abandoned ahead of the Muslim army. After little more than a week, Saladin was compelled to withdraw. In frustration, he turned on Kerak.[106]

Siege of 1183

Far more is known about Reynald's actions in the Levant than any other lord of Transjordan, thanks in no small part to his proximity to William of Tyre and Saladin's celebratory biographers. Despite this, his contributions to the architectural development of Kerak are hard to discern. The most detailed picture of the lordship during his tenure is provided by a charter issued in November 1177 to the Hospitallers, in which Reynald and Stephanie confirm what had been granted to the order by Maurice in 1152. In the region of Montreal, this included: the village of Benisalem, along with its free inhabitants on either side of the principal wadi; the formerly mentioned Syrian, Caissar, along with his heirs and possessions; land between the vineyards of Seguin and William the Ass; and a house in Montreal, presumably the one between those of Caissar and that which belonged to the viscount of Nablus. In the region of Kerak, this included: the village of Cansil, along with its associated rural lands and settlers, and the adjacent ruined settlement of Hable, which is not found in the earlier charter; land next to the vineyard that had belonged to John the castellan and then the archbishop of Petra; a house in Kerak; and the boat that the Hospitallers were permitted to use to transport goods duty free across the Dead Sea. Additionally, the order was recognized to possess a small garden that had been donated by Stephanie, perhaps following the death of Miles, as she apparently made this grant on her own. Reynald and Stephanie also added at this time some partly cultivated lands that had belonged to Lord Theobald of Bethune prior to his death.[107]

Aside from what was added to that which the Hospitallers had received in 1152, the confirmation issued in 1177 contains some noticeable omissions. There is no mention of the fortifications at Kerak – the tower and barbican – that had been granted to the order. The most obvious explanation would appear to be that ongoing building efforts led to the replacement or reconfiguring of these defensive structures, or that they were otherwise relinquished by the Hospitallers at some unrecorded point in time. It is possible, if unlikely, that the tower, having lost its military value, might be associated with the nondescript house (*domus*) in Kerak, which is mentioned for the first time. All things considered, however, this house was probably located in the town.

Also missing from the 1177 confirmation is the tax that the Hospitallers were entitled to collect on goods and booty captured from Muslims, once the Church had received its share. This may relate to an ongoing dispute between the order and the archbishop of Petra, which was not settled until 1181. The eventual agreement established the tithe owed on all Hospitaller property in the diocese at 40 bezants. An additional provision stipulated that half the standard tithe was to be levied on all property subsequently acquired by the order, excluding animal fodder, vineyards and gardens, so long as the order financed the costs associated with the harvest, and that the archbishop had not previously collected a tithe from these lands.[108] It seems, however, that the position of the Hospitallers had declined somewhat at Kerak, as there is no mention of the order during any of the attacks made against the castle in the following years.

Shortly after Saladin's return to Damascus in the middle of October 1183, Frankish fears that he would strike again were realized. Reynald had already made his way to Kerak by the time Saladin arrived with his army. Security concerns might have contributed to Reynald's return to Transjordan, but so too was his presence required to host a celebration: the marriage of his stepson, Humphrey [IV] of Toron, to Isabella of Jerusalem, the king's half-sister. If William of Tyre is correct, and Isabella was 8 at the time of her betrothal in October 1180, she would have been 12 at this moment, the minimum required age for girls to marry. Saladin's army may have arrived at Kerak on the very day that the wedding was celebrated.

Saladin had set out from Damascus on 22 October. His move into Transjordan appears to have had the double objective of capturing the castle and using the occasion of the siege, which drew together figures from both Syria and Egypt, to make certain administrative rearrangements. Following Saladin's acquisition of Aleppo earlier in the year, his younger brother, al-'Adil, had made a request to swap his position in Cairo, where he administered Egypt in his older brother's absence, for Aleppo and northern Syria. An attack against Kerak provided Saladin with a convenient opportunity to facilitate this exchange and replenish his army, replacing Syrian and Mesopotamian troops whom he had released following the incursion into Palestine with well-rested forces from Egypt. Responding to his brother's summons, al-'Adil led not only a portion of the Egyptian army into Transjordan, accompanied by his personal treasure and family members, but also a large party of merchants, who used the protection afforded by the army to make the journey to Syria.[109]

Saladin's main force, moving south from Damascus, paused at Rabba, 10km north of Kerak, where it regrouped before moving in and surrounding the stronghold. Reynald, aware that Baldwin IV would have been kept apprised of events in the region, tried to delay the inevitable siege of his castle, providing as much time as possible for a Frankish relief force to muster in Palestine and march to his position. Accordingly, he opted to defend the town north of the castle, making use of the local townspeople and Syrian Christians from the surrounding region who had sought refuge behind its walls. Although William of Tyre would criticize Reynald for this, the historian's own description of the town and its defensibility suggests it was a sensible decision.

Clustering on the outskirts of this fortress, on the site of the earlier city, was now a village whose inhabitants had placed their homes there as a comparatively safe location. East [south] of them lay the fortress, the best of protection, while on the other side rose the mountain itself, encompassed, as has been said, by deep valleys. Thus, if the village had even a moderately low wall, the inhabitants need not fear any hostile attack. At two points only was there any possibility of reaching the top of the mountain, and these could be easily defended by a few men even against large hostile forces. The other sides were supposed to be impregnable.[110]

As preparations took place in the town, Reynald had those cavalry forces at his disposal harry elements of the advancing Muslim army, slowing its approach.

The military force based at Kerak was evidently meagre. Despite the town's natural defences, the Muslim besiegers were able to force their way in quite quickly. A panicked retreat into the castle ensued, during which the bridge that spanned the fosse between the town and the castle was dislodged, preventing the defenders from subsequently launching any sallies against the Muslim forces that took up positions in the town. The situation was crowded inside the castle, exacerbated by the guests and entertainers who had come to Kerak for the wedding of Humphrey and Isabella. One contemporary source contends that Stephanie of Milly, mother of the groom, sent down some of the wedding feast to Saladin, who in turn asked in which tower the wedding couple would be spending the night, so he could direct his men not to assail it.[111]

The sources all mention Saladin's use of artillery at this siege. William of Tyre's account twice notes that Saladin prepared throwing machines and other siege engines ahead of time, which he brought with him to Kerak. Six of the sultan's trebuchets were set up in the town, which would have been used against the northern front of the castle, and another two were erected outside at a place called *Obelet* – the only other location where it might seem reasonable to set up artillery against the castle would appear to be the spur to the south. Ibn al-Athir placed the number of trebuchets at a close seven, similarly noting that the siege was pressed from within the town. Another point that the sources unanimously agree on is the lacklustre progress of the siege; having taken control of the town quickly, Saladin's forces failed to make any significant progress against the castle.

Although it was widely reported that the besiegers' artillery played against the castle incessantly, day and night, it had little impact. These were not the great wall-smashing engines that would appear a century later, but rather much smaller machines that posed little threat to fortified masonry, as is evidenced by this siege.[112] Despite the planning that went into this operation, Ibn al-Athir was compelled to suggest that Saladin had not brought enough trebuchets with him. This is a strange remark when considering that this is the largest complement of such engines that the historian places at any siege of a Frankish stronghold up to this point in his grand history. Although William of Tyre claimed Saladin's artillery threw stones of a great size, he emphasized the danger that these posed to people who exposed themselves beyond their places of shelter, rather than the walls of the castle. In an illuminating anecdote, thanks to the suppressing cover provided by these engines, some of the besiegers were able to use ropes to descend into the great northern ditch and slaughter the livestock that the townspeople of Kerak had left there, providing the Muslim army with fresh meat.

Those inside the castle apparently had no defensive artillery, as at one point a group attempted to construct such an engine. It seems they tried to assemble the machine on a tower or stretch of the castle's battlements, but the besiegers were able to target this party of builders, and the incoming stones persuaded them to give up their efforts and rather endure the incoming barrage. Meanwhile, the houses of the town were occupied by the besiegers, including large numbers of non-combatants who accompanied Saladin's army and provided it with various goods and services. The Muslims found the houses full of grain and other provisions, stockpiled ahead of the approaching winter, all of which had been left behind during the chaotic retreat into the castle.

Al-'Adil reached Kerak on 22 November. Although the arrival of Egyptian forces enhanced the size of Saladin's army, and invigorated the market that had sprung up in the occupied town, this seems to have had minimal impact on the progress of the siege. Meanwhile, in Jerusalem, factional squabbling delayed the Frankish relief effort. Guy of Lusignan faced criticism for his reluctance to engage the Muslim army following Saladin's invasion of Galilee two months earlier. Without Reynald's support, Guy found himself at the mercy of his rivals. The king, having recovered somewhat from his most recent bout of illness, revoked Guy's regency powers. As partisan rivalries continued, Baldwin IV arranged a coronation for his 5-year-old nephew, Baldwin V, who became co-king on 20 November, cementing the line of succession. This pleased everyone except Guy. For Raymond of Tripoli and his allies, this denied any legitimacy to arguments or actions Guy might take to claim the throne for himself upon the death of Baldwin IV. For Joscelin and Agnes of Courtenay, it likewise ensured the succession of Baldwin V and kept the crown in their family. Even Sibylla would probably have been quite happy, as her son's position was secured. With this settled, and a measure of consensus established among the baronage, efforts could finally be focused on the relief of Kerak. Shortly after the coronation of his nephew, Baldwin IV himself led Frankish forces towards Transjordan. Upon reaching the Dead Sea, the king entrusted command of the army to Raymond of Tripoli.

With the approach of Frankish forces, Saladin was compelled to give up his siege efforts against Kerak on 3 December 1183. After about five weeks of work, the besiegers had little to show for their efforts, and were forced to destroy the engines they had employed. Saladin appears to have had no desire to engage the Frankish relief army; instead, he completed his administrative shuffle, sending Taqi al-Din, his nephew, to replace al-'Adil as his deputy in Egypt, while al-'Adil would receive responsibility for Aleppo and a region of northern Syria that included Manbij. The Franks reached Kerak the following morning, at which point Saladin withdrew with the remainder of his forces, reaching Damascus on 12 December. The Frankish army likewise returned to Jerusalem.

Kerak had been tested, withstanding what was probably its first significant siege, and the castle had performed well. With neither a bridge over the northern ditch to facilitate sallies nor defensive artillery to harass the besiegers, the castle's natural defences, the deep northern ditch, and its solid northern wall proved sufficient to hold back the attackers and at no point does it appear to have been at risk of falling.

The Ernoul account provides a strange and otherwise uncorroborated anecdote relating to this siege. It is in this account that Stephanie of Milly is said to have brought down some of the wedding feast to Saladin, and he in turn spared the tower in which the newlyweds were sleeping. Saladin is presented as having a soft spot for Stephanie, who, the author claims, took this occasion to remind Saladin that he had once held her in his arms years earlier when he was a prisoner in the castle. The only suggestion that Saladin was at one time held captive in Kerak is found earlier in the same history, where it is suggested that he was detained during the reign of Amalric before Shirkuh came to power in Egypt, i.e. between early 1163 and the start of 1169.[113] Saladin was born between September 1137 and September 1138, and few details of his early life are known until he accompanied Shirkuh to Egypt for the first time in 1164. Stephanie is first mentioned in a charter dated to 3 July 1155, leaving at most seventeen years of age between them. Philip of Milly acquired Kerak in 1161, when Stephanie was at least 6, and Amalric came to the throne two years later, leaving Stephanie too old to have been held in the way that is suggested if she met Saladin at Kerak. Saladin's presence can also be accounted for from 1164 onwards, and no Syrian raids into Transjordan are documented in the early 1160s, providing no known opportunity for him to have been imprisoned in the castle while Stephanie was there, even in the final years of Baldwin III's reign. It is possible, if unlikely, that Saladin was briefly captured during an earlier campaign further north, when Philip of Milly still held his lands around Nablus, though there is no evidence at all to suggest this.

That this anecdote should appear in a somewhat disorganized Frankish account, which places the earlier meeting impossibly at Kerak, and that none of the many biographies of Saladin mention such an episode of captivity, or indeed any encounter between the sultan and the Franks prior to 1164, leave it very unlikely that there is any truth behind the story. Instead, this seems to have been part of a myth relating to Saladin's younger years that was circulating around the time of the Third Crusade (1189–92). A similar and likewise uncorroborated episode appears in the anonymous *Itinerarium Peregrinorum*, a contemporary account of the Third Crusade. Among the background information provided in the early chapters, it is claimed that Saladin, when he came of age, was knighted by Humphrey of Toron.[114] Although the author of this account almost certainly had in mind Humphrey II, the constable of Jerusalem, who died in 1179, it is possible that this fanciful story instead refers to Humphrey the younger; if so, it might be another suggested link between Saladin and Kerak.

Siege of 1184

Saladin's siege of Kerak in 1183, and the incursion into Galilee that preceded it, mark a transition in Saladin's foreign policy priorities. Having established his authority across Syria and most of the Jazira by early 1183, he finally identified the Franks as his primary target. Saladin had spent a decade justifying campaigns against fellow Muslims as a necessary step on the way to pushing the Franks out of the Levant; it was time to start backing up this rhetoric. Kerak had none of the religious significance held by certain places in Palestine; instead, it had considerable strategic value, which was not lost on its Frankish lord.

So long as Kerak remained under Latin control, its garrison and any other Frankish forces operating from the stronghold could threaten the free movement of merchants, pilgrims and armed contingents between Saladin's power centres. This sentiment was detailed by Baha' al-Din when reflecting on this period:

The place caused great trouble to the Muslims, for it cut communications with Egypt, so that caravans were only able to move with sizeable military escorts. The sultan was very concerned about it, to make the route to Egypt passable (may God facilitate that, to Him be praise and gratitude).[115]

These same qualities led al-Qadi al-Fadil, head of Saladin's chancery in Egypt, and an apparent observer of the siege of Kerak in 1184, to pen a more poetic description of the castle in one of his letters:

> It is the anguish that grips the throat, the dust that obscures eyesight, the obstacle that strangles hopes and waits in ambush to halt courageous resolutions. It is the wolf that fortune has posted in the valley, and the excuse of those who have abandoned the duty of pilgrimage prescribed by God.[116]

The fact that Kerak was a possession of Reynald of Châtillon, whose daring raids into Arabia had made him the face of the Frankish threat, only added to Saladin's desire to capture the castle. Accordingly, after withdrawing from Kerak near the end of 1183, Saladin spent the following months planning another campaign against the stronghold. In the meantime, the Franks of Transjordan continued to launch raids and otherwise pursue the aggressive policy that Reynald was known for. Responding to reported Frankish attacks, a caravan set out from Egypt in April 1184 to reinforce and bring weapons and horses to the Muslim garrisons at 'Aqaba and Sadr, in the Sinai.[117]

By the end of May 1184, armed contingents from Anatolia and the Jazira had begun to gather at Aleppo, responding to a summons issued by Saladin to join a new campaign against the Franks. These forces accompanied al-'Adil south to Damascus; after a short rest, they continued onwards to Transjordan. Saladin had opted not to wait for these northern elements to join him; having assembled his forces outside Damascus at Ra's al-'Ayn, he set out for Kerak on 13 July. Ibn Jubayr, a pilgrim from al-Andalus who was travelling through the region at this time, was surprised to see how merchants and others continued to move back and forth between Frankish and Muslim lands, even as Saladin set out to besiege Kerak.[118] The traveller claims to have seen Saladin leave Damascus in Jumada I (10 August–8 September), but it seems he misdates this by a month, or that it was instead al-'Adil whom he saw set out for Transjordan.

At Kerak, Saladin was met by additional forces from Egypt under Taqi al-Din, accompanied by certain members of al-'Adil's family, who had been detained or otherwise remained in Egypt the previous year. Letters had arrived around the start of May ordering the Egyptian army to march into Transjordan with as much infantry as possible – Saladin had recently purged the Fatimid army of much of its traditional infantry. Having mustered the army, Taqi al-Din set out from the environs of Cairo on 23 July, arriving at Kerak on 30 July, only a few days after Saladin. Al-'Adil and the northern forces subsequently passed through Amman, on about 17 August, and reached Kerak around 21 August. Saladin may have ordered these northern elements to linger in the Hawran for a while, which would have deterred the Franks from raiding towards Damascus while his main Syrian army connected with Taqi al-Din and coordinated siege operations outside Kerak.

With his army at full strength, Saladin had the castle surrounded. Nine trebuchets were reportedly set up against the town, which, after a brief but intense period of fighting, was stormed by the besiegers. Saladin's artillery was then brought inside the town and set up to assault the northern defences of the castle, as had been done the previous year. The great obstacle faced by Saladin's army, according to the various Muslim sources, was the ditch that divided the northern end of the castle from the town. It is here that Ibn al-Athir provides an estimate of the depth of the fosse: 60 cubits (about 28–30m). To overcome this obstacle, the besiegers set to work attempting to fill the gorge. Saladin's forces initially made slow progress due to the showers of arrows, crossbow bolts and stones sent forth by the castle's defenders. The Muslims resolved to dig trenches for protection, but found this difficult due to the hard volcanic stone upon which the castle and town were perched. This led Saladin to order the manufacture of bricks and the collection of wood, which was used to build three walled paths, complete with protecting roofs, from the safety of the town right up to the edge of the ditch. This added greatly to the comfort and confidence of those endeavouring to fill the fosse. Meanwhile, the besiegers' artillery played against the castle's ramparts, chipping away at their battlements and impairing the garrison's ability to interfere with the engineering efforts at the edge of the ditch below.[119]

Although the sources provide a fairly clear overall impression of the siege, there is some confusion regarding the dating of certain events. In one of his letters, 'Imad al-Din placed efforts to start filling the castle ditch on 16 August, a Thursday, roughly two weeks after siege efforts began. Baha' al-Din noted that it was not until a week later, on 23 August, that the castle and town were surrounded, at which point Saladin's artillery was erected. Al-Maqrizi, the great historian of the early fifteenth century, who made use of numerous contemporary sources, similarly recorded that earnest efforts to besiege the castle began only after al-'Adil had arrived at Kerak, but that the artillery was not ready until 3 September, a Monday, though he calls it a Thursday. These engines, he wrote, played against the castle through the night, until the Franks arrived the following day, a Tuesday, which he called a Monday. There is evidently some confusion in al-Maqrizi's rendering of things, but resolving this is difficult because the contemporary sources provide so few dates for events.

Despite these issues, there is agreement on the circumstances surrounding the end of the siege. Facing the threat of an attack while his forces were occupied assailing the castle, Saladin opted to lift the siege and move against the Frankish army that was approaching from the north. The Franks are said to have halted at a place called al-Wala.[120] Saladin took his forces to Hisban, in the Balqa', where he hoped to lure the army of Jerusalem into an engagement. The Franks, however, remained committed to their tactic of refusing battle, and they instead continued on to Kerak, setting out from al-Wala, according to Baha' al-Din, on 4 September. Having passed by the Franks, leaving no army between his own and Palestine, Saladin resorted to raiding. Detachments were sent west of the Jordan to pillage Samaria, where they plundered the region around Nablus and attacked the small Frankish stronghold at Jinin. After acquiring some loot, these forces recrossed the Jordan ahead of Saladin's entrance into Damascus on 15 September 1184. Some of the raiders reached the city with news of the campaign before Ibn Jubayr set out on 13 September. Unsurprisingly, it was the raiding activities that the traveller, and most likely his sources, were most interested in recounting.[121]

William of Tyre's account provides plenty of detail relating to the events leading up to this siege, but it ends shortly before it began. Following his return from Transjordan in December 1183, Baldwin IV had remained quite upset with Guy of Lusignan, allegedly going so far as to demand Heraclius, the patriarch, annul Guy's marriage to Sibylla. When news of this reached Guy, he made for Ascalon and his wife, from where he refused to answer the king's summons. This led the king to confiscate Jaffa, part of Sibylla's dowry and thus Guy's county, and call a council of the barons at Acre. Reynald, who is conspicuously absent from these events, appears to have remained at Kerak between the sieges of 1183 and 1184. Guy's position was advocated instead by Heraclius and the masters of the Templars and Hospitallers. The king's favour had clearly swung away from the old court party, and when Baldwin IV would not agree to return Guy to his favour, Heraclius simply left Acre. The impudence shown by Guy and Heraclius would appear to reflect the king's failing health – Guy recognized that he, as stepfather of Baldwin V, was in line to assume power, and Heraclius was willing to risk the enmity of the king in his final days, appreciating the strength of the alliance he had with those who would presumably rule once Baldwin IV died. Following the patriarch's departure, Raymond III of Tripoli was once more named regent of the kingdom.[122] Although this is where William's history ends, it was almost certainly Raymond who led the relief army towards Kerak near the end of summer 1184. Ironically, it was thus Raymond who was responsible for employing the same tactic of avoiding battle while leading the army to Kerak that had contributed to Guy's loss of favour a year earlier.

The only contemporary account of the siege from a Frankish perspective is contained in a letter that Baldwin IV sent to the patriarch and masters of the military orders. These figures had been sent to Europe to solicit support for the Frankish principalities, and their mission doubled as a convenient way for the king to remove Guy's most senior clerical allies from the kingdom. The siege of Kerak and subsequent Muslim raid into Samaria are the focus of the letter. It states that Saladin set out for Transjordan on 9 or 10 July, from which point he plundered Frankish territory until the Muslims broke into the town of Kerak on the eve of the feast of St Peter in Chains (31 July). A four-week siege ensued, during which the besiegers employed fourteen trebuchets, which would appear to confirm that the engines were deployed inside the town, as had been the case in 1183. These, however, are the only details provided relating to the siege. No mention is made of the condition of the castle, when the relief army arrived, or anything else to this effect. The general timing and course of events aligns with that found in Muslim accounts, and considerable attention is given to the raid that followed, where it is confirmed that the Muslims reached Nablus, Sebastia and Jinin.[123] No mention is made of Reynald, Raymond, Guy, or the internal political issues of the kingdom.

Despite this being Saladin's second siege of Kerak in as many years, and the attention that was evidently devoted to siege works and engines, there is no hint in the sources that the castle was at any point in real danger. The emphasis placed on efforts to fill the ditch in Arabic accounts has led some historians to conclude that the north wall of the castle had been destroyed by Saladin's artillery, but this was certainly not the case.[124] The ditch was the point of focus because it was the immediate challenge that the besiegers were unable to overcome before the Frankish relief army arrived; had the siege been interrupted after the fosse had been sufficiently filled, there is every reason to assume that the stoutness of the northern wall would have received comparable notice. Those scholars who suggest that the north wall was destroyed also fail to explain why efforts were made to fill the ditch, when a far simpler, cheaper and faster method of crossing the gorge would have been to use basic improvised bridges. But what is fundamentally neglected in such theories is a sound appreciation of the development of contemporary mechanical artillery; these engines were nowhere near powerful enough to breach fortified masonry at this point in time.[125] Revealingly, the sources specify that Saladin's trebuchets targeted the castle's ramparts, indicating these were primarily antipersonnel weapons, or at the very most were used to steadily damage battlements. The efforts to fill the fosse instead indicate that the northern wall remained a defensible barrier.

It was necessary to fill the ditch in order to provide Muslim sappers with a platform to work on at the level of the wall's foundations, as they attempted to prise these out, an easier task than attempting to excavate a cavity in the bedrock, just below them (still quite a height from the floor of the fosse). If the gorge could be filled sufficiently, a sturdy penthouse might be pushed forward to shelter the sappers and greatly facilitate their efforts.[126] Unfortunately for Saladin, it seems his sappers were unable to attack the northern wall before the siege was lifted.

This second siege of Kerak in as many years appears to have done little to curb Frankish aggression. In September 1184, reports circulated in Lower Egypt that a Frankish army was moving against Faqus, leading the citizens of Bilbays to abandon their homes and a brief exodus from the metropolitan area of Cairo-Fustat-Giza. An army was sent to counter the Franks; upon reaching Bilbays, some soldiers took the opportunity to loot the abandoned town. The reports were evidently exaggerated as this proved to be little more than a raid. The Frankish expedition, which is not mentioned in any Latin source, captured a number of prisoners and livestock before returning without ever having made contact with any Egyptian forces.[127]

The opportunistic action, which took advantage of Saladin's absence from Egypt, could have been organized by Reynald, who seems to have remained in Kerak after the Frankish relief army withdrew from his castle only days or weeks earlier. Such an action would certainly fit with his pattern of behaviour. It is also possible, however, that the raiders had instead travelled along the coast from Ascalon, which might explain why Faqus, about halfway between Bilbays and Tinnis, was said to be the target of the raid. This would allow for the possibility that the raiders had been Guy's men. One of the final events recorded by William of Tyre is a raid led by Guy in early 1183 against the Bedouin tribes the king had permitted to graze around Darum. Still out of favour, might Guy have launched a much more daring expedition the following year? A third possibility is that these were Templars from Gaza. The order's master, Arnold of Torroja, had accompanied the patriarch of Jerusalem to Europe, where he died around the time this raid took place. The seneschal of the Templars, Gerard of Ridefort, was entrusted with most affairs in the Levant and would shortly be elected the order's next master. When considering that Reynald, Guy and Gerard were close allies, it is even possible that all three had advance knowledge of the raid, regardless of who organized it.

Collapse of the Kingdom

When Ibn Jubayr passed through Acre in October 1184, he observed that Raymond III of Tripoli was the most powerful man in the kingdom of

Jerusalem. Raymond continued to enjoy his position of paramount influence following the death of Baldwin IV in March 1185. Baldwin had arranged for Raymond to continue acting as regent of the kingdom on behalf of his nephew, Baldwin V. To compensate the count's costs, Raymond was given the revenues drawn from the lordship of Beirut, still a royal possession. Although Guy of Lusignan was marginalized, a power-sharing agreement had clearly been negotiated. Joscelin of Courtenay was appointed the young king's guardian, as the boy's closest male relative but outside the line of succession, and royal castles and citadels were similarly placed under the control of the Templars and Hospitallers. Even Reynald, of whom little is heard during these critical times, was a party to this arrangement, which saw Raymond receive ultimate executive power, but his traditional political rivals in most other positions of influence. Raymond, with the consent of the barons, concluded a peace with Saladin in the winter of 1185, following which the sultan set out for northern Syria and then the Jazira, crossing the Euphrates in the middle of April. This provided an obvious opportunity for Reynald to return to Palestine, if he had not been there already. When Raymond of Tripoli confirmed a grant on behalf of Baldwin V, on 16 May 1185, Reynald appears first among the witnesses, with Joscelin of Courtenay second; Guy was not present.[128]

The reign of Baldwin V lasted only about a year and a half. The young king died in the summer of 1186, a few months before his ninth birthday. This left his mother, Sibylla, as heir to the throne and led to an open divide among the nobles of the kingdom of Jerusalem. Heraclius, the patriarch, and the masters of the Templars and Hospitallers, Gerard of Ridefort and Roger of Moulins, supported Sibylla, and through her, her husband, Guy of Lusignan. The couple was also backed by Guy's brother, Aimery, the royal constable, and Joscelin of Courtenay, the kingdom's seneschal. Aside from these holders of important offices, the only significant baron among this party was Reynald of Châtillon, who, having returned to Kerak, made for Jerusalem to offer his support. This group pushed forward with the coronation of Sibylla, despite the objections of Raymond III of Tripoli and his baronial allies, who refused to attend. On the day of the ceremony, Reynald is said to have addressed the congregation that had gathered in the Church of the Holy Sepulchre, announcing that it was Sibylla's right by birth to inherit the kingdom. After a crown was placed on her head, Sibylla promptly exercised her right to crown her husband, Guy, as king.

Reynald's party had initially formed a decade earlier around Agnes of Courtney, Amalric's first wife. Raymond of Tripoli and his allies drew support from Amalric's second wife, Maria Komnene. She had remarried around 1177, choosing Balian of Ibelin, one of Raymond III's closest allies – it was Balian who carried young Baldwin V to his second coronation in 1185, which had been overseen by Raymond. In opposition to Guy and Sibylla, the barons gathered at Nablus, once Melisende's base of power and by this time the centre of Maria's dower lands. They prepared to crown a rival monarch, putting forward the claim of Isabella, Maria's daughter with Amalric, who was about 14 years old. It was during the siege of Kerak in 1183 that Isabella had married Humphrey [IV] of Toron, heir to the lordship of Transjordan and Reynald of Châtillon's stepson. Given this connection, it is revealing that Reynald remained such a staunch supporter of Guy, evidently believing he would continue to command more influence and prestige with his traditional friends. Humphrey, as it turned out, was not the strong figure that his grandfather had been. Rather than accept the kingship that was offered to him by Raymond and his allies at Nablus, Humphrey slipped out of Nablus and made for Jerusalem. He promptly presented himself before Sibylla, who forgave him, then swore an oath of homage to Guy. Humphrey's betrayal of the barons at Nablus may have prevented a civil war, and it certainly averted the ire of his stepfather. Following the defection of their alternative to Guy, the barons submitted. Aside from Raymond of Tripoli, the only lord of the kingdom who refused to pay homage to Guy was Baldwin of Ramla, lord of Ramla and brother of Balian of Ibelin. It was Reynald of Châtillon, Guy's principal and ranking supporter, who was charged with summoning him, though Baldwin opted to leave the kingdom instead.[129]

Not since the early 1150s, when Baldwin III attempted to assert his sole authority, had the kingdom of Jerusalem been so divided. Saladin, meanwhile, returned to Aleppo in April 1186, and arrived back in Damascus on 2 June. His first significant action upon his return to Syria was to shuffle his family administration. Reports had arrived from Egypt that Saladin's eldest son, al-Afdal 'Ali, was interfering in the governance of his strong-willed cousin, Taqi al-Din. The sultan opted to send his brother, al-'Adil, back to Cairo, as he had considerable previous experience handling Egyptian affairs. With him, Saladin sent one of his younger sons, al-'Aziz 'Uthman, on whose behalf al-'Adil would rule. Taqi al-Din was compensated with considerable lands in northern Syria, and al-Afdal was given nominal authority over Damascus. Saladin placed a third son, al-Zahir Ghazi, in Aleppo. While Saladin balanced the interests and abilities of the senior members of his family, whom he relied on to rule his extensive lands, he was consciously grooming his sons to eventually take power, choosing al-Afdal to be his ultimate heir and head of the family.[130]

In the background to these events, hostilities resumed. Muslim sources assert that Reynald agreed to a peace with Saladin at some point after the siege of Kerak in 1184. Although they present this as distinct from the accord negotiated by Raymond III on behalf of Baldwin V in 1185, it seems more likely that Reynald was simply a party to the royal truce – the Muslim delegates may have been keen to have Reynald's explicit agreement, considering his history of organizing bold raids from Transjordan. The peace concluded in the name of Baldwin V would have ended with the young king's death; as might be expected, Reynald can be found raiding caravans passing through his lands thereafter.

According to 'Imad al-Din, Reynald seized a particularly large caravan, which was accompanied by a sizable group of soldiers, at some point before March 1187. Although this does not appear in Baha' al-Din's record of events, a similar reference can be found in the *Eracles* continuation of William of Tyre's history, where it is related that a spy informed Reynald of the movement of the caravan between Cairo and Damascus. Setting out from Kerak, Reynald intercepted the caravan, which was said to have been accompanied by no less a figure than Saladin's sister. Saladin subsequently protested this action to Guy, citing the peace that had been concluded with the representatives of Baldwin V. Guy is said to have ordered Reynald to relinquish the caravan and the captives that he had taken, to which Reynald replied that he recognized the existence of no such truce with Saladin. This anecdote seems to have been inserted into the narrative at a slightly later time, as it does not appear in the contemporary Ernoul version. The author had the clear intention of vilifying Reynald, and like 'Imad al-Din's account, this was used to justify or explain Saladin's incursions into the kingdom beginning in the spring of 1187.[131]

Reynald was not the only baron of the kingdom acting with a degree of impudence. Muslim historians relate that Raymond of Tripoli concluded a peace with Saladin following the latter's return to Syria in 1186, around the same time that Guy had come to power, usurping Raymond's place as de facto leader of the kingdom. As the autonomous count of Tripoli, Raymond was well within his rights to conclude his own foreign policy; however, there are suggestions that he extended this agreement to include his lands in Galilee, which he held on behalf of his wife, and for which he owed homage to the king of Jerusalem. The sources, both Frankish and Muslim, assert that there was almost open war between Guy and Raymond in the late part of 1186. As part of his alliance with Saladin, Raymond may even have welcomed a force of Muslim fighters to help defend Tiberias. As much as anything else, observed Ibn al-Athir, this disunity among the Franks led to their downfall.[132]

In the spring of 1187, Saladin was thus in an opportune position to exploit affairs west of the Jordan. Aware that Muslim forces were assembling outside Damascus, Guy called the leading barons and clergy together at Jerusalem. Saladin's first action was to set out near the end of March for the Hawran. He took up a position near Bosra and sent advance forces further south into

Transjordan, discouraging Reynald or anyone else in Kerak from attacking the annual pilgrim caravan as it returned from the Hijaz. As one contemporary remarked, 'this wolf [Reynald] detected the scent of the lion [Saladin], it was not long before he re-entered his fortress lest his soul escape his body.' Accompanying the caravan were members of Taqi al-Din's household, who had initially remained in Egypt but were now ready to join him in Aleppo, as well as one of Saladin's nephews, the son of his full sister. It is tempting to suggest that this was the inspiration behind the fanciful story that Reynald had captured one of Saladin's sisters during an attack launched against an earlier caravan. When the pilgrims had passed safely, Saladin moved into Frankish territory, where he was met by al-'Adil at the head of the Egyptian army. These forces then raided Frankish Transjordan, while at least a detachment attacked Kerak. The castle was probably subjected to no more than a loose blockade; Saladin had come to appreciate the considerable effort that it would take to capture the stronghold, so had most of his forces pillage the early crops, destroying what they could and tying down the Frankish forces in Kerak and Montreal for about two months. Meanwhile, to the north, Saladin had Taqi al-Din lead Aleppan forces through the Sarmada Pass to Harim, from where they could threaten Antioch and similarly discourage Bohemond III from leading the full army of Antioch south to assist the gathering Frankish forces in Palestine.[133]

While Saladin raided around Kerak, Reynald was with Guy and the assembling army in Jerusalem. Although Reynald is blamed for carrying out raiding activities between Guy's coronation and Saladin's move into Transjordan, it is possible that he was in Palestine the entire time. On 21 October 1186, Reynald witnessed charters issued by Guy in Acre. Indicative of the lingering political divide, the other signatories included the patriarch and a number of bishops, as well as Gerard of Ridefort and Roger of Moulins, the masters of the Templars and Hospitallers respectively, Aimery, the kingdom's constable, and Miles, the royal butler, but not one other prominent baron. Joscelin of Courtenay may have been in Beirut until the following spring – following the death of Baldwin V, he seized the city on behalf of Sibylla, his niece, denying Raymond of Tripoli any opportunity to try to retain control of the lordship.[134]

Events accelerated in the spring of 1187. Although reports must have been arriving of Saladin's activities in Transjordan, the army of Jerusalem remained in Palestine because another Muslim force was gathering to the east, under al-Afdal, at Ra's al-Ma, outside Damascus. Testament to the severity of the developing situation, Raymond of Tripoli was the only baron of the kingdom who did not answer Guy's summons. The masters of the military orders, who set out for Tiberias to persuade Raymond to join the army, came across a large detachment of scouts that al-Afdal had sent into northern Palestine. On 1 May, the small group of Templars and Hospitallers rashly attacked this much larger party and were soundly defeated near the springs of Cresson. According to one account, Raymond had allowed the Muslim forces to enter his lands, provided they withdraw back across the Jordan by sunset and take nothing from any town or house. Having defended themselves against the Frankish attack, the members of this armed scouting party were able to continue their way east and honour this agreement.[135]

Having been limited to raiding in Transjordan, this was precisely the kind of development that Saladin had been waiting for. Leaving some of the Egyptian army behind to continue blockading Kerak and Montreal, Saladin rushed north, arriving at 'Ashtara, east of the Sea of Galilee, on 27 May. There he was met by al-Afdal and a stream of other figures who brought armed forces from northern Syria and the Jazira. In late June, Saladin began to move his forces towards the Jordan. It was only at this point, according to Ibn al-Athir, that Raymond of Tripoli renounced his alliance with Saladin. Around the start of July, the Muslim army crossed into Frankish territory and attacked Tiberias, issuing a direct challenge to the Franks to defend their lands.[136]

Reynald of Châtillon had remained with Guy at Acre following Saladin's departure from Transjordan. When the Muslims began marching westward, the Frankish army advanced to Saffuriyya, north of Nazareth and about halfway between Acre and the Lower Jordan. In the popular version of events that followed, that found in the *Eracles* continuation of William of Tyre's history, Raymond lobbied to sacrifice Tiberias, while Reynald and Gerard of Ridefort argued that the army should continue moving east to engage Saladin and relieve the town. This account relies heavily on the contemporary Ernoul account, which is generally favourable to Raymond; however, a report sent to the pope from Genoa around the end of September 1187 claims that it was instead Raymond, rather than Reynald and Gerard, who advocated the army attempt to rescue his wife in Tiberias.[137]

Regardless of whose plan it was to move to Tiberias, Saladin was able to intercept the army of Jerusalem and force a battle near an extinct volcano known as the Horns of Hattin. The engagement was a disaster for the Franks. Raymond, in command of the vanguard, was able to break through a Muslim division, which then closed ranks against the main army behind. Balian of Ibelin and Joscelin of Courtenay, who commanded the rearguard, were similarly able to flee westward when the gravity of the situation became apparent. Few of those with the main force in the centre of the Frankish army were able to escape.[138]

Guy of Lusignan and many of the kingdom's nobles were taken captive, prizes to be ransomed later. Saladin had a different plan for Reynald of Châtillon, the man who orchestrated his defeat at Montgisard in 1177 and had led numerous daring raids into Muslim lands since. Reynald had become a symbol of opposition, the face of Frankish aggression and the Christian challenge to the image the sultan was cultivating for himself as a great *mujahid*. Frankish and Muslim sources unanimously agree regarding what came next. Following the battle, Saladin called Guy, Aimery and Reynald to his tent. While the sultan berated Reynald for his un-princely conduct, he offered Guy a cup of refreshing sherbet. When the king proceeded to pass the cup to Reynald, Saladin quickly clarified that it was not he who had offered Reynald this gesture of hospitality. Reynald and Guy were summoned again later in the day. It was at this point that Saladin, having resolved on a course of action, drew his sword and swung it down on Reynald's neck at the shoulder. While Guy looked on in shock, others finished the job of severing Reynald's head from his body. Reynald of Châtillon is the only man known to ever have been executed personally by Saladin, such was the infamous reputation the lord of Kerak had developed over the preceding years. Although summary execution was also the fate of the captive brothers of the military orders, Gerard of Rideford was spared, allowing him to be ransomed in the weeks that followed.[139]

Saladin's victory at Hattin avenged his earlier defeat at Montgisard. Far more significantly, his ability to finally draw the Franks into an engagement, allowing him to utilize the numerical superiority of his forces, led to the destruction of the army of Jerusalem and the near collapse of the Frankish kingdom. With no army to relieve them, the cities of Palestine, including Jerusalem, fell one by one over the following months. By the end of 1187, Tyre was the only city of the kingdom that remained in Frankish hands. The following year, Saladin led his forces through the county of Tripoli and conquered a large portion of the principality of Antioch. Meanwhile, the largest inland castles of the kingdom of Jerusalem became islands of Frankish authority as Saladin's influence washed over Palestine. In November 1188, Saladin set out to personally oversee efforts against the Templar castle of Safed, which surrendered on 6 December. He then went to Belvoir, a newly built stronghold of the Hospitallers, where the garrison similarly agreed to terms on 5 January 1189. This left Beaufort the only remaining Frankish outpost in Palestine other than Tyre. Thanks to some trickery on the part of the castle's lord, Reynald of Sidon, Beaufort's garrison held out until April 1190 before finally surrendering.

When Saladin left Transjordan in May 1187, al-'Adil remained behind with a considerable portion of the Egyptian army. Al-'Adil led most of these forces north once news of the victory at Hattin reached him, reinforcing his brother in Palestine. The man assigned the task of continuing efforts against Kerak was Sa'd al-Din Kamshaba, a mamluk of the late Shirkuh, who had gone on to marry one of al-'Adil's daughters. The garrison of Kerak posed little threat, and the crushing defeat suffered by the Frankish army meant that there was no prospect of a Latin relief force showing up to rescue the castle's defenders. This allowed the besiegers to take a fairly relaxed approach and simply wait until those within the stronghold ate their way through their provisions. When considering the troubles that Saladin had encountered in his attempts to take the castle in 1183 and 1184, there was little incentive to invest men and money in an attempt to accelerate the garrison's inevitable surrender. One of the greatest initial obstacles was probably trying to convince the garrison of what had happened at Hattin and impress upon them the reality of their situation.

Reynald of Châtillon appears to have continued to exercise authority as the lord of Transjordan up until his death. His stepson, Humphrey [IV] of Toron, the rightful heir to Transjordan, had also been at Hattin and was one of the many Frankish barons taken captive. Humphrey's mother, Stephany of Milly, and his wife, Isabella, were in Jerusalem when the city surrendered to Saladin in early October 1187. They are said to have been received by the sultan, who heard their petition to release Humphrey, and Saladin reportedly summoned the young lord from Damascus so that he could be reunited with his mother and wife. It was agreed that Stephanie would arrange for the surrender of Kerak and Montreal, following which, Humphrey would be released. When she arrived in Transjordan, however, neither garrison was willing to acquiesce. Eventually, when provisions ran out, the garrisons were left with no other options. In November 1188, more than a year and a half after Saladin had first imposed a loose blockade, the defenders of Kerak surrendered the castle. Saladin was at this time leading his main army up the coast of northern Syria, while al-'Adil was overseeing affairs in Palestine from Toron (Tibnin), roughly halfway between the remaining Frankish garrisons at Safed and Beaufort. Montreal held out until the following spring, when it too was surrendered. The garrisons of the smaller strongholds of Transjordan, including al-Wu'ayra, had similarly submitted by this time. Despite holding out for so long, the defenders of Kerak and Montreal were given free passage to Frankish lands and their lord, Humphrey [IV] of Toron, was also set free.[140]

Arabic reports of affairs in Transjordan in the months following Hattin are fairly sober, reserving more dramatic language for descriptions of Saladin's conquests to the north. Frankish accounts, by comparison, are more sensational. The garrison of Kerak is said to have eaten all of the dogs, cats and other animals in the castle; it is even claimed that the defenders sold their wives and children to their attackers in return for food, though Saladin helped find and buy them back after the siege. At Montreal, the siege dragged on so long that the men inside the castle reportedly went blind due to a lack of salt in their diet. Looking beyond these anecdotes, the various sources agree that Saladin was most hospitable to the Frankish defenders following their surrender.[141] Despite the length of the sieges, and the trouble this caused, guaranteeing the liberty of the obstinate garrisons was a small price to pay to control securely the inland route between Egypt and Syria. These were, by all accounts, passive sieges, limited to blockading efforts without the use of siege engines. This freed Saladin to allocate his resources elsewhere, while ensuring Kerak fell to him in a good state of repair. The castle, less than fifty years old when it was surrendered, would never again come under Frankish rule.

What's in a Name?

Although Kerak came to be known by a variety of names, the root of these is reasonably apparent. Known locally as Kerak, this was rendered into Latin as variants of *Crac* or *Chrac*. Its designation as *Petra Deserti* or *Crac de Petra* dates from the 1160s, when the Latin metropolitan see of Petra was re-established at Kerak. Likewise, variations of *Crac de Montreal* reflect the shift in political power, from Montreal to Kerak.[142] The lordship itself continued to be named after Montreal, and lords most often styled themselves as 'lord of Montreal', even though Kerak became the main seat of power in Transjordan. William of Tyre noted at one point that the region was known as *Petracensis*, similarly rendered as *Civitas petracensis* on the seal of Reynald of Châtillon, where he is given the title lord of Montreal (*dominus Montis Regalis*). This seal would have been created at precisely the same time as William was writing his history.[143]

While the equation of Petra with Kerak was common by the late twelfth century, it seems Burchard of Mount Sion had trouble distinguishing Kerak from Montreal a century later, no doubt due to the variety of names used to refer to the castle and the particularly confusing *Crac de Montreal*. Intriguingly, this latter label appears to have crept into the Arabic tradition, as some later sources refer to the castle as *Karak al-Shawbak*.[144]

Significance and Extent

In the decades that followed Saladin's conquests, Transjordan was remembered as one of the great lordships of the twelfth century. James of Vitry, writing around 1220, placed it on his list of the kingdom's eleven most important lordships. A few decades later, John of Ibelin questioned whether it had been one of the kingdom's four principal baronies, ranking alongside the county of Jaffa-Ascalon (to which he attached Ramla, Mirabel and Ibelin), the principality of Galilee, and the lordship of Sidon-Caesarea-Bethsan. Rather than Transjordan, John favoured the county of Tripoli as the fourth barony, as it was said to owe the king at least 100 knights, and Transjordan only 60 (40 from Kerak and Montreal and another 20 from Hebron), while the counts of Tripoli also had their own constable and marshal. Despite this, Transjordan ranks fourth on the lists he drew up of military service owed by each lord of the kingdom and the lords who had judicial franchises – the county of Tripoli does not appear on these lists. Intriguingly, the archbishop of Petra, according to John of Ibelin, was one of only three bishops who was not required to provide a levy of sergeants during times of emergency – the other two were the bishops of Beirut and Banyas. The neighbouring bishop of Hebron, for comparison, owed 50 sergeants. This exemption may have been due to the isolation of Kerak and the lack of a significant Frankish population in Transjordan.[145]

Transjordan was clearly an important and extensive lordship, but determining further details is tricky. Oliver of Paderborn, a participant of the Fifth Crusade, recorded that there were seven Frankish strongholds, in addition to Kerak and Montreal, that merchants passed as they travelled to or from Mecca, though he does not name them, which has caused historians to speculate as to which he might have had in mind.[146] Even more definitive twelfth-century references to some Frankish centres in the region have not yet been validated by archaeologists. For example, Amman was part of the lordship of Transjordan by at least 1161, as it is mentioned in Baldwin III's grant to Philip of Milly, and then in Philip's donation to the Templars in 1166. These charters suggest that Amman was the centre of a secondary administrative unit, which almost certainly had a fortified seat of power of some kind, though none of the site's fortifications have yet been linked to a period of Frankish occupation.[147]

In his account of Saladin's conquest of Transjordan, 'Imad al-Din, and Ibn al-Athir following him, listed the captured strongholds of the region as: Kerak, Shawbak (Montreal), Hurmuz, al-Wu'ayra and al-Sila'.[148] To these can be added a number of towns and *casalia* mentioned in surviving charters, such as Tafila, Benisalem and Cansir, which can be identified with varying degrees of certainty. Below Kerak and Montreal, the lordship's principal seats of authority, a number of smaller power centres acted as bases of Frankish influence; unfortunately, we know little about most of them.

St Catherine's in Sinai

The most distant part of the lordship of Transjordan was, at least nominally, the Monastery of St Catherine in southern Sinai. When Baldwin I travelled to 'Aqaba in 1116, Albert of Aachen, writing in Europe, claims that the king intended to continue on to Mount Sinai. The king was dissuaded from doing so, however, by messengers sent by the monks, who feared the presence of the Franks might rouse the anger or suspicion of the Fatimids, as Cairo was a journey of only four days from there. Although the Franks would claim St Catherine's as part of the re-established bishopric of Petra, and the Ernoul account states plainly that beyond Kerak 'is Mount Sinai, in the land of the lord of Kerak', Sinai appears to have remained subject to greater Egyptian authority. In 1134, a document was issued to the monks of the monastery in the name of the Fatimid caliph, al-Hafiz, confirming their traditional privileges. Thirty-five years later, these rights were recognized once more in one of the few surviving decrees issued by Shirkuh, between his rise to power as vizier in January 1169 and his death that March.[149]

During his tenure as lord of Transjordan, Philip of Milly is said to have visited the monks of Mount Sinai, who gave him a relic of St Catherine, the early fourth-century saint after whom the monastery was named. Philip reportedly sent this back to Europe at a later date, along with a splinter of the True Cross that he had received from Manuel Komnenos, presumably during his visit to Constantinople in 1169, shortly before his death. The pilgrim Thietmar, who passed through Transjordan on his way to the monastery in the second decade of the thirteenth century, relates a story in which an unnamed noble of 'Petra, or al-Shawbak,' had at one time attempted to carry off the body of St Catherine. This plan, however, was foiled by a number of divinely inspired natural disasters. Although no names are provided, the implicated lord was most likely either Philip of Milly, perhaps in recollection of his pilgrimage in the 1160s, or Reynald of Châtillon, who is not known to have visited the monastery, though it is perhaps not difficult to imagine him dreaming up such a daring plot.[150]

Although the lords of Kerak may have exercised no real authority over Sinai, there were clear links between the monastery and the lordship of Transjordan. In August 1217, around the time of Thietmar's visit, Pope Honorius III replied to a request from the local bishop, who was also the abbot, that the monastery gain papal protection. The extensive list of properties belonging to the monks, which stretched from Egypt to Constantinople, and Damascus to Cyprus, included vineyards and olive groves at Wadi Musa, Montreal and Kerak, as well as houses at the latter two and an oven at Montreal.[151]

'Aqaba

The Franks first visited 'Aqaba in 1116, the year after work on Montreal began. As Pringle has highlighted, there is no evidence that the Franks established a castle at 'Aqaba at this time; in fact, there is no known reference to a Frankish stronghold at the site until one fell to Saladin in 1170.[152] The remains of four fortification programmes can still be seen in and around the modern town of 'Aqaba. The oldest consists of sections of a town wall constructed during the Roman occupation. 'Aqaba fell under Muslim rule in the early seventh century and a fort was subsequently built along the coast during the Umayyad period. Excavations in this complex have produced few finds attributable to the twelfth century, suggesting it was abandoned around the time the Franks first arrived. To the south, a smaller fort was built in the fourteenth century, during the reign of al-Nasir Muhammad. This sits on an earlier khan, which excavators have dated to the late twelfth century or the thirteenth, corresponding with the period when the Ayyubids controlled the site. This first fort may have been remodelled by Baybars, prior to the rebuilding efforts undertaken during the reign of al-Nasir Muhammad. The khan was abandoned or otherwise fell into a state of disrepair during the late Mamluk period. It was rebuilt in the first decade of the sixteenth century, with further alterations carried out by the Ottomans in 1587–88. It was once believed that the fort might rest on top of an earlier Frankish castle; however, excavations have yielded no evidence to support this.[153]

The primary Frankish outpost at 'Aqaba appears to have been located on Jazirat Fara'un, otherwise known as Pharaoh's Island or Isle de Graye. This is the stronghold that Thietmar saw when he passed through the region in the early thirteenth century. Positioned on an island close to the western shore of the Gulf of 'Aqaba, this would appear to correspond with the accounts of Saladin's capture of the Frankish castle in 1170, and the subsequent blockade of an offshore castle by a part of Reynald's force during the famous Red Sea raid a decade later. Initial excavations were carried out during the Israeli occupation of Sinai, though no definitive evidence was found linking the structure to the twelfth century. Subsequent rather drastic efforts to clear and 'restore' the castle have left scholars in general agreement that little more can be discerned concerning its history.[154]

Wadi Musa

In the decades following Baldwin I's initial visit to Wadi Musa in 1100, a Frankish presence developed in this area. The first reference to a stronghold in the immediate region is found among events dated by William of Tyre to 1144. The historian relates that a force of Turkmen, aided by a group of locals, captured the Frankish castle and killed certain Christians there. In his first military campaign as king, Baldwin III led a contingent of the Frankish army to deal with the situation. Apparently unable to recapture the castle through conventional means, the Franks began destroying the surrounding olive groves, from which the locals made their living. This persuaded those in the stronghold to surrender on terms that secured their freedom and no further consequences.[155]

It is often suggested that the first fortification efforts at Wadi Musa probably followed Baldwin II's trip to the region in 1127, rather than one of Baldwin I's earlier visits. Whenever the site was fortified, there are indications that the region remained a royal possession for some time. For example, William of Tyre noted that it was the king who installed a garrison when the local stronghold was retaken in 1144, rather than some other lord, though a casual remark like this should not be given undue weight. It is clear in Baldwin III's grant of Transjordan to Philip of Milly in 1161 that Wadi Musa was not part of the lordship of Montreal prior to that point. The wording of the charter may imply that Wadi Musa, and the surrounding region, had previously been granted to Ulrich, viscount of Nablus, and had since been inherited by his son, Baldwin. Ulrich was viscount of Nablus under Baldwin II and Fulk, serving in this role until at least 1138. It is possible that he was removed from this post and given Wadi Musa, though neither he nor his son, nor any other figure in the Latin East, is ever referred to as 'lord of Wadi Musa' or 'viscount of Wadi Musa'. Aside from this, a connection between Transjordan and Nablus can be traced back to the days of Roman of Puy, and it was presumably Ulrich's house in Montreal that is mentioned, in 1152, as belonging to the viscount of Nablus. If indeed Ulrich, and Baldwin after him, held a lordship of the king centred on Wadi Musa, it was not the only one in the region. A charter issued around the same time as Philip was invested with Transjordan records the grant of a village, Hara, in the region of Wadi Musa, to the Hospitallers by two brothers. They had inherited the settlement from their father, who had received it from Baldwin II.[156]

Two strongholds have been identified in the Wadi Musa region: al-Wu'ayra, slightly more than 2km to the northeast of the centre of the classical town of Petra, and al-Habis, perched on a peak that overlooks the heart of the ancient city from the west. Al-Wu'ayra sits along the side of a ridge, which falls away to the east. It is roughly rectangular, about 100m long, north–south, and around two-thirds as wide, with a number of towers that project only slightly or not at all from the curtain walls. The plan of al-Habis, the core of which at least is considerably smaller, was dictated by the form of the steep rise on which it was built. At the very top, a tower, about 8.5m by 5m, crowns the site, while at least one irregular enceinte surrounds it at varying levels below. A cistern, fairly large in proportion to the structure, is perhaps the best surviving element of the stronghold. While al-Wu'ayra may have offered better access to the main north–south road running to the east of Petra, al-Habis provides a spectacular and commanding view of the ancient settlement. There is general agreement that al-Wu'ayra should be associated with the Frankish stronghold referred to simply as Wadi Musa. A number of scholars have proposed linking al-Habis with Frankish *Celle*, because Yaqut, in the thirteenth century, noted the presence of a stronghold of a similar name in Wadi Musa, clearly distinct from al-Wu'ayra, which he placed outside Wadi Musa. The prevailing opinion today, however, is that *Cella* corresponds with al-Sila', along the road south of Tafila. Both al-Wu'ayra and al-Habis were captured by Saladin during his conquest of Transjordan, and neither served as an important outpost thereafter.[157]

A possible third defensive position has also been identified in Wadi Farasa, just south of the main basin of the ancient town. The remains amount to some pottery dated to the twelfth century and a wall that was apparently built to restrict access along the route up the wadi to Jabal al-Madhbah and the High Place of Sacrifice. How exactly this site might have fit into the broader defensive arrangements, or to what degree it was occupied by the Franks, remains unknown.[158]

Hebron

Known to the Franks as St Abraham and Muslims as al-Khalil, Hebron was the most significant and perhaps last appendage added to the lordship of Transjordan. The ancient settlement was captured by Godfrey of Bouillon during his short reign, though how it was ruled thereafter is a subject of debate. Godfrey is said to have given Hebron to Gerard of Avesnes, following the knight's release after a brief period of captivity in 1099, during which Gerard was crucified by the defenders of Arsuf when the town was attacked by Godfrey. Gerard died a few years later during the Second Battle of Ramla in 1102. Complicating matters, Geldemar Carpenel reportedly retired to Hebron in 1100 around the time of Godfrey's death, after a failed attempt to acquire Haifa from Tancred. Geldemar was among those who supported Baldwin I's right to the throne following Godfrey's death, and Baldwin subsequently rewarded Geldemar by granting him Haifa when Tancred went north to assume the regency of Antioch. Geldemar's position in Hebron is unclear, though he evidently held certain lands in the region, as he is found making a gift to the Hospitallers of one *villanus* in Hebron and another in Jericho prior to his death at the First Battle of Ramla in 1101.[159] Confronting the apparent possession of Hebron by both men, Riley-Smith proposed that Gerard was not given Hebron, but rather a nearby castle, freeing Hebron to be held by Geldemar. Mayer, however, has rejected this, arguing that Gerard was instead the royal castellan. Whatever the truth, both men were dead by 1102.[160]

A certain Hugh of Hebron appears next, mentioned by Albert of Aachen in 1105. Only a few years later, however, Albert recorded that Hebron was held by Walter Mahumet, who had received it from the king following the death of Rorgus of Haifa, which Albert placed among the events of 1106. Although Walter Mahumet appears frequently in charters of the time, these documents do not identify him as being the lord or castellan of Hebron. From 1115 to 1136, Baldwin of Hebron appears as a witness to many charters. Walter last appears in the historical record as a witness to the first of these documents, leading to the suggestion that Baldwin may have replaced Walter. The number of royal charters witnessed by Baldwin of Hebron indicates that he, like Ulrich of Nablus, was a close supporter of Baldwin II. When considering that Ulrich and other prominent viscounts are typically identified as such, it seems Baldwin, who is not, more likely held Hebron as a lordship.[161] Further complicating things, another Hugh of Hebron was responsible for granting Bethgibelin to the Hospitallers at the behest of Fulk in 1136. Hugh had evidently not replaced Baldwin as lord of Hebron because the latter is named among the witnesses, along with Pagan the Butler and a number of other senior royal officials.[162]

Intriguingly, Humphrey II of Toron, the kingdom's future constable, made a donation of land to the order of St Lazarus from the region of Hebron in 1148. In July 1149, a certain Castellan Humphrey of Hebron appears on a different charter.[163] Mayer has argued that the two men are the same: Humphrey of Toron served as castellan of Hebron before Baldwin III elevated him to the position of constable in 1152, at which time he relinquished Hebron. Tibble has instead maintained a more traditional and easily supportable position, proposing that Hebron was the seat of a lordship from the start of the twelfth century, each of its early lords having apparently been unrelated, while Humphrey of Toron merely held lands in the region.[164] Indeed, it is quite plausible that following the death of Baldwin of Hebron, the lordship was retained by the crown and only then was a castellan installed to administer things on behalf of the monarchy. As for Humphrey of Toron, William of Tyre made no mention of him holding any position associated with Hebron. It is perhaps of considerable significance that William referred to Humphrey as one of the major lords of the kingdom with Fulk at Montferrand in 1137, noting Humphrey's youth and inexperience, but also implying that he had succeeded his father as lord of Toron by that time. As lord of Toron, it is extremely unlikely that Humphrey would also have served as castellan of Hebron. Likewise, when noting Humphrey's appointment as constable of the kingdom fifteen years later, William remarked that Humphrey controlled considerable lands in the Lebanese mountains east of Tyre (the lordship of Toron), but added no indication of any association with Hebron.[165] Accordingly, this appears to be simply another example of a lord holding lands in a different lordship.

Regardless of whether, or when, Hebron was a lordship or a viscounty, it was eventually bestowed on the lords of Kerak, though like much of its administration leading up to this, it is unclear when exactly the transition took place. It is tempting to suggest that Hebron was given to Philip of Milly when the lordship of Transjordan was greatly enlarged and authority in the region consolidated. The only evidence to indicate this, however, is a confirmation issued by Amalric to the Templum Domini in 1166, which includes two *gastines* (abandoned settlements) belonging to the region of Hebron that had been donated by Philip. This proves only that Philip held lands in the region, which he may have inherited from his father, and does not even confirm that the donation was made after Philip became lord of Transjordan.[166]

When Hebron and Kerak came under the authority of the same lord, the ecclesiastical jurisdiction of the two centres remained distinct. In 1168, around the same time that the bishopric of Petra was re-established, and perhaps not entirely unrelated to this, Hebron was elevated to the status of a diocese. The new bishop, Reynald, was a suffragan of the patriarch of Jerusalem, rather than the neighbouring archbishop of Kerak.[167]

By the first half of 1177, Hebron was held by Reynald of Châtillon, lord of Transjordan. While Reynald held Transjordan through his wife, Stephanie of Milly, and on behalf of her son, the young Humphrey [IV] of Toron, it is quite possible that Baldwin IV granted Hebron to Reynald to hold in his own right – Reynald stood to lose Transjordan when Humphrey came of age, but Hebron may have been his to hold and pass on to any children he might sire.[168] This, however, would only have been possible if Hebron had not previously been held by Philip of Milly. There were natural ties, both ethnic and commercial, that had existed between Hebron and Kerak long before the arrival of the Franks. Likewise, following the end of Latin rule, Hebron would often remain a part of the administrative region ruled from Kerak.

By the early 1180s, Reynald had entrusted Hebron to John Barzela, who served as his castellan.[169] The main stronghold of Hebron, what the Franks referred to as the castle of St Abraham, is the complex known today as the Haram al-Khalil. The structure lies over the caves associated with the final resting place of the three Biblical Patriarchs, Abraham, Isaac and Jacob, along with their wives Sarah, Rebekah and Leah. The large blocks used to enclose the holy site suggest they date to the time of Herod the Great, following which the site was further fortified. Although all but the northeast wall and western corner were demolished in the twentieth century, there is evidence that the site was further fortified during the early Mamluk period.[170]

Bedouin

The Bedouin deserve special notice, as their influence in Transjordan was perhaps more significant than in any other region of the Frankish Levant. The nomadic tribes of the area could help or hinder the movement of people, including pilgrims, merchants and soldiers, through this corridor between Syria to the north and Egypt and Arabia to the south. The kings of Jerusalem seem to have retained, at least nominally, the right to tax the trade that moved through the region and authority over much of its Bedouin population. In reality, the local ruler in Kerak probably maintained closer ties with these groups, and it was they to whom the Bedouin paid a portion of the tax or protection money they charged those moving through their lands.[171] Likewise, Muslim figures had an interest in securing cordial relations with these groups. The ruler of Damascus, in particular, was liable to have his image tarnished if the Bedouin interfered with the annual *hajj*.

In the final third of the twelfth century, the lords of Kerak appear to have enjoyed a close working relationship with at least some of the local Bedouin groups. Following his expedition into Transjordan from Egypt in 1173, Saladin presented this campaign as primarily an action against the Bedouin. By driving them from Frankish lands, he argued, it would deny the lords of Transjordan of their traditional guides and force the Bedouin to return to what he called the side of Islam. To this end, Saladin asked Nur al-Din to grant the Bedouin a number of *iqta'at* in Syria, from which they could support themselves. Two years earlier, when Saladin had invaded Transjordan, only to learn that Nur al-Din had intentions of meeting him, one of the excuses that Saladin offered was that his force had taken heavy losses at the hands of Bedouin in alliance with the Franks.[172] Although the Bedouin may have been implicated as a convenient excuse or explanation on both occasions, some were almost certainly assisting the Franks. The force that Reynald led into northern Arabia around the start of 1182, for example, was probably accompanied by Bedouin guides, while the camels that carried Reynald's prefabricated boats down to the Red Sea a year later would have been provided, if not also led, by local Bedouin.

The tensions between Saladin and the Bedouin stretched beyond the willingness of some in the Transjordan region to assist the Franks when it served their interests. For example, different Bedouin communities were implicated in the revolts that broke out in Upper Egypt in 1171 and 1174.[173] These actions were, to at least a degree, a result of Saladin's broader efforts to disenfranchise the Bedouin and limit their influence in Egypt. Within a couple years of becoming vizier, Saladin reduced the Bedouin contingent of the Egyptian military by more than 80 per cent.[174] In this light, it is understandable

Kerak from the east. (*Library of Congress, LC-DIG-matpc-06951*)

South end of the castle from the southeast. (*Alexander Hornstein*)

Eastern front of the castle, looking south. (*Alexander Hornstein*)

West end of the northern
front from the inside, 2010.
(*Marla MacKinnon*)

West end of the northern
front from the inside.
(*Alois Musil*)

Western entrance to the town from the outside. (*Library of Congress, LC-DIG-matpc-01693*)

Burj al-Zahir from the west.
(*Henry Sauvaire*)

Burj al-Zahir from the south.
(*Henry Sauvaire*)

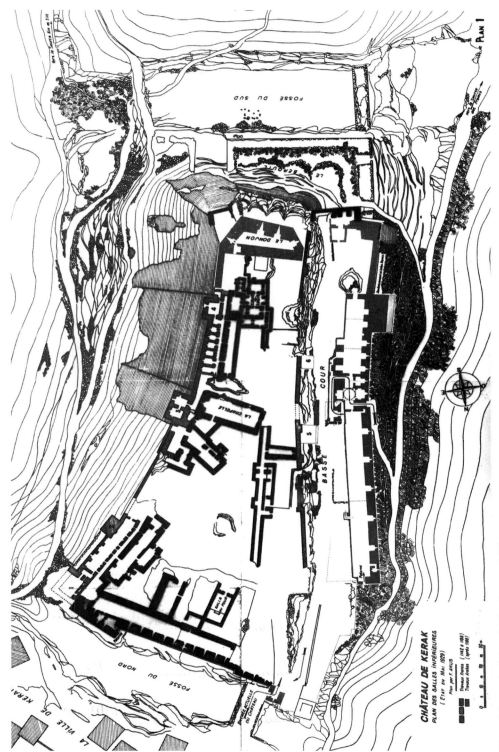

Plan of the castle. (*Anus for Deschamps, 1939*)

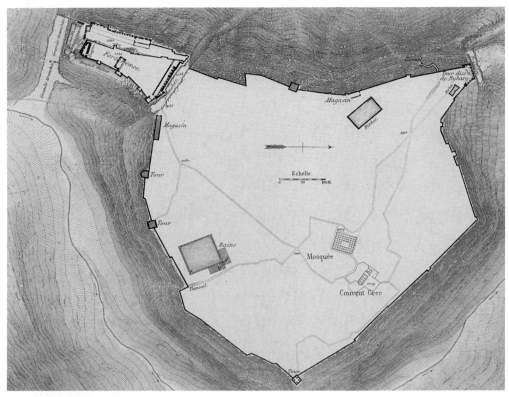

Plan of the town. (*Mauss for Luynes, 1874*)

Plan of the town. (*Musil, 1907*)

why certain Bedouin figures may have been increasingly willing to work with the Franks following Saladin's rise to power, and why some were only too eager to attack what remained of Saladin's army as it fled west across Sinai following his defeat at Montgisard in 1177.

Identifiable People

Aside from the lords of Transjordan and Archbishop Guerric, it is hard to identify many individuals who may have lived in or helped administer the region. The inscription found at Montreal, noted above, appears to attest to a certain Hugh, who was viscount there in 1118, but this is a unique example of epigraphic evidence prior to the Ayyubid period of occupation. Most Frankish names associated with the lordship are instead found in the surviving charter evidence.

Baldwin III's grant of Transjordan to Philip of Milly in 1161 names four prominent royal vassals who had held lands in the region. The first is Pagan the Butler, whose fief formed the core of the larger lordship created for Philip. The next two are Viscount Ulrich of Nablus and his son, Baldwin, mentioned above. Ulrich was dead by this time and Baldwin relinquished the lands he had inherited from his father in Transjordan to the king in exchange for others, removing him from the region and adding these lands to those Philip was to receive. The fourth is John Gothman, a royal vassal whose service was transferred to Philip, and who thus continued to hold lands in Transjordan from 1161. John was evidently a man of some years by this time, as he witnessed a confirmation issued by Baldwin II in 1126, appearing seventh on the list, ahead of Ansketin (Anschitinus), the viscount of Jerusalem, and behind Rohard, the future viscount of Jerusalem. Ten years later, he was among a long list of figures, including Pagan the Butler, Ulrich of Nablus and Baldwin of Hebron, who witnessed Hugh of Hebron's gift of Bethgibelin to the Hospitallers. John is the last lord on this list, ahead of John the chamberlain and Sado the marshal, both royal officials. Given the timing of his appearance in the charter evidence, and then virtual disappearance until 1161, John probably owed his rise to Baldwin II, and may have been granted his lands in Transjordan around the same time as Pagan the Butler received his more substantial lordship. John appears thus to have been a minor royal vassal, though a man of not insignificant rank, which is supported by the marriage of his daughter, Elizabeth, to Hugh of Caesarea, a man of considerable standing. Although the reshaping of Transjordan in 1161 had a direct impact on John, he was not a witness to the charter; he was at that moment a prisoner of war. John had accompanied the army that Baldwin III had marched to relieve

Banyas in 1157, and was among those captured when Nur al-Din surprised this relief force. Later in 1161, John and his family are found selling a number of villages to the canons of the Holy Sepulchre to help raise funds for his ransom.[175]

The grant issued by Maurice to the Hospitallers in 1152 bears the names of a number of other figures.[176] In addition to the viscount of Nablus, presumably Ulrich, who had a house at Montreal, a certain Seguin is noted to have possessed a nearby vineyard, while another plot of land was held by William the Ass, and John the castellan had another vineyard close to a main road in the region of Kerak. John and Seguin appear first and second respectively on the list of witnesses. John was almost certainly the castellan of Kerak, and

Witnesses to Maurice's grant to the Hospitallers, 1152	Witnesses to Reynald's confirmation to the Hospitallers, 1177
Johannes castellanus	*Original witnesses:*
Seguinus	frater Ascenardus
Rabellus	Seguinus
Stephanus de Arens	Martinus vicecomes
Ayraldus castellanus Montis Regalis	Johannes Tyberiadensis
Martinus vicecomes	Eraudus castellanus
Johannes Tiberiadis	Martinus de Melida
Assenardus frater Templi Domini	Balduinus de Taroana
Johannes Crassus	Garinus de Hobelet
Gauterius Parmentarius	Johannes Mahomet
Simon de la Carta	magister Raimundus
Composed by Reinardus capellanus	magister Martinus
	and many others from Montreal and Petra
	Those who had died:
	Seguinus
	Martinus vicecomes
	Johannes Tyberiadensis
	Eraudus castellanus
	Current witnesses:
	dominus Guerricus Latinorum primus
	Petracensis archiepiscopus
	dominus Godescalcus
	Evenus castellanus
	Seherius
	Rangotus
	Girardus de Betarrasa
	Johannes de Terroda
	Balduinus frater ejus
	Composed by Willelmus capellanus Rainaldi
RRH nos. 279, 551, pp. 71, 146–47; Cart. Hosp. nos. 207, 521, 1:160, 355–56.	

perhaps the second most influential secular figure in the lordship. Seguin was also a man of some standing, and later appears as a witness to Walter of Beirut's donation to the Order of St Lazarus in 1167.[177] Third on the list of witnesses of the 1152 document is Rabel, who later witnessed a grant issued by Baldwin III at Sidon in January 1160, where he is found as 'Rabel of Montreal'.[178] This royal charter may represent the brief period when Kerak passed back to the crown between the lordships of Maurice and Philip, leaving it possible that Rabel had been appointed to serve as the royal deputy in Montreal. It is at least as likely, however, that Rabel simply took his name from the stronghold, in which case he may have been the son of one of the early figures who were granted lands in the region by Baldwin I. Stephen of Arens, who is otherwise unknown, appears fourth, followed by Ayrald, castellan of Montreal.

The sixth witness to Maurice's grant was a certain Viscount Martin. Another man of this name is found witnessing a confirmation issued in 1115, while Baldwin I was overseeing the initial construction of Montreal.[179] This would appear to be a certain Martin of Nazareth, who is frequently found in the company of William of Bures, prince of Galilee, and not the same man noted in 1152. This later Martin may have been an otherwise unmentioned viscount based somewhere else in Transjordan, perhaps at Wadi Musa; alternatively, he might have been Maurice's deputy in Montreal, or simply a visitor from elsewhere. The seventh witness was John of Tiberias, whose name represents another apparent link between Transjordan and the interior regions of central

Witnesses to Walter's grant to the order of St Lazarus, 1167	Witnesses to Humphrey [IV]'s grant to the order of St Lazarus, 1183
Guerricus, Petracensis ecclesie Latinorum primus archiepiscopus	dominus Guerricus Petracensis archiepiscopus
Seherinus de Mamedone	dominus princeps Reinaldus
Seherinus de Waise	comes Jocelinus
Siguinus	Guido comes Joppensis
Girardus de Beteras	Hagne
Guarinus de Hobelet	frater Guido Hospitalis
Girardus de Spineto	Girardus de Beteras
Inguanius	Johannes de Broies
Petrus de Hasard	Seherius Juvenis
Osmundus de Belnaco	Seherius de Sancto Habraham
magister Martinus	magister Raimundus
magister Raimundus	magister David
Herricus de Leodio	Bricius senescallus
Herricus filius ejus	*Composed by* frater Willelmus
Composed by Laurentius domioni Galterii capellanus	
RRH nos. 454, 628, pp. 119, 166; UKJ nos. 321, 439, pp. 558–59, 749–50.	

and northern Palestine. John's presence in the lordship might relate to an association that Pagan the Butler appears to have had with the principality of Galilee. In 1132, Pagan witnessed a grant made by William of Bures to the Church of the Holy Sepulchre, where he is listed as 'Pagan of Montreal', yet he is identified as among those representing Tiberias, perhaps indicating that he held lands in eastern Galilee.[180] The eighth witness to Maurice's grant, a certain Brother Ascenardus, was a member of the Templum Domini, which speaks to their continued presence and influence in the lordship.

A generation later, in 1177, Reynald of Châtillon confirmed Maurice's grant to the Hospitallers. Intriguingly, a list of original witnesses is provided, though it differs from that found on the earlier charter. The names of Ascenardus, Seguin, Martin, John of Tiberias and Ayrald appear first, though a note following this list of original witnesses reveals that all but Ascenardus had since died, while Rabel and John the castellan are noticeably absent. Rabel seems to disappear from official records, suggesting he died or otherwise left the region, but John was evidently still alive. John was one of seven witnesses to a grant issued by Reynald and Stephanie in 1180; three of the seven witnesses are identified as relatives of Reynald, indicating that John may have been tied closely to his most recent lord. Although John was clearly still alive, the 1177 confirmation reveals that his vineyard, noted in Maurice's original grant, had since passed to the archbishop of Petra. Among the remaining figures identified as the original witnesses, Garinus of Hobelet, whose name does not appear on the 1152 charter, can be found on Walter's grant to the order of St Lazarus in 1167. His lands would appear to be associated with the place where William of Tyre claims Saladin erected some of his artillery when besieging Kerak in 1183.[181]

The list of later witnesses to the confirmation issued in 1177 begins with Archbishop Guerric. The first two secular figures, a certain Lord Gottschalk and Evenus the castellan, presumably of Montreal, seem otherwise unknown. Seherius, who appears next, would seem to be either Seherius the Younger or Seherius of Hebron, both of whom are found on a grant issued in 1183 by Humphrey [IV] of Toron to the order of St Lazarus. This was made for the benefit of the souls of his grandfathers, Philip of Milly and Humphrey the constable, as well as that of his father, Humphrey the Younger, and in honour of his mother and her husband, Reynald. The partisan nature of the kingdom's politics at the time is evidenced by the leading witnesses, who were none other than Archbishop Guerric, Reynald, Joscelin of Courtenay and Guy of Lusignan, then count of Jaffa-Ascalon. Two men with similar names, Seherinus of Mamedone and Seherinus of Waise, appear on Walter of Beirut's earlier grant to the order in 1167. A person found on all three documents is Gerard of Betera.[182]

Aside from those figures who appear as witnesses to charters issued by the lords of Kerak, a few other individuals can be tied to the lordship. For example, a certain Martin held a lordship centred on Tafila, about 40km south of Kerak. He is found as a witness to the resolution of a dispute between Amalric, viscount of Nablus, and the abbey of St Mary of the Valley of Jehoshaphat in February 1177. The names of a few other individuals also suggest they either held lands in Transjordan or were born there before moving on to serve elsewhere. A number of figures also appear to have taken their name from Hebron. In addition to Hugh and Baldwin, both of Hebron, who are found on the same charter of 1136, Norman of Hebron was a witness to a charter issued by Hugh, castellan of Hebron, around 1150. Likewise, John Barzela, castellan of Hebron, appears on the same charter as a certain Letard of Hebron about three decades later. Seherius of Hebron, noted above, is yet another example.[183]

In addition to the archbishop of Petra, the names of certain lower-ranking clerics have survived. These include a number of chaplains to the lords of Kerak, who, as members of a small literate minority, were often relied upon to draft documents. The first of these to appear is Reynard, chaplain of Maurice, who drew up the grant to the Hospitallers in 1152. Fifteen years later, Laurence, chaplain of Walter, formerly lord of Beirut and at this time lord-regent of Transjordan on behalf of his daughter, Beatrice, drafted the gift made by Walter to the order of St Lazarus in memory of his wife, Helena. Reynald of Châtillon's chaplain, during his tenure as lord of Kerak, was William, a member of a religious order, most likely the Templum Domini. Reynald's wife, Stephanie of Milly, had her own chaplain, a certain Nicholas. The agreement concluded between Archbishop Guerric and the Hospitallers in 1181 names another seven clerics associated with the bishopric of Petra: Stephen, a dean; Godfrey, an archdeacon; Lidinus, a cantor; Arnold, Engelric and Bernard, priests; and William, a subdeacon. Five of these men witnessed an earlier agreement between the archbishop and the monks of St Mary of the Valley of Jehoshaphat concerning the payment of tithes for certain villages belonging to the order in Transjordan. An additional figure, Elias, is also named among the canons of Kerak on this earlier document.[184]

Ceramic and Faunal Evidence

One of the best ways to gain a sense of what life was like for those living in Transjordan in the twelfth century is to look closely at the ceramic and faunal remains – the bits of broken pottery and animal bones that are recovered through archaeological digs and surveys. Until comprehensive excavations are undertaken at Kerak, we are forced to rely on the scant evidence that has been collected in and around the castle, as well as that which has been found and studied at contemporary sites where we can imagine similar populations lived. One of the big challenges, however, is that the current sequencing of the ceramic record is still far from precise. This makes it hard to say with certainty whether most pieces (or sherds) of pottery date to the Frankish period or sometime slightly earlier or later. Although there are some exceptional diagnostic types, typically vessels imported from elsewhere, most pottery found in the area datable to the twelfth century is fairly generic. Difficulties are only enhanced when looking at handmade wares, the least studied and roughest category, which often make up a majority of the pottery sherds in assemblages that appear to date to the Frankish period. Until the scholarly understanding of the ceramic record improves, dating will remain imprecise and conclusions based on connections between sites will continue to rely on a considerable measure of conjecture.[185]

Some of the earliest modern excavations in Frankish Transjordan were carried out at al-Wu'ayra. The vast majority of ceramic finds that have been dated to the Frankish period are fragments of fairly rough handmade vessels, most of which were of a closed form or shape. Those revealing decoration feature simple linear or geometric patterns. Unfortunately, the decoration style and forms of these vessels appear to have been in use for an extended period of time, both before and after the Frankish presence. This suggests that these vessels were produced locally, though no direct evidence of this has yet been found. In general, luxury pieces are very rare; although a fair quantity of wheel-thrown pottery has been identified, this appears to predate the Frankish occupation of Wadi Musa.[186] Sinibaldi has noted similar pottery trends at nearby smaller sites. At Wadi Farasa, to the south of the Petra *siq*, all of the ceramics dated to the Frankish period are handmade; almost all are unpainted and most belong to vessels that had a closed form. Likewise, at Bayda, about 5km north of Petra, the twelfth-century ceramics are almost all handmade and unpainted, and most vessels once had a closed shape.[187] Collectively, the simplicity of these assemblages speaks to fairly local economies, and suggests Frankish rule probably had minimal influence on the means and methods of pottery production in the region.

Montreal, the other main castle in the region, presents a context that was perhaps more like that of Kerak, given the size, status and presumably similar function of the stronghold. The pottery assemblage from a large vaulted structure in the northwest of the castle, which the excavators have identified as a Frankish 'palatial' building, is quite different to those found at the smaller contemporary sites around Petra. Some 7,506 fragments of pottery have been recovered in Frankish and Ayyubid layers, belonging to a minimum of 2,698 vessels. Around two-thirds of the sherds discovered were wheel-thrown, while handmade wares made up less than 10 per cent of the minimum number of vessels. Despite the much higher quantity of wheel-thrown wares, fancier glazed and stone-paste pottery accounted for less than 1 per cent. The remainder of the assemblage, found in secondary deposition and dubbed 'residual', was primarily wheel-thrown and believed to predate the arrival of the Franks.[188] Although the pottery of Montreal suggests a greater level of affluence, indicated by the proportionally higher number of wheel-thrown vessels and much lower proportion of handmade ones, the limited evidence of imported high luxury wares is interesting.

There are similar trends when looking at the faunal evidence. Assemblages from Montreal show that sheep and goat provided most of the meat consumed by the inhabitants of the castle during the Frankish period. Most of the animals were slaughtered at between 10 and 24 months of age, indicating that they were raised to be eaten, though the remains of some older animals reveal that some were used in secondary industries, providing things like milk or wool/hair. Pigs were also raised under Frankish rule, while the quantity of cow consumed in the castle, which was never a lot, apparently increased during the Ayyubid period. There is evidence to suggest that wild boar was hunted in the surrounding region, as was large game, such as gazelle, and the appearance of wild kite bones may be the result of falconry. A significant number of parrotfish bones have also been discovered, as has evidence of sea urchins and molluscs. These would have come from the Red Sea, more than 120km away; their presence is an indication of the considerable trade that moved along the King's Highway.[189]

The twelfth-century inhabitants of al-Wu'ayra appear to have had a similar diet to those at Montreal. Sheep and/or goat bones are most common, though considerable numbers of pig, cow and parrotfish bones have also been discovered. The pigs were slaughtered at a young age, providing further evidence that the local population was predominantly Christian. The quantity of fish bones at al-Wu'ayra is higher than that at Montreal, probably due to the former's closer proximity to the Red Sea and the affordability of fish as a lower status food product. Another difference is the discovery of a significant number of chicken bones at al-Wu'ayra; the age of the birds suggests they were raised primarily to lay eggs. Evidence of hunting is also less obvious when compared with Montreal, which seems to speak to the lower status of the site.[190] Nearby, Wadi Farasa provides a similar picture. Goat and sheep bones are again most numerous; the majority were slaughtered before the age of 2, though some were used for secondary industries. Like the other sites, the evidence suggests that the garrison fed on prime cuts of meat, as a disproportionately high number of long bones appears in the assemblage. A large quantity of parrotfish bones were also found. When compared with remains from earlier settlement periods, it seems the quantity of fish consumed in Transjordan rose considerably during the twelfth century. As at Montreal, no eggshells or bird bones have yet been found in a medieval context at Wadi Farasa.[191]

Two general trends appear when considering the ceramic and faunal evidence. First, there were certain obvious commonalities linking the sites. When considering the pottery, there seems to have been a local tradition of producing handmade wares that went on uninterrupted. Likewise, the animal bones reveal that most meat that was consumed came from sheep and goats, a trend that existed independent of the Frankish presence. The quantity of pork that was eaten probably rose with the arrival of certain Frankish figures, but there may have been an existing tradition of pig rearing, as the Franks settled in areas that had existing Christian populations. The presence of fish bones, particularly Red Sea parrotfish, is interesting, but whether or not the apparent increase in the consumption of fish was tied to the arrival of the Franks is unclear. The other obvious trend is the similarities between the smaller sites in the Petra area and their shared differences with Montreal. These differences, such as the finer quality of the pottery found at Montreal, the more obvious practice of hunting there, and the lower consumption of fish, appear to reflect the discrepancy in status between a main centre of power and smaller outposts. Future excavations at Kerak will hopefully allow for comparisons with these other Frankish sites; in the meantime, the collections from Montreal should be considered the closest examples of the types and proportions of finds that we might expect to discover at Kerak.

Later Perceptions

When Kerak and Montreal surrendered in 1188 and 1189 respectively, their garrisons, and any other Franks who had taken refuge in the castles, were allowed to evacuate the region for what lands remained in Latin hands. Although Transjordan would never again fall under Frankish rule, most local Christians probably remained. Likewise, some Franks, for whom Kerak had always been their home, or who had married into the local Syrian community, may have decided to stay behind.

An invaluable account of the region has been provided by Thietmar, a Latin pilgrim who travelled through Transjordan in 1218 on his way to the Monastery of St Catherine in Sinai. Having crossed the Jordan north of the

Dead Sea, Thietmar made his way south past Kerak. He describes it as a 'large city sited on a high mountain and fortified with walls and towers'. Nearby, he was entertained by a poor Orthodox woman, and was that evening visited and blessed by a figure whom he identified as the Orthodox bishop. He continued southward:

> I left to the right-hand side vast rugged places and to the left very huge mountains. I came to the mountain that is called *Petra* in Latin, *Montreal* in French, and al-Shawbak (*Scobach*) in Saracen. On the summit of that mountain is placed an excellent castle, enclosed step by step by three walls and so solid that I have never seen stronger. It belongs to the sultan of Babylon [*Cairo*]. Saracens and Christians live in its suburbs. There I was hospitably received by a certain French widow, who gave me information about the journey and the way of travelling through the desert to Mount Sinai. She provided me with twice-cooked bread for the journey, cheese, dried grapes, figs and wine. She also brought to me the Bedouin with camels [who would accompany me] to Mount Sinai, because the way through the desert is not known by other people. Indeed, it came about that they swore and bound themselves by their religion and law to bring me back alive or dead.

He goes on to call the country he passed through fertile, as he made his way from Montreal to Petra, then down the 'Araba towards 'Aqaba and Sinai.[192]

Thietmar's encounter appears to be the only known reference to Franks continuing to live in Transjordan. When considering that Montreal had hosted an ethnically European population for three-quarters of a century, this probably produced a mixed community as certain Frankish men married local Syrian women. A similar process may have taken place at Kerak, but the community at Montreal was a generation older, allowing more opportunity for a sense of local entrenchment to develop. As power shifted to Kerak from the 1140s, social and geographical ties may also have helped maintain stronger links between the Franks of Kerak and those in Palestine. Regardless of how many Franks may have opted to remain in Transjordan, both Kerak and Montreal continued to support large Syrian Christian communities. A majority of the inhabitants of Kerak were Christian at the end of the sixteenth century, though the proportion of Christians at Montreal had declined by this time; nevertheless, Abu'l-Fida' observed that most of Montreal's population was still Christian in the early Mamluk period.[193]

Thietmar's travels are somewhat exceptional when considering that Transjordan was an area of peripheral interest to most medieval European pilgrims. The region was primarily associated with the wandering of the Israelites, before their entry into the Promised Land. Wadi Musa was believed to have been *Cadesbarne* (Kadesh-Barnea), where Moses struck a rock, producing a spring, and nearby Jabal Harun is still associated with Mount Hor, where Aaron died (Numbers 20:1–29, 33:37–38). For the few Frankish pilgrims who passed through the region, like Thietmar, these were of secondary importance, waypoints on their way to Sinai and St Catherine's Monastery.

Despite the continued Christian presence in Transjordan, Latin pilgrimage east of the Dead Sea almost ceased following the region's return to Muslim rule. A pilgrimage guide, composed around 1260, notes that the road beyond Jericho was closed: 'you can go no further by that road.' To the west of the Dead Sea, Hebron was still accessible, though the Franks had not controlled any territory in the interior of southern Palestine since 1244. Pringle has observed that the main Latin pilgrimage route to Sinai shifted during the Mamluk period. Whereas pilgrims had once crossed the Jordan near Jericho, making their way south through Transjordan and then across Sinai from 'Aqaba, they came to instead travel along the coast via Gaza and al-'Arish, before turning south and moving between the oases of Sinai on their way to the Monastery of St Catherine.[194]

By the late thirteenth century, the irregular and inconsistent names that were used to identify formerly Frankish sites in Transjordan were leading to confusion. This is evident in the work of Burchard of Mount Sion, a German monk who spent some time in the Levant around 1280 and authored an influential description of the Holy Land. Whereas William of Tyre mistakenly associated Petra with Kerak, and Thietmar incorrectly equated Petra and Montreal, Burchard combined all three. In his presentation of greater Syria, he followed the established tradition of dividing the southern part into the three Arabias. The capital of the third and southernmost, he wrote, 'is Montreal (*Mons regalis*), which is called Kerak (*Krach*), and was formerly called Petra of the Desert (*Petra deserti*), sited above the Dead Sea'. Although this remark is clearly meant to refer to Kerak, given its proximity to the Dead Sea, it seems Burchard failed to appreciate that there was a second significant stronghold in the region; rather than simply mixing up the names, he failed to grasp that Kerak and Montreal were two different castles. Later in his work, he again refers to Kerak as Montreal, noting that it was called *Petra deserti* in antiquity, but was then known as *Krach*. Combining the history of the two sites, he noted that the castle had been built by Baldwin I, true of Montreal rather than Kerak, and that at the time he was writing it was used by the sultan of Egypt as his treasury, more accurate of Kerak than Montreal.[195]

Continued Claim to the Lordship

The last vestiges of Frankish authority in Transjordan were removed in 1189, but certain figures maintained their claim to the lordship. Although Reynald of Châtillon appears to have acted as the lord of Transjordan throughout the final decade of his life, he ruled on behalf of his stepson, Humphrey [IV] of Toron. Like his wife, Isabella of Jerusalem, Humphrey must have been at least 12 years old at the time of his wedding in 1183, placing his birth no later than 1171, though William of Tyre's remarks seem to imply Humphrey was slightly older than his bride. His adolescence is confirmed in the donation made to the order of St Lazarus on 21 April 1183, shortly before his wedding. Although this was issued in Humphrey's name, it states clearly that the grant was made with the agreement of his mother and Reynald, who is called 'lord of the lands of Montreal and Hebron'. The legal age of majority for men in the kingdom of Jerusalem was 15, and Humphrey would have been at least 16 when he took part in the Battle of Hattin, yet he seems not to have begun acting as lord of Kerak.[196]

Intriguingly, Reynald appears on official documents as 'lord of Montreal' for the last time on 16 May 1185. He witnessed three more charters before his death, all of which were issued by Guy of Lusignan on 21 October 1186, where he is referred to as *domnus princeps*, a simplified title attributed to Reynald on a number of previous occasions.[197] It is possible that Humphrey came of age sometime after the middle of May 1185, though nowhere is the young man referred to as 'lord of Montreal'. Humphrey seems to have been a somewhat timid character, and when considering the environment of heightened political tension, and Reynald's considerable influence at court following the death of Baldwin V, Humphrey may have offered little protest to his stepfather's continued rule. This was certainly not without precedent, as Melisende famously continued to wield power years after her son, Baldwin III, came of age. Had things transpired differently in 1187, it is a safe assumption that Guy would have found Reynald, then around 60 years old, an alternative position in the months or years that followed, allowing Humphrey to claim his patrimony. Alternatively, Reynald may have stood to continue ruling Hebron, which might explain why his possession of the lordship appears so frequently as a part of his already quite extensive title – often given as 'Prince Reynald, lord of Montreal and Hebron'.

Humphrey [IV] had every reason to expect that he would eventually inherit Transjordan. Testament to this, the young heir gave up his patrimony, or rather it was relinquished on his behalf, to secure his claim to the region. Following the death of his father, Humphrey stood to inherit not only Transjordan through his mother, but also Toron from his paternal grandfather, Humphrey

II the constable. When the elder Humphrey died in 1179, Baldwin IV refused to allow Humphrey [IV] to claim both Toron and Transjordan, which would allow the young lord, and Reynald in the meantime, to control two significant lordships. Perhaps able to lean on the example provided by Philip of Milly, and possibly also Walter of Beirut, an agreement was struck whereby the young lord would relinquish his claim to Toron, most likely in exchange for some kind of nominal compensation. William of Tyre, as royal chancellor, claims to have drafted this document himself, though neither it nor its details have survived.[198]

Like many other lords of the kingdom of Jerusalem, Humphrey was freed in the months following his capture at Hattin. His release was secured with the surrender of Kerak and Montreal, while Guy of Lusignan's liberty was a term of Ascalon's surrender. Shortly after the Battle of Hattin, while both Guy and Humphrey were still prisoners, Conrad of Montferrat, the brother of Sibylla's first husband, William, arrived at Tyre, where he assumed command of the city's defence. Upon gaining his freedom, Guy was placed in a desperate situation when Conrad refused to relinquish control of Tyre, the only city of the kingdom that remained in Frankish hands. This led Guy to launch a bold attack against Acre in late August 1189, initiating what would become a two-year siege and the defining struggle of the Third Crusade, as thousands of Europeans, reacting to Saladin's capture of Jerusalem in 1187, made their way to the Levant. As the struggle for Acre dragged on, many died of disease in the besiegers' camp, including Sibylla and her daughters. The city was finally captured in 1191, following the arrival of Philip II of France and Richard I of England.[199]

Guy's claim to the throne of Jerusalem had come through Sibylla, Amalric's eldest daughter. As the third and only remaining child of Amalric, it was not long until Isabella was put forward as the rightful monarch. Her husband, Humphrey [IV] of Toron, however, was not considered a worthy candidate to be king; his decision to refuse the crown when it was offered to him by the barons in 1186 had not been forgotten. Humphrey was instead pushed to dissolve his marriage, freeing Isabella to marry Conrad of Montferrat. Much as Agnes of Courtenay, Amalric's first wife, may have been instrumental in developing a party of supporters around her young son, Baldwin IV, Maria Komnene, Isabella's mother and Amalric's second wife, is cast as a leading figure advancing Isabella's claim and the loudest voice pushing her daughter to renounce her husband. Both Humphrey and Isabella eventually acquiesced and their marriage was annulled by the archbishop of Pisa, who was among those who had joined the crusaders' siege camp outside Acre. Isabella, who is presented as a reluctant participant to her mother's plans, seems to have genuinely loved her husband or at least felt guilty; although only about 19 years old, she had been married to Humphrey for the last seven years. This probably explains her subsequent decision to restore Humphrey's patrimony to him, the lordship of Toron, though it was at that time under Muslim rule.[200]

The succession was formally resolved following the conclusion of the siege of Acre. Conrad and Isabella were recognized to be the king and queen of Jerusalem, while Guy of Lusignan was compensated with Cyprus, which Richard I of England had conquered from the Byzantines on his way to Palestine earlier in 1191. Isabella would marry twice more, becoming a widow for the third time before the age of 30 and ultimately outliving all four of her husbands. Her final marriage, in 1198, was to Aimery of Lusignan, who had by that time inherited the crown of Cyprus from his younger brother, Guy. Isabella thus died queen of Jerusalem and Cyprus. The former title passed to her eldest daughter, Maria, who had been conceived with Conrad of Montferrat prior to his death in 1192.

Humphrey [IV] of Toron died childless in 1198, leading his claim to Toron and Transjordan to pass to his natural sister, Isabella of Toron. Reynald of Châtillon had arranged for Isabella, his stepdaughter, to marry Roupen III of Armenia, with whom she had two daughters, Alice and Philippa. Following Isabella's death, the Frankish claim to Transjordan passed to Alice, whose second husband was Raymond IV, the son of Bohemond III of Antioch and the person to whom Raymond III of Tripoli had willed his county. Their son, Raymond-Roupen, ruled Antioch from 1216 until 1219. Raymond-Roupen had married Helvis of Lusignan, the daughter of Aimery of Cyprus by his first wife, making her the stepdaughter of Isabella of Jerusalem. When a peace agreement saw northern Palestine return to Frankish control in 1229, Alice claimed her patrimony in northern Galilee.[201]

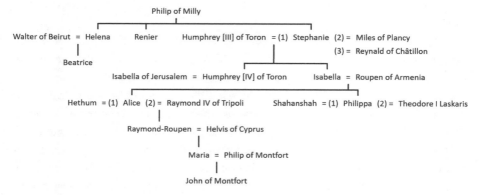

Fig. 1. Descendants of Philip of Milly.

In 1239, more territory in Palestine was returned to the Franks; following this, a list was drawn up of lands that had once been held by the Franks but were still under Muslim rule. Included on the list are a number of places that had once been held by the lords of Transjordan:

7. Towards Arabia and in Arabia he retains Hebron, which is now called St Abraham and is an episcopal seat.
9. Likewise the renowned castle that is called Tafila (*Traphyla*).
10. Likewise the city of Petra (*Petracensem civitatem*); and it is an archiepiscopal seat, which is now commonly called Karak (*Cracum*).
11. Likewise the castles of Montreal (*Montis regalis*) and al-Sila' (*Celle, Sela*) along with many other castles whose names I do not know, with their appurtenances; and this land ought to belong to the daughter of Prince Ruben and it extends five days' journey from Jerusalem.
12. Likewise Wadi Musa (*Vallem de Messa, Moussa*), which is part of Idumæa, and this is towards Damascus there are many castles and towns whose named I do not know, and it ought to belong to the young lady mentioned above.[202]

Although Transjordan would never again fall under Frankish rule, the family claim was kept alive by Alice's granddaughter, Maria of Antioch, the daughter of Raymond-Roupen and Helvis of Lusignan. Maria of Antioch married Philip of Montfort, lord of Tyre, bringing to their marriage Toron as well as her claim to Transjordan, which would pass to her eldest son, John of Montfort. By the time of John's death in 1283, the Franks once more faced an existential threat. The Mamluks had replaced Saladin's descendants as the masters of Syria, and the Franks could do little against such a formidable opponent. Antioch had been taken in 1268 and the Franks held little beyond the coast by the end of 1271. The dream of reclaiming Kerak had ended, replaced by more modest hopes of simply holding on.

Saladin's conquest of Transjordan also had ramifications for the Church. Around the start of 1198, as Innocent III took the papal tiara, challenges to the boundaries of patriarchal authority resurfaced.[203] Traditionally, Tyre and Petra had fallen under the authority of the patriarch of Antioch; however, following the arrival of the Franks and the establishment of Latin bishops, both were placed under the authority of the patriarch of Jerusalem. The resurgence of this controversy had practical implications for Tyre, which remained a Latin possession from 1124 until 1291. This issue carried less significance east of the Jordan, as the archdiocese of Petra had fallen from Frankish control along with Kerak, and prospects for its recapture were bleak.

In the years following 1187, titular bishops continued to be appointed for most sees that had once been under Frankish rule, but as Hamilton has observed, Petra was the only Latin bishopric of the twelfth century that had not been restored by the end of Innocent IV's papacy in 1254. The only apparent reference to a bishop of Petra after Guerric's death in 1190 is a vague mention in papal documents dating to 1238.[204] The apparent failure to appoint a titular bishop seems to represent a realistic assessment of the unlikelihood that Kerak, the seat of the diocese, would ever be recaptured. It was simply too far away and too exposed.

Chapter 3

Ayyubid Period

Al-Karak is a very strongly fortified castle on the borders of Syria, towards the Balqa', and in the mountains. It stands on a rock surrounded by wadis, except on the side toward the suburb. Al-Karak is situated midway between Jerusalem and 'Aqaba, on the Red Sea. It stands on a high hill.[1]

Yaqut al-Hamawi (d. 1229)

Kerak was ruled by members of Saladin's family – the Ayyubids – for about seventy-five years. In January 1189, following his capture of the great Hospitaller castle of Belvoir and only weeks after the garrison of Kerak had surrendered, Saladin discussed the administration and defence of the lands he had acquired since the Battle of Hattin with his brother, al-'Adil. They visited Jerusalem before the end of the month, then continued on to Ascalon, which had been granted to al-'Adil following the city's surrender on 5 September 1187. Saladin took back Ascalon from his younger brother at this time, compensating al-'Adil with Kerak and Montreal; although the latter had not yet been surrendered, this was expected at any moment.[2] These arrangements were part of Saladin's long-term succession plan: his eldest son, al-Afdal 'Ali, was 18 and already based in Damascus; his second son, al-'Aziz 'Uthman, was back in Egypt and almost 17; and a third son, al-Zahir Ghazi, now 15 years old, was in Aleppo.[3] As Saladin handed more authority to his sons, he carved out a secondary sphere of influence for his brother, which consisted of significant marginal lands, notably Transjordan and a large zone of influence in the Jazira. Both were important regions, but neither commanded the prestige of the great urban centres of Cairo, Damascus and Aleppo.

For the moment, al-'Adil continued to hold considerable authority in Egypt, on behalf of his brother and nephew, but this was acknowledged to be temporary. Transjordan, the link – and potential buffer – between Egypt and Syria, was in many ways an ideal place for Saladin to base his experienced brother while his own sons matured. When Saladin subsequently tweaked things further, taking some regions held by al-'Adil on the west side of the Euphrates in exchange for others to the east, Transjordan was excluded from these rearrangements. Later in 1189, al-'Adil made his first confirmed visit to Kerak. He is said to have commissioned some refortification efforts before setting out for his other powerbase in the Jazira.[4]

Al-'Adil

Under Ayyubid rule, Kerak remained a reasonably important centre. Along with the castle, al-'Adil was responsible for the interior corridor between Cairo and Damascus, which included the southernmost Syrian portion of the *hajj* route. The Franks also continued to regard the stronghold with an element of reverence. Following Saladin's capture of Jerusalem in the autumn of 1187, the cross that the Franks had placed on the Dome of the Rock (the *Templum Domini*), was taken down. According to rumours found in one continuation of William of Tyre's history, this cross was taken to Kerak.[5] The story appears a few decades after Kerak fell into Ayyubid hands, and may reflect the fact that the castle began to function almost immediately as an Ayyubid treasury – employed as such by al-'Adil and those who held it after him.

Al-'Adil's acquisition of Transjordan in 1189 had as much to do with Saladin's interest in gaining direct control over Ascalon as it did with finding a suitable place to base his brother. Unlike Kerak and Montreal, Ascalon's position along the coast exposed it to assault by European crusaders, a vulnerability that became all too apparent as noteworthy elements of the Third Crusade began arriving in the Holy Land later that year. The main event of the Third Crusade was the protracted siege of the port city of Acre. This lasted for almost two years between the summers of 1189 and 1191, finally ending in the weeks that followed the arrival of Philip II of France and Richard I of England. Although the French king departed for Europe shortly thereafter, Richard remained, hopeful that Jerusalem might be returned to the Franks. When negotiations between Richard and Saladin began in the autumn of 1189, one of the main stumbling blocks was said to have been 'Crac of Montreal' – Kerak – which Richard wanted destroyed as a term of any peace agreement.[6] It seems the English king had been made aware of the strategic value of the great castles of Transjordan. Saladin was resolutely opposed to this; indeed, Kerak was to prove a valuable Muslim possession the following year. Informed that Egyptian forces were gathering at Bilbays, where they prepared to escort a large party of merchants to Palestine, Richard dispatched a contingent of his army to intercept this convoy. When the Muslim force was attacked on 23 June 1192, its various elements were scattered. In the chaos, some fled back to Egypt while others, notably al-'Adil's forces and 'loyal' Bedouin, escaped to Kerak.[7]

The departure of Richard I of England and the final elements of the Third Crusade in late 1192, followed by Saladin's death early the next year, ushered in a new status quo in the Levant. While Frankish power would henceforward be concentrated primarily along the coast, Saladin's realm was divided among his sons, now in their early twenties, solidifying a tripartite division of Ayyubid authority between the centres of Cairo, Damascus and Aleppo.

Al-'Adil was at Kerak when he received news that his brother had died. He was provided an opportunity to avoid showing any disproportionate favour to one of his nephews when his northern lands in the Jazira came under threat by 'Izz al-Din Mas'ud, the Zankid ruler of Mosul, who was emboldened to expand his lands after receiving word of Saladin's death.[8] Following this temporary distraction, al-'Adil was quickly pulled into his nephews' struggle for power. He initially acted as an arbiter between them, before ultimately taking power himself, first in Damascus and then Cairo. Throughout, he retained control of Kerak, which continued to act as the administrative centre for the broader region of Transjordan.

Although only a secondary seat of power, Kerak remained a place of some importance and al-'Adil appears to have continued patronizing the castle. Epigraphic evidence reveals that a certain emir, Sarim al-Din Barghash al-'Adili, carried out building work there on his behalf in the 1190s.[9] In addition to serving as a treasury, Kerak was also used as a prison. 'Izz al-Din Usama al-Salihi, who had been entrusted with the strongholds of Belvoir and 'Ajlun, was among those confined in the castle after al-'Adil moved against him in 1211–12.[10]

Al-Mu'azzam 'Isa

Towards the end of his life, al-'Adil divided his lands among his sons. Egypt was placed under al-Kamil, who stood to become head of the family; southern Syria, including Damascus, Palestine and Transjordan, was allocated to al-Mu'azzam 'Isa; the northern regions, apart from Aleppo, which had been retained by Saladin's son al-Zahir Ghazi, were divided between al-Ashraf Musa, Shihab al-Din Ghazi, and al-Hafiz Arslanshah. With al-'Adil's death in 1218, Kerak thus passed to al-Mu'azzam 'Isa, who used the castle, along with Jerusalem, 'Ajlun and Damascus, as one of his principal armouries.[11]

Al-'Adil's death took place during the Fifth Crusade.[12] This expedition had been the project of Pope Innocent III, who died a year before armies began setting out from Europe in 1217. The crusaders attacked Egypt in the summer of 1218, besieging the port town of Damietta, near the mouth of the main eastern branch of the Nile. Al-'Adil died on his way to Egypt to offer assistance to al-Kamil, who was already acting as his deputy there. While al-Kamil defended Egypt, al-Mu'azzam 'Isa lent support to his brother, though

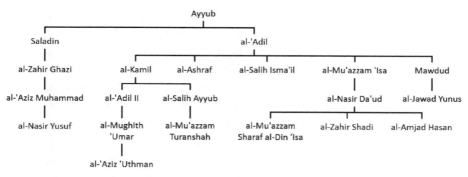

Fig. 2. Ayyubid family.

he watched things with concern when back in Syria, particularly with the fall of Damietta on 5 November 1219.

During and then after the lengthy siege of Damietta, which lasted more than 500 days, delegations began moving back and forth between al-Kamil and the crusaders. Al-Kamil was prepare to return Palestine to the Franks if the crusaders would leave Egypt and give up Damietta. Negotiations stumbled when things came to Transjordan, much as they had during the Third Crusade: al-Kamil was willing to facilitate the return of lands that had formerly belonged to the kingdom of Jerusalem prior to Saladin's conquests, but he refused to include Kerak and Montreal. Aware of these negotiations, and the lingering threat that the Franks might turn on Syria, regardless of their success in Egypt, al-Mu'azzam 'Isa had the walls of castles across Palestine pulled down. These slighting efforts extended to the town walls of Jerusalem, leaving the city defenceless. Revealingly, Kerak and Montreal were spared this destruction. Al-Mu'azzam 'Isa was evidently committed to the defence of these strongholds, having faith in their ability to resist a siege should Palestine pass back to the Franks; he may also have been informed of his brother's negotiation strategy, which specifically excluded the two castles. As the walls of Jerusalem were pulled down, leaving the city defenceless, many of the Muslim inhabitants left, heading for Egypt, Damascus and Kerak.[13]

Meanwhile, negotiations continued in Egypt. Al-Kamil's offer came to include not only the lands conquered by Saladin, but the return of Frankish prisoners, the fragment of the True Cross that Saladin had captured at Hattin, funds to help the Franks refortify Jerusalem, and an annual subsidy in exchange for retaining Transjordan. This was ultimately rejected by the Christians, who demanded more money and the surrender of Kerak.[14] The offer, however, was not unanimously opposed by the various components of the Latin army. Most European crusaders were said to have been inclined to accept al-Kamil's proposal, as this would fulfil their ultimate aim of seeing Jerusalem return to Christian rule. Some with longer-term interests in the region, notably the military orders, the Italian merchant communities and the Patriarch of Jerusalem, pointed to the practical challenges of trying to hold Jerusalem if the Transjordan corridor remained open. Critically, little had changed in the three decades since Richard I of England had declined to attack Jerusalem, believing the city could not be held so long as certain regions, Transjordan in particular, remained firmly under Muslim control.

As neither side was willing to consent to a peace agreement that excluded their possession of Kerak, negotiations ultimately failed. The Christian army finally marched out of Damietta in July 1221, heading for Cairo. The crusaders were halted at Mansura, where they encountered the Egyptian army on the other side of one of the distributary branches of the Nile. Unable to push onwards, the crusaders were eventually compelled to begin a withdrawal back to Damietta in late August, which quickly turned into a chaotic flight. Those who had been left in Damietta, and those who survived to join them there, promptly surrendered the town and left the region. The Fifth Crusade, having lasted three years in Egypt, was a complete failure. For al-Kamil, this was a moment of triumph. Not only had he been able to fend off the Franks, but he had successfully called on and received help from his brother, al-Mu'azzam 'Isa, reinforcing his position as the supreme figure in the Ayyubid realm. For al-Mu'azzam 'Isa, this had been an equally threatening situation, having faced the very real prospect that his brother might consent to return all of Palestine to the Franks.

The Ayyubids' steadfast reluctance to give up Kerak begs the question: why was it considered so valuable? Milwright has identified three attributes that contributed to this. First there was the productivity of the land. This included a regular agricultural surplus and the specialty crops grown in around the Dead Sea, as well as mineral resources. Second was the importance of the Bedouin. In addition to their livestock, which included goats, sheep, horses and camels, the Bedouin could also be employed as auxiliary troops, scouts and for more general intelligence gathering. Third was the defensibility of the castles of Kerak and Montreal. The confidence placed in Kerak in particular led al-'Adil, and many subsequent rulers, to use the castle as a treasury.[15] To these might be added a fourth attribute: Kerak and Montreal continued to dominate the secondary corridor between Cairo and Damascus, as well as the Transjordan section of the *hajj* route.

Following Saladin's conquest of Palestine in 1187, the coastal *via maris* became the main artery for traffic moving between Egypt and Syria, taking travellers via Gaza. This route, however, was more exposed to Frankish interference from their remaining bases of control along the Palestinian coast. The King's Highway was a somewhat less comfortable option, and potentially vulnerable to hostile Bedouin, but it continued to offer an alternative. More importantly, if Palestine were lost to the Franks, this corridor would once more become the main link between Cairo and Damascus. When considering the polemics that had developed during the reigns of Nur al-Din and Saladin, it is also not hard to imagine that many Muslims viewed the prospect of handing control of a critical section of the pilgrim route back to the Franks as unacceptable. Reynald of Châtillon's ability to dominate the region, let alone his daring raids towards the Hijaz, would not have been forgotten.

Rather than slight Kerak, al-Mu'azzam 'Isa, like his father before him, saw to the castle's improvement. Above the outer gateway of the western tunnel entrance to the town, an inscription dates building work to 1227. The emir who supervised this development of the town's fortifications was Shams al-Din Sunqur al-Mu'azzami.[16] Around the castle, fruit trees were planted and the gardens came to resemble those of a Syrian capital. Other sites in Transjordan also benefitted from the patronage of al-Mu'azzam 'Isa.[17]

Meanwhile, with the collapse of the Fifth Crusade and the disappearance of any immediate threat posed by the Franks, divisions began to reappear among the Ayyubids. As the struggle for power continued, tensions rose between the brothers al-Mu'azzam 'Isa, al-Kamil and al-Ashraf Musa; the latter initially sided with al-Kamil, the more distant power, but by 1226 had shifted his allegiance to al-Mu'azzam 'Isa.[18] The Franks were fairing little better as succession issues continued to plague the kingdom of Jerusalem. Maria of Jerusalem died around the age of 20, shortly after giving birth to a daughter, her heir and successor, Isabella II. The young queen was later betrothed to the Holy Roman Emperor, Frederick II, whom she married in 1225, around the time of her thirteenth birthday. Isabella II died giving birth to her first and only child, a son, Conrad, in 1228, leaving behind another infant as titular monarch of Jerusalem.[19]

Emperor Frederick II had committed himself to go on crusade prior to the Fifth Crusade, but he repeatedly delayed setting out. Despite his initial reluctance to travel to the Holy Land, the emperor built up a rapport with al-Kamil over the years through a fairly regular exchange of letters. Responding to the increasing threat posed by al-Mu'azzam 'Isa and his growing group of allies, al-Kamil went so far as to make Fredrick much the same offer as he had presented to the leaders of the Fifth Crusade. Al-Kamil was prepared to see those lands Saladin had conquered returned to the kingdom of Jerusalem, with the explicit exclusion of Transjordan, in order to gain a military alliance against his brother. Although this was a considerable gesture, al-Kamil stood to lose little: Palestine was in the zone of influence of al-Mu'azzam 'Isa, and by shifting focus there he helped weaken the case of those in Europe advocating another crusade to Egypt. Then, just as Frederick II was preparing to finally fulfil his crusading vow, al-Mu'azzam 'Isa died in November 1227.[20]

Al-Nasir Dawud

Al-Mu'azzam 'Isa was initially succeeded in Damascus by his son, al-Nasir Dawud.[21] Al-Kamil used the death of his brother to promptly demand that his nephew turn over Montreal. When this was refused, the sultan marched out of Egypt, taking control of Jerusalem and Nablus, and with them Muslim Palestine. In search of support, al-Nasir Dawud called on al-Ashraf, his uncle and former ally of his father, while smaller Ayyubid figures similarly took sides. To al-Nasir's misfortune, his uncles came to an understanding that excluded him. Al-Kamil and al-Ashraf met in southern Palestine in November 1228, where they agreed that al-Ashraf should hold Damascus and southern Syria, while al-Nasir would be compensated from al-Ashraf's lands east of the Euphrates. Refusing to accept this, al-Nasir found himself besieged in Damascus, first by al-Ashraf and then by both his uncles. Making matters worse for al-Nasir Dawud, much of his father's treasure was out of reach in Kerak. When al-Kamil sent a small detachment to Transjordan, al-Nasir's mother, who was then at Kerak, organized a successful counterattack that drove off the hostile forces. The two emirs who had led this detachment were captured and reportedly remained prisoners in the castle until their deaths. An agreement was eventually reached in June 1229: al-Nasir would give up Damascus and Montreal, but would be allowed to keep Kerak, and with it northern Transjordan, the Jordan Valley, and Nablus, while the fortress of Sarkhad, in the Hawran, would be retained by al-Nasir's senior emir and trusted advisor, 'Izz al-Din Aybak al-Mu'azzami. Al-Ashraf duly took power in Damascus, while those lands beyond the Euphrates that had earlier been offered to al-Nasir instead passed to al-Kamil.[22]

While al-Nasir Dawud was held up in Damascus, Frederick II finally arrived in Palestine, leading what is known as the Sixth Crusade. Since the death of al-Mu'azzam 'Isa, al-Kamil no longer had need of Frederick's assistance, and the emperor's presence was now much more threatening than helpful. Reacting to the dynamic situation in which he found himself, al-Kamil, who led negotiations with Frederick while his brother initially dealt with their nephew, offered to hand Jerusalem over to the emperor as the main clause in a ten-year peace agreement. This was accepted.[23]

Besides Frederick and al-Kamil, and to an extent al-Ashraf, whose approval was necessary, this solution pleased few. For Christian critics, Frederick had effectively accepted less than what had been offered during the Fifth Crusade. For many Muslims, it seemed as if the holy city had been simply given away. Although the surrender of Jerusalem was a blow to the images of al-Kamil and al-Ashraf, it was a practical move. Thanks to al-Mu'azzam 'Isa's slighting efforts, Jerusalem was indefensible, meaning the Franks would effectively hold it at the pleasure of their Muslim neighbours. Furthermore, while the Franks stood to gain control of the city, al-Haram al-Sharif (the Temple Mount) and with it its holy places, notably the Dome of the Rock and the al-Aqsa Mosque, were to remain under Muslim authority. From a Frankish perspective, the symbolism of regaining Jerusalem had propagandistic value, but no effort was made to address the practical matter of how the city might be retained once the peace expired. As was highlighted in the contemporary Ernoul account, *Crac de Mont Roial* remained in Muslim hands.[24]

From 1229, following al-Nasir Dawud's surrender of Damascus and his relocation to Kerak, Transjordan became a semi-independent principality. In some ways, Kerak reassumed the status that it had held under al-'Adil, before he usurped his nephews. In this instance, however, al-Nasir more obviously held his authority by the will of the ruler of Egypt, his uncle, al-Kamil. Al-Nasir never lost hope of reclaiming Damascus, his patrimony, but he was convinced that the support of the sultan of Egypt was required to do this. Al-Kamil had a similar interest in securing the loyalty of his nephew, who now acted as a buffer between Egypt and the potential machinations of al-Ashraf Musa in Damascus.

In 1231, al-Kamil had a marriage contract drawn up between one of his daughters, 'Ashura Khatun, and al-Nasir Dawud.[25] This was part of an effort to build a network of alliances and forge a broader Ayyubid coalition, which the sultan promptly put to work in 1232. After assembling the Egyptian army, al-Kamil moved into Syria, collecting al-Nasir at Kerak in April and other forces to the north as he made his way towards the Euphrates. The campaign culminated in a siege of Amid (Diyarbakir), which surrendered in October.[26] A few years later, in 1235–36, al-Kamil returned to the Jazira, pressing his claim to the lands he had gained from al-Ashraf Musa in the agreement they had struck during the Sixth Crusade, which also saw al-Nasir relegated to Kerak. Al-Kamil's eldest son, al-Salih Najm al-Din Ayyub, who had already been granted Hisn Kayfa, was given authority over these lands in the Jazira, but he was not his father's favourite. It was al-Kamil's younger son, al-Adil, named after his grandfather, who was designated heir apparent in Egypt.[27]

In Syria, al-Kamil's dominance led to a growing sense of resentment, which in turn inspired a number of reactionary policies targeting potential opponents. This extended to al-Nasir Dawud, who was made to renounce the marriage agreement with the sultan's daughter. Al-Nasir was so afraid that al-Kamil might seize Kerak that he appealed in person to the caliph in Baghdad. As most of the Ayyubids joined together against al-Kamil, al-Nasir found himself in the middle, politically and geographically. Despite his fears and previous treatment, he still opted to side with Egypt, believing an alliance with Cairo provided the best chance of recovering Damascus. This decision initially seemed to pay off when al-Kamil named him the rightful heir to Damascus and renewed the marriage contract with his daughter. Meanwhile, in Syria, al-Ashraf Musa died in August 1237. Without a son to succeed him, al-Ashraf willed his lands to one of his younger brothers, al-Salih Isma'il, who had been ruling the Syrian city of Bosra. Things appeared to be falling into place for al-Nasir, who quickly set out with al-Kamil to challenge control of Damascus. The siege was successful and al-Salih Isma'il was forced to cede the city to his older brother at the end of December, for which he was compensated with his former possession of Bosra along with Baalbek. To the great disappointment of al-Nasir, al-Kamil opted to hold Damascus himself for the time being. This arrangement, however, did not last long. Still in Damascus, al-Kamil died on 9 March 1238.[28]

The deaths of al-Ashraf and al-Kamil ushered to power a new generation. In Egypt, al-Kamil's designated heir, al-'Adil II, duly took power, while al-Salih Najm al-Din Ayyub continued to rule the Jazira. In Damascus, their cousin, al-Jawad Muzaffar al-Din Yunus, another grandson of al-'Adil, was selected to hold power on behalf of al-'Adil II as his deputy (na'ib), deliberately excluding al-Nasir Dawud. Frustrated, al-Nasir brought his army into the field, moving on Gaza. Unfortunately for al-Nasir, his disappointments would continue. In July 1238, he was decisively defeated by al-Jawad in northern Palestine, forcing al-Nasir to flee back to Kerak.[29] Despite his victory, al-Jawad Muzaffar al-Din Yunus quickly came to believe that he had lost the trust of his cousin, al-'Adil II. Before the end of 1238, he appealed to al-Salih Ayyub, who agreed to exchange Sinjar and other regions in the Jazira for Damascus. Meanwhile, al-Nasir Dawud, still believing an alliance with Egypt offered the best chance of recovering Damascus, went to Cairo to curry favour with al-'Adil II. This set the stage for yet another showdown between brothers – al-'Adil II in Cairo and al-Salih Ayyub in Damascus – with Kerak on the side of Egypt and most of Syria in alliance with Damascus.[30]

Al-Nasir Dawud set out with an army from Egypt on behalf of al-'Adil II in the summer of 1239. For siding with his brother, al-Salih Najm al-Din Ayyub moved into northern Palestine and began distributing the lands that al-Nasir had held there since surrendering Damascus a decade earlier. Unfortunately for Al-Salih Ayyub, his Syrian alliance was not as solid as he believed. His uncle, al-Salih Isma'il, who had briefly held Damascus in late 1237, took advantage of his nephew's departure from Damascus to seize control of the city for himself around the end of September. This sudden coup of sorts caused a wave of uncertainty to wash over al-Salih Ayyub's remaining allies, most of whom abandoned him. Isolated, al-Salih Ayyub was himself captured by al-Nasir Dawud, who proceeded to send his cousin to Kerak. Once more, the castle was used as a high-status prison.[31]

This turn of events was convenient for al-'Adil II: the threat posed by his brother, al-Salih Ayyub, had disappeared, while al-Salih Isma'il recognized his nominal authority. This also freed the Egyptian troops to turn their attention towards a growing number of crusaders who had recently arrived in Palestine, contingents of what is known as the Barons' Crusade. Some of these crusaders were bested near Gaza in November 1239.[32] Following this, al-Nasir Dawud, who was forced to look on in anger as yet someone else had come to power in Damascus, attacked Jerusalem – the ten-year peace concluded between al-Kamil and Frederic II had expired by this time. Jerusalem's Frankish defenders surrendered around December 1239, after a siege of about three weeks, though the only defensible part of the city at the time was the citadel, known as the Tower of David. Jerusalem had little military value, even less since its walls had been pulled down, but it still carried considerable symbolic weight, and al-Nasir could claim to have liberated Jerusalem for Islam, correcting the wrong committed by his uncle a decade earlier.[33]

Tensions remained high among the Ayyubids. With al-Salih Najm al-Din Ayyub in his custody, al-Nasir Dawud was in a particularly strong position. Al-'Adil II demanded that his brother, al-Salih Ayyub, be turned over to him. Al-Nasir leveraged his captive to demand the sultan first recognize his right to rule Damascus, a claim he had maintained since the death of his father, al-Mu'azzam 'Isa, in 1227. Meanwhile, al-Salih Isma'il, who continued to rule Damascus, sought to avoid provoking al-Nasir, lest this push his nephew into an alliance with al-'Adil II that could threaten his position. But perhaps the most influential voice was the closest one to al-Nasir, that of his captive cousin, al-Salih Ayyub, who might be particularly indebted should he be set free. With al-'Adil II threatening to march on Kerak, al-Nasir Dawud struck a deal with al-Salih Ayyub and released him. In the spring of 1240, the two cousins met in Jerusalem, where they were joined by al-Muzaffar of Hama, and together they agreed to a division of power: al-Salih Ayyub would replace al-'Adil II as ruler of Egypt and al-Nasir would finally reclaim Damascus.

Before a confrontation could take place, al-'Adil II was overthrown by a group of his own emirs in Egypt. Al-Salih Najm al-Din Ayyub was summoned to take his brother's place; two weeks later, he assumed power in Cairo on 18 May 1240.[34]

The change of rulers in Cairo was to leave al-Nasir Dawud disappointed yet again, as it quickly became apparent that al-Salih Ayyub had little interest in seeing him restored to power in Damascus. This pushed al-Nasir Dawud to turn against his former ally, and at times side with al-Salih Isma'il. The Ayyubid world remained divided between the men who held Cairo and Damascus, with Kerak once more in the middle, though more often on the side of Damascus. It was at this time that al-Salih Isma'il, in search of allies, returned much of Palestine to the Franks. Not all Franks approved of an alliance with Syria, leading another faction to conclude a similar peace agreement with al-Salih Ayyub in Cairo – it cost al-Salih Ayyub nothing to acknowledge the Franks' possession of the lands ceded to them by al-Salih Isma'il.[35]

Over the following years, a number of engagements took place between the various parties. Al-Nasir Dawud was defeated by al-Salih Isma'il east of the Jordan, but he was able to overcome an Egyptian force near Jerusalem in mid-1241. In the meantime, al-Jawad Muzaffar al-Din Yunus, al-Adil II's former administer in Damascus, was for a time a prisoner in Kerak. Having lost his lands in the Jazira, al-Jawad set out for Egypt. He was captured by, or perhaps defected to, al-Nasir Dawud, who confined him for a while before releasing him, introducing yet another player into the mix. Al-Nasir Dawud also attempted to recover Montreal during this period, though his effort was unsuccessful.[36]

Despite a number of brief and failed alliances, the situation in 1244 looked much as it had four years earlier, with Kerak and Damascus in partnership against Cairo. The Syrian faction secured Frankish assistance by confirming their possession of Jerusalem, while al-Salih Ayyub summoned help from the Khwarizmians, offering them lands in Syria in exchange for their support. The Khwarizmians were nomadic Turkmen, originally from the central Asian Steppe, who had been pushed west by the Mongols, leading them to take a significant part in the politics of the Jazira during the 1230s. In his younger years, al-Salih Ayyub had made extensive use of their services while ruling beyond the Euphrates; since that time, their influence had come to be felt as far west as Aleppo. When the Khwarizmians reached Palestine in the middle of 1244, they forced al-Salih Isma'il to withdraw back to Damascus and al-Nasir Dawud to Kerak. They proceeded to sack Jerusalem in July on their way to Gaza. In October, the Khwarizmians, backed by a contingent of Egyptians led by Rukn al-Din Baybars, who had been a prisoner alongside al-Salih Ayyub during his incarceration in Kerak, defeated the allied Syrian-Frankish army at the Battle of Forbie. The army of Kerak had been lined up on the allied left, with the Franks making up the right, opposing the main Khwarizmian force. In the aftermath of the battle, al-Nasir lost all of his lands west of the Great Rift, while al-Salih Isma'il was compelled to give up Damascus and content himself with his old possession of Baalbek, along with Bosra and the Sawad.[37]

Although al-Salih Ayyub rewarded the Khwarizmians with lands in Palestine, they believed they had been promised more. Seeing an opportunity, al-Nasir Dawud reached out to the Turkmen. With their support, he appropriated Jerusalem, Nablus and the rest of the lands he claimed in Palestine. The Khwarizmians, however, soon outstayed their welcome in Syria. Following a failed siege of Damascus, they were defeated in May 1246 by the army of Homs, supported by Aleppan contingents, while Egyptian forces moved against them from the south. Al-Salih Isma'il fled Baalbek, which was subsequently occupied in the name of al-Salih Ayyub. The remaining Khwarizmians gathered around al-Nasir Dawud, but they were defeated in the Balqa' by Egyptian forces on 11 September 1246. Pressing their advantage, the Egyptians moved in to attack Kerak. Al-Nasir bought peace with his besiegers by promising to surrender the Khwarizmians that were with him at that time.[38]

During the 1230s and 1240s, al-Nasir Dawud was an influential figure in the Levant. Kerak, however, was more than anything a means to an end for him; it was the secondary centre from which he hoped to one day regain control of Damascus. Although his ambitions lay elsewhere, it is very likely that al-Nasir Dawud developed the castle during the two decades in which it served as his base of power. Brown has identified the main palatial complex, which still stands in the southern portion of the castle, as dating to his reign. In the valley below, there was evidently a guesthouse, where Ibn Wasil (d. 1298) was accommodated for a time. The great historian was a young man in the early 1230s when he enjoyed the patronage of al-Nasir Dawud. Around the same time, another of the great Ayyubid historians, Sibt ibn al-Jawzi, spent a number of years in Kerak, having left Damascus in protest when Jerusalem was surrendered to the Franks in 1229. To have attracted such men of letters, Kerak must have been, to at least some degree, a centre of learning and intellectualism.[39]

Al-Salih Ayyub

Al-Nasir Dawud's tenure in Kerak ended in 1249. In the half-decade leading up to this, al-Salih Najm al-Din Ayyub had established himself as the dominant figure in the Near East. Al-Nasir Dawud allegedly proposed to surrender Kerak to his powerful cousin in early 1249, as the latter returned south from a campaign in northern Syria. The wily ruler of Kerak, however, ended up backing out of this arrangement when he learned the sultan's health was failing, and that another great crusading army was poised to attack Egypt. Later in the year, al-Nasir Dawud went north to solicit the support of one of his more distant cousins, al-Nasir Yusuf of Aleppo. While he was away, al-Nasir entrusted Kerak to his favourite son, al-Mu'azzam Sharaf al-Din 'Isa. Two of al-Nasir's older sons by another wife, al-Zahir Shadi and al-Amjad Hasan, resented the favour shown to their younger half-brother and resolved to seize the castle while their father was away. Once they were in control, al-Zahir Shadi remained in place, while al-Amjad Hasan went to Egypt to negotiate the castle's surrender to al-Salih Ayyub, hoping the sultan would award them with lands greater than those they might hope to inherit from their father. The brothers were duly rewarded, and Badr al-Din al-Sawabi was sent to administer Kerak and Montreal (as *na'ib*) on behalf of al-Salih Ayyub.[40]

By the time al-Amjad Hasan had reached al-Salih Ayyub in Egypt, it was September. In June, Louis IX of France had organized the landing of a large crusading force in northern Egypt. This, the Seventh Crusade, saw Damietta occupied virtually unopposed. After a delay of a few months, the crusaders made their way south, by which time al-Salih Ayyub was quite ill. The sultan died in late November 1249, leaving others to lead the defence of Egypt.

Found in the history of al-Nuwayri is a letter believed to have been written by al-Salih Najm al-Din Ayyub shortly before his death to his son, al-Mu'azzam Turanshah. Although father and son had a strained relationship, the letter makes clear how important Kerak was seen to be.

My son, if the nobles of Aleppo try to make you hand over Kerak to al-Nasir [Yusuf], give him [instead] Shawbak [Montreal]. And if he is not satisfied with that, increase it [to include] al-Sahil [the littoral] for his satisfaction. But do not allow Kerak to leave your hand. By God, heed my recommendation because you do not know the plans of your accursed Enemy [the crusaders]. Perhaps – God forbid it – if he advances to Egypt, Kerak will be your refuge, and it will protect your person and your *harim*. Egypt does not possess such a fortress, and gather there you have an army with which you can advance against the enemy and retake Egypt. But if you do not have a refuge like Kerak your soldiers will disperse from you. I have decided to transport there money, supplies, the *harim*, and everything that is precious to me. And I will make it my refuge and will be strengthened by it. By God, my heart was not strong and my back not firm until I had it [Kerak] in my possession. Praise be to God alone, and blessing and peace to His Prophet Muhammad and on his family and his companions.[41]

As Milwright has observed, al-Salih Ayyub had first-hand knowledge of Kerak, having spent seven months there a decade earlier as al-Nasir Dawud's prisoner. The extreme measures that al-Salih Ayyub advised his son to take to retain control of the castle, as well as his apparent immediate use of it as a treasury, a role that can be traced back to al-'Adil, speak to the strength and perceived value of the castle in the mid-thirteenth century. It is peculiar in some ways that the importance of Kerak should be so clearly and consistently emphasized by contemporaries following the arrival of a considerable force of crusaders.[42]

Al-Mu'azzam Turanshah

Al-Mu'azzam Turanshah was at Hisn Kayfa when news of his father's death reached him in December 1249. In a strange parallel, it seems that al-Salih Ayyub had sent his son to the distant Jazira to keep him from interfering in the affairs of Egypt, much as his own father, al-Kamil, had sent him to the same region for similar reasons decades earlier. Setting out for Egypt, al-Mu'azzam Turanshah reached Damascus in early January, where he paused for a while. Continuing onwards, he sent some of his men to secure Kerak, and his father's treasure there, while he himself reached Mansura on 24 February 1250.[43]

Mansura was where the Egyptian army had halted the progress of the Fifth Crusade in 1221, and the Seventh Crusade had similarly stalled there in late December 1249, having left Damietta a month earlier. Little more than two weeks before al-Mu'azzam Turanshah's arrival, the crusaders managed to ford the distributary that separated the two armies. Although this was an accomplishment that their predecessors had not managed, supply issues, impetuous actions and swelling opposition prevented the crusaders from pressing any advantage. Unable to push southward, the Seventh Crusade ended much like the Fifth: a series of unproductive negotiations preceded a chaotic retreat northwards to Damietta, during which the French king and many others were captured and far more were killed. Louis IX subsequently ransomed himself and remained in Palestine for a few years, where he helped develop the fortifications of a number of Frankish towns along the coast.[44]

In Egypt, al-Mu'azzam Turanshah's reign was brief. He immediately proved unpopular, showing little favour to those who had risen to power under his father. It was a group of his father's mamluks (the private companies of slave soldiers upon whom the Ayyubids were becoming increasingly reliant) who murdered the new sultan in May 1250, while the French king was still a prisoner.[45] The mamluks subsequently took power themselves, establishing a new ruling regime in Egypt.

Al-Mughith ʿUmar

At the time of al-Muʿazzam Turanshah's death, al-Mughith ʿUmar, son of al-ʿAdil II, was a prisoner in Montreal – it was naturally feared that he might harbour resentment following the overthrow of his father in 1240. With the uncertainty that accompanied the slaying of the new sultan, al-Mughith ʿUmar was set free by Badr al-Din al-Sawabi, the man to whom al-Salih Ayyub had entrusted the administration of Transjordan. Al-Mughith ʿUmar took up residence in Kerak and turned the castle back into the seat of power of an autonomous Ayyubid principality, which once more included Montreal. From his base in Transjordan, and with the remnants of al-Salih Ayyub's treasure in Kerak, he was able to resist both the new Mamluk regime in Egypt and al-Nasir Yusuf of Aleppo, who extended his authority across Ayyubid Syria following al-Muʿazzam Turanshah's murder.[46]

A balance of power between al-Nasir Yusuf and the Mamluks, led by ʿIzz al-Din Aybak al-Salihi, was established in the early 1250s. The Mamluks, however, were not a naturally united group, being composed of a number of different companies or regiments. Disputes and distrust eventually led the Bahriyya regiment, led by Rukn al-Din Baybars, to flee Egypt for Syria, where they initially found service with al-Nasir Yusuf. When relations cooled between al-Nasir Yusuf and the Bahriyya in 1257, Baybars offered his support to al-Mughith ʿUmar. On behalf of the ruler of Kerak, Baybars led two failed expeditions against the Mamluks of Egypt. Displeased with the failure of the second, which he had been persuaded to accompany, al-Mughith ʿUmar refused to allow the Bahriyya to enter Kerak following their return in the spring of 1258, forcing them to camp outside the town. By early 1259, Baybars and the Bahriyya had left al-Mughith's service and reconciled themselves with al-Nasir Yusuf. This reunion, however, was short-lived; a failed attempt on the life of al-Nasir Yusuf saw Baybars leave Syria and finally make amends with the Mamluks of Egypt, now led by Sayf al-Din Qutuz.[47]

Meanwhile, al-Nasir Dawud returned to Transjordan. Since departing Kerak in 1249, he had bounced back and forth between Aleppo and Baghdad. While in Iraq, he developed a relationship with the caliph, who ultimately sent him to Syria to raise an army that could help defend Baghdad against the advancing Mongols. The shockwaves created by the westward advance of the

Mongols had been felt in Iraq, the Jazira and even Syria for decades, but these regions came under direct threat in the 1250s. When he arrived at Kerak, al-Nasir was promptly detained by al-Mughith 'Umar until the caliph ordered his release. Al-Nasir Dawud was still in Syria when the Mongols captured Baghdad in February 1258. It was outside Damascus, the city he had tried for so many years to reclaim, that al-Nasir subsequently died of disease.[48]

Like al-Nasir Dawud, al-Mughith 'Umar contributed to the development of Kerak. An inscription found outside the western walls of the town, recording the construction of a certain structure, bears the date 1253. The building project was overseen by a certain Jamal al-Din Natr, though the name of the commissioning patron was deliberately damaged to the point of illegibility. Rather than an attempt to obscure who commissioned this work, the defacement appears to have been a personal attack, as the name of the ruler's father and grandfather remain, confirming it was al-Mughith 'Umar who was responsible. It seems the final Ayyubid ruler of Kerak was subject to a *damnatio memoriae* of sorts when the castle fell under Mamluk rule. Despite this evidence of building, of which nothing more is known, Milwright is quite justified in his observation that most of al-Mughith 'Umar's funds were probably directed towards paying troops, rather than financing construction projects.[49]

Arrival of the Mongols

A Mongol army crossed the Euphrates in late 1259. From the start of 1260, it overran most of Ayyubid Syria. This Mongol force was led by Hulagu, brother of the great khan, Mongke.[50] Having taken the city of Aleppo, and while still subduing a remnant of resistance in the citadel, Hulagu sent a portion of his army under his leading general, Kitbuqa, to occupy southern Syria. Shortly after receiving the surrender of the citadel of Aleppo, Hulagu returned east. He had received news that Mongke had died, so made for Azerbaijan in order to better defend his lands from any challenges and keep apprised of news relating to the succession. Meanwhile, Kitbuqa occupied Damascus unopposed; al-Nasir Yusuf abandoned the city ahead of his arrival, fleeing towards Gaza. As Mongol raiders spread through Palestine, the Hawran and as far as Wadi al-Mujib, al-Nasir Yusuf found himself deserted by most of his followers. He was eventually captured and compelled to order the surrender of the Ayyubid forces still defending 'Ajlun and Subayba.[51]

Kerak enjoyed quite a different fate. Al-Mughith 'Umar, like many other Middle Eastern rulers, had sent a delegation to the Mongols before they arrived in Syria. William of Rubruck claims to have met this envoy from Kerak at Karakorum in 1254. William was a Franciscan friar and papal envoy, who had accompanied the Seventh Crusade to the eastern Mediterranean and from there set out for the Mongol court. The envoy was reportedly a Damascene Christian, who offered al-Mughith 'Umar's support to Mongke.[52] This was a prudent gesture, as it placed al-Mughith 'Umar in the Mongols' good graces should they reach Syria, and there were few drawbacks if their expansion was halted at some point to the east.

As the Mongol army advanced westward, Kamal al-Din ibn al-Tiflisi had been sent to Kerak to receive al-Mughith 'Umar's submission. The ruler of Kerak responded by sending his young son, al-'Aziz 'Uthman, and a number of senior emirs back to Hulagu, whom they met at Tabriz, in Azerbaijan. Hulagu duly acknowledged the local authority of al-Mughith 'Umar and recognized his claim to Hebron, which forces from Kerak had captured years earlier from al-Nasir Yusuf. Al-'Aziz and the delegation from Kerak were then sent back with a Mongol representative (*shahna*), who would presumably oversee affairs in Transjordan on behalf of Hulagu. This party had made it as far as Damascus when news arrived of the Mongol defeat at 'Ayn Jalut, about 140km to the southwest. Panic quickly spread through the city, leading al-'Aziz and those with him to barricade themselves in the house where they were staying, resisting efforts by certain Mongol figures to take the young prince with them as they fled.[53] In the meantime, thanks to his diplomatic prudence, al-Mughith 'Umar had not only retained control of Kerak, but his lands had been largely immune from Mongol raiding activities.

It was a Mamluk army that defeated the Mongols on 3 April 1260 at 'Ayn Jalut, in the Jezreel Valley, about 30km south of the Horns of Hattin. In November 1259, with the Mongols poised to invade Syria, Qutuz had overthrown the 17-year-old son of Aybak, in whose name he had been ruling Egypt. Joined by Baybars and other leading Mamluk figures, Qutuz led the army of Egypt into Palestine the following summer. They made camp outside Acre, with the blessing of the Franks, before pushing onwards and defeating the Mongol force Hulagu had left in Syria. Pressing their advantage, the Mamluks extended their authority northward, filling the vacuum of power as the Mongols withdrew. Kitbuqa had been among those slain at 'Ayn Jalut, while Hulagu, unable to launch any serious counterattack at the time, could do little but execute the Ayyubid prisoners he had with him, including al-Nasir Yusuf.[54]

The defeat of the Mongols gifted Syria to the Mamluks, though Qutuz was killed by a group of Mamluk emirs less than two months after his great victory. Baybars had been a leading figure in the murder of al-Mu'azzam Turanshah back in 1250, and it was he who apparently took the leading role in the death of Qutuz. As the next Mamluk sultan, Baybars solidified and extended Mamluk authority.

Chapter 4

Mamluk Period

Al-Karak is a celebrated town with a very high castle, one of the most unassailable of the castles of Syria. About a day's march from it is Mu'ta, where are the tombs of Ja'far at Tayyar and his companions. Below al-Karak is a valley, in which is a *hammam*, and many gardens with excellent fruits, such as apricots, pears, pomegranates, and others. Al-Karak lies on the borders of Syria, coming from the Hijaz. Between al-Karak and Shawbak is about three days' march.[1]

Abu'l-Fida' (d. 1331)

K erak remained the last vestige of independent Ayyubid rule in Syria until 1263.[2] In 1261, as the Mamluks were still consolidating their hold over much of Syria, Baybars dispatched Badr al-Din al-Aydamuri to acquire Montreal. The castle was taken with little apparent resistance and Sayf al-Din Balaban al-Mukhtassi was installed as governor. Kerak, which was attacked by another Mamluk force under Jamal al-Din al-Muhammadi, proved a greater obstacle. Although isolated, with no independent party in Damascus to play against the Mamluks of Egypt, al-Mughith 'Umar enjoyed the support of Kurdish Shahrazuriyya troops, who had been displaced from their homeland in Iraq by the Mongols. In the years following their arrival in Syria, from around the end of 1257, the Shahrazuriyya's loyalties had shifted between al-Nasir Yusuf, al-Mughith 'Umar and the Mamluk sultans of Egypt.[3]

In the spring of 1263, Baybars moved into Palestine from Egypt, and al-Mughith 'Umar was persuaded to join him at Baysan, in northeastern Palestine. Although promised safe conduct, the Ayyubid ruler was arrested upon his arrival. To justify this breach of protocol, a number of letters that had been exchanged between al-Mughith 'Umar and the Mongols were produced. In these, the emir of Kerak encouraged the Mongols to conquer the Levant, while Hulagu's response recognized al-Mughith 'Umar's authority over a large part of southern Syria and made a promise of men to assist with an invasion of Egypt. Whether or not things played out this dramatically is debatable, but Amitai has persuasively argued that there is no reason to doubt that al-Mughith 'Umar maintained a correspondence with the Mongols in the years leading up to 1260. For Baybars, these letters served to legitimize the deception of his former patron. Following his apprehension, al-Mughith 'Umar was sent to Cairo, where he would later die.[4]

Baybars

From Palestine, Baybars set out for Transjordan. Accompanied by his army, as well as a number of builders and masons, the sultan reached Kerak on 4 May 1263. Although Baybars appears to have been prepared to besiege Kerak – as the army approached, ladders were brought from various places in the Balqa' – this proved unnecessary. Al-Mughith 'Umar's sons appreciated their situation and came down from the castle to surrender that evening. In exchange for their quick show of submission, they and those with them were pardoned equally promptly. Mamluk forces then occupied the stronghold, while Baybars himself made his way up to the castle the next morning.

Sitting in the hall built by al-Nasir Dawud, the sultan organized affairs. The governing administration of Kerak was left largely in place, after local officials and the leading townspeople swore an oath of allegiance – this included a number of Christians, who were made to swear their oaths on a Bible. The castle was then provisioned with supplies and 'Izz al-Din Aydamur, *ustadh al-dar* (master of the palace), was made *na'ib*, with authority also over Montreal and the broader region. Leaders of the local Bedouin, the Banu Mahdi and Banu 'Uqba, were also summoned and charged with maintaining the loyalty of the region's nomadic groups, as well as security more generally in the desert corridor down to the Hijaz. Baybars then made a tour of the town and castle, ordering certain improvements. About six days after his arrival, he left Kerak, the newest part of the Mamluk realm.[5]

It is quite probable that it was during these initial improvements, as has been suggested by 'Amr, that al-Mughith 'Umar's name was removed from certain dedicatory inscriptions.[6] The town defences of Kerak were certainly improved during Baybars' reign, as Burj al-Zahir, the great northwestern tower named after Baybars, and rounded Burj Banawy display inscriptions to him. Epigraphic evidence at Montreal confirms it too was developed under Baybars' rule.[7]

Although Kerak would never rival Damascus in regional importance, it was a significant, if secondary, part of the Mamluk realm. When Baybars sent a force into Arabia against Khaybar in 1264, the governor of Kerak was ordered to support this expedition by sending Arab emirs and some of the Bahri soldiers stationed with him. From the governor's correspondence, it seems this administrative region was similar to the late Frankish lordship of Transjordan – Kerak was the centre of power with secondary seats at Montreal and Hebron. The castle also continued to function as a treasury and arsenal, roles it had come to take on during the Ayyubid period. When Caesarea was captured from the Franks in 1265, the siege engines that had been employed in the taking of the citadel were sent to Kerak, 'Ajlun and similar arms depots. The captive defenders of Caesarea were also sent to Kerak, from where they most likely travelled onwards to Cairo.[8]

Mamluk rule was more centralized than the system of Frankish lordships and more unified than the collection of Ayyubid principalities. Baybars' authority was more akin to that of Saladin, stretching across the Mamluk realm. Although some regional deputies would try to assert their autonomy, all were technically, and most were in effect, subject to the sultan's will. This allowed Baybars the power to intervene in local affairs and divert funds as he saw fit, as he did in 1269, when he ordered the treasury of Kerak to finance a large annual shipment of grain (valued at more than 200,000 dirhams) to Medina.[9] Likewise, he had the authority to appoint and remove the local official (na'ib) as he saw fit.

Initial Mamluk *nuwwab* of Kerak	
1263 – 1271	'Izz al-Din Aydamur al-Zahiri
1271 – 1279	'Ala' al-Din Aydakin al-Fakhri
1279 – 1283?	'Ala' al-Din Aydughdi al-Harrani al-Zahiri
1286	'Izz al-Din Aybak al-Mawsili al-Mansuri
1286 – 1291	Rukn al-Din Baybars al-Mansuri
1291 – 1310	Jamal al-Din Aqush al-Ashrafi

Baybars made a number of trips to Kerak during his reign. In 1266, on his way there from Damascus, he fell from his horse. Three years later, the sultan embarked from the castle on a secret pilgrimage. Having sent provisions ahead to Kerak, Baybars set out for Transjordan under the pretence of a hunting trip, reaching the castle on 2 July 1269. He departed five days later, making for Montreal and Arabia beyond. On his return, Baybars left Mecca on 13 August, reaching Kerak seventeen days later. He stayed only one night before setting out for Damascus after the Friday prayer on 31 August, the first day of the Islamic New Year. Worried about potential unrest in Syria, Baybars made a secret journey from Cairo to Kerak in September 1271, reaching the castle on 13 September, ten days after his departure. Following his arrival, the sultan transferred governorship of Kerak to 'Ala' al-Din Aydakin al-Fakhri, who also assumed the position with the rank of *ustadh al-dar*, while 'Izz al-Din Aydamur was promoted to governor of Syria. This was the first leg of a journey that would take the sultan to northern Syria in October. Baybars visited Transjordan again in the late summer of 1274, staying almost two weeks at Kerak before returning to Cairo. In late May 1276, the sultan set out on another secret journey from Cairo to Kerak, this time to counter a plot, having been informed that a party was intent on overthrowing his representatives there.[10] This was Baybars' last visit to the castle before his death in July 1277.

Qalawun

Baybars was initially succeeded by his son, Baraka, who took the name al-Sa'id. In the summer of 1279, the new sultan was deposed and replaced by his younger brother, Salamish, known as al-'Adil, a puppet of the man who was really in charge, al-Mansur Qalawun al-Salihi. Like Baybars, Qalawun had been a mamluk of al-Salih Ayyub and one of the many figures who influenced the course of early Mamluk history. Qalawun served as regent for only a few months before he usurped the young ruler in late 1279, taking power in his own name. Kerak was to serve as the place of royal exile for the deposed sons of Baybars. For good measure, Qalawun also ordered the imprisonment of the sons of al-Nasir Dawud, former ruler of Kerak, the following February. Meanwhile, 'Izz al-Din Aydamur, whom Baybars had installed in Kerak and then Syria, fell from power and was imprisoned amidst this transfer of power in 1279. He was replaced by Shams al-Din Sunqur al-Ashqar, who would quickly prove resistant to Qalawun's authority and display ambitions to become sultan himself.[11]

The dispossessed sons of Baybars attracted others who had lost out with Qalawun's rise to power. These figures, including many of Baybars' Zahiri mamluks, flocked to Kerak, where they benefitted from the treasure that had been stored there over the years. Al-Sa'id was able to quickly extend his influence southward to Montreal. To the north, Qalawun's interests were secured by Jamal al-Din Aqush al-Ashrafi, who was appointed to administer Salt and the Balqa' in January 1280. In mid-February, Qalawun sent a force from Egypt to restore his authority in southern Transjordan. Led by Badr al-Din Bilik al-Aydamuri, this detachment successfully compelled the surrender of Montreal a month later.[12]

A further blow was dealt to the opposition in Kerak with the death of al-Sa'id in mid-March 1280, following a tournament accident. The leadership role fell to another of Baybars' sons, Najm al-Din Khidr, who took the name al-Mas'ud. An ally was also found in Shams al-Din Sunqur al-Ashqar, who was based in Damascus. When Qalawun learned of the coordination between these two parties, he sent another force to Syria under 'Izz al-Din Aybak al-Afram. This army, which set out around the start of May, is said to have 'frightened' those in Kerak along its way. 'Izz al-Din Aybak had insufficient forces to attack Shams al-Din Sunqur, so he fell back on Gaza, where he was joined by Badr al-Din al-Aydamuri on his return from capturing Montreal. Together, the two emirs defeated a force sent against them by Shams al-Din Sunqur. 'Alam al-Din al-Halabi and Badr al-Din al-Fakhri, who had formerly governed Kerak before it was given to al-Sa'id, were subsequently sent from Egypt to reinforce Qalawun's army in Syria. Collectively, this group of emirs went on the offensive and ultimately reclaimed Damascus for Qalawun. Shams al-Din Sunqur, having been pushed out of Damascus, established himself to the north at the castle of Sahyun (Frankish Saone) in the Syrian Coastal Mountains, where he remained a rallying point for opposition to Qalawun.[13]

Having lost the support of Shams al-Din Sunqur, al-Mas'ud opened negotiations with Qalawun. The Mamluk prince hoped to secure for himself a sizable administrative region, like that once ruled by al-Nasir Dawud. The situation, however, was quite different than that of the late Ayyubid era. Al-Nasir Dawud had been able to carve out a semi-autonomous principality in Transjordan thanks to the rivalry between the rulers of Cairo and Damascus; without the presence of a figure in Damascus who might oppose the power of the sultan in Egypt, al-Mas'ud had little leverage. In exchange for ending his opposition and submitting to Qalawun, al-Mas'ud was allowed to retain possession of Kerak, and close members of his family were permitted to join him there, though his authority was confined to the Kerak plateau. This established a state of peace in the summer of 1281.[14]

Peaceful relations between Qalawun and the descendants of Baybars at Kerak lasted two years. In the summer of 1283, Qalawun sent an army to Syria with Badr al-Din Baktash al-Fakhri. This force camped outside Kerak for some time, but proved unable to compel the Zahiri to return to obedience, even after the army began living off the surrounding region.[15] The breach between Kerak and Cairo continued for another three years.

In late February 1286, Qalawun dispatched Husam al-Din Turuntay to Transjordan at the head of an army. A blockade was imposed against Kerak and siege engines, brought from the strongholds of Syria, were set up against it. In the face of this new threat, the sons of Baybars, al-Mas'ud Najm al-Din Khidr and al-'Adil Badr al-Din Salamish, quickly agreed to terms, some of their supporters having already deserted them. Qalawun sent none other than the emir and historian Baybars al-Mansuri to deliver a letter of safe conduct to the brothers, who had requested this as a term of their surrender. Following the castle's capitulation around the start of April, Husam al-Din Turuntay, carrying out the Sultan's wishes, appointed 'Izz al-Din Aybak al-Mawsili al-Mansuri to rule Kerak; he had previously been governor of Montreal and had joined Husam al-Din's force as it marched on Kerak. Command of the castle was bestowed on Badr al-Din Baktut al-'Ala'i, and 'Izz al-Din Aybak al-Najmi was selected to govern the town. Kerak, meanwhile, was provisioned with men and supplies, and once more became a treasury and armoury of the ruler of Cairo. The sons of Baybars were escorted to Egypt, where they were initially treated well. When rumours began to circulate of a Zahiri plot, the brothers were arrested. They would remain prisoners until 1291, when Qalawun's son and successor, al-Ashraf Khalil, sent them and their mother to Constantinople, where they became guests of the Byzantines. Al-'Adil Salamish died abroad; his brother, al-Mas'ud, survived to return to Cairo, where he died in 1308–9.[16]

At the end of August 1286, a few months after Husam al-Din Turuntay and his party had returned to Cairo, Qalawun set out for Syria with the army of Egypt. He stayed a while at Gaza before crossing southern Palestine, leaving the bulk of the army behind. The sultan reached Kerak around the start of October and quickly set about inspecting the castle and seeing to its needs. He ensured there were sufficient supplies and reissued the *iqta'at* of the local Bedouin emirs. He also commissioned certain repairs, including the cleaning out of a pool, which was near the still unidentified 'victory gate'. Qalawun then returned to Gaza, or perhaps instead the hunting grounds further north around Arsuf. Once reliable reports arrived that the Mongols were not in a position to invade northern Syria, he released most of his army, then set out for Cairo, where he arrived in December.[17]

It was during this visit to Kerak in 1286 that Qalawun installed Baybars al-Mansuri as *na'ib*, replacing 'Izz al-Din Aybak al-Mawsili al-Mansuri, who was shifted first to Gaza and then to Safed. Baybars al-Mansuri provides the text of his investment, the final clause of which covers the benefits he was granted:

> The noble good opinion has necessitated that the high, masterly, sultanic, kingly, Mansuri, Sayfi, may God increase it in greatness, effectiveness and execution, order go forth to be applied to his *iqta'* fief, in accordance with the *iqta*'s that have been drawn up for him in the Syrian districts, for his private retinue, and for those with him, those reliable known troops he would employ in service, in perfect submission, and complete provision, after his relinquishing what was in his possession in the Egyptian homelands, and the number of his retinue, and 80 horsemen (*tawashi*) coming from the property and endowment of the emir 'Alam al-Din Sanjar *al-dawadar* al-Salihi as usual in al-Darbsittiyya. This is for the field produce for the year 685 [1286].[18]

Baybars al-Mansuri reports that Kerak had suffered over the past few years due to the recurring siege activities. The lands had been devastated, some fields were left fallow, and the attitudes of locals had been affected. Perhaps unsurprisingly, he notes that prosperity returned to the region from the point he arrived, though he asserts that repeated rains were in no small part responsible for this, allowing him to give credit to God.[19]

Compared to the early 1280s, things were quiet in the region of Kerak in the half-decade following 1286. The castle continued to serve as a prison for high-ranking officials, but not much more is reported during this period.[20] This would hardly have disappointed Baybars al-Mansuri, who continued to serve as Qalawun's deputy in the region for the remainder of the sultan's lifetime. The emir still held this post close to five years later when he joined the assembling army of Qalawun's son and successor, al-Ashraf Khalil, ahead of the great siege of Frankish Acre in 1291.

Following the Mamluks' capture of Acre, which saw the Franks abandon what few footholds they had retained along the Palestinian coast, Baybars al-Mansuri claims al-Ashraf Khalil ordered him to return to Kerak. The emir, however, asked to instead join the sultan's service and accompany him to Egypt. Regardless of whether this was a genuine request or instead the historian's way of glossing over the sultan's decision to replace him with one of his own men, Kerak was entrusted to Jamal al-Din Aqush al-Ashrafi, a mamluk of the new sultan and one of his leading emirs. Baybars al-Mansuri speaks highly of his replacement, whom he notes was purchased for al-Ashraf by his father, Qalawun.[21]

Jamal al-Din Aqush appears to have administered Transjordan for almost two decades. Baybars al-Mansuri notes that Aqush was granted a further seven villages when al-Ashraf Khalil passed through the region in 1293. The emir was still based at Kerak in 1309, where he welcomed al-Nasir Muhammad when the sultan began his second exile. This marked the end of Aqush's tenure in Kerak. Following his dismissal by al-Nasir, Aqush briefly held the governorship of Damascus from 1311 until his arrest the following year. The emir's downfall was orchestrated once more by al-Nasir, who arranged for power in Damascus to pass to one of his own mamluks, Sayf al-Din Tankiz.[22]

Al-Ashraf and His Successors

During Jamal al-Din Aqush's time as *na'ib* of Kerak, an earthquake shook the region. The tremors were felt across southern Syria in early 1293, bringing down minarets in Ramla and Gaza. It was apparently particularly intense in the region of Kerak, and three of the castle's towers are said to have been destroyed.

'Ala al-Din Aydughdi al-Shuja'i and a team of builders were dispatched from Damascus to repair the damage at Kerak and undertake necessary rebuilding work.[23]

Also in the first half of 1293, al-Ashraf Khalil prepared his army to move into Syria. Ahead of this, al-Muzaffar Mahmud of Hama and his uncle, al-Afdal 'Ali, the cousin and father of the historian Abu'-Fida' respectively, were summoned to Cairo, reportedly taking post horses and completing the journey, via Kerak, in only eight days. As the Egyptian army then followed the main road towards Damascus, the sultan, accompanied by the emir of Hama, proceeded by fast camels to Kerak. There he met Aqush, inspected the castle and settled affairs in the region. Al-Ashraf then continued to Damascus, where he arrived in mid-May, three days ahead of his army.[24]

Having devoted consideration to Kerak, it is interesting that al-Ashraf Khalil subsequently ordered 'Izz al-Din Aybak al-Afram to slight Montreal. The emir objected, but bent to the sultan's wishes. Ibn al-Furat sided with the position of 'Izz al-Din Aybak: 'Castles and fortresses are the refuges of Islam, the treasures of the Muslims, and it is in them that they take refuge during difficult times, sieges, and when enemies appear, so this was an unbelievable matter.'[25] When considering the sultan's apparent suspicion of Baybars' sons, and his father's troubles wresting the castles of Transjordan from them, he may have judged Montreal to be more of a risk than an asset should it fall to an enemy. Kerak, by contrast, was much more than just a military outpost; it was a significant regional administrative centre.

Al-Ashraf Khalil was murdered in December 1293 and two decades of instability followed. Leading Mamluk emirs struggled for power, often using young princes as pawns or puppets. Al-Ashraf was initially succeeded by his 8-year-old brother, al-Nasir Muhammad. The young sultan was pushed aside in 1294 by Zayn al-Din Kitbugha al-Mansuri, one of Qalawun's powerful mamluks, until he was ousted in turn by Husam al-Din Lajin, who was himself killed in January 1299. This allowed for the return of al-Nasir Muhammad, the son of Qalawun who had initially succeeded his older brother, al-Ashraf Khalil. Following his fall from power, al-Nasir Muhammad had been sent to Kerak, and it was from there that he was recalled. Al-Nasir's second reign lasted ten years and was dominated by the emirs Rukn al-Din Baybars al-Jashnakir and Sayf al-Din Salar. In March 1309, on the pretext of making a pilgrimage, the sultan left Cairo and returned to Kerak, effectively abdicating. This led Baybars (II) al-Jashnakir to assume the role of sultan, taking the name al-Muzaffar.[26]

In late 1299, during al-Nasir Muhammad's second reign and his temporary absence from Kerak, the Mamluks faced another significant Mongol invasion.

Avenging the previous generation's defeat at 'Ayn Jalut, the Mongols overcame a Mamluk army at the Battle of Wadi al-Khazindar, or Third Battle of Homs, on 23 December 1299. Mongol forces then raided southward; facilitated by the pasturage provided by the winter rains, some pushed as far south as Gaza. Although some Mongol detachments may have reached the lands of Kerak, most raiding took place west of the Jordan and the Dead Sea.[27] Unlike the Mongol campaign into Syria in 1260, there appears to have been no serious attempt to hold territory on this occasion. The Mongols regrouped at Damascus in March 1300, from where they made for the Euphrates, before the gathering Mamluk army had even left Egypt. As the invaders withdrew from Syria, Mamluk authority was reintroduced behind them.[28]

Al-Nasir Muhammad's second period of exile would not be as long as the first. In January 1310, he set out from Kerak for Damascus, accompanied by some of Qalawun's emirs and a large group of Syrian Bedouin, with whom he forged a close bond during his time at Kerak. Having rallied further support he moved on to Cairo, which he occupied, becoming sultan for a third time. The deaths of Baybars II and Sayf al-Din Salar followed shortly thereafter. This ushered in a period of stability that lasted until al-Nasir Muhammad's death in 1341, following which instability returned.[29]

According to the contemporary emir Abu'-Fida', when facing the advance of al-Nasir, Baybars II had offered to abdicate peacefully if he were granted Kerak, Hama or Sahyun, along with 300 mamluks. Al-Nasir Muhammad promised him Sahyun, a defensible site but the least important politically, and 100 mamluks; however, the former sultan was apprehended outside Darum while attempting to flee Egypt for northern Syria. Sayf al-Din Salar, meanwhile, was initially granted Montreal, before he too was arrested a few months later. In the shuffling of administrative positions that continued over the following year, Jamal al-Din Aqush al-Ashrafi, who had governed Kerak since 1291, was invested with Damascus. Aqush was arrested in 1312, though he was apparently held in comfortable confinement until he was released in 1315. Although his rank is said to have been elevated at this point, Aqush does not seem to have held a significant position thereafter. Baybars al-Mansuri, who had held Kerak decades earlier, rose to become *na'ib* of Egypt, but his time in this office was similarly brief. Amidst the reordering, Asandamur al-Kurji, who held Hama for a period before it passed to the emir and historian Abu'l-Fida' in 1310, found himself a prisoner of Kerak from 1311.[30]

Al-Nasir Muhammad would visit Kerak a number of times over the following years. He passed through in late April 1313 while completing a pilgrimage from Damascus, and he stopped again for a few days on his return in mid-May. Four years later, he made a trip to Hisban, in the Balqa', where he met a number of Syrian emirs. This would have taken him via Kerak, where, according to Abu'l-Fida', he released Sayf al-Din Bahadur, who had been arrested in 1315. In early 1320, al-Nasir made a trip from Cairo to Kerak, where he made a withdrawal from his treasury, before returning to Egypt.[31] The castle's role as a prison, treasury and seat of regional administrative power continued.

Development under the Qalawunids

Kerak enjoyed the patronage of both Baybars and Qalawun, but it was under al-Nasir Muhammad that the castle came to hold its greatest degree of importance during the Mamluk period. It was here, during his lengthy first exile, that al-Nasir gained the base of support that would later return him to power in 1310. Leading up to this, he almost certainly patronized and developed the institutions, structures and services in Kerak. He may also have seen to any necessary repairs following an earthquake that shook Egypt and southern Syria in 1303, just a decade after the previous one.[32] Al-Nasir continued to invest in Kerak following his return to power in 1310, as it was at this time that a number of new buildings were commissioned. These included a mosque, *maristan* (hospital), *madrasa* (religious school), *sabil* (public fountain), *khan* (caravan hostel), and *qasr* (palace). All but perhaps the last of these would have been constructed in the town, rather than the castle, though remains of none of these town buildings have been identified.[33] It is to this initiative, said to have been undertaken in 1311, that Brown dates the so-called *qa'a al-nahas* (hall of copper). This was the palace where al-Nasir Muhammad stayed when visiting the castle, and it was where a later sultan, al-Zahir Barquq, would be imprisoned.[34]

Beyond these reports of building efforts in the town, and the probable construction of a palace in the castle, contemporaries offer few additional insights into the development of Kerak around this time. Ibn Battuta, the renowned traveller, composed a short description after passing by Kerak in September 1326 on his way to the Hijaz. He emphasized the castle's impregnability and its strong topographical position, noting also its recent function as a refuge for sultans, referring to the exile of al-Nasir Muhammad. Al-Dimashqi confirms that the castle continued to serve as a Mamluk treasury, but his description provides little that cannot be found in earlier accounts.[35]

With the shift from Frankish to Muslim rule, Montreal continued to occupy a secondary position in the administrative region dominated by Kerak. Despite this, more epigraphic evidence has survived relating to building efforts at Montreal. In the nineteenth century, Sauvaire recorded an inscription on a marble plaque over the door of a shrine outside the castle. Construction of this monument was attributed to an emir named Sharif al-Din 'Isa ibn al-Khalil ibn Muqatil in the year 646AH (1248–49), during the reign of al-Salih Najm al-Din Ayyub. Certain improvements to the castle were subsequently commissioned by Baybars, following his acquisition of the stronghold in 1261. The most dramatic refortification efforts, since the castle was lost by the Franks, were carried out in the late 1290s, during the reign of Husam al-Din Lajin, which saw the addition of Montreal's four conspicuously large towers. These works were overseen by the emir 'Ala' al-Din Qubrus al-Mansuri.[36] Lajin's building campaign was probably necessary following al-Ashraf Khalil's decision to slight the castle in 1293. Although there is more epigraphic evidence surviving at Montreal, at least as much attention was probably devoted to Kerak, which remained the more important centre of political power in the region.

Mamluk Administration

The Mamluk administration of Syria was divided into provinces, each run by a figure known as a *na'ib* (short for *na'ib al-saltana*, 'vice-sultan', pl. *nuwwab*), the deputy of the sultan in Cairo. The principal regional power centres were Damascus, Aleppo, Tripoli, Hama, Safed, Gaza, and Kerak. As power and regional dynamics shifted, some lesser centres fell under the authority of their larger neighbours, while others gained importance and rose to join their ranks. The borders of these provinces shifted over time, as did internal regional divisions. For example, the Balqa', north of the Kerak plateau, was at times administered from Kerak and at others from Damascus.[37]

Each *na'ib* was held by an emir, with more prominent figures often receiving the most important and prestigious posts. An emir of the first degree was theoretically responsible for supporting a force of 100 private mamluks; an emir of the second degree, forty; and an emir of the third degree, ten. Each emir was granted an *iqta'* – essentially, the tax revenues of a given region – the value of which was proportionate to the size of the force he was expected to maintain. The numbers of emirs of each class and their incomes varied over time, though the value of the most lucrative Egyptian *iqta'at* was consistently greater than those *iqta'at* held by the most prominent emirs based in Syria. Each *na'ib* was supported by a number of emirs and mamluks, as well as many figures who might be labelled bureaucrats. Below the *na'ib*, the provincial administration typically included the chamberlain (*hajib*), who was second in command, the commander of the army (*atabak*), and the commander of the citadel (*na'ib al-qal'a*), all of whom were emirs.[38]

The Bedouin continued to exercise considerable influence in Transjordan. During the early Mamluk period, Kerak and Montreal served as places of interaction between the agents of Mamluk authority and these nomadic groups, who provided a vital source of livestock to both the ruling regime in Cairo and local sedentary populations. Bedouin support could be as overt as the assistance that was offered to al-Nasir Muhammad, or as subtle as allowing the annual *hajj* to pass unmolested. Milwright has argued that a critical motive behind Baybars' regular visits to Transjordan in the 1260s and 1270s was a desire to develop relations with the Bedouin; his ties to local tribes stretched back to his exodus from Egypt in 1254. Baybars provided *iqta'at* to the Banu 'Uqba and Banu Mahdi, incorporating them into the defensive administration of the region around Kerak and Montreal. Despite these efforts, complete internal security was never achieved, as references to attacks against caravans continue to appear in the sources.[39]

The Beginning of the Decline

Following the third reign of al-Nasir Muhammad, Transjordan entered a period of decline. Ironically, this was due in part to Mamluk military successes. The final defeat of the Franks and repeated repulsions of the Mongols, with whom relations improved in the 1320s, saw the region's strategic significance decrease. Greater security in Palestine drew traffic away from the interior corridor through Transjordan, which was a harsher route between Cairo and Damascus and one still vulnerable to Bedouin harassment. Accordingly, as trade between Egypt and those areas under Mongol rule increased, most commerce flowed through Palestine.

Al-Nasir Muhammad died in 1341 and four decades of power struggles ensued. The eldest son of al-Nasir Muhammad, Ahmad, who was in his early

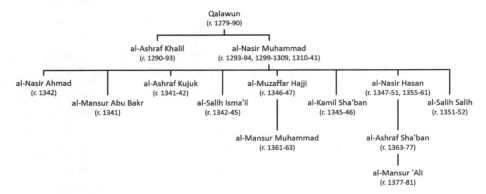

Fig. 3. Qalawunid sultans.

or mid-twenties when his father died, was initially overlooked in favour of his younger brother, al-Mansur Abu Bakr. After only two months, Abu Bakr was dethroned by Sayf al-Din Qawsun, al-Nasir Muhammad's most powerful emir and son-in-law. Qawsun appointed another of al-Nasir Muhammad's young sons as sultan, and Abu Bakr's death in Upper Egypt followed not long after. Meanwhile, Ahmad took up residence it Kerak, where he had spent portions of his young childhood and where his father had taken refuge during his periods of exile. Like his father, Ahmad also built support among the locals of Kerak and the Bedouin of the region, allowing him to resist Qawsun's attempts to dislodge him.

In October 1341, Qawsun sent an army against Kerak. This force, however, chose to instead support Ahmad, joining a number of Syrian emirs in revolt against Qawsun. In Egypt, Qawsun was forced out of Cairo and Ahmad was proclaimed sultan, taking the title of al-Nasir. Al-Nasir Ahmad appears to have been distrusting of leading figures, and was quickly at odds with many of them. The two men who had been most responsible for his rise to power were Tashtimur al-Badri (nicknamed *Hummus Ahdar*, Green Chickpeas) and Qutlubuga al-Fahri. They were duly appointed to administer Egypt and Syria respectively, but were quickly arrested and sent to Kerak, where they were apparently executed.

After only about a month in Cairo, al-Nasir Ahmad left for Kerak. Taking with him his father's treasure, huge numbers of livestock and the royal insignia, he planned to transfer the Mamluk capital to Kerak. This move was far from popular in Cairo and it was only a matter of months until, in June 1342, Ahmad was declared deposed and another of his brothers, al-Salih Isma'il, was proclaimed sultan in his place. Thanks to the strength of the castle and the support that he enjoyed from the locals, Ahmad continued to reside in Kerak for another two years, resisting seven attempts to remove him, until he was finally betrayed and subsequently killed in 1344.[40]

The new regime's initial inability to capture Kerak, and with it Ahmad, was not for lack of effort; instead, it was symptomatic of growing internal issues. Al-Nasir Muhammad had been able to consolidate power, but his emirs prevented his sons from doing the same. In 1345, al-Salih Isma'il died, apparently of natural causes, at the age of 19. His brother, al-Kamil Sha'ban, ruled for a year before he was toppled by a revolt, leading to the accession of a younger brother, al-Muzaffar Hajji, who was overthrown and killed in July 1347, having 'ruled' for less than a year. Next to the throne was al-Nasir Hasan, another minor, who was forced to abdicate after a few years, making way for al-Salih Salih, the eighth son of al-Nasir Muhammad to become sultan. Al-Nasir Hasan would later regain power, but he was killed following an attempt to flee Cairo for Kerak in 1361.[41] During this period, real authority was often wielded by influential emirs, some of whom sought to secure their position by ruling through the sons of al-Nasir Muhammad. For many of these young sultans, the grandsons of Qalawun, Kerak came to represent a place of refuge. This was where their father had been exiled, only to build up a base of support and return to power, and it was where their brother, Ahmad, had been able to resist the authority of the dominant emirs in Cairo for a number of years.

The second downfall of al-Nasir Hasan had been brought about by Yalbugha al-'Umari al-Khassaki, a Circassian and the most powerful Mamluk emir at the time. Yalbugha continued the practice of ruling through young Qalawunids, elevating al-Mansur Muhammad, a son of al-Muzaffar Hajji in 1361, then replacing him two years later with al-Ashraf Sha'ban, the 10-year-old son of al-Nasir Hasan. Al-Ashraf Sha'ban outlived Yalbugha and remained in power until he was killed in 1377, leading to the accession of his infant son, al-Mansur 'Ali. The tradition of powerful emirs pretending to rule through Qalawunid sultans, however, was coming to an end. Following the death of 'Ali, and the brief elevation of another child-ruler, al-Salih Hajji, power changed hands. In 1382, al-Zahir Barquq, the most powerful of the Yalbughawi mamluks, took the title of sultan for himself, marking the transition to the Burji (or Circassian) period of Mamluk history.[42]

Mamluk *nuwwab* of Kerak during the reign of Barquq	
1385 – 1386	Damurdash al-Qushtamuri
1386 – 1387	Altunbugha al-Jubani al-Yalbughawi
1387 – 1389	Ma'mur al-Qalamtawi al-Yalbughawi
1389 – 1390	Husam al-Din Hasan al-Kujkuni
1390 – ?	Qadid al-Qalamtawi al-Yalbughawi
? – 1394	Shihab al-Din Ahmad ibn al-Shaykh 'Ali
1394 – 1398	Batkhash al-Suduni
1398 – 1400	Sudun al-Zarif al-Zahiri al-Shamsi

This change of ruling regimes was far from seamless. Barquq faced simmering tensions until finally a number of emirs revolted in 1389. The opposition was led by Yalbugha al-Nasiri, the *na'ib* of Aleppo, who found an ally in Tamurbugha al-Afdali al-Ashrafi. The latter, better known as Mintash, was *na'ib* of Malatya and had already broken away from the sultan with the support of many Ashrafi mamluks. By early March, Barquq had reportedly lost control of all the power centres of Syria, save Damascus, Baalbek and Kerak. The Egyptian army sent to Syria by the sultan arrested the *na'ib* of Gaza, Aqbugha al-Safawi, who was sent to Kerak, and Gaza was placed under Husam al-Din ibn Bakish. Barquq's army was defeated shortly thereafter, leading Damascus to fall to Yalbugha al-Nasiri. This also persuaded Husam al-Din ibn Bakish, as well as Ma'mur al-Qalamtawi, *na'ib* of Kerak, to abandon the sultan's cause and join the revolt. Barquq's loss of Gaza and Kerak, which dominated the two corridors between Egypt and Syria, was a serious blow. Possession of Kerak, meanwhile, strengthened the position of the opposition party, as it continued to serve as an armoury, in addition to accommodating a number of political prisoners. The Syrian emirs invaded Egypt in May and Barquq's remaining support quickly evaporated. Cairo was taken before the end of the month and Barquq was apprehended. Yalbugha al-Nasiri declined to become sultan himself; instead, the young sultan whom Barquq had usurped, al-Salih Hajji, was briefly returned to power.[43]

In June 1389, Yalbugha al-Nasiri installed Husam al-Din Hasan al-Kujkuni as *na'ib* of Kerak, replacing Ma'mur al-Qalamtawi, who was summoned to Cairo. Barquq was then sent to Kerak, where he was reportedly imprisoned in the *qa'a al-nahas* (hall of copper). Meanwhile, in Egypt, Yalbugha al-Nasiri was overthrown by Mintash, leading to disorder in Cairo and a breakdown of authority across Syria. This pushed Husam al-Din al-Kujkuni to release Barquq and offer the former sultan his support. Barquq also received the backing of the Banu 'Uqba and the people of Kerak, while an increasing number of Syrian emirs also lent their support to his cause. The armies of Mintash and Barquq clashed near Damascus in early January 1390. Although the engagement was fairly indecisive, Barquq was able to capture al-Salih Hajji, who duly abdicated in favour of his captor. Prior to this, during the confusion of the battle, when it had looked like Barquq was losing, Husam al-Din al-Kujkuni was among a number of Syrian emirs who had fled the field. This led Barquq to appoint Qadid al-Qalamtawi as *na'ib* of Kerak before making his return to Cairo.[44]

Once restored, Barquq was initially quite forgiving of many who had taken part in his downfall, as a good number of these emirs were obvious allies against Mintash, who remained a threat in Syria. Two of Kerak's qadis, the brothers 'Ala' al-Din al-Karaki and 'Imad al-Din Ahmad, were also promoted in recognition of the kindness they had shown the sultan during his period of exile; the former was promoted to the position of confidential secretary of Egypt (*katib al-sirr*) and the latter was named chief qadi of Egypt. Over the following years, Barquq manoeuvred to place his own men in positions of power. By the end of 1394, according to Ibn Taghribirdi, every *na'ib* in Syria was one of his mamluks, while the last of the influential Yalbughawi emirs died a prisoner in Alexandria in 1399.[45]

In the background, Kerak remained a step from which ambitious emirs might reach the highest positions of authority. During his first reign, Barquq appointed Altunbugha al-Jubani, a Yalbughawi, *na'ib* of Kerak in January

1386. The man he replaced was Damurdash al-Qushtamuri, who appears to have returned to Egypt, where Mintash later gave him some of the responsibilities of acting interim *na'ib* of the citadel of Cairo in December 1389. Altunbugha al-Jubani, already an emir of some importance before his arrival at Kerak, was promoted to the role of *na'ib* of Damascus little more than a year later. Symptomatic of the tumultuous political environment, Al-Jubani's predecessor in Damascus had served as *na'ib* of the city for less than a year, and al-Jubani himself was arrested around the end of October 1388 and sent to Alexandria. Altunbugha al-Jubani was freed the following spring with the ousting of Barquq, and reportedly played an important role in the capture of the sultan, who, despite ordering his arrest only months earlier, looked to the emir as an ally. This trust was not entirely misguided, as al-Jubani was said to have been among those who were against executing the sultan, advocating he be exiled instead. Balancing relationships, it was Altunbugha al-Jubani who escorted Barquq out of Cairo as the deposed sultan began his trip to Kerak in 1389, shortly before the emir was granted a prominent position in Egypt under the new regime.[46]

When Altunbugha al-Jubani went to Damascus in the autumn of 1388, he was apparently replaced in Kerak by Ma'mur al-Qalamtawi, who was *na'ib* by the time the Syrian emirs revolted against Barquq shortly thereafter. Ma'mur al-Qalamtawi was another prominent figure; he had married a daughter of Yalbugha al-Khassaki and had previously served as *na'ib* of Tripoli. He initially remained loyal to Barquq, though the successes of Yalbugha al-Nasiri saw him switch sides in the spring of 1389. Following Barquq's exile, the emir's wife was said to have cared for the deposed sultan during his time at Kerak. In June 1389, with the fall of Barquq, al-Nasiri summoned Ma'mur al-Qalamtawi to Cairo, where he was made an emir of the first degree and appointed grand chamberlain of Egypt. Like Altunbugha al-Jubani, he was one of Yalbugha al-Nasiri's leading supporters during the open fighting that broke out in mid-August 1389 between those emirs loyal to al-Nasiri, primarily the established Yalbughawi mamluks, and the Zahiris and Ashrafis led by Mintash. The victory of the latter led to Ma'mur al-Qalamtawi's capture and imprisonment, a fate shared by Yalbugha al-Nasiri and Altunbugha al-Jubani.[47]

Yalbugha al-Nasiri had chosen Husam al-Din Hasan al-Kujkuni to succeed Ma'mur al-Qalamtawi as *na'ib* of Kerak. Al-Kujkuni set out from Cairo in mid-June 1389, a week before al-Zahir Barquq's departure for Kerak, giving the emir little time to settle in before he received his high profile prisoner. As political stability broke down in Egypt, al-Kujkuni was left in the unenviable position of trying to ensure he ended up backing the man who would come out on top. Mintash was able to gain power in Cairo with the support of

Barquq's Zahiri mamluks, who expected the release of their master should their side prevail. Mintash, however, had no intentions of freeing Barquq and began persecuting the Zahiris as they turned against him. It was during this phase of unrest that Mintash apparently dispatched an assassin to Kerak with instructions that al-Kujkuni was to assist with the murder of Barquq. In light of the opposition Mintash was facing in Cairo, and the support shown by the people of Kerak towards Barquq, al-Kujkuni seems to have waited as long as possible before picking a side, ultimately betting on the rising strength of the deposed sultan. Although he was among those who later fled during the clash between the forces of al-Zahir Barquq and Mintash on 2 January 1390, al-Kujkuni appears to have remained loyal to Barquq in the months that followed.[48]

Having fled what turned out to be an indecisive battle, and a political victory for Barquq, Husam al-Din Hasan al-Kujkuni was replaced as *na'ib* of Kerak by Qadid al-Qalamtawi, an emir of the second degree. Qadid al-Qalamtawi had been among those still loyal to Barquq in February 1389, when he marched out of Egypt against the Syrian emirs who would shortly overthrow the sultan. He then took part in the fighting in Cairo six months later. Little more is said of him until he is found serving as *na'ib* of Alexandria, an office that was stripped of him on 17 March 1397, following which he was made to retire to Jerusalem, where he died in late 1398. His time as *na'ib* of Kerak may have been the pinnacle of his career, though it remains unclear how long he held this post.[49]

Meanwhile, on 2 February 1390, Barquq ordered the release of seventeen senior emirs who had been imprisoned by Mintash, many of whom had played a role in the sultan's deposition the previous year. These included such prominent figures as Yalbugha al-Nasiri and Altunbugha al-Jubani, as well as Ma'mur al-Qalamtawi. A few days later, Barquq appointed al-Jubani commander of the emirs (*atabak al-'asakir*) and second in command of the armies of Egypt a few days later, and in mid-March the emir was named *na'ib* of Damascus for a second time. Less than a week later, on 19 March, Ma'mur al-Qalamtawi was installed as *na'ib* of Hama. Both men were charged with carrying on the sultan's fight with Mintash in Syria. When the armies of Barquq and Mintash subsequently faced each other, Altunbugha al-Jubani, who commanded one of the three divisions of Barquq's army, was killed by conspirators who had infiltrated his forces. The conspirators also captured Ma'mur al-Qalamtawi, who was subsequently executed by being cut in two at the waste. For both men, Kerak had served as a prominent step as they rose to positions of considerable influence.[50]

A year after abandoning al-Zahir Barquq in battle, Husam al-Din Kujkuni, along with Kumushbugha al-Hamawi, who had been *na'ib* of Kerak and Aleppo respectively, arrived in Cairo and presented themselves before the sultan. Both men were received honourably and Kujkuni was given an *iqta'* in Egypt commensurate with his status as an emir of the first degree. Best remembered for his part in setting Barquq free from Kerak, he reportedly remained one of the sultan's leading emirs, though little more is said of him prior to his death in 1398–99.[51]

In November 1394, while pausing at Damascus on his return to Cairo from Aleppo, al-Zahir Barquq appointed Batkhash al-Suduni *na'ib* of Kerak. The man he replaced was Shihab al-Din Ahmad ibn Shaykh 'Ali, who became grand chamberlain of Damascus. At what point Ahmad replaced Qadid al-Qalamtawi is unclear, leaving it possible, if unlikely, that someone may have held the post in between them. Batkhash al-Suduni had previously been *na'ib* of Safed and then grand chamberlain of Egypt. He had also risen to the status of an Egyptian emir of the first degree before he took control of Kerak. These men, like those who had earlier held the position of *na'ib* of Kerak during the reign of al-Zahir Barquq, were among the most prominent figures in the broader Mamluk military-administration. A few years later, in October 1398, another Egyptian emir of the first degree, Aqbugha al-Lakkash, was appointed *na'ib* of Kerak. This, however, appears to have been a ruse, as he was arrested once he reached Gaza. The emir was confined briefly in Subayba before he was restored to favour and named *na'ib* of Gaza the following spring.[52]

By late 1389, Barquq had shuffled his emirs in such a way that every prominent *na'ib* was one of his personal mamluks, with the exception of Ahmad ibn Shaykh 'Ali, whom Ibn Taghribirdi notes was brought up by Barquq. Ahmad was by that time the *na'ib* of Safed, though he would not hold the position much longer. The following April, the sultan ordered his arrest. Ahmad's imprisonment was short and he was appointed commander of Damascene forces at the end of May 1399.[53] The *na'ib* of Kerak was by this time Sudun al-Zahiri al-Shamsi, known as al-Zarif. He had been appointed in November 1389, in the wake of the arrest of Aqbugha al-Lakkash at Gaza. Unlike many of his predecessors, al-Zarif does not appear to have held a prominent office prior to his arrival at Kerak. Only months earlier, in August, he had been appointed to a post of minor head of guards.[54]

Following the death of al-Zahir Barquq in 1399, a period of civil war accompanied the succession of the sultan's teenaged son, al-Nasir Faraj. In the spring of 1400, Batkhash al-Suduni was reportedly appointed to replace al-Zarif as *na'ib* of Kerak, apparently taking up the office for a second time. Like many other emirs, Batkhash al-Suduni had endured a period of imprisonment during the two decades associated with the rule of Barquq – he had been confined in Damascus for less than two months in the spring of 1399. An emir named Jumaq was installed as *na'ib* of Kerak at the end of July 1402, though nothing is known of his actions while he held the post. Batkhash al-Suduni died as a prominent emir of Damascus two years later in 1404.[55]

Conflict continued during the years that followed. Jumaq, no longer *na'ib* of Kerak, was arrested in Syria in the late summer of 1407, and he was executed in Cairo at the end of September. On 31 August 1409, al-Nasir Faraj appointed Sudun al-Jalab *na'ib* of Kerak, only to see him quickly join a group of Syrian emirs in revolt. The Syrian opposition was led by Nauruz al-Hafizi and Shaykh al-Mahmudi, while one of the emirs found leading the sultan's forces against them in December 1410 was Sudun al-Zarif, former *na'ib* of Kerak. Nauruz and Shaykh subsequently invaded Egypt; on their return to Syria, they travelled via Transjordan. Finding themselves shut out of Montreal, the rebels continued northward and established themselves at Kerak, where they paused to consolidate their position. During their stay at Kerak, an attempt was made on the lives of Shaykh al-Mahmudi and a number of other emirs during a visit to the baths. This was reportedly organized by the chamberlain of Kerak, Shihab al-Din Ahmad. It is unclear whether the location for the attempted assassination was the *hammam* noticed by Ibn Wasil, below the castle, or perhaps another bath complex in the town, remains of which were identified in the nineteenth century.[56]

Kerak was subsequently attacked by the sultan and the rebellious emirs were subjected to a siege that lasted about a month, between March and April 1411, until a negotiated compromise was reached. Sudan al-Jalab had left Kerak before the siege, following a falling out with Shaykh and Nauruz, though he returned to join their cause the next year when hostilities with the sultan resumed. He was with the Syrian army that defeated and subsequently deposed al-Nasir Faraj in the spring of 1412. Leading up to this, the sultan launched a wave of persecutions against his father's Zahiri mamluks. Sudun al-Zarif was among a number of prominent emirs to be arrested, leading to his execution on 25 November 1411. Meanwhile, the broader contest for power in the Mamluk realm continued through the following decades.[57]

Material Culture and Life at the Time

Looking beyond political developments and powerful figures, it is harder to see how life might have changed for those living in and around Kerak during the transition from Ayyubid to Mamluk rule. Quite broadly, the thirteenth and fourteenth centuries are viewed as an era of prosperity, which gave way to decline in the fifteenth century. This characterization is based in part on textual references, but even more so on the material evidence.

The population of Kerak, so often relied on by exiled sultans, remained predominantly Christian. In 1301, a number of restrictive ordinances were passed against Christians and Jews living under Mamluk rule. Christians were obliged to wear a blue turban, those of Jews and Samaritans were to be yellow and red respectively, and all were forbidden from riding horses and mules. As often accompanied the periodic introduction of such legislation, a number of churches and synagogues were vandalized and others destroyed. Revealingly, al-Maqrizi recorded that the one area exempt from these laws was Kerak. Because the population was predominantly Christian, Jamal al-Din Aqush al-Ashrafi was able to excuse the region, and the Christians of Kerak and Montreal were not forced to dye their turbans.[58] Beyond such anecdotes as this, little is known of the people of Kerak.

One of the more obvious crises of the fourteenth century was the arrival of the Black Death. It reached Alexandria in the autumn of 1347, from where it spread across Egypt and Syria. Although few senior Mamluk figures seem to have died from the first wave of the epidemic, recurring outbreaks of plague would be reported well into the fifteenth century. The specific effects felt in Kerak are hard to determine.[59]

As the fourteenth century gave way to the fifteenth, one of the functions that the castle retained was its role as a high-status prison.[60] Thanks to the centralization of Mamluk authority, prisoners might be kept in a range of places, including: the citadel of Cairo, close to the centre of power; Alexandria, where many were sent in the late Mamluk period, or alternatively Damietta; or in relative exile in one of the strongholds of Syria, such as Subayba or Marqab (Frankish Margat). Kerak represented a middle ground between the prisons of Egypt and the other castles of Syria; it was far enough to keep the influence of confined figures out of court politics, but close enough to keep well informed of events in and around the castle. It is still unknown how prisoners were treated in Kerak, or where most were kept, but it seems safe to assume that the emirs confined in the castle were kept reasonably comfortable.

Sugar

While disease killed some, others enjoyed the economic rewards that accompanied the expansion of Transjordan's sugar industry. By the early thirteenth century, sugarcane appears to have become the most profitable agricultural product in the Jordan Valley and around the south end of the Dead Sea, just west of Kerak. It is still not entirely clear when sugarcane first came into cultivation in the Levant, having been imported from South Asia, but there are indications that this process may have started in the eleventh century. Pringle's survey of secular buildings identifies two sugar production sites northwest of Kerak, near the mouth of Wadi al-Karak, and a number of others further south in and around Safi, near the entrance to Wadi al-Hasa.[61] Although some of the ceramics at certain sites date back to the twelfth century, it was during the thirteenth and fourteenth centuries that the cultivation and refinement of sugarcane was at its peak, with production declining during the fifteenth century.

Contemporary sources, including the Egyptian historian al-Nuwayri, describe the process of refining sugar at this time. First the sugarcane was harvested, chopped up, and then crushed in a factory before it was squeezed in a press. The juices that were released were then repeatedly boiled and strained, reducing this to a syrup. When most of the water had evaporated, the syrup was poured into ceramic moulds. These moulds were conical, tapering towards the bottom, where one or more small holes allowed excess liquid to drain into jars placed below, while the sugar in the cones crystalized. This left a cake of sugar in the mould and some extra syrup in the jar below, which could be reboiled or sold as it was. The sheer quantity of broken moulds at sites associated with sugar production has led to the belief that moulds were intended for single-use and broken when the cake of crystalized sugar was removed.[62] Although this was a reasonably specialized industry, and remained concentrated to the west of the Kerak plateau, it would have accounted for a significant portion of the agricultural wealth produced in the broader region of Kerak during the Mamluk period.

Sugar production, at least in significant quantities, appears to postdate the period of Frankish rule in Transjordan, though there is evidence that the region's later association with sugar was appreciated in Europe. In the first half of the fourteenth century, Francesco Balducci Pegolotti refers to powdered sugar of *Cracco* or *Cranco di Montreale*, which he claims was inferior to the sugar of Cyprus, Rhodes and Syria (undefined), but better than that of Alexandria.[63] Given the variety of names assigned to Kerak and Montreal, particularly from the thirteenth century onwards, and the more suitable geography for sugar cultivation just west of Kerak, it seems this, rather than Montreal, was the place identified.[64]

Linked with sugar cultivation was the production of copper. A centre of copper mining was Faynan (Byzantine Phaino), to the northwest of Montreal. This had been a centre of copper production prior to the Muslim conquest of the region in the seventh century. While copper extraction continued elsewhere, it seems not to have resumed at Faynan until the Ayyubid period, from which time production continued into the fifteenth century. The conspicuous correlation between the rise and decline of sugar and copper production suggests certain linkages. In the broadest sense, both were export industries reliant on investment and regional trade. More directly, the cauldrons in which sugar was boiled were typically made of copper, leaving it possible that the development of the sugar industry to the north might have created the demand that gave new life to the copper industry in Wadi 'Araba.[65]

Ceramics

Milwright's study of the ceramics collected in and around Kerak supports the idea of a thriving economy during the Ayyubid and Mamluk periods. In the countryside, the number of sites where pottery dated to the thirteenth and fourteenth centuries has been found is indicative of a vibrant village culture and a level of sedentary occupation unseen since the Byzantine period, around eight centuries earlier. Most of the pottery found at these small sites across the Kerak plateau was handmade, rather than wheel-thrown. Although inferior in technical respects, handmade wares could be readily produced locally with limited specialized equipment. Thus the quantity of the ceramics indicates economic prosperity, though the nature of the pottery suggests these villages and rural communities had limited access to the export trade goods of the urban centres of Syria and Egypt.[66]

A minority of sherds dating to the Ayyubid-Mamluk period recovered from the Kerak plateau reveal evidence of glazing. When present in assemblages, these glazed wares are usually found at sites close to the castle and those along the King's Highway. At peripheral sites, where influence from Kerak would have been at its lowest, there is a near complete absence of glazed wares. Brown has suggested a similar pattern probably extended to other non-ceramic goods. Kerak's declining importance in the later Mamluk period can also be seen in the ceramic record; a near complete shift to handmade, non-glazed types of pottery had taken place by the end of the fifteenth century.[67]

Kerak was naturally the economic hub of the surrounding region, and the pottery fragments found in and around the castle, consisting of more than 8,000 sherds, are quite different than most of those found in the countryside. Whereas most ceramics discovered at rural sites are handmade and unglazed, handmade wares account for only a small proportion of the castle assemblages. This has been interpreted as indicative of a 'palace culture'. Unlike the surrounding villages, the castle, and to an extent the adjoining town, was occupied by elites. Whereas the inhabitants of villages and other smaller sites made use of locally produced handmade wares, those in the castle used wheel-thrown vessels, many of which were probably imported. This corresponds with the results of Brown's excavation in the castle's southern palace complex, which has yielded the only stratigraphically secure ceramic evidence from the site to date.[68] The castle pottery also indicates a period of particular prosperity from about the mid-thirteenth century to the mid-fourteenth century. This is suggested by the presence of stonepaste wares, which were probably produced in Damascus, as well as Chinese imports, while the variety of decorated glazed wares, as well as petrofabric analyses, reveal trade links with various regions of the Levant.[69]

Trade

Transjordan had long been a conduit of trade between Syria, Egypt and the Hijaz. When he passed through the area in the early thirteenth century, the pilgrim Thietmar remarked on the active Red Sea trade that connected Egypt and India, the benefits of which would have flowed north through Transjordan to Syria.[70] The staple exchange goods produced in the region surrounding Kerak were agricultural products, the majority of which were traded and consumed locally. Beyond the plateau, Kerak's primary trade partners were in southern Palestine, Hebron being the closest point of exchange with Jerusalem and Gaza beyond, and Damascus to the north. There were also strong trade links between Kerak and 'Aqaba to the south, but there is surprisingly little in the ceramic evidence to support close commercial ties with Egypt. Most long-distance and high-value trade goods originating in Transjordan came from the south end of the Dead Sea, sugar being the most profitable industry.[71] A variety of mills, making use of the natural streams flowing in the wadis west of Kerak, testify to more modest, but essential, local agriculture.

Documents found in Jerusalem speak to a carpet industry in Transjordan during the Mamluk period. An endowment of the late fourteenth century to *madrasa al-Taziyya* includes carpets from Hawran, Kerak and Shawbak; another of the same period also mentions carpets from Shawbak. These carpets were presumably woven of wool or goat hair procured from local herders.[72] With this apparent carpet industry in mind, it is tempting to draw connections with an industrial complex at Montreal, which abuts the western side of the castle's lower church. It has been suggested that this was a dyeing facility, though the excavators have also pointed to its similarities with an Ottoman soap workshop.[73]

Period of Transition

Although Kerak received a boost in importance thanks to its association with Barquq during his period of exile, its significance declined following his death as power continued to concentrate in Egypt. In Syria, the *na'ib* of Damascus commanded by far the most prestige and the largest military force, with Aleppo an equally clear second. Tripoli, Hama and Safed were another rung lower, while Gaza's importance surged near this level during periods of revolt in Syria due to its position.

Ibn Sasra recorded who stood to receive the Syrian provinces when the new regime reorganized affairs following Barquq's initial fall from power in 1389, but Kerak is not among the eight he listed. It reappears on a list corresponding with the end of 1395, where Batkhash al-Suduni is found as *na'ib*. The man Batkhash replaced, Shihab al-Din Ahmad ibn Shaykh 'Ali, had not been promoted *na'ib* of Damascus, as Altunbugha al-Jubani had been in 1387, but rather chamberlain of Damascus.[74] Over time, the status of the men to whom Kerak was entrusted declined, as did the size of the military forces they commanded. Once a step for emirs on the rise to the highest positions of influence, it fell to a secondary category of appointments in the mid-fifteenth century. Many of the emirs who had served as *na'ib* of Kerak during the reign of Barquq had been emirs of Egypt; with time, the post was more commonly held by emirs based in Syria, further from the centre of power. This trend can be seen during the reign of al-Zahir Jaqmaq.

When the sultan came to the throne in 1438, Kerak was held by Khalil ibn Shakin al-Shaykhi. Prior to his appointment as *na'ib* of Kerak in September 1437, Khalil had served as *na'ib* of Alexandria for a year and a half from the start of June 1434, and then he briefly acted as vizier of Egypt for a month from late March 1436. Following the succession of al-Zahir Jaqmaq, Khalil was appointed commander of the forces at Safed. He held a number of similar lateral positions over the following years, including *na'ib* of Malatya and then *na'ib* of Jerusalem, before he was ultimately named a Syrian emir of the first degree in March 1447.[75]

Mamluk *nuwwab* of Kerak during the reign of Jaqmaq	
1437 – 1438	Khalil ibn Shakin al-Shaykhi
1438 – 1439	Aqbugha al-Turkmani al-Nasiri
1439 – ?	Mazi al-Zahiri Barquq
? – 1452	Hajj Inal al-Yashbaki
1452	Tughan al-Sayfi Aqbirdi Minqar
1452 – 1460	Yashbak Taz al-Mu'ayyadi

The man who replaced Khalil in Kerak was Aqbugha min Mamish al-Turkmani al-Nasiri, an emir of the third degree. In the months leading up to his appointment, Aqbugha had served as emir of the pilgrimage – it was his misfortune that the annual *hajj* caravan was attacked and pillaged that year. The emir served as *na'ib* of Kerak from late 1438, but he was removed and imprisoned in the castle prior to his death in late May 1440. Control of Kerak passed to Mazi al-Zahiri Barquq, an emir of Damascus, who took over from Aqbugha in late October 1439. Like Khalil ibn Shakin al-Shaykhi, Mazi would rise to become an emir of the first degree in Damascus.[76]

In July 1452, Sayf al-Din Hajj Inal al-Yashbaki was confirmed as *na'ib* of Kerak. A week later, he was given Mazi al-Zahiri Barquq's *iqta'*, as the latter had been placed under house arrest. After only about a month, Hajj Inal al-Yashbaki became *na'ib* of Hama, replacing Sudun al-Abi Bakri al-Mu'ayyadi. The latter was compensated with the Damascene *iata'* that had been given to both Hajj Inal and Mazi al-Zahiri Barquq. Hajj Inal al-Yashbaki seems to have had a more traditional career path: he was still *na'ib* of Hama in January 1453, but had become *na'ib* of Tripoli by February 1459, at which time he was installed as *na'ib* of Aleppo. His elevation to the top job in Aleppo was part of a waterfall effect of promotions to replace the *na'ib* of Damascus – the *na'ib* of Aleppo went to Damascus, the *na'ib* of Tripoli to Aleppo, Hama to Tripoli, Safed to Hama, Gaza to Safed, and an emir of the first degree from Damascus became *na'ib* of Gaza. Hajj Inal al-Yashbaki died in Aleppo on 27 May 1462. In his death notice, Ibn Taghribirdi mentioned that he had been *na'ib* of a number of Syrian provinces, including Hama, Tripoli and Aleppo, but left out Kerak. His death caused another waterfall of promotions reaching down to the *na'ib* of Gaza. Kerak was noticeably excluded from these chains of promotion in both 1459 and 1462.[77]

Tughan al-Sayfi, a mamluk of Aqbiri al-Minqar, assumed control of Kerak in August 1452. Perhaps indicative of Cairo's declining authority and influence in Transjordan, Tughan was killed by locals of the Kerak area in late October the same year. The emir was reportedly still quite young, having been one of the younger mamluks that Sultan al-Zahir Jaqmaq had chosen to elevate in the early part of his reign. News of his death reached Cairo on 1 November; a week later, orders were issued investing Yashbak Taz al-Mu'ayyadi as the new *na'ib* of Kerak.[78]

Yashbak Taz, originally an emir of Damascus, had been chamberlain of Tripoli from the spring of 1448. Following his time in Kerak, he went on to command the Mamluk forces of Damascus around the end of 1459, not long before his death in the late spring of 1460. After Yashbak Taz al-Mu'ayyadi, Kerak was entrusted to Taghribirdi al-Ashrafi in January 1460. Taghribirdi was an emir of the third degree prior to holding Kerak, though he had been promoted to that position only seven months earlier.[79] This seems a long way from such prominent men as Altunbugha al-Jubani, Ma'mur al-Qalamtawi and Batkhash al-Suduni, or even earlier figures like Baybars al-Mansuri.

Although the importance of Kerak declined during the fifteenth century, the castle still served as the seat of power of the regional Mamluk administrator, and the town benefited from the presence of the bureaucracy and the military forces that supported him. The position of *na'ib* of Kerak remained a relatively prestigious office, but its significance and the real authority of the men who held this title continued to decline. In addition to political instability in Cairo, there were a number of factors that contributed to Kerak's decreasing importance during the Burji period.

Symbolically, Kerak had drifted further away from the court culture and centre of power in Cairo under the Qalawunids, as it came to represent an idealized way of life associated with the Bedouin. This left it marginalized when the new rulers did not share these romantic notions. Further isolating Kerak from the mid-fourteenth century were economic difficulties brought about by natural phenomena. These events included the resurging waves of plague as well as regular droughts and accompanying periods of famine. In addition to cycles of drought, which were particularly well documented by contemporaries in Egypt, analyses of tree rings have revealed that there was a more general trend in Transjordan towards desertification from the late fourteenth century. Higher temperatures and reduced rainfall, coupled with changing political dynamics, saw once cultivated fields fall into disuse.[80]

No longer able to sustain themselves by their traditional agricultural practices, due to failing crops, the breakdown of established trade links, increasing insecurity, or a combination of these factors, some who inhabited the Kerak plateau adopted a more pastoral lifestyle. As many people came to mix subsistence agriculture and herding, some villages were occupied only seasonally and by much smaller portions of their original populations. While it can be said with confidence that there was a dramatic decrease in the number and size of settlements, to what degree this reflected an overall drop in population, versus widespread internal migration and the adoption of a less sedentary lifestyle, is difficult to discern. Across the plateau, close to 90 per cent of sites occupied at some point during the Mamluk period had been abandoned by the start of the sixteenth century. Despite the dramatic shift in lifestyle, archaeologists have not yet been able to identify a cataclysmic event that might have caused this transition, suggesting a collection of less sensational factors were responsible. Walker's efforts to synthesize this information has led her to stress the regionalism of this transition.[81]

One obvious consequence of this process was the collapse of the sugar industry in the fifteenth century. Once the area's most profitable agricultural export, sugar fails to appear on the region's tax records in the early sixteenth century.[82] Agriculture, however, remained the primary economic activity of the region. Whereas two-thirds of early Ottoman revenues drawn from Montreal, to the south, came from the herding activities of the Bedouin, taxes from Kerak were levied from agricultural produce.[83]

The political marginalization of Kerak saw the influence of the Bedouin increase. At the end of the eleventh century, when the Franks first established themselves in Syria, local tribal groups appear to have had reasonably free reign in the region. Following the spread of Frankish authority, there are few indications of hostilities between the Bedouin and the Catholic rulers of Kerak; on the contrary, members of these nomadic groups were instrumental in assisting certain Frankish actions, most famously the raids organized by Reynald of Châtillon in the early 1180s. When Transjordan passed back under Muslim rule, efforts were made to impose greater influence and authority over the Bedouin, fostering opposition during the centuries that followed. The breakdown of centralized Mamluk influence provided local tribal groups with greater freedom, contributing to the political environment in which Tughan al-Sayfi was killed. The influence of the Bedouin had reached such a level by the early sixteenth century that Sibay, the powerful emir who ruled Damascus, assembled an army to move against the Bedouin of Kerak and Montreal in 1507 and then again in 1508.[84]

The help of the Bedouin of Transjordan had proven instrumental in returning certain deposed sultans to power. Al-Nasir Muhammad had directly benefitted from their support, and the Banu Numayr and Banu Rabi' had helped preserve Ahmad's independence prior to his capture in 1344. Bedouin forces had similarly assisted al-Zahir Barquq reclaim power from Kerak in 1389–90. This relationship, however, turned increasingly hostile as Bedouin groups came to act with greater autonomy. When considering possible factors behind the escalating raiding activities of the Bedouin, Milwright has highlighted the lack of personal meetings between the Mamluk sultans and Bedouin leaders, which had proven so useful in the time of Baybars and the Qalawunids. Against a backdrop of Cairo's increasing disinterest in the region's affairs and the dwindling availability of natural resources, Kerak's Mamluk officials were finding it hard to simply retain control by the start of the sixteenth century.[85]

Chapter 5

Ottoman Period

Karak is an impregnable fortress, standing high on the summit of a mountain. Its fosses are the valleys around it, which are very deep. They say it was originally, in Roman days, a convent, and was turned into a fortress. It is now the treasure-house of the Turks. Of its dependencies is ash-Shawbak, a well-fortified town, with fruits in plenty, and copious springs.[1]

al-Dimashqi (d. 1327)

In August 1516, Ottoman forces defeated a Mamluk army at the Battle of Marj Dabiq, north of Aleppo. As took place after the Battles of Hattin and 'Ayn Jalut, a significant restructuring of the power dynamic in Syria followed. The Ottoman sultan, Selim I, led his forces southward and entered Damascus in early October, its Mamluk governor having already fled the city. Selim went on to conquer Egypt the following year.

One of the early Ottoman governors of Damascus was originally a Mamluk. Janbirdi al-Ghazali served as *na'ib* of Kerak and later Hama, and fought against the Ottomans during their push into the Levant. He subsequently offered his services to the new regime, and was appointed governor of the Ottoman *eyalet* or *wilaya* (province) of Damascus in 1520, which included Kerak. During his short time in this position, Janbirdi al-Ghazali attempted to secure the *hajj* route through Transjordan, which he did with relative success. He was killed in early 1521 during a failed revolt following the death of Selim I a few months earlier.[2]

As Ottoman authority set in, power in southern Syria remained focused on Damascus, which was ruled by a *beylerbey*. A number of regional officials, most often a *sanjaqbey*, administered *liwas* (smaller districts) from prominent towns. Kerak seems to have fallen into the *liwa* of 'Ajlun, along with the rest of Transjordan. The importance the area had due to the *hajj* and caravan traffic, however, may have led to the appointment of a *sanjaqbey* in Kerak, who would have overseen the three *nawahi* (tax zones, sg. *nahiya*) of Kerak, Jibal al-Karak and Shawbak. Testament to the nature of power in the region, the *beylerbey* in Damascus appears to have appointed Kerak's *sanjaqbey* from among leading local families. The Ottomans had few incentives to commit resources and attention to Transjordan so long as commerce and, more importantly, pilgrims were able to move freely through the area. This allowed the negative socio-economic trend to continue, and the rapid decline of direct Ottoman authority in and around Kerak followed.[3]

Marginalization

A factor that contributed to the further economic and political decline of Kerak's significance during the early Ottoman period was an alteration to the path followed by the *hajj* through Transjordan. Ibn Battuta, who accompanied the annual pilgrim caravan in 1326, left an account of the traditional route. From Damascus, the caravan made its way to Bosra, where there was a pause for four days to allow anyone who might have been delayed in Damascus to catch up. Pilgrims then continued onwards along the King's Highway towards the former Roman fortress of Lajjun, and then on to Thaniyya, a few kilometres east of Kerak. They paused there for four days, allowing for a rest and visit to Kerak to purchase supplies before continuing onwards through the increasingly arid landscape. The next notable town was Ma'an, from where the caravan left Syria and pushed into Arabia, heading for Tabuk, al-'Ula and then the holy cities of Medina and Mecca. Ibn Battuta's remark that Christians ventured no further than al-'Ula speaks to the presence of Arab Christian merchants who accompanied and helped facilitate the travels of the Muslim pilgrims.[4]

During the reign of Suleiman the Magnificent (1520–66), the *hajj* route was moved eastward, from the King's Highway to the Desert Road, known then as the *tariq al-bint*.[5] This more eastern path, later chosen for the route of the Hijaz railway at the start of the twentieth century, saw pilgrims pass through Qatrana, more than 30km east of Kerak. This shift marginalized Kerak further, reducing its political importance and denying it many of the economic benefits associated with the *hajj*. By comparison, when Baybars made his secret pilgrimage to the Hijaz in the summer of 1269, passing through Kerak on his way there and return, he would have interacted directly with the local economy and leading figures, reinforcing the importance of both the town and those influential people who dwelt there.[6] Three centuries later, this significance had eroded considerably.

Kerak's declining importance is also evident when looking at the countryside around the town. In general, agriculture and settled populations continued to decline, with sedentary communities concentrated in the highlands along the southwestern fringe of the plateau. People certainly inhabited other regions, but they embraced a more nomadic or seasonal lifestyle. Some moved around during the year, as their focus shifted between localized agriculture and herding;

others came to rely entirely on pasturage. Between the late sixteenth and late nineteenth centuries, permanent settlement density may have declined more than 70 per cent.[7]

Ottoman tax records from 1596, which were studied by Hütteroth and Abdulfattah, provide a breakdown of the Kerak district (*liwas*) and its three *nawahi* – Kerak, Jibal al-Karak and Shawbak – from a fiscal perspective. Kerak consisted of a town (Kerak) and thirteen smaller villages, which included Safi and Mazra'a, on the south coast of the Dead Sea, and Tafila and Shajara, situated along the King's Highway south of Wadi al-Hasa. There were apparently also another sixteen distinguished *mazari* (agricultural units that were typically not occupied year-round, sg. *mazra'a*) and twenty-eight *mazari* listed together as a single tax entity. To the south, Jibal al-Karak was recorded as having seven villages and four *mazari*. Shawbak, the southernmost of the three, included a town (Montreal), as well as seven villages, six *mazari* and two *qita' ard* (lit. 'pieces of land', usually smaller or less productive than *mazari*, sg. *qit'at ard*). Twelve nomadic groups were also listed in association with Shawbak, from whom flat fees were collected.[8]

With a stipulated tax rate of 25 per cent, the district yielded a modest 279,100 *akçes* (or *aqja*, silver coins that served as the Ottoman unit of account).[9] The *nahiya* of Kerak contributed almost half, 134,400 *akçes*, with only 15,000 drawn from the town of Kerak itself – less than a few of the smaller villages of the broader district. To the south, the *nawahi* of Jibal al-Karak and Shawbak yielded 60,000 and 84,700 *akçes* respectively. For the latter, Montreal, the only other town of the district, yielded 14,000 *akçes*. The nomadic groups of the *nahiya*, noted above, appear to have paid an amount comparable to that provided by the villages. Fiscal figures are provided for seven of these groups: six paid between 5,200 and 5,500 *akçes*, and another provided 2,000. The most profitable agricultural good throughout the district was wheat, accounting for 28 per cent of the total tax revenue. Taxes were also drawn from barley, summer crops, olive oil, vineyards, fruit trees, goats and bees. An additional financial tax was levied from the town of Kerak, and various legal fees and fines were collected from all sedentary communities, amounting to 84,700 *akçes* across the district.[10]

The town of Kerak also supported a market, from which 2,500 *akçes* were collected. Although modest, it was probably the largest market on the east side of the Great Rift south of Damascus, yielding a return two-thirds greater than the market at Salt, the only other one in Transjordan. The taxes drawn from the commerce of nearby centres in southern Palestine, however, were considerably greater. The market of nearby Hebron, for example, paid 35,000 *akçes* into the Ottoman coffers. A bit further west, Gaza, the largest market

Kerak from the south. (*Matthew Dalton, copyright APAAME*)

Kerak from the southeast. (*Robert Bewley, copyright APAAME*)

Kerak from the east. (*Robert Bewley, copyright APAAME*)

Kerak from the northwest. (*David Kennedy, copyright APAAME*)

Kerak from the west. (*Robert Bewley, copyright APAAME*)

Kerak from the north. (*David Kennedy, copyright APAAME*)

East end of the northern front and northeast gate. (*Michael Fulton*)

West end of the northern front and modern entrance. (*Michael Fulton*)

Upper northern vault, looking west. (*Heather Crowley*)

Northern vaults, looking east.
(*Michael Fulton*)

South end of the upper ward from the east end of the chapel. (*Michael Fulton*)

Western front of the upper ward, looking southeast from the lower ward. (*Michael Fulton*)

Lower ward, looking south from the northern structure. (*Michael Fulton*)

Central eastern tower and eastern glacis from the south. (*Michael Fulton*)

Castle chapel, looking west. (*Michael Fulton*)

South *iwan* of the southern palace complex. (*Michael Fulton*)

East *suffa* of the southern palace complex with opening to the mosque behind. (*Michael Fulton*)

Southern pavilion, looking southwest. (*Heather Crowley*)

Upper level of the eastern corridor of the upper ward, looking south. (*Michael Fulton*)

South *iwan* of the small *qa'a* of the upper ward, looking southwest. (*Michael Fulton*)

Central corridor of the upper ward, looking south towards the chapel. (*Michael Fulton*)

Room with the western oven. (*Michael Fulton*)

The Majaly sensed an opportunity and joined an alliance led by the Banu Sakhr, which also included the Banu Hamida and the Hijaya. Collectively, this group pushed the 'Amr out of the region. By manipulating a series of subsequent conflicts between rival tribes, the Majaly were able to secure their own prominence in the environs of Kerak. In the early nineteenth century, Sheik Yusuf al-Majaly, nephew of the Majaly sheik who had initially helped drive the 'Amr from Kerak, facilitated the return of the 'Amr, but only so they could be crushed by the Banu Hamida. This allowed the Majaly sheik to show benevolence to the 'Amr, permitting them to occupy some poor lands in the northeast of the plateau; the 'Amr would intermarry with the Muslims of Kerak thereafter. The Majaly then persuaded the townspeople of Kerak to attack the Banu Hamida. This so weakened the latter that the Majaly could drive them from the area around Kerak, forcing them to settle in the northwest of the plateau and the Balqa' beyond. The Majaly then occupied these vacated lands north of Kerak, allocating some to allied Christian tribes. The Majaly, under Sheik Yusuf, were the dominant tribe from this time, with the Banu Hamida as their main rivals. Despite their regional pre-eminence, the Majaly continued to pay tribute, in the form of gifts, to the powerful Banu Sakhr.[17]

From the start of the nineteenth century, information begins to appear in the travel records composed by Western adventurers. Among the details found in Burckhardt's account is the observation that Yusuf al-Majaly recognized the nominal authority of Ibn Sa'ud of the Wahhabis in 1808. The sheik was, in turn, sent gifts and granted the title of 'Emir of all the Bedouins to the south of Damascus, as far as the Red Sea'. This would appear to have been an alliance of convenience. It allowed Ibn Sa'ud to claim that his influence stretched into Syria and Ottoman lands, while the Majaly similarly benefitted from their association with the powerful Arabian Wahhabis. For the Majaly, this association came at little cost. They reportedly declined to send the full tribute required by Ibn Sa'ud, ignored calls to make war against the Ottomans, and made no effort to force their Christian allies to pay any additional tax. Just two days before Burckhardt arrived at Kerak, two Wahhabi tax collectors had visited from Medina. Although the Wahhabis left with no money, the townspeople had made a show of praying regularly, something few of them, with the exception of the sheik, were apparently in the habit of doing.[18]

Irby and Mangles, who visited in 1818, noted an anecdote of tribal fighting in which the Wahhabis are said to have attacked Kerak, encamping on the hill to the south of the castle for a number of days. The people of Kerak boasted of having killed about forty of their attackers with their muskets from the embrasures of the castle. Kerak's inhabitants were armed in so much as each man was said to have possessed a pistol and long gun. During his tour of the castle in 1806, Seetzen noticed a swivel gun, adding that two others had been acquired by the Wahhabis from there.[19]

While the Majaly were masters of Kerak, they controlled little beyond. Western travellers heading to Petra via Kerak were compelled to seek not only the support of the Majaly sheik, but also the permission and protection of the sheiks of Shawbak, Wadi Musa, and often certain Bedouin groups. Layard was attacked and robbed while ascending Wadi Kerak in 1840, despite travelling with permission of Sheik Abu Daouk, a leader of the Huwaytat. Ahmad, the son of the Majaly sheik, assigned a small bodyguard to accompany Layard beyond the environs of the town, lest the Englishman be accosted again when he set out to join a group of the Banu Sakhr, whom he would accompany northward. Even beyond the plateau, the tribes of Kerak had a reputation for thievery. Conder, while at Hisban, had some of his donkeys stolen by thieves from the Kerak region. Although the Majaly acknowledged the theft, they refused to offer any recompense unless Conder and his party presented themselves in person at Kerak.[20]

In 1834, trouble came to Kerak following a revolt in Palestine led by Qasim al-Ahmad. The uprising was symptomatic of the instability and setbacks the Ottomans were facing all over their empire. The roots of this particular episode stretch back to 1798, when the French, led by General Napoleon Bonaparte, invaded Ottoman Egypt. The French were pushed out by the British, who themselves left in 1803. Into the vacuum stepped Muhammad 'Ali Pasha, who ruled Egypt fairly autonomously from 1805, only nominally recognizing the authority of the Ottoman sultan in Constantinople. From 1831 to 1833, Ibrahim, the son of Muhammad 'Ali, effectively conquered Ottoman Syria. Kerak reportedly submitted reasonably quickly, and an Egyptian garrison was installed in the castle.

According to local accounts, the inhabitants of Kerak rose up one night and killed the soldiers billeted in the town, said to number 460, while another 600 who were in the castle surrendered after a short period, agreeing to leave the town. This appears to correspond with the revolt of Qasim al-Ahmad in 1834. When the uprising failed in Palestine, Qasim al-Ahmad fled to Kerak, which he probably saw as an attractive place of refuge, and he may even have regarded the Majalys as natural allies, given their nominal ties to the Wahhabis, who were opponents of both Muhammad 'Ali and the Ottoman sultan. Tribal Kerak, however, was no match for Ibrahim Pasha and his father's armies. The Majaly sheik, presumably Yusuf, fled Kerak and sought refuge with the Huwaytat, the pre-eminent tribe of the Transjordan region. This proved a miscalculation, as the Huwaytat, who had little affection for the Majaly, handed the sheik over to Ibrahim Pasha, leading to his execution. Meanwhile, Kerak was besieged by Egyptian forces for a period of seventeen days. As punishment for this resistance, parts of the town and surrounding region were destroyed following the defenders' surrender – this included an oil mill in the valley, which was pointed out to Luynes by Sheik Muhammad in 1864. A significant number of the town's inhabitants and a large portion of the Christian community were said to have left for Jerusalem and Hebron during this period of hostility. Power in Kerak passed to the brother of the executed sheik, who agreed to recognize Egyptian suzerainty and pay a small tribute, but no garrison nor administrative official was stationed in the town. Conflict flared up a few years later, leading to the defeat of Ibrahim Pasha and his withdrawal from Syria in 1841. This left Kerak virtually free of imperial influence until 1893.[21]

The defences of Kerak were certainly damaged during the siege of 1834, but the location and extent of this destruction is hard to determine. Klein and his party were informed that one of the neighbouring hills, which he identifies as 'Jalamet es-Sabeha', was where Ibrahim Pasha positioned his guns, and he observed that it offered a splendid view of the town. De Saulcy, who visited Kerak in 1851, entered the town through a 'breach' in the wall, rather than by one of the two town gates, both of which were still in use at the time. Tristram, who followed in 1872, mentions leading his party through the Christian quarter and then scrambling over a gap in the wall somewhere in the northeastern part of the town, from which they led their horses down a zigzagging path into one of the wadis, suggesting the breach had become a secondary point of entrance into the town. Whether this breach was the same one used by De Saulcy is hard to say. De Saulcy, among others, observed destruction surrounding him as he walked along the streets, which he attributed to the wrath of Ibrahim Pasha. Although this would seem quite sensible, it may be worth considering the words of Irby and Mangles, who spent time in the town in 1818, and reported seeing ruins and foundations everywhere. Mauss and Sauvaire noted possible damage inflicted by the Egyptian forces during their visit in 1866, but added no specifics.[22]

Sheik Muhammad al-Majaly was the pre-eminent figure in Kerak from the mid-nineteenth century. Although the Ottomans exerted no real authority in Kerak, Muhammad supported nominal imperial rule in the region, even inviting the Ottomans to send soldiers to help ensure security for travellers. He asked Luynes to appeal on his behalf to the Ottoman official in Jerusalem for 50 cavalry, whom he would pay, in order to defend himself from his enemies and demonstrate his loyalty. Mauss and Sauvaire describe a similar instance in which a force of 500 horsemen was requested from Damascus, in exchange for which a sum of tax revenue would be paid – taxes had evidently not been collected, or at least paid to the Ottomans, since the time of the

Egyptian invasion of Palestine more than two decades earlier. This fits with Tristram's characterization of the leading sheik of Kerak as an Ottoman appointed official, a colonel responsible for collecting taxes; by comparison, he cast the sheik of the Banu Sakhr as an Ottoman vassal, who provided military support when summoned and collected a tribute from the sheik of Kerak in exchange for providing regional security. Klein, who made the acquaintance of Fendi'l-Faiz at Hisban, sheik of the Banu Sakhr, similarly described him as the Ottomans' representative of the various tribes of the Balqa'. It was during this conversation with Fendi'l-Faiz, in August 1867, that Klein learned of the recent migration of the Banu Sakhr into the Balqa', a region formerly dominated by the 'Adwan, whose great sheik, Dhi'ab, was then a prisoner of the Turks.[23]

Muhammad al-Majaly's interest in maintaining good relations with the Ottomans fit into the broader web of regional alliances and feuds that dominated the politics of Transjordan in the late nineteenth century. In the 1860s, the Majaly had led a coalition against the Banu Sakhr, successfully pushing them into the Balqa'. Luynes noted that the Majaly had engaged in a feud with the more nomadic Banu Sakhr shortly before his visit in 1864; the cause of this was said to have been the murder of an ally of the Banu Sakhr, perpetrated by Salih, son of Sheikh Muhammad al-Majaly. Clashes continued over the following decades, part of a broader pattern of violent tribal warfare that saw raids launched by and against the Banu Hamida of the plateau to the north of Kerak, as well as the Banu Sakhr, the Huwaytat, and others. When Klein visited the region a few years after Luynes, he found the people of Kerak locked in a feud with the Banu Hamida. This, he was led to believe, stretched back to the efforts of the Duc de Luynes to acquire a certain basalt stone featuring an inscription found near Wadi al-Mujib. He claims the sheik of Kerak agreed to acquire this stone secretively, which outraged the Banu Hamida when they found out, and a blood feud ensued. Ironically, Klein would discover the famous Mesha Stele (or Moabite Stone) only days later while encamped near Dhiban, just north of Wadi al-Mujib. Sensing potential profits, a man from Kerak brought news of the stone's discovery to the Westerners in Jerusalem, though he was probably only one of a number to do so. The monument was subsequently destroyed by the Banu Hamida, who were coming under pressure from the Ottomans to produce the stone for the Germans, the Turks' European allies. Fragments subsequently found their way to Jerusalem, an operation that Doughty claims was facilitated by the sheik of Kerak, who sought a reward for his efforts. Western enthusiasm for antiquities only added to the existing conflict and animosity between the Banu Hamida and the tribes of Kerak.[24]

In the 1870s, the Ottomans renewed efforts to impose their authority in Transjordan. This began with the Balqa' and resulted with the installation of a local administrator and a Turkish garrison at Salt in 1876. Pressing their advantage, the Ottomans defeated the 'Adwan further south and subsequently captured their leader, Dhi'ab. Two years later, fighting again broke out between the Ottomans and the 'Adwan, who were supported by the Banu Sakhr and Banu Hamida in an alliance of convenience. Unfortunately for the allies, however, this resulted in another Ottoman victory. Although an attempt was made to extend Ottoman administrative reforms south of Wadi al-Mujib, it proved impractical to enforce these and Kerak continued to be governed fairly autonomously.[25]

Meanwhile, a particularly bloody phase of tribal fighting took place to the south in 1877. This came about when the Majaly encouraged the Banu 'Attiya, who had helped them in their conflict with the Banu Sakhr, to move against the Huwaytat. Like most of these conflicts, this involved a complex network of alliances that stretched from Ma'an and Wadi Musa in the south to the Balqa' in the north. In Kerak, a personal rivalry was also set to develop between Salih and Khalil, the son and brother of Sheik Muhammad respectively. Salih would eventually succeed his father in 1886, but his authority would be undercut by his formidable uncle, who commanded considerable prestige and support.[26] In the background to these local conflicts was a growing awareness that change was on the horizon, heralded by increasing Western interest in the Middle East.

Era of Western Travellers

Beginning in the early nineteenth century, a number of adventurous Europeans visited Kerak. The accounts of these figures, still frequently referred to as 'Franks' by the local inhabitants, shed light on the castle's state of preservation, the substance of the town, and provide various details relating to the people of Kerak from an outsider's perspective.

Population

Many early Western visitors tried to provide a sense of the size of Kerak's local community and its religious composition. Seetzen, who passed through in 1806, estimated there were around 120 Muslim and 80 Christian houses in the town. Families would often share homes, with married couples each occupying a small room; due to this, the Muslims were reportedly able to provide 600 or 700 fighters and the Christians 400. Six years later, Burckhardt observed that Kerak hosted 500 families, 100 of which were Christians, attributing 400 and

250 rifles to the Muslim and Christian inhabitants respectively. He observed that the Muslims, whom he called Turks, came from all over southern Syria, but principally from Hebron and Nablus, while most Christians were the descendants of refugees from Jerusalem, Bethlehem and Bayt Jala. Burckhardt saw little difference between the local Muslims and Christians, who enjoyed what he saw as almost the same customs and laws. Irby and Mangles, who visited another six years on, similarly observed that the Christians seemed to enjoy equal footing to their Muslim counterparts. If Kerak's Muslim population did not attend religious services with noticeable regularity, the same could be said of their Christian neighbours – according to Burckhardt this was because they did not understand the Greek liturgy. A number of visitors also noted that Kerak continued to serve as a titular episcopal see, though its Orthodox bishop lived in Jerusalem and rarely, if ever, visited.[27]

In 1840, following the disturbance that had taken place less than a decade earlier, Layard placed Kerak's population at about 800 or 900. This included 300 Christians, who attended a small church serviced by a single priest. Layard did not note the military strength of the population, but mentioned that the people of the region had been considerably disarmed by Ibrahim Pasha. Lynch, who spent less than twenty-four hours in Kerak eight years later, placed the population at 300 families, three-quarters of which he reckoned were Christians. Whereas Burckhardt claimed Christians enjoyed the same rights as Muslims, Lynch noted that the former paid an annual tribute, but otherwise lived amicably with the Majaly tribe, most members of which were camped outside the town at the time of his visit. Despite this characterization, Lynch, like Layard before him, cast the Christians as an oppressed group. Mauss estimated that the population was about 7,000 in 1866, though later in his account this is amended to a total of about 8,000, specifying that roughly 6,000 were Muslims and 1,800 were Christians. He noted that the people of Kerak possessed around 2,000 long guns (a figure twice as high as those provided by Seetzen and Burckhardt), though this is similarly refined later to 2,000 rifles belonging to Muslim inhabitants and 500 to 600 carried by Christians.[28] From these observations, it seems safe to assume that a significant portion of Kerak's population was still Christian, probably somewhere between a fifth and a third of those living in the town. Most of these Christians, however, appear to have traced their ancestry to migrants from southern Palestine, rather than the Christian community that had occupied the town during the Frankish period.

An issue with any of these estimates was the seasonal shift in settlement dynamics. Klein, who visited in February 1872, made note that there were said to be at most 514 Muslim and 270 Christian families in Kerak, observing these people came from an assortment of backgrounds. Tristram, who accompanied the same expedition as Klein, observed that there were nowhere near the number of Christians then in Kerak as had been observed during the stay of Mauss and Sauvaire six years earlier, postulating that many were at that time camping in the countryside with their flocks and herds. Bliss, who spent four nights in Kerak in March 1895, placed the population of Kerak at between 8,000 and 10,000, including, in his words, 'those who never live in the town'. He estimated the number of Christians to be a few hundred. Similar figures are provided by others around the same time: Meistermann placed the population at 7,000, among whom 1,200 were Greek Christians and 300 were Catholics; Dowling estimated the population to be about 10,000, including 2,000 Orthodox Christians. Gautier, however, believed there to be 22,000 people living in the town following his visit in 1899.[29]

The people of Kerak were organized by tribe, each with its own sheik. Burckhardt noted the Christians had two sheiks in Kerak, who directed the affairs of the Christian community in coordination with the Orthodox priest. Irby and Mangles, followed by Lynch and De Saulcy, mention only one Christian sheik, Abd 'Alla, who must have held this position from at least 1818 to 1851. A person's religion, however, was not an exclusionary or necessarily defining quality, as there are numerous references to Christians in the entourages of the Majaly sheikhs.[30]

Although the members of most tribes adhered to the same religion, there were exceptions. Likewise, the Christian community was not a cohesive group. By 1847, a church had been built to offer services to a number of Christians who had adopted the Greek Catholic rite. Another division took place around 1875, when a Roman Catholic mission was established in the town, attracting converts from both the Greek Catholic and Orthodox congregations. It seems disputes, rivalries and identity politics were in part responsible for some of these conversions, as almost the whole 'Azizat tribe adopted Roman Catholicism. This pluralism caused tensions to rise among the Christian community, as each sect feared the decline of its own influence. Eventually about 150 families, from three Christian tribes, including the 'Azizat, left Kerak.[31] Many appear to have gone to Madaba, where a Catholic mission was established in 1880 – both Conder and Bliss noted that many of its supporters had come from Kerak. Back in Kerak, a Greek priest continued to administer to the Orthodox congregation. When Luynes visited in 1864, the priest was assisted by two others, who, he noted, were to be relieved every two years. Other Western visitors observed the presence of only one additional priest or deacon, though at some times the priest was evidently unsupported.[32]

European missionaries moved into Transjordan from around the middle of the nineteenth century. Both Catholics and Protestants focused initially on

Salt, where they benefitted following the imposition of more direct Ottoman authority. These figures often offered rudimentary educational and medical services, which were valued by the Ottomans. To the south, those who established themselves in Kerak operated with limited outside support. The Latin mission continued to function following the exodus to Madaba, even though the Christian population of the town was almost entirely Orthodox from that time. During his visit in 1896, Musil stayed with the priest who ran the mission and its associated school for boys and girls. The previous year, Dowling noted that 120 boys and 60 girls attended this school. There was also a Protestant missionary presence in Kerak from the 1880s, namely the English Methodists William Lethaby and his wife, who were joined for a period by Mary Arnold. In 1894, following the imposition of direct Ottoman rule, the Church Missionary Society took over Protestant activities in the town, though its presence in Kerak was maintained only until 1908. The Latin mission, meanwhile, was still in existence when Deschamps studied the castle in 1929. Deschamps placed the population of Kerak at around 10,000 during his stay, though he estimated this included only 200 Christians. When Jordan's first census was conducted in 1948, the inhabitants of the town numbered almost exactly 4,000, while the population of the district of Kerak was just under 40,000.[33]

Life in the Town

Despite the relative fertility of the area around Kerak, it was far from a wealthy region by the nineteenth century. Testament to the extent of the shift towards a semi-nomadic lifestyle, most Western visitors remarked on the locals' habit of camping around the town. While a number of families would remain outside the town year-round, tending livestock, much of the otherwise urban population would join them in tents in the fields during the summer.[34]

Wheat and barley remained staple crops. The harvest, according to MacMichael, was deposited in the castle, where it was ground using oxen and horses, though other visitors noted smaller stockpiles in caves and underground storage places. Just about every family kept goats or sheep. The availability of livestock was such that it made the sale of butter shameful, while these animals served as a convenient currency. Yusuf al-Majaly and his son, Ishmael, told MacMichael that the sheik was owed every tenth sheep or goat and every twentieth camel that was born to the members of his tribe. Most trade was with neighbouring Bedouin groups, who relied on the semi-sedentary population for grain. There was also a regular caravan route south of the Dead Sea, connecting Kerak with Hebron and Jerusalem. In April 1806, Seetzen accompanied a group of merchants returning westward, who were led by Arab guides. This trade provided the people of Kerak with staples like rice, coffee and tobacco, as well as manufactured goods, such as furniture and clothing, which were sold in a few shops run by merchants from Hebron. In addition to the town's merchants, there were a few artisans – a blacksmith, a shoemaker and a silversmith. During his brief visit, Layard encountered a Jewish peddler from Hebron who traded small items with the Bedouin between Kerak and Damascus.[35]

Despite the significant reduction in trans-regional trade since the early Mamluk period, Irby and Mangles encountered a merchant from Hebron as well as another from Damascus. A trade in slaves also continued. Burckhardt observed that many, both Muslims and Christians, owned slaves of African ancestry whom they had bought from the Bedouin, who had in turn acquired these people from the slave markets of Jedda and Mecca, while MacMichael identified the source of the sheikh's slaves as Egypt. There were also at that time a few free families of African background. Two of the first men whom Irby and Mangles encountered when ascending the wadi up to Kerak from the west were of sub-Saharan ethnicity, while in his first meeting with Tristram, Sheik Muhammad was preceded by a mounted slave, who acted as his herald among other things.[36]

A common theme among most accounts composed by Western travellers was their distaste for the houses of the town. These were typically single-level structures without any windows, and only some appear to have had a noticeable vent through which smoke from a central hearth could escape – they are described as being blackened inside. While the walls were constructed of stone, roofs consisted of rushes and mud. The floors of most houses sunk well below the street level, due partly to the slope of the ground in places, but more generally a result of centuries of rebuilding and deposition. This led some visitors to accidentally walk, or even ride, onto the roof of a house. The Christian quarter, along with the Orthodox church, was in the northern part of the town, though there was little in the eyes of the Westerners to distinguish any of the houses from one another. During his visit in 1899, Gautier observed that only five houses in the town could be rightfully labelled as such: the new houses built for the Ottoman governor and garrison commander, the Greek convent, and two others. A large part of the area within the walled town also seems to have been unoccupied throughout the nineteenth century.[37]

Although these early Western travellers devoted little attention to gender dynamics, Irby and Mangles noted that the women of Kerak did not typically cover their faces. Their observation appears to imply that this was exceptional or otherwise uncommon. MacMichael elaborated that women often wore blue cotton robes, which Klein calls common to the Bedouin of Transjordan, with a black veil of silk below the face, adding that many displayed a nose ring. Those women with whom the travellers spoke seemed quite comfortable conversing with them, to the point that some even felt it appropriate to entertain these foreign men.[38]

Rule of the Majaly

The Majaly dominated the affairs of Kerak during the nineteenth century, but their hegemony relied on the support of a network of local tribes. In the town of Kerak, their rule was endorsed by about half of the Muslim population, but they could rely on the backing of most of the Christians.[39] While the Majaly were said to have extorted a tribute from the communities around the Dead Sea to the west, they in turn were often compelled to pay a protection fee to the nomadic Huwaytat and Banu Sakhr. This protection money discouraged the Bedouin from pillaging the farmlands around Kerak as they passed through the region.[40]

Nineteenth-century Western travellers rarely characterized their time in Kerak as a positive experience, due in no small part to the treatment they received from the Majaly. Seetzen and Burckhardt, who travelled incognito, were welcomed warmly by the local Christians, with whom both stayed during their visits. Unlike Seetzen, who travelled less conspicuously, Burckhardt made the acquaintance of Sheik Yusuf. The adventurer had few nice things to say about the man, who forced Burckhardt to wait almost three weeks in Kerak before continuing on his journey, and only after compelling the traveller to pay him to serve as his guide. Irby and Mangles were less resentful, calling Sheik Yusuf plain, blunt and honest. They too were compelled to pay the sheik to guide them as they continued southward from Kerak, but they had fewer issues with this.[41] If Yusuf was regarded as an unsavoury character by certain Western visitors in the early nineteenth century, his successors were to prove no more pleasant in the eyes of many later travellers.

Layard, who visited six years after the Palestinian uprising of 1834, found himself at odds with Ahmad, whom he identified as the son of the Majaly sheik, then absent from Kerak. Unfortunately, Layard does not provide the name of Ahmad's father, and Ahmad himself seems to disappear from written records after this. A decade later, neither the people of Kerak nor Sheik Muhammad endeared themselves to de Saulcy in 1851. Aware of the troubles faced by his predecessors, to which can be added the confrontational experience of Lynch in 1848, Luynes took considerable care to make arrangements with Sheikh Muhammad before his party began its assent up Wadi Kerak in 1864. In subsequent conversations, the sheikh acknowledged that he had earned a poor reputation among Westerners, though he denied having deserved this.

Following in the steps of Luynes, Mauss and Sauvaire also enjoyed a relatively smooth visit two years later, and Sheik Muhammad put at their disposal the first level of a small house facing the Greek church, which they used as their workshop. Though they were grateful for receiving the good grace of the sheik, which allowed them to work quickly and relatively efficiently, they identified with the experiences of de Saulcy. When leaving, Mauss reflected on their good fortune, noting that their stay of fifteen days was longer than that of any European before them, apparently excluding Burckhardt. In 1872, Tristram had perhaps the most confrontational encounter yet. Having entered the town and set up camp in the open space behind Burj al-Zahir, his party was effectively held there under guard by order of the sheik's son, presumably Salih. Tensions eased the following day with the arrival of Sheik Muhammad and, more importantly, the son of the great sheik of the Banu Sakhr, who had been contracted to guide the Westerners through the region north of Kerak. In 1890, the Hills similarly fell victim to Salih. The couple were detained for a period of days, being forced to pay all they could, before they were allowed to continue on to Madaba. They felt considerable relief when they crossed Wadi al-Mujib and entered the care of the Banu Hamida.[42]

Kerak's relative independence through the nineteenth century contributed to its reputation, among both Europeans and many Syrians, as a place of brigandage. Basic cultural differences, however, accounted for most of the displeasure experienced by Western travellers. While it was the attempts to extract money from them that consistently drew the ire of Westerners, it was the particularly abrasive manner in which this was done by the Majaly that set them apart. The extraction of wealth was a means to both show and sustain dominance; on the flip side, largess was expressed through hospitality and gift giving. The appropriate amount to be offered or extracted was judged in proportion to the perceived means of the individual or group.

Montreal

For most nineteenth-century travellers who left descriptions of Kerak, the town was a waypoint on a longer journey, rather than their destination. Burckhardt was heading for Egypt, but would happen across Petra on his way; the abandoned Nabataean-Roman town would then be the objective of many subsequent travellers passing through Kerak. Some, including Irby and Mangles, Mauss and Sauvaire, Hornstein, Lagrange, and Libbey and Hoskins, made their way to Montreal, or Shawbak as it had continued to be known to the local community and broader Muslim world.

Seetzen described Montreal as ruined, though he was nevertheless impressed by the strength of the castle's position, noting it was worth visiting. Mauss reported that the stronghold's battlements had been dismantled, and sections of certain walls had been destroyed, the gaps having been filled with rough masonry. Mauss and Sauvaire were told that this destruction, or at least the latest phase, had been carried out by Ibrahim Pasha, who slighted the castle during his conquest of Syria, with the demolition carried out by a certain Sheik Sa'id Abu Dis. They also noted the remains of a wall, near the base of the castle hill on the opposite side of the valley to the northwest of the stronghold, which they were informed was the remains of an old bazaar. Unfortunately, their visit was brief, cut short by fighting between tribal groups. This limited their study of the castle's defences to tracing the outline of the walls. They noted that there appeared to be periods of destruction and rebuilding, supported by a number of Mamluk inscriptions. About three decades later, Hornstein observed that there were between fifty and seventy houses then within the walls of the castle.[43] Like Kerak, Montreal remained a node of settlement, with the influence of the local tribes who dominated the castle limited to the surrounding area.

Direct Ottoman Rule

Kerak's period of tribal rule ended in 1893. Prior to this, most of the taxes raised by Sheik Muhammad, and Sheik Salih after him, which were collected mainly from the inhabitants of the town, remained in the region. A portion of these revenues could be used to support the small groups of Ottoman troops who were occasionally sent to assist them. For all of their efforts to preserve good relations with the Ottomans, the Majaly were fiercely determined to preserve their autonomy. Hill, who visited Kerak in the final years of this era of local rule, remarked:

> The Keraki can muster from sixteen hundred to two thousand well-armed horsemen; and [the castle] being thus protected by nature, and having long enjoyed independence, have come to believe themselves invincible, and express contempt for the Turkish Government, who hitherto have let them alone.[44]

Things, however, were on the threshold of change. By 1890, the Majaly harboured fears of an Ottoman advance on Kerak.[45]

Having established their authority in the Balqa' a generation earlier, the Ottomans renewed efforts to impose direct rule over central and southern Transjordan. The initial plan was to turn Ma'an, a town on the *hajj* route southeast of Wadi Musa, into the centre of regional authority, but local events saw focus settle instead on Kerak. When hostilities broke out between the Majaly and the Banu Sakhr, both, as nominal Ottoman subjects, appealed to imperial authorities for assistance. This pretext for intervention persuaded the Ottomans to alter their plans. Compared to Ma'an, Kerak supported a much larger urban population and its leading figures had closer economic and political ties to southern Palestine and even Damascus. A military force was duly sent to Kerak in October 1893. After a brief show of resistance by locals, the Ottoman forces, accompanied by administrative figures, were welcomed into the town.[46]

To the south, Montreal was subsequently occupied and garrisoned as well. Violence broke out there in May 1895, only a few months before Hornstein's visit. This allegedly began when Turkish soldiers told a local woman to draw water for their horses, which caused objections from the men of the town. The soldiers were subsequently chased out, leading a small Ottoman force to bombard the town from the opposite hill with two field guns. Small skirmishes with the local Bedouin ensued over the following days. Eventually the Ottomans retook control of Montreal and another garrison was billeted in the castle.[47]

Kerak's occupation by Ottoman forces in 1893 saw the introduction of administrative reforms across Transjordan. The town became the seat of power of a *mutasarrif*, whose authority encompassed the Balqa' to the north down to the region around Ma'an in the south. This figure answered to the *wali* of Syria, who was based in Damascus. The first *mutasarrif* of Transjordan was Hussein Bey Effendi, but he had been succeeded by Rashid Pasha by the time Gautier made the latter's acquaintance in March 1899. Although power had shifted in Kerak, local politics continued. In the interest of preserving peace, and ensuring caravan routes remained open and unhindered, prominent local figures received a small stipend from the *mutasarrif*. Despite this aspect of continuity, the town began to change under direct Ottoman rule. A prominent government building was erected in front of the castle, and construction efforts extended to the establishment of a post office, telegraph station, and military hospital. A new Turkish school was also built using stone harvested from one of the town's Mamluk towers. The introduction of Turkish officials, and a sizable garrison, probably contributed to a slight rise in trade activity, and merchants from Damascus are reported to have visited twice a year.[48]

For visiting Westerners, direct Ottoman rule brought a more familiar environment – their letters of introduction from imperial officials carried much more authority, and institutional affiliations outweighed personal connections with tribal figures. Despite being shot at on their way, the Hills' second visit to Kerak in 1895 was considerably more pleasant than their experience five years earlier. Appreciative of the shift, Bliss reflected on how different his experience was compared to those who had passed through Kerak before him, highlighting the sums that had been extorted from de Saulcy, Tristram and others by the Majaly, a practice swiftly brought to an end with the imposition of Ottoman authority. At the time of Bliss's visit, the Majaly were camping near Qasr al-Rabba, north of Kerak. As he approached the town, Bliss was met by a young sheik of the Banu Sakhr, who turned out to be the son of the figure who had helped Tristram escape from under the thumb of the Majaly two decades earlier.[49]

Following their occupation of Kerak, the Ottomans slighted the town defences. Two gaps were opened in the eastern wall: one in the southeast, near the castle ditch, and another to the north, beyond the eastern gate. These had the effect of mitigating the strategic value of the town's two renowned tunnel entrances, which had fallen into disrepair by this time. The demolition was sufficient for Musil to report that a rider could comfortably enter the town on horseback in 1896, something that had not previously been possible, though all paths into the town remained somewhat cumbersome.[50]

With the arrival of the Ottomans, the castle regained a measure of military significance. Although the official government office was located in the town, just beyond the northern ditch, the military detachment assigned to Kerak was based in the castle. The garrison reportedly numbered 1,200 in 1896 (three regiments, each consisting of 400 soldiers), while estimates two years later placed it around 2,000 men, mostly infantry, along with a force of cavalry and two modern pieces of artillery. Testament to the declining importance and use of the castle during the preceding tribal period, it was necessary for the soldiers to clear out centuries' worth of debris. These units appear to have then bunked in the vaults below the lower ward. The castle had not been entirely uninhabited, as various stages of small houses were reported, though there was not the complete occupation of the castle by townspeople as was seen at Montreal. Musil reported that casemates, presumably those along the southern section of the eastern wall, were used as prison cells by the Ottoman garrison. At the very south end of the castle, he noticed that stones from the glacis were being robbed for building works elsewhere, threatening the integrity of the fortifications rising above. A few years later, Gautier observed ongoing repair efforts inside the castle.[51]

Human actions were certainly responsible for some of the damage sustained by the castle following the end of Mamluk rule, but so too were earthquakes. Tremors shook the region in 1546, 1834 and, most recently, in 1927; unfortunately, the impact of these earthquakes is hard to determine. The outward faces of the castle's northeastern tower had collapsed by the time it was photographed by Sauvaire in 1866, exposing what were once at least four levels.[52] Destruction on this scale was most likely caused by natural disasters.

End of Ottoman Rule

Although Western travellers benefitted from the greater stability and security provided by the Ottomans from 1893, Turkish policies were less popular with the local people of Kerak, who saw a rise in taxes and the imposition of certain restrictions. Following revolts elsewhere in the Near East, there was an uprising in Kerak in 1910. This was a response to a renewed push by Sami Pasha, the *wali* in Damascus, to bring the region under tighter control. Taxes were to be increased, breach-loading firearms confiscated, land registered and a census to be conducted to facilitate conscription efforts. Despite the arrival of more soldiers to help carry out these reforms, the sheiks of Kerak, whose stipends had been reduced ten years earlier, resolved to revolt. Like the trouble that resulted in the brief siege of Montreal in 1895, the Ottoman garrison was initially overrun, but the uprising was quickly suppressed with the arrival of reinforcements, ahead of whom resistance quickly melted away. A punitive tax was imposed in the aftermath of the revolt, but this was reduced the following year and cancelled the year after that. Although the uprising had cost the lives of a number of locals, their resistance helped ensure Ottoman conscription was never introduced in the region before the empire collapsed. In the bigger picture, this slowed the integration of Kerak into the growing socio-economic sphere of the Near East.[53]

Meanwhile, the breakdown of sedentary communities or shift towards a more semi-nomadic lifestyle from about the fifteenth century was being reversed; the nineteenth century saw a shift back towards settled agriculture. By 1939, before the widespread mechanization of farming practices in the region, Jordanian farmers were producing large quantities of cereal grains, almost all of which was wheat or barley, and close to half of which was a surplus. Much of this was sold to the Bedouin, who would purchase their stores in the summer; others sold to merchants west of the Dead Sea. Until the introduction of trucks and more reliable roads in the mid-1920s, tribal contractors were relied upon to transport this grain to Palestine using pack animals.[54]

Kerak saw little direct involvement in the First World War and the Arab Revolt. Some locals joined the Ottoman army, while others were paid to conduct irregular operations against Bedouin who supported the Arab resistance. With the collapse of the Ottoman Empire, Kerak, as a regional administrative centre and one of the largest towns in Transjordan, was drawn into the political discussions that followed. In 1918, Faisal, the son of the Sharif of Mecca, Hussein ibn 'Ali, took control of Damascus following its capture from the Ottomans, claiming authority over Syria in the name of the Arabs. While debates carried on in Damascus, Kerak returned to a period of tribal rule, which continued following the French initiative to assert control over Syria and push Faisal from power in 1920. Kerak next found itself a part of the British-backed Emirate of Transjordan, led by Abdullah ibn Hussein, Faisal's older brother. It was a number of years before effective centralized authority was reimposed in Kerak, though by the time Deschamps visited in 1929 he observed that the local police force, led by English officers, provided all latitude to travellers who arrived to visit the castle. Not until after the Second World War did most people living in and around Kerak identify with the broader region of Transjordan, but as tribal leaders who maintained positions of authority were drawn into national politics, so too were these brought to the local level. The Majaly, who cultivated a relationship with Abdullah, retained their position of paramount influence in Kerak, while their traditional rivals naturally tended to offer their support to the opponents of Abdullah.[55]

The end of direct British influence in Transjordan from 1946 had little real impact in Kerak. Far more significant were the demographic shifts that followed the Second World War, which were felt throughout Jordan. The pressures and reforms that accompanied the large wave of Palestinian immigration in 1948, a result of the Arab-Israeli War, and the death of Abdullah in 1951 in many ways marked the end of the traditional tribal government. As emir and then king from 1946, Abdullah had been a figure with whom tribal leaders could identify. The recent demographic shift, the ultimate succession of Hussein, Abdullah's son, in 1952, and broader globalization trends ushered in processes of modernization, or Westernization, that extended to Kerak. Perhaps the most obvious result was a surge of investment in infrastructure and various other construction projects, which radically changed the appearance of Kerak. By the 1960s, the town would have been almost unrecognizable to those who knew it a generation or two earlier. Administrative and social reforms would continue over the following decades. Politically, Kerak has continued to act as a local centre of power, serving as the centre of one of Jordan's *muhafatha* (regional governates).

Further demographic shifts accompanied the Six-Day War of 1967, Lebanese conflicts in the 1970s and 1980s, the Iraqi invasion of Kuwait in 1990 and subsequent Gulf War. The Iraq War from 2003 brought as many as a million displaced refugees to Jordan, a figure eclipsed a decade later by the migration of millions of Syrian refugees from 2011.[56] Meanwhile, Kerak has been impacted by the broader forces of globalization and trends in technological advancement like many other towns of comparable size throughout the Levant. In the face of all these changes, the great castle has continued to dominate the town. Ever evolving in response to local demands, it has taken on a new role, retaining its importance and contributing to the success of the surrounding community in a new way.

Once the seat of power of great crusader lords, Ayyubid princes, occasionally Mamluk sultans, and Arab sheiks, the castle has little political or military value in the modern world. The stronghold's new significance, the origins of which can be traced back to the Western travellers of the nineteenth century, is tourism. Starting in the late twentieth century, tourism has emerged as one of the leading sectors of the Jordanian economy, and today Kerak is one of the many marvels that draw millions of visitors to Jordan from around the world each year.

Chapter 6

The Castle

The castle, partly cut out of, and partly built upon, the mountain-top, presents the remains of a magnificent structure; its citadel cut off from the town by a ditch-ravine. It seems to be Saracenic, although in various parts it has both the pointed Gothic and the rounded Roman arch. A steep glacis-wall skirts the whole. The walls, now partly standing, are composed of heavy, well-cut stones; and there were seven arched store-houses, one above the other, with narrow slits for defence. The part used as the chapel was evidently built in the times of the crusades; and the east end, where the altar stood, was least demolished. [...] From the narrow embrasures of the vaulted chambers we looked down into the ravine, green with fields of grain and grass, and the shrubbery of oleanders, and upon part of the sea in the distance.[1]

W.F. Lynch (visited 1848)

As it stands today, Kerak is a conglomerate of Frankish, Ayyubid and Mamluk masonry, with evidence of Ottoman repair work and more recent restoration efforts. The castle's development is attested in the historical sources, but rarely is it clearly stated when certain parts of the castle were constructed or who was responsible for building which components. There is also limited epigraphic evidence – the imposing inscription striped across the outside of the southern tower is a unique example of a ruler taking credit for the construction of one of the castle's features. In the absence of such specific evidence, it is necessary to examine the various architectural elements and the sequence of building phases observable in the various walls, towers and internal structures of the castle. Some rebuilding work was carried out to strengthen the castle, other construction efforts were probably responses to natural disasters, such as earthquakes, while some projects were undertaken simply to add to the grandeur of the mighty fortress, to make it a more opulent and comfortable place to live, and further awe visitors.

Kerak is one of the largest and best preserved castles in the Levant. It is an imposing structure, more than 200m long, north–south; at the south end, it is about 50m wide, east–west, and more than twice this at the northern end. The eastern portion forms an upper ward, with a lower bailey to the west.[2] Despite the castle's impressiveness and historical importance, no detailed comprehensive archaeological or architectural study has yet been carried out.

The first and still most detailed modern investigation was conducted by Paul Deschamps in 1929, the results of which were published ten years later. In the early 1990s, Denys Pringle, the eminent archaeologist of Frankish Palestine, noted how little detailed study Kerak had received since. Robin Brown's dig in the palace complex, which was carried out over the course of a week in 1987, remains the only archaeological excavation in the castle to date. Brown's efforts focused on a small area inside the southern palatial structure, with the aim of dating the complex. Around the end of the twentieth century, Marcus Milwright examined the pottery that had been collected in and around the castle over the years, though all of this, except the small quantity unearthed by Brown, was found outside a stratigraphic context.[3]

A closer examination of some of the architectural elements was carried out by Thomas Biller, Daniel Burger and Hans-Heinrich Häffner around the same time, and Micaela Sinibaldi has since added further interpretations. Most recently, Lorenzo Fragai has examined the standing Mamluk palatial elements in detail.[4] Although each study has had its limits, as does any, collectively they have helped emphasize how much more the castle has to share. The great problem is that the same factors that make the castle so impressive also create considerable challenges for archaeologists. Beyond being one of the largest medieval structures in the southern Levant, much of the castle remains buried, presenting enormous logistical and funding challenges, as well as equally daunting responsibilities to ensure standing architecture and finds are properly studied, conserved and made available to the academic community and interested members of the public.

Early Interpretations

The grandeur of Kerak has attracted the interest of visitors for centuries, leading to a range of interpretations concerning its various elements and their origins. In 1806, Seetzen hypothesized that the castle was Byzantine, noting the church and the remains of paintings found within. Following his visit in 1812, Burckhardt suggested that the stronghold probably came into being under Islamic rule in the aftermath of the First Crusade, prior to its occupation and development by the Franks. Irby and Mangles similarly concluded that much of the castle predated the chapel, while Lynch, who also judged much of the fortified complex to be of Muslim construction, saw certain Roman influences. More assertively, Tristram noticed indications of Roman occupation and suggested the revetment of the castle's glacis might date to at least the Herodian era (around the year 0). Bliss, who visited while Kerak hosted an Ottoman garrison, similarly believed that much of the stronghold predated Frankish occupation, attributing the rough masonry to this earlier period and the finer limestone work, including the entire lower bailey, to the Franks.[5] From Deschamps onwards, however, scholars have associated the rougher masonry, consisting of stone quarried on site, with Frankish construction phases; the finer limestone, quarried from nearby seams, was employed by later Muslim masons. This general identification is in part made easy by comparing the masonry used to construct the chapel, a clearly Christian element, with the masonry of the great southern tower, which displays a prominent Arabic inscription dating to the Mamluk period.[6]

As a number of early Western visitors observed, *spolia* can be found incorporated into the walls of the castle.[7] Among the more decorative examples that were reused are a relief sculpture, an ornate column capital, and some rosettes. There are also indications that the Franks may have made use of building stones that had once belonged to earlier structures on the site. Some of the oldest Frankish masonry displays a mixture of stones, all of a relatively small size, and although all appear to have been harvested on site, the varying colour and consistency may suggest that they were initially sourced and employed in different places around what became the castle complex.[8] Later Frankish building phases tend to display a more consistent type of stone and often longer blocks, possibly indicating that the stone was newly quarried as part of these construction efforts.

It is relatively easy to distinguish the masonry of the earliest Frankish building phases from Muslim work a century later. The former is evident in the earliest stages of the castle's construction, including the chapel, a building of clearly Frankish provenance. The latter is generally finer, exemplified in the work dating to the early Mamluk period, which includes the great southern tower. Whereas the Franks appear to have used stone found on site, much of it probably excavated from the northern ditch, the finest Mamluk work consists of limestone sourced from a nearby vein. It may be that this change in building material marks the shift from Frankish to Muslim rule; however, it is not yet possible to rule out with certainty that some of the early Ayyubid work resembles that of the Franks, before a preference was shown for the finer limestone. This transition in building materials had taken place by 1227, as evidenced by the outer entrance to the town's western tunnel, and the dated inscription above, which seems to provide a clear *terminus ante quem*.[9]

Eastern Front

Kerak is perhaps most impressive when viewed in profile from the east, with the great glacis sloping down from the wall of the castle at the top of the ridge. The earliest eastern wall, however, originally ran less than 10m behind the present curtain. This is revealed by a number of embrasures, or arrow slits, that once pierced this line of walls. One of these embrasures can be found in the apse of the chapel and another in the eastern wall of the adjoining sacristy. To the south, another embrasure is discernable in the eastern wall of the long vaulted hall, which has come to be known as the hall of rosettes, and one more can be seen in a structure that appears to have been used as a mosque at a later date. The embrasures were blocked around the time the present eastern curtain was constructed, rendering the slits in the now interior walls redundant.

This phasing, identified by Deschamps, was emphasized in a review by Brooker and Knauf, who drew attention to the reused materials visible in this earliest phase of construction. Biller, Burger and Häffner have concluded that this line of walls predates the arrival of the Franks, due to the presence of the pre-Frankish decorative elements, which they judge to be early Islamic, rather than Byzantine, as Deschamps proposed.[10] The earlier suggestion advanced by Brooker and Knauf, however, that this is instead *spolia*, has yet to be disproven, and has merit when considering that these decorative elements, which would have appeared on the outer face of the original wall or structure, would not have been clearly discernable from the base of the slope outside the castle.

The present outer eastern wall and its three mural towers were built at some later point in time. The towers are rectangular and are set longitudinally to the line of the wall, with eastern (external) faces 10–15m wide. The walls of the towers and sections of curtain connecting them vary in thickness from about 1.5m to 2m.

The southernmost of the three eastern mural towers stands immediately east of the earlier tower-turned-mosque. Embrasures visible from the outside suggest that the tower contains two internal levels. The lower storey, which is inaccessible at the moment, displays two east-facing embrasures, while the level above has a single opening in the eastern wall. Above, at the current ground level, nothing more has survived. The neighbouring curtain wall, which extends to the north, has similarly not survived above the level of the modern pathway. Below this, the wall is pierced by six embrasures, each accessed by a casemate stretching back from the outer wall. These casemates were apparently being used as Ottoman prison cells when Musil viewed them in the mid-1890s.[11] Between the casemates and the hall of rosettes to the west, a vaulted corridor was created facilitating movement north–south in this area of the castle, and providing access to the southern mural tower.

To the north, the central mural tower of the castle's eastern front is due east of the chapel. Its lowest level is divided into a northern and southern casemate, with a doorway between them. Each of the two rooms was provided with two embrasures: one in the eastern wall and another in the other exterior wall. The curtain stretching northward from the central tower has been largely altered and rebuilt. The northern mural tower appears to be solid at the first level; the second consists of a single room with two discernable openings in each external wall.

Beyond the northern tower, two levels of vaults run along the northernmost stretch of the eastern curtain, with embrasures piercing the outer wall at each level. At the northeast corner of the castle stands another tower. It contains three internal levels, each covered by a barrel vault aligned north–south. The outer eastern wall and part of that to the north have collapsed, exposing the interior of the tower. Deschamps attributed this destruction to an earthquake that shook the region in 1927, two years before his visit, though a photograph taken by Mauss reveals that the exterior of the tower had collapsed at least six decades earlier. A few courses of what appear to be Mamluk, or at least post-Frankish, fine limestone masonry still crown the southwestern corner, the tallest surviving part of the tower.[12]

From the time of Deschamps onwards, the outer line of eastern defences has been attributed to the Franks. This judgement is based on the masonry style, which is similar to, yet distinct from, the earliest Frankish work. Like the masonry of the chapel, the advanced line of defences makes use of the hard bedrock of the castle plateau, though the blocks appear purpose-cut, rather than reused. The simple plans of the towers provide few indications of who commissioned them; however, when considering what appear to be later efforts to refortify the northern end of the castle, using the same local stone, it seems safe to date these defences to the Frankish period of occupation.

One of the most dramatic features of the castle is the great glacis. Masonry revetment covered the slope from the bases of the eastern and southern walls down to the valley below. This would have served to make the slope harder to climb, keeping attackers away from the walls while disguising the natural bedrock. Although the most obvious parallels for such work are at sites fortified under Muslim rule, such as the citadels of Aleppo and Homs, the work has traditionally been attributed, with few questions or explanations, to the Franks. Much of the glacis, including the entire northern half of the eastern section, was rebuilt in the twentieth century.[13]

Northern Front

The northern side of the castle faces the town, making it the most approachable front to any attacker who is able to overcome the town defences. To secure this front, a ditch was cut across the bedrock of the plateau. The excavation of this great trench probably provided much of the purpose-cut stone used to build many of the Frankish components of the castle. According to Ibn al-Athir, writing in the early thirteenth century, the ditch was 60 cubits (about 30m) deep. Ibn Shaddad would repeat this figure a couple of generations later, in the late thirteenth century, and Abu'l-Fida', another generation on, noted that the floor of the fosse was almost 50 cubits (about 25m) below the bridge that spanned it.[14] The ditch is roughly 20–25m wide and currently contains centuries of build-up and debris, leaving its true depth unclear. This, along with the wall behind it, was what stopped Saladin in 1183 and 1184.

The castle's outer northern wall, which rises from the scarp of the ditch, is slightly more than 20m high and about 4m thick. A projection is to be found at each end of the wall, creating the impression of shallow towers. The western salient, which has been largely destroyed, displays evidence of rebuilding under Islamic rule. The eastern salient presents an outward face of about 25m. In its western flank, and slightly recessed, is a small gate, about 2m wide. Two small openings can also be seen along the base of the wall between the two projections. The northern wall and its eastern salient are faced with what appear to be elongated regular blocks with rough faces. Deschamps described the wall as having been built using unfaced blocks, though Sinibaldi, like Bliss before her, has astutely noticed that most are rather ashlars with narrow, deeply recessed margins and unfinished bosses.[15] Despite the rugged appearance of the wall, the stones form even courses, though the height of these varies course to course.

Two long barrel vaults, one on top of the other, run behind the stout northern wall. Both are about 6m wide internally and display the remains of transverse arches in places. The bedrock was evidently cut away in places to provide a flat surface during the construction of the lower storey, as parts of the rear (southern) wall can be seen to rise directly from exposed bedrock, which forms the lowest portion of the wall in certain areas. A number of embrasures through the northern wall are accessible at each level, and additional arrow slits were provided in the projections at either end. A staircase in the thickness of the northern wall connected the upper and lower levels. The vaults are currently about 70m long; each once connected to structures on either end. The terrace above the upper vault would have provided a broad fighting platform stretching back from the parapet. Due in part to the slope of the ground, the towers, or structures, at either end of the northern wall supported three internal levels, as well as an open fighting platform above. To the south, additional buildings abut the lower vault. Many of these remain below the current ground level, allowing visitors to walk out on top of them from any of the three openings in the southern wall of the upper vault.[16]

The masonry of the northern wall and its two salients is fairly similar. Despite this, a number of different construction phases are evident. The original eastern wall of the castle appears to have terminated with a tower, which incorporates an earlier, possibly Nabataean, bas relief sculpture. This tower was subsequently enhanced with the construction of the broader eastern salient in a later building phase. Less of the western salient has been preserved, and parts of what still stand were heavily restored in the second half of the twentieth century; however, photographs taken before the First World War reveal that there had been a similar tower at this end of the wall until it was remodelled into the larger salient. This was not a mere matter of elongating these towers and presumably reinforcing the wall connecting them. As Sinibaldi has noted, the masonry style suggests these alterations were undertaken around the time that the eastern defences of the castle were redeveloped, but the outside of the northern wall also displays more than one building phase, indicating multiple efforts to rebuild or remodel the face of the wall opposite the town.[17]

A close look at the exterior masonry of the castle's northern front suggests that the two salients, as well as the easternmost portion of the northern wall between them, were part of the same building phase. Beginning a few metres west of the eastern salient, however, the courses of the northern wall are interrupted, and from this seam the courses become shorter and the outward faces of the stones are slightly more rugged, with fewer displaying marginal drafting. This appears to represent a different building phase, though whether this work was undertaken before, after or around the same time as that on either side is hard to determine at this time.

Arguments that this slightly different masonry represents an effort to repair damage inflicted during one of Saladin's sieges in the 1180s are unconvincing for a few reasons. First, the 'repair' work goes all the way down to the bedrock, and runs between two fairly clean seams. Given the threat that Saladin posed in the 1180s and the regularity of his attacks, it is inconceivable that the Franks would have so completely deconstructed the castle's most approachable defences in order to rebuild them afresh at such a time of heightened insecurity. A more expeditious method of patching a breach would be expected if indeed this was necessary. Second, it seems extremely unlikely that a section of the central northern wall would need to be rebuilt so completely, while no apparent damage was sustained by either of the neighbouring salients. Third, there is the means of how such a section of wall might have been destroyed to consider. Contemporary artillery technology was nowhere near powerful enough to damage such a wall to the point that it would require such drastic rebuilding. While sapping would have been a way to do this, the sources are quite clear that Saladin's miners were never able to access the wall of the castle.

The exposed bedrock all along the northern front also reveals that it had not been compromised, confirming the wall had not been brought down by sappers removing the stone below the wall. Looking beyond Saladin's siege activities, miners are not mentioned to have worked against the castle at any other siege prior to the end of the Mamluk period.[18]

Today, visitors to the castle cross a modern bridge over the northern ditch and enter the stronghold through a gateway built into the eastern side of a projection at the western end of the western salient. Scholars, from Deschamps onwards, have judged this western projection to be Muslim work, though some of the lower masonry is similar to that found elsewhere along the exterior faces of the castle's northern end. Beyond this, at the extreme western end of the northern front, are what appear to be the remains of a tower. Although included on Deschamps' plan, this northwestern tower has received little attention due to its poor state of preservation.

Main Gate

Due in no small part to the destruction of much of the northwestern corner of the castle, there has been a longstanding debate concerning the original location of the stronghold's main entrance. Historical records reveal that there was a significant entrance in the northern front of the castle, which could be accessed from the town via a bridge over the northern ditch. It was across this bridge that people fled into the castle when Saladin's forces broke into the town in 1183. William of Tyre, when lamenting that this bridge was knocked down by the fleeing defenders, calls this the only means of passage across the ditch. This appears to have been the same entrance used by al-Nasir Muhammad in March 1309, when he crossed the bridge over the fosse in a processional entrance into the castle. It seems the bridge was still temporary or removable, as it collapsed just as the sultan reached the gate on the far side. Thirty-five mamluks and a number of the town's inhabitants fell into the northern ditch on this occasion, though only one of the mamluks reportedly died. Due to the depth of the fosse, ropes and rigging were required to hoist out those who had fallen.[19]

Some accounts appear to misleadingly present one of the two tunnel entrances into the town as a gateway to the castle. Both Ibn Shaddad, in the late thirteenth century, and Ibn Battuta, in the early fourteenth century, describe gaining entrance by way of a long tunnel hewn from the rock. No indications of such a tunnel entrance have been found along the northern side of the castle, or anywhere else around its trace. Although Ibn Battuta, who visited Kerak while heading for Mecca in September 1326, claimed the fortress had only one entrance, presumably referring to the eastern entrance to the town, it is quite likely that he simply failed to notice the western entrance on the opposite side of the town. Centuries later, Layard similarly described entering the castle via a vaulted passage cut into the rock, though his description clearly confirms that this was the western tunnel into the town, rather than a gateway belonging to the castle proper.[20]

The main entrance to the castle was in its present location, at the northwest corner of the tower, by the time Europeans began arriving at Kerak in the nineteenth century. There was apparently no need for a bridge by 1896, as Musil observed that the western end of the ditch had been filled, providing a causeway between the castle and the town.[21] One of the most detailed descriptions from the nineteenth century was provided by Rey, who relied on the earlier notes made by Mauss. He placed the main gate in its current location, noting that it was once secured by a portcullis and leaf doors, ahead of another two gateways, each with a portcullis, before access was given to the upper ward of the castle. Above this passage, presumably aligned perpendicular to it, were the vaults running along the northern exterior wall.[22] This is quite the elaborate entranceway, and may have been influenced by the accounts of Ibn Shaddad and Ibn Battuta, though it is worth emphasizing that Rey did not himself visit the castle. It is not inconceivable that evidence of portcullises may have been noted by Mauss; although the portcullis is associated primarily with Frankish fortifications, there are some readily apparent Mamluk examples, such as those at Subayba.

In his influential history of medieval warfare, Oman provided his own interpretation of Rey's remarks, and thus a third-hand description of what he believed the original entrance to the castle looked like. Oman associated the entrance passage noted by Rey with the long vaulted ranges backing the castle's northern wall. Because he interpreted, quite mistakenly, the southern wall of these vaulted ranges to be another line of defences, he argued the castle's Frankish designers, by employing more than one line of walls, had been influenced by what he believed were superior Eastern fortification principles.[23]

Since Deschamps published his study in 1939, the original main entrance has instead been associated with the small gate in the western flank of the eastern salient. This, in no small part, is because it is the only medieval gateway of any size still surviving along the northern front of the castle.[24] The small size of the opening, however, has been disconcerting to some, leading to a theory that its scale is a reflection of the confidence that the Franks placed in the town's defences. Observing that the gate was too small to ride through, Mayer has proposed that the castle's Frankish defenders left their horses in the town, implying they had considerable faith in their animals' safety there. Sinibaldi has similarly suggested that the gate's simple design and small size may indicate that the Franks placed considerable faith in the defensibility of the town.[25]

From a military perspective, there are issues with both interpretations. Regarding the former, the Frankish military elite was fundamentally a body of mounted warriors. Even if the inhabitants of the town were a fairly trusted community of local Christians, it is inconceivable that the Frankish garrison would have left their horses, the most expensive part of any knight's military equipment and one essential to their social status and fighting style, outside a castle as large as Kerak, regardless of the perceived defensibility of the town. It is also noteworthy that Saladin's men found livestock in the castle ditch, which the Franks had driven there during the siege of 1183, but no mention is made of horses. Furthermore, stone mangers can still be found inside the castle – the garrison's costly warhorses would have been the first animals brought within the stronghold. If the small gate in the eastern salient was indeed the castle's main entrance during the Frankish period, it seems reasonable to suggest that riders simply dismounted as they approached. Turning to the latter, rather than a weakness, a small gate was a strength when evaluated in terms of defensibility. Accommodating fleeing townspeople, as became an issue in 1183, would not have been a leading consideration in the minds of the castle's designers; quite the opposite, a small gateway would deliberately restrict the rate at which a large group of people could enter the castle, helping ensure that a retreat did not turn into a route. The outer Frankish gates of 'Atlit, built in the early thirteenth century, are similarly small and likewise placed in the flanks of towers, as are the gates of the outer bailey of Subayba and numerous examples elsewhere.[26]

Biller, Burger and Häffner have put forward a different theory, suggesting that the main Frankish gate was instead along the western side of the upper ward, close to the north end of the castle.[27] This is based primarily on conjecture, and no physical evidence has yet been found of an outer gate in this section of the castle. When considering the circumstantial evidence, however, it seems quite possible, if not likely, that the main entrance was somewhere around the western end of the northern front from at least the start of the fourteenth century. If al-Nasir Muhammad was able to ride into the castle, he was not entering by the small northeastern gateway; yet if a bridge collapsed behind him, he was clearly crossing the northern ditch. The degree to which the northwestern corner of the castle has been destroyed may indicate that it was targeted by the Ottomans during their efforts to slight the stronghold. If so, the extent of the damage might be justified if this is where the main entrance to the castle had been. Moving further into the realm of speculation, if there was an entrance in this part of the castle in 1309, it is quite possible that there was one in the same place during the Frankish period. While it might be worth reiterating that no archaeological evidence has yet been found to indicate the presence of a Frankish entrance in this part of the castle, so too is it worth highlighting the clear preference shown by medieval castle builders to develop existing gateways rather than move them.

Complicating the matter of locating the Frankish main entrance to the castle is the presence of a barbican by 1152. The existence of such is revealed in a charter issued to the Hospitallers, which granted the order a certain tower to the left of someone entering the castle, and the space (the barbican) extending up to a certain 'tower of St Mary'.[28] In the Frankish Near East, a 'barbican' was an outer wall, or more exactly the space between the main wall and an outer wall, rather than a confined entryway with multiple gates and a 'kill zone' in between. Those who suggest the main gate was at the eastern end of the northern front are forced to fit this into the existing architecture. Mayer, for example, has proposed that the so-called tower of St Mary may be the eastern mural tower just beyond the apse of the castle chapel.[29] It is possible that a space was initially left between the original eastern wall and the line built slightly beyond it, before this was covered in a subsequent building phase. Alternatively, if the main gate was always at the western end of the northern front, or even near the north end of the western wall, as suggested by Biller and his colleagues, the tower given to the Hospitallers would appear to have been the original northwest tower of the castle. In this scenario, the gateway must have been located to the west of the tower, placing it on the left of someone approaching the castle from the town, while what was once the Frankish barbican beyond has been completely obscured.

It is perhaps easiest to imagine the barbican on the western side of the castle because less has survived in this area, allowing for endless possibilities of what may once have stood there. Likewise, it is unclear what the lower ward of the castle may have looked like before it was completely rebuilt (or simply built) following the end of the Frankish period. It still remains to identify the tower of St Mary, which Pringle once proposed may even have been the Frankish predecessor of the great Mamluk tower at the very south end of the castle.[30] Another candidate might be the shallow tower projecting from about the middle of the upper western wall, which is roughly opposite the west end of the chapel and its main entrance.

Western Front (Upper)

The wall running along the western side of the upper ward of the castle appears to date to the original Frankish fortification effort. The wall is about 2m thick and the masonry consists of somewhat smaller stones than the longer ones used when the eastern defences were advanced. The nature of the masonry led Deschamps to conclude that the wall had been destroyed during a siege and rebuilt, though which siege he had in mind is a mystery.[31] A number of small salients, resembling buttresses, project from the outward face of the wall. The stones used for the corners of these display marginal drafting.

West of the chapel, below a section of missing curtain wall, a talus rising up the slope from the lower ward of the castle may have formed the base of a lone Frankish tower along this front. A later tower, built of limestone and presumably of Muslim provenance, was added against the north side of this earlier tower, projecting slightly further. On the outward (western) side of this addition, the remains of six corbels are visible near the top of the tower. These are the remains of a box machicolation – the ends of the corbels would have supported a slight protrusion from the face of the wall, while the spaces between the corbels would have been left open, allowing defenders to shoot or drop things down on anyone at the base of the tower. The northern side of the entrance to this, as well as the springer and first few voussoirs, are still in place, while the southern side, now missing, was captured in one of Tristram's images.[32] Directly below each corbel, four courses lower, is what appears to be a putlog hole. To the south of this central western tower, a smaller tower of limestone construction was also added, further strengthening this front of the upper ward.

Although the original western wall appears to have been built by the Franks, there is evidence of rebuilding under Muslim rule. A significant portion of the northern stretch of the western curtain is clearly of Muslim construction. The original wall was levelled, five to seven courses above the sloping bedrock, and rebuilt anew. Twenty-one to twenty-six courses of this new wall remain, displaying two levels of embrasures, arranged in vertical alignment. What stood above is unknown. Between this rebuilt northern section of the western curtain and the central tower, a staircase has taken shape between the upper and lower wards. The present stairs facilitate the circulation of tourists around the castle; however, a path and stairs could be found here since at least the nineteenth century. It is quite likely that there was some sort of connection between the upper and lower wards in this area from at least the Mamluk period, though what it originally looked like, and whether it was encased in some sort of tower, is hard to discern at this time.

South Front

Occupying a narrowing tongue of land that extends south from the plateau of the town, the shape of the castle was dictated by the local topography. South of the castle, the ground falls away as it continues to narrow, before rising and spreading outwards. A large ditch, about 30m wide, was dug across the narrow neck of this depression to further isolate the stronghold from the rise beyond. A path of natural rock was preserved along the eastern side of the ditch, while a similar rock bridge may initially have been left on the western side, though this had been replaced with a masonry wall by the late nineteenth century.[33] The obstructions at either end have led to suggestions that this might have served as an open pool, filled each year by the winter rains. Whatever the case, they would have provided paths across the ditch and served to restrict movement around the southern end of the castle.

North of the ditch is a large enclosure, traditionally identified as an open-air reservoir or *berquil*. This is more than 50m long, east–west, with a vaulted entranceway along the western side. It may have provided a source of usable non-drinking water, as well as an obstacle to anyone attempting to attack the castle from the south. The enclosure boasts thick walls, which were crowned with a parapet, and corbels once protruded about eight to twelve courses above the bedrock, from which box machicolations would have risen. Deschamps judged the reservoir to be of Frankish construction; however, machicolations of this style, which can be found in later Ayyubid, Mamluk and even Frankish masonry, have all been dated to the thirteenth century, suggesting these almost certainly belong to a Muslim building phase.[34] The corbels can be seen in the photographs taken by Sauvaire, but had been robbed by the time of Musil's visit three decades later in 1895.

From the north side of the reservoir, the southern portion of the glacis rises to the castle plateau above, though much of the revetment was rebuilt in the twentieth century. The glacis terminates at what has often been identified as the Mamluk 'donjon'.[35] Foundations, which can be seen slightly ahead of the base of this monumental facade and connect to the south end of the western curtain wall, indicate that there once stood an earlier Frankish structure here. Projecting from the southeast corner, the base of what was once a tower of some description still stands out awkwardly from the grand structure behind. The masonry of this small southeastern tower displayed multiple building phases, though heavy 'restoration' saw it effectively rebuilt in the early years of the twenty-first century.

A large, roughly trapezoidal tower, the Mamluk 'donjon', crowns the castle's southern defences. The exterior of the tower's broad southern face measures

25m across. At either end, another face extends back at an obtuse angle, the southwest face for 11m and the southeast face for 17m. The rear (northern side) of the tower measures 36m east to west. The southern section of the eastern curtain appears to have been rebuilt at the time of the tower's construction, allowing it to join the tower seamlessly. On the other side, there does not seem to have been a similar effort to join the western side of the tower to the southern end of the western curtain.

The great southern tower consists of three internal levels. The lowest may be solid, as it reveals no openings along its exposed exterior fronts; its northern face, however, remains below ground level, leaving it possible, if unlikely, that an entrance to an open basement may yet be found. The second level is accessed by a doorway near the eastern end of the northern wall. Within, four embrasures, extending from casemates, two to the south and one each to the southwest and southeast, pierce the walls, which are up to 6.5m thick. These surround a grand two-storey open space. The northern and southern walls, which display the same bossed masonry as the exterior faces of the tower, rise to the height of a single level and support a pointed barrel vault, running east–west, that reaches up through the third level. The considerable thickness of the tower's external walls is reduced at the third level, allowing for ledges along the southwest and southeast sides, which provide access to two slots through each of the tower's angular faces. A narrow corridor also runs behind the southern side of the vaulting that spans the tower's main room, offering access to three more south-facing embrasures at the third level. Outside the tower, a small external staircase, just east of the main doorway, leads to another ledge that runs along the northern face of the tower at the third level. This passes five blind arches inserted into the thickness of the tower's northern wall; the westernmost of these contains a door that leads to the internal ledge at this level and the southern corridor behind the vaulting of the main room.

On top of the tower is a terrace, the fourth level, around which runs a double-level parapet. The thick lower level of wall is pierced by casemates servicing embrasures: three to the southeast; four to the south; and two to the southwest, though one of these has almost disappeared. Above, the breadth provided by the casemates created a wall walk that ran behind a crenellated parapet. Although these topmost battlements have all but vanished, the remains of five broad merlons, each pierced by an embrasure, can still be discerned along the southern side. The tower thus offers an increasing number of embrasures at each level, and these were arranged in a manner so that no two are in direct vertical alignment.[36]

Wrapping around the three southward exterior faces of the tower, between the second and third rows of embrasures, is a long inscription, carved into two otherwise smooth courses of masonry. Although hard to read, it looks to attribute credit for the tower's construction to Baybars.[37] The tower bears unmistakable similarities to that built at the northwest end of the town, Burj al-Zahir, which displays a similar inscription to Baybars. The masonry of the tower is fairly uniform, though seams and slight differences reveal that it is the product of a number of building phases; this does not, however, rule out the possibility that these were part of the same construction initiative. For example, the exterior face of the northern wall was built with ashlars featuring shallow bosses at the second level, but smooth masonry above at the third level. When considering that the type of stone appears to be the same, as are the size of the blocks, this might be explained as simply a preference for two different aesthetic styles. When viewed from the west, however, it becomes apparent that the second level of the wall was built first, as the western end of this wall was left unbonded to the remainder of the tower that was built around it. It is the northern edge of this earlier wall that provides the external walkway in front of the five blind arches. Contrary to the suggestion of Biller, Burger and Häffner, who propose this wall was built by the Franks, the masonry style suggests that it was instead constructed under Muslim rule. This initial phase of the southern tower seems to rest on even earlier masonry, which makes up the first level of the northern wall. Although dating this lowest building phase is quite difficult, Fragai has proposed that at least some of it may date to the Ayyubid period.[38]

The great southern tower dominates the landscape and still awes any onlookers approaching the castle from the south. This would appear to have been one of the guiding motives behind the design of the tower, not unlike the one built at the northwest end of the town, which would have similarly impressed those approaching from the wadi to the west. It has occasionally been proposed that the tower was designed to shield the castle from artillery erected on the rise to the south, or even that the earlier Frankish tower built at this end of the castle had been destroyed by Saladin's trebuchets during one of the sieges of the early 1180s. Such suggestions, like those offered to explain evident refortification efforts at the north end of the castle, seem to misjudge the power of contemporary siege engines.[39]

Extending north from the eastern side of the great southern tower is a section of curtain wall that looks to have been built around the same time. The remains of this wall display five casemates with embrasures that align with the second level of the neighbouring tower. Above, corbels linked by shallow arches indicate the presence of a wall walk that could have been accessed from the terrace on the tower to the south. Three embrasures are discernable at this level, while another three, further north, pierce the wall at descending elevations. These more northern embrasures, however, can only be identified from outside the castle. Although both sides of the wall were constructed using very similar masonry, the exterior face of the wall was evidently built first; subsequent remodelling on the interior side, perhaps when the lower casemates were built back from the exterior of the wall, blocked these three descending embrasures.[40]

Interior Structures

Much of Kerak still lies underground. More accurately, the apparent ground level of the upper ward is artificial, the product of debris and fill building up over the years as the top parts of structures were torn down or collapsed, disguising much of the lowest storey. Below are a series of dark passageways and vaulted rooms, dimly lit by openings in the ceiling through the ground above. The chapel and southern palatial complex have drawn the most attention over the years, while most other areas still await close examination, and many are simply still inaccessible.

Chapel

In the centre of the castle stands a church, which was probably one of the earliest structures built on the site by the Franks. Internally, it measures 25m by about 8.5m. An arched doorway in the western wall provided access, and there was a rounded apse at the eastern end. There were reportedly once four narrow lancet windows, though only one of these survives, in the western portion of the southern wall, and it has been heavily restored. The north wall, the best preserved, shows no evidence of fenestration, leading Pringle to suggest that there may have been a second window in the now collapsed eastern portion of the southern wall, as is found on Mauss's plan. To these can be added the embrasure in the apse and another in the sacristy adjoining the chapel to the north. Only the western half of the barrel vault that once covered the space stands today, though the remains of a central transverse arch can still be seen on the northern side. A number of columns were evidently found on or near the site, as these were incorporated into the walls of the chapel, their ends being visible in the rough courses of fairly small stones. In about the centre of the eastern side of the northern wall, a short staircase leads down into what was once a sacristy or side chapel. This is about 7.5m east–west and 5m north–south, covered by a pointed barrel vault aligned with the long axis of the structure. An embrasure, which was subsequently blocked, pierces the centre of the eastern wall. A small niche on the south side of the embrasure and a compartment nearby, built into the thickness of the northern wall closer

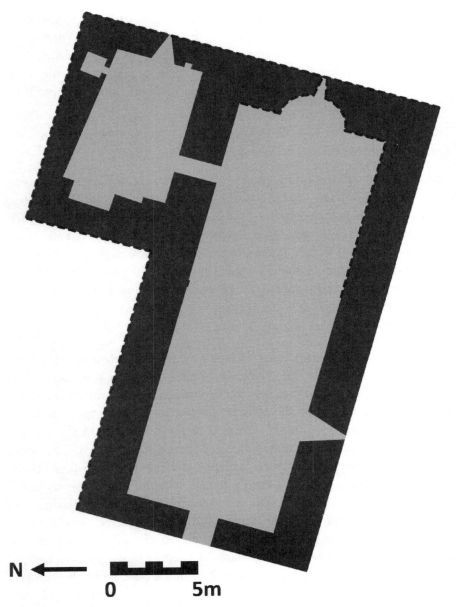

Fig. 4. Castle chapel (after Pringle).

to the floor, have been identified by Pringle as a credence niche and an aumbry respectively. A straight staircase, beginning to the west of the doorway, rises up the southern wall, before turning north and continuing to climb the western wall, over a pointed arch. This would have once continued through the vault, giving access to a now obscure upper level or some other lost structure.[41]

The interior of the chapel was originally covered in white plaster, which once displayed frescoes. Although the paintings are now lost, traces of the plaster can still be seen. When Burckhardt visited in the early nineteenth century, the images were already in a poor state of preservation and little was clearly distinguishable. Irby and Mangles confirmed that the paintings appear to have been of groups of men, proposing that one figure may have been a king wearing armour and another a martyr being disembowelled. Some Latin writing was still discernable at this time, though not enough to make out more than a few letters. Thirty years later, in 1848, Lynch observed what he believed to be a female saint painted on the ceiling. Another two decades on, Mauss and Sauvaire, followed by Tristram, could make out only a haloed head; the former claimed that Sheik Majaly had ordered the paintings destroyed, though this is uncorroborated.[42]

Southern Palace (Qa‘a)

The chapel roughly divides the upper ward of the castle into northern and southern halves. In the centre of the southern portion is a significant complex, which has long been characterized as a palace. Deschamps identified this as the residence of the Frankish lords of the castle; however, Brown's excavations have conclusively shown this complex postdates the period of Frankish occupation. She has instead identified this as a *qa‘a* – the principle hall of an Islamic palace during the Ayyubid and Mamluk periods. The central feature of a *qa‘a* was the open court, the *durqa‘a*, which was faced on each of its four sides by an *iwan*, a similarly sized room, or a smaller alcove, called a *suffa*. Among its various functions, this space often served as a formal reception area. Historical records suggest that Kerak had at least two palatial structures: one commissioned by al-Nasir Dawud and another dating to the reign of al-Nasir Muhammad.[43]

Much of this palatial structure is currently below the surrounding ground level. Visitors typically approach from the north, descending a modern staircase that leads to an entranceway, over which is mounted a now badly damaged inscription. The doorway is composed of finely shaped stones, with a tall lintel, above which sits the inscription. Behind the lintel is a pointed arch of finely shaped voussoirs. This entrance leads to a corridor that runs south along the northwest part of the palace complex. Two doorways are found on the eastern side of the passage: the northern of the two opens to a barrel-vaulted hall; the southern doorway, as well as another in the southern wall of the northern hall, provides access to a vestibule, from which a doorway to the south leads to the *qa‘a*.

The central *durqa‘a* is open to the sky; no traces of vaulting or any other type of ceiling have yet been identified. Vaulted *iwans* are to be found to the

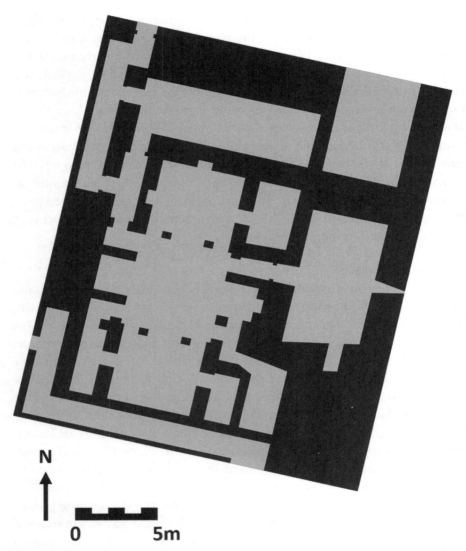

Fig. 5. Southern palace complex (after Brown).

north and south of the central court, each featuring a large central entrance and a smaller portal to either side, though these were at least partly filled at a later date. The north *iwan* contains a small alcove in the western wall, and another in the northern wall appears to have been filled. On either side of the central atrium is a *suffa*. These, unlike the *iwans*, are narrower than the *durqaʿa*, providing space on either side for a small doorway and passage. The northwestern passage leads to the entrance vestibule; the southwestern passage opens to a narrow room connected to the western side of the south *iwan*; the southeastern passage may have mirrored that of the southwest, though it also came to provide access to an exit passage to the southeast had this not been one of its original functions. Each of these three passages makes an initial 90-degree turn to the north or south, but the fourth, to the north of the eastern *suffa*, is straight. It leads to an earlier structure, against which the *qa'a* was built, which appears to have been turned into a mosque. The southern wall of this abutting structure is conspicuously out of alignment, perhaps to indicate the appropriate direction of prayer, and a large niche in the wall may have served as a *mihrab*. An embrasure, blocked from the outside, is a prominent feature in the eastern wall, indicating that this was once an exterior wall, quite likely of Frankish construction.

The *qa'a* is fairly symmetrical. Each face of the *durqa'a* displays three openings, while the northern and southern halves of the complex almost mirror each other. The northwest vestibule, west of the north *iwan*, is similar to the narrow rooms on either side of the south *iwan*, though the vestibule is not directly connected to the north *iwan*. Likewise, a doorway in the eastern wall of the north *iwan* leads to a room that is slightly larger than those on either side of the south *iwan*. Although the somewhat rough masonry of the *qa'a* is underwhelming, traces of plaster reveal that the walls would once have been coated and probably decorated. Excavations also revealed a plaster floor. Brown has proposed that the south *iwan* may have been where the primary dignitary sat, receiving guests who entered from the northwest. The north *iwan* could have been used for more domestic purposes, with the northeastern chamber perhaps functioning as a bedroom.[44]

Brown's excavations were carried out along the western side of the south *iwan* in 1987. Results initially led to the conclusion that the *qa'a* was commissioned during the Mamluk period; however, a subsequent re-examination of the finds has led the excavator to instead favour an Ayyubid genesis. Pottery confirms that the structure was in use during the Mamluk period, and fragments of fine imported table wares support the idea that luxurious meals were once served in this area. More generally, the material finds indicate that although the *qa'a* may have remained a place of social importance during the Ottoman period, the wealth and status of those who used the structure declined noticeably as Kerak's significance waned.[45]

Taking into consideration the limited excavation finds, and similar Ayyubid and Mamluk structures elsewhere, Brown has suggested that this may be the *Qa'a al-Nasiri* of al-Nasir Dawud. This preference for a thirteenth-century date of origin is in no small part due to the greater similarities between the structure's plan and those of similar Ayyubid rather than Mamluk parallels. The Ayyubid *qa'a* at Montreal, which was probably built a generation earlier, is proximately closest, though there are a number of similar examples elsewhere in greater Syria.[46]

Southern Pavilion Area

To the south of the southern palace, still mostly below the current ground level, is another complex or collection of buildings, most of which remain largely inaccessible. The main feature in this area is a quadrangular pavilion: a large groin-vaulted structure with four corner pillars, a wide open arch in each cardinal direction, and a square opening in the centre of the ceiling. The southern arch of the pavilion opens to a large vaulted alcove, on top of which was built the second level of the northern wall of the great southern Mamluk tower. East and west of this structure, there is evidence of walls belonging to other buildings. To the north, a number of vaulted rooms and halls are discernable, which probably connected in some way to the nearby southern palace.

Dating this early complex and its various components is difficult, in no small part due to their state of ruin. Fragai has suggested that the alcove to the south of the pavilion may be a vestige of the earliest Ayyubid palace complex, built by al-'Adil or al-Mu'azzam 'Isa. At the very least, it predates the castle's acquisition by Baybars. The abutting pavilion, Fragai proposes, was built by al-Nasir Muhammad, in the early fourteenth century, and that its construction involved the tearing down of neighbouring buildings to the east and west.[47]

Hall of Rosettes, Southeastern Gallery and Small Qa'a

Stretching north from what became the mosque of the southern palace is what is commonly called the hall of rosettes. The western wall is the original element, displaying large regular ashlar and the decorative rosettes that lend their name to this structure. A hall was created with the addition of a wall to the east and vaulting spanning the space in between. At the northern end is a doorway, the exterior portion of which is very finely fashioned and appears to date to a later building phase. To the east of the hall of rosettes, another vaulted passageway provides access to six casemates along the outer eastern wall, as well as the southernmost of the eastern mural towers. The masonry of this gallery, including the doorway at the northern end, is much more ragged.

Both the hall of Rosettes and the southeastern gallery terminate at what has been identified as another *qa'a*. This, however, is nowhere near the size of the main palace space to the south; instead, it is more a vestibule with two small *iwans*. Despite its limited scale, the masonry is very fine. The back wall of the north *iwan* features a decorative geometric engraving, and a similar artistic element may have adorned the centre of the south *iwan*, as there is conspicuous damage where it would have been. This southern wall of the south *iwan* rests on top of the outer arch of the northern doorway into the hall of rosettes. The floor of the *iwan* seems to have been removed, revealing a small staircase that descends, west to east, down to the entrance of the earlier hall. On the western side of the small *durqa'a*, a vertical line of decorative muqaranas has been carved into the masonry on either side of what appears to have been a doorway. Today, a staircase of later construction rises from the threshold of this doorway up to the west. This passes through masonry ruins that abut the elaborate vestibule, before reaching the current ground level above, just south of the chapel. Although it is hard to date the small *qa'a*, most attribute its construction to the Mamluk period.[48]

Opposite the western doorway of the small *qa'a* is a doorway to the east. This leads to a room that extends to the north, making it about twice the size of the *qa'a*. An opening in the southern wall of this room provides access to the north end of the southeastern gallery. The room's eastern wall is overgrown and hard to examine, though there is evidence of what was once vaulting. The topmost portion of this wall was rebuilt in the twentieth century to stabilize the neighbouring walkway above. The northern wall of the room corresponds with the eastern part of the chapel's southern wall, and displays the ends of a number of columns, similar to those found elsewhere in the walls of the chapel.

Vaulted Corridors

From the northern end of the room east of the small *qa'a*, a narrow passageway runs west, behind the rear wall of the north *iwan*. The northern wall of this corridor consists of bedrock and the lowest courses of the south wall of the Frankish chapel; on the southern side, a masonry wall supports a half-vault above. There were apparently structures accessible to the south of the corridor, but these are currently obstructed. As it continues to follow the bedrock, the passageway turns north around the southwestern corner of the chapel above. The northern portion beyond is considerably wider, and the ceiling becomes much higher just north of the chapel, from about the point where the corridor passes the central tower of the western front. Continuing northward, there is a slight bend to the west passing the rebuilt section of the upper western curtain, before the passageway returns to its original orientation, bringing it into alignment with the western end of the castle's north front, and any gateway that might once have been positioned there. This north–south part of the corridor probably served as a main artery along the western side of the upper ward. Access was provided to vaulted rooms on both sides, while its masonry is quite heavy and reveals different building phases, as well as modern repair work. At the place where the level of the ceiling rises, there is a staircase on the western side. This leads up to the current ground level and the place where the modern external path down to the lower western bailey begins.

To the east of the western passageway, the bedrock of the northern portion of the upper ward continues to rise. Running down the middle of this is another north–south corridor, at a higher elevation. This central area of the castle north of the chapel has not yet been studied – it does not appear on Deschamps' plan of the castle nor any since. The surviving section of this central corridor extends for roughly the middle third of the distance between the great vaults along the northern front of the castle and the chapel to the south. The masonry of this central passageway displays multiple phases, some of which are similar to that found around the southern pavilion. Like the passage to the west, this was a reasonably lofty corridor and doorways on either side provide access to a number of adjoining rooms. Some of these entrances feature a simple lintel, while others were spanned by arches.

A third significant north–south corridor can be found further east. The northern half of this, which extends south from a room to the east of the great northern vaults, is in a good state of repair. East of the passageway is the second level of the gallery that stretches southward from what was once the northeastern corner tower. These three covered avenues would have facilitated movement around the northern portion of the upper ward, and provide an indication of the degree to which the central parts of the castle were built up – this was far from a ring of walls enclosing an otherwise open yard.

The underground passageways and vaulted rooms were a feature of the castle that frequently attracted the notice of Western visitors in the nineteenth century. More than one was impressed by the number of vaulted storeys – Mauss observed that there were up to five or six levels, presumably assuming the upper court rose from the level of the lower bailey in places. Today, few structures display clear evidence of more than two internal levels – the northwestern tower, with its three barrel-vaulted storeys, is one of these exceptions. Some of these subterranean rooms accommodated the living quarters of Turkish soldiers during the brief period when the castle was garrisoned by the Ottomans from the end of the nineteenth century. Most, however, were evidently filled with debris, much as they remain today. Amongst the rubble, Deschamps reported seeing Byzantine sculptures, distinct from the Nabataean figure incorporated into the eastern section of the northern wall and the rosettes featured on the wall that later became part of the hall named after them. What else might be hiding in the fill remains to be discovered.[49]

Kitchens

A few rooms associated with food production can be found near the great vaults at the northern end of the castle. Aligned between the central and western corridors, a reasonably large barrel-vaulted room contains an oven at its northern end. The oven is quite large, built across the entire width of the room, allowing it to have fed a considerable number of people. The masonry appears to be Frankish, but this remains far from certain without further archaeological evidence. A second, smaller oven can be found in a similar vaulted structure just to the east. Further east again, on the western side of the eastern passageway, there are the remains of what appears to have been a kitchen complex. A number of workspaces are visible along the walls, and two large millstones can be found in the middle of the floor. Accessed from one of the western doors is a smaller room, almost half of which is occupied by a third oven.[50] It is not yet clear what the specific purpose or role of each oven was, if indeed more than one of them was in use at the same time, which appears probable.

Given the size of the castle, its evident bread-making capabilities and abundant space for storing provisions, it is peculiar that an obvious source of drinking water has not yet been identified. Burckhardt observed that there was a 'deep well' in the castle; Lynch reported that there were seven wells as well as cisterns; and Mauss similarly noted numerous cisterns in the castle. Bliss, however, was unable to find any of these at the end of the nineteenth century.[51] It is impossible that a castle of this size and importance did not have a source of reliable drinking water; it simply remains to be found. Likewise, certain essential buildings, such as a stable, have not yet been located definitively.

Lower Bailey

To the west of the upper ward, at a considerably lower elevation, runs the lower bailey. It is more than 200m north–south and about 20–30m east–west. The fine limestone masonry indicates that what exists today postdates the Frankish occupation of the site. Deschamps was first to notice a different style of masonry around the base of the southwestern corner, which he identified as being Frankish. As Pringle has highlighted, if Deschamps is correct, it is possible that earlier Frankish work here might correspond with the barbican granted to the Hospitallers in 1152. Building on this notion, Milwright has proposed that if there was a western bailey of some kind during the early Frankish period, the tower of St Mary, which is mentioned in the charter to the Hospitallers, may have been at the south end of the lower ward. As for most of what is standing, Korn has suggested this is Ayyubid work, while Biller, Burger and Häffner, as well as Milwright, propose that it was instead commissioned by the Mamluks.[52]

The lower bailey, in its present form, provides a broad terrace along most of the western side of the castle. A double-level parapet crowns much of the outer western wall: casemates with embrasures are provided below, which support a wall walk and battlements above. The latter consist of narrow crenels between merlons pierced by embrasures. The southern stretch of the wall presents five casemates, beyond which the continuous line of casemates is interrupted by the rear of a tower, which survives to the same height as the neighbouring walls. In the centre of the east face of the tower is a simple doorway, covered by a lintel. This opens to a long room, beyond which are four shooting chambers along the western side; each was provided with an embrasure to the west, while the northern and southernmost include a second in the flank of the tower. The plan of the tower, which appears to be solid below this level apart from a postern at its base, shares clear similarities with others built by the Mamluks in the late thirteenth century.

North of the tower, the outer wall runs at roughly the same level for another sixteen casemates. A vaulted structure, about 35m long, occupies the northwestern corner of the lower bailey proper – this currently functions as the castle museum. Entrance to this vaulted northern space is provided by a door in the southern wall; inside, there are three casemates along the western wall and one to the north. The roof of this structure provides an elevated platform. The western parapet rises up to this terrace from the south and wraps around it, providing six more casemates to the west and one to the north.[53]

At the very southern end of the lower ward is another structure, vaulted east–west, which was built against the outer southern wall. This section of wall features four levels of surviving embrasures: one at the basement level; three accessible from the main storey of the structure, which would have been roughly level with the terrace of the bailey to the north; two in casemates of the lower level of the parapet; and a familiar line of pierced merlons above. The lower level of the parapet would have been accessed from the structure's roof, where a third, westernmost casemate provides access to two simple single-slot machicolations, which may have served as latrines.

As in many other sections of the castle, multiple building phases are evident at the south end of the lower bailey. The main southern wall joins the rising bedrock of the upper ward to the east. To the west, quite significant repair efforts were carried out in the twentieth century, obscuring what was once at this end of the wall. Today, the wall simply ends, leaving a clean edge and a space between it and another wall, which continues to the west a few metres behind. The east end of this slightly more northern wall abuts the vaulted structure built against the main southern wall, blocking the northern half of the western end of the structure but leaving the southern part open to the outside. These two sections of southern wall were probably once joined by a short north–south wall, which may even have contained a postern.

The more northerly section of southern wall runs west for a few metres before turning north, from which point it becomes the western wall of the lower bailey. North of the corner, near the south end of the west wall, there is a noticeable change in the dressing of the masonry. The shift in dressing reflects modern efforts to replace the facing of the wall, which had fallen away by the early twentieth century. This once damaged section of wall is located below the spot where the most southerly casemate of the western wall had once been located – the facing of the wall was replaced, but the parapet above was not rebuilt. While rebuilding efforts such as these at the southern end of the western ward have helped prevent the walls from crumbling further, they complicate efforts to discern how elements originally related to one another and the order in which they were built.[54]

In the middle of the lower court is a small building. This accommodates a staircase that connects the upper and lower levels of the western bailey. Deschamps postulated that the machicolations of the central western tower of the upper court, which look down on the northern side of this little structure from a few metres to the north and east, were meant to help defend it.[55] Although possible, such a simple and direct link seems unlikely given their relative positions to one another.

In the centre of the lower level, below the terrace of the western ward, is another large *qa'a*. There is a niche in the rear of the east *iwan*, while the west *iwan* has a niche in each of its sides and an embrasure in the back wall. Two rooms, or vestibules, of a similar size to the north and south of the central *durqa'a* allow visitors to travel through this space. The staircase up to the terrace above is accessed from the eastern side of the southern chamber, while a shooting room with a single embrasure is to be found to the west of this southern component. Above the *durqa'a*, supported by pendentives between the four arches, runs a decorative ring of large muqarnas. There seems to have been nothing above this when Deschamps visited, only a hole, 7m wide. Modern restoration efforts have seen the addition of six courses of a dome, though the centre remains open to the terrace above. Fragai, who has conducted the most detailed investigation of this part of the castle to date, has concluded, primarily on the basis of analyses of the masonry, that the *qa'a* dates to the Mamluk period. Given its proximity to the western side of the castle, he has associated this with the *qa'a al-nahas* (hall of copper), from where Sultan al-Zahir Barquq was said to have gazed towards Jerusalem and Hebron during his period of exile in 1389.[56]

At the northern and southern ends of this lower level are long vaulted rooms. To the south, the room is 8m wide and almost 40m long. Three embrasures were provided in the northern half of the western wall, spaced similarly to the lower level of the parapet above, though none are found to the south, due to the presence of the outer western tower. Today, this hall extends only half the distance to the southern curtain, leaving it unclear what is further south, though embrasures can be seen south of the western tower from outside the castle. On the other side of the *qa'a*, a long room of similar width stretches for about 80m. There are only six embrasures in the western wall of this northern hall, which are spaced much further apart. The northern half of this room mirrors the hall above, though it is provided with a postern at the northern end. A latrine is also to be found at the northern end of the western wall, similar to the level above, which is accessible from the side of the northernmost casemate. Bliss reported that these large vaulted halls had not yet been cleared of debris when he visited in 1895.[57]

The *qa'a* between the two long vaulted rooms, with its ornate muqarnas, served as part of an entrance way. The passage up to the terrace above is accessed from the eastern side of the southern chamber, while a similar corridor in the western side of the northern room leads down to an external gate. The gateway is only about 2.5m wide, though it sits in a slightly wider blind arch that reaches all the way up to the upper internal level above, giving the entranceway a monumental appearance while keeping the actual entrance small and easy to defend. Despite the simple architectural splendour of the gate, and the large *qa'a* that it led to, it is questionable whether this entrance ever received significant use – it was certainly not the one through which al-Nasir Muhammad rode in procession in 1309.

Like the great southern tower of the upper ward, and the grand northwest tower of the town, the design of the western gate suggests that it was meant to impress viewers as they approached the castle from a distance. The slope around the gate is too steep for this to have been the main point of access for visitors coming from the west, via the south end of the Dead Sea; the western entrance to the town was probably preferred. Likewise, those approaching from the King's Highway, to the east of the castle, would most likely have entered via the town's eastern portal, before making their way to the northern entrance to the castle. The only practical way to reach the outer western gate is to move along the base of the western wall from either the north or the south, but such an approach completely obscures the majesty of the blind arch – it was perhaps meant to be seen more than it was to be used. Although this was the most ornate external gateway of the lower ward, there were two others: the postern at the end of the northern hall, and another postern in the southern flank of the outer western tower.

Only from outside the castle can the section of masonry belonging to the outer bailey that Deschamps identified as Frankish be viewed.[58] Extending north from the southwest corner is a talus, from which extends a low stretch of wall. The closest parallel to this masonry appears to be found in surviving parts of the original glacis. If Deschamps' theory is correct, and this early work was commissioned by the Franks, most of the lower ward of the castle would appear to rest on earlier Frankish foundations. While possible, the lack of evidence to indicate Frankish work elsewhere urges caution.

North of the apparently Mamluk vaulted halls of the lower ward, and west of the tourist-friendly ramp that leads up to the modern entrance to the castle, the northwestern corner of the stronghold is in a state of considerable ruin. A wall extends from the northern end of the long hall of the lower ward, before turning east, then north again, roughly following the terrain. To the east of this wall, the dilapidated remains of structures are evident. At the very northern end, this front terminates with the base of the castle's northwestern tower, little of which remains. North of this tower is the westernmost end of the great northern ditch; to the east are two more staggered salients, the easternmost of which contains the modern castle gate in its eastern flank. The northwestern area of the castle is in such a state of ruin that few scholars have tried to date the remains of its various structures.

Like most medieval castles, Kerak is the product of numerous building phases. Over the years, its defences were augmented and even rebuilt, while internal components were added, remodelled and replaced. What exactly the castle looked like at any given moment is still hard to determine. Likewise, questions remain relating to how some structures were used, what thinking led to the design and decoration of various elements, and how different people interacted with the space over time. While future excavations may offer some hints into mysteries such as these, what can be said without any reservations is that it is certainly a misnomer to refer to Kerak as simply a 'crusader castle'.

Chapter 7

The Town

The ancient wall surrounding the town is in ruins, but it can be traced all along the line. In places it stands for a considerable height. Besides the great castle at the south-east, there are four towers. These latter all date from Crusading times, and are in distinct contrast to the main part of the wall. The towers are built of hard yellow limestone cut in the usual style of the Crusaders; the wall is built of flint and sandstone; the stones themselves are not large, but are peculiarly long and thin; the courses are often not continuous. Between the towers there are small turrets, some of Crusading work and others of the style of the main wall. This latter style also occurs at the great castle; here we also find the long thin stones, only much larger; many, but not all, are drafted. The style of boss is peculiar, especially at the quoins, where it often projects for more than a foot, with a long square set back, ending in a rough mass. It is thus a unique combination of rough boss and smooth boss, giving the corners an extraordinary effect. From the point of view of defence, as well as of architecture, these projecting bosses, up which anyone could climb, seem an extremely stupid arrangement.[1]

Frederick Jones Bliss (visited 1885)

The town of Kerak had been inhabited for centuries before the castle was built. Despite its long history, very little is known about its layout and appearance prior to the arrival of the Franks, and few internal structures predating the Ottoman era can be identified with any degree of certainty. One shift that can be observed, however, is the formation of a Christian quarter at the north end of the town. This was a product of evolving demographic and settlement dynamics during the centuries following the end of Latin rule. At what point the declining Christian population came to concentrate where it did is unclear, though it is not unreasonable to suggest that this started fairly early, as influential Muslim figures, who supported the local Mamluk and even Ayyubid administrations, came to occupy spaces in the town that were closest to the castle – the seat of power.

With Kerak's declining importance from the late Mamluk period, the town's fortifications eventually fell into disrepair. The Ottomans contributed to this process at times, during their efforts to impose imperial authority, while stone robbing would have been a more constant factor – the increasingly dilapidated walls provided a quarry of pre-cut stone for local builders. Although fairly ruinous by the nineteenth century, Tristram was able to observe that in no place were these defences completely demolished, while in some they were perfectly preserved.[2] There had almost certainly been a town wall during the twelfth century, and it is possible that the earliest phases of the town's fortifications predate the Muslim conquests of the seventh century. Dating most components of the walls, however, will remain extremely difficult until excavations are carried out. Fortunately, there is epigraphic evidence to help identify some of the most impressive Ayyubid and Mamluk elements.

The best preserved parts of the town defences, Burj al-Zahir and Burj Banawy, present bold inscriptions that date their construction to the reign of Baybars in the late thirteenth century. These towers display the same type of limestone masonry that was used for the construction of certain Mamluk structures in the castle. Some nineteenth-century figures, however, remained convinced that this finer masonry should be attributed to the Franks. Mauss, for example, proposed that Baybars had simply added his name to existing towers. The fairly detailed description composed by Bliss near the end of the century (featured at the start of the chapter), is equally inaccurate in its interpretations. Nevertheless, Bliss's remarks are valuable in so much as they speak to the widespread rebuilding efforts undertaken by Muslim figures to repair, rebuild and augment the town's defences, even if he misjudged who was responsible for what work. Much of the less impressive masonry, including the rougher sections that probably predate 1188, has already fallen victim to the forces of urban sprawl.[3]

Tunnel Entrances

Until the end of the nineteenth century, access to the town was controlled by two entrance systems, one on the eastern side of the town and one on the western side. Each consisted of a fairly long tunnel cut into the bedrock below the town. These rather unique gateways attracted the attention of many visitors from about the fourteenth century. Most twelfth- and thirteenth-century historians fail to mention the tunnels; however, epigraphic evidence dates the western one to the 1220s, and it is possible that their origins may be much earlier.

The town's western entrance connected Kerak with the route to southern Palestine that passed south of the Dead Sea. The approach was rough and steep, compelling visitors of the late Ottoman era to dismount and scramble over and around large boulders as they neared the passageway. The outer entrance consisted of a simple arch, above which was an inscription dating its construction, or perhaps improvement, to 1227. This work took place during the reign of al-Mu'azzam 'Isa and was overseen by one of his mamluks, a certain Shams al-Din Sunqur al-Mu'azzami. The tunnel beyond made two turns before emerging behind the line of the town walls. How far the tunnel extended, and thus where exactly it emerged, is hard to determine. Estimates of its length varied: Lynch reckoned it to be 80 feet; Tristram 50 yards; Bliss 70 yards, though he thought it may have originally extended about 125 yards; and Deschamps believed it to have been 80 yards.[4] What the interior entrance to the tunnel looked like remains a mystery.

There was a similar tunnel entrance on the eastern side of the town. This eastern portal connected Kerak with the King's Highway, the main route between Damascus and 'Aqaba, with Egypt and Arabia beyond. It was this entrance to the town that was observed by Ibn Battuta and most who visited Kerak while completing the *hajj*. The gateway received less attention from nineteenth-century Western travellers, who most often approached Kerak from the west. Both tunnel entrances fell from use in the late nineteenth century.[5]

Due to the difficult approaches to the town gates and their deteriorating condition, a number of paths eventually formed over dilapidated sections of the enceinte, where the town wall was low or had disappeared entirely. Tristram noted two such pathways in the northeast section of the town in 1872. The eastern tunnel remained passable, if treacherous, near the end of the nineteenth century, but it was blocked completely by 1902. Photos from the 1930s reveal the extent to which the town walls had further disappeared, a result of accelerated stone robbing and the urban development that accompanied direct Ottoman rule and then heightened European influence following the First World War. Both Bliss and Deschamps alluded to their being other entrances to the town, in addition to the two tunnels, though their remarks leave it unclear as to where, or how old, they may have been.[6]

Burj al-Zahir

At the northwest end of the town, dominating the approach to the western tunnel entrance, is Burj al-Zahir. The largest of the town's surviving towers, it was built to awe visitors arriving from the west. Along the inside of the central wall is a bold inscription, announcing to all who was responsible for the structure's construction. Although de Saulcy, and Mauss and Sauvaire following him, had trouble making out some of the text, it was clear to all who could read Arabic that it attributed credit for the tower's construction to Baybars. The inscription provides a lengthy list of the sultan's titles, but no date or any other hint of when exactly the work was carried out or who might have overseen building efforts.[7]

The tower bears a likeness to the great southern tower of the castle, similarly presenting three prominent faces. The outward face of the broad central wall extends for 40m, with another wall on each end extending back at less than a 90-degree angle. The main difference is that Burj al-Zahir is not really a tower; it has no rear wall, allowing for no significant internal space. The wall at the lowest level of the tower, which is the height of two normal storeys, is about 8m thick and accommodates a small internal passage or gallery. The thickness of the wall provides a platform at the next level, which is the height of two storeys above. Although much shallower than the terrace on top of the great southern tower of the castle, it similarly provided access to casemates. Six courses below this platform, and about twenty above the ground, runs the dedicatory inscription to Baybars. A third level was enclosed in the thickness of the wall above the casemates. Through this ran a gallery that serviced a continuous line of machicolations. Little survives of what was once above this level, but there was almost certainly a parapet of some description. At the inward end of each of the side walls, a turret, the full width of the structure, extended upwards from the platform of the second level. These were once at least as high as the top of the surrounding parapet. In front of the tower, a ditch was cut into the bedrock to separate the town from the northwestern tip of the plateau beyond, which falls away less dramatically than elsewhere.[8]

At the end of the nineteenth century, the tower was quarried for stone. Photographs by Mauss and Sauvaire, taken in 1866, and Hornstein, in September 1895, reveal little change and feature clear evidence of the third level. By Musil's first visit, in August 1896, everything above the corbels of the machicolations had disappeared; this was the state of the tower when Gautier viewed it in 1899. Just three years later, when Libbey and Hoskins photographed the tower, in 1902, everything down to the platform, which formed the base of the second level, had been removed. This was in part due to redevelopment initiatives in this part of the town following the Ottoman occupation – Musil forecast that the tower's stone was to be used to rebuild the town mosque, which might account for the final destruction phase. The tower provided an accessible source of cut stone, some of which was probably used to build the new military hospital, school and perhaps also the mosque.[9] For more than a century, the tower has stood in much the same condition.

Other Defences

The remains of four other impressive towers were still noticeable along the trace of the town walls in the nineteenth century, though none of these were as monumental as Burj al-Zahir. Starting in the southeast, there was a vaulted structure that began at the castle ditch and extended along the town wall to the northeast. Musil called this Khan el-Kebaz, and it clearly predates the Ottoman building phase from the late nineteenth century, which has led to the remodelling and disappearance of certain sections of the structure.[10]

Further along the town wall to the northeast, about 150m from the northeastern corner of the castle, is Burj al-Banawy. Striped around the outside of this rounded tower is an inscription to Baybars, similar to the one found on Burj al-Zahir. Two levels of this tower can still be seen, each with embrasures arranged around a central room.[11] The use of towers of different shapes is not uncommon in early Mamluk architecture. At Subayba, for example, large rectangular and rounded towers of a comparable size were both constructed during Baybars' reign, while Qalawun added a stout quadrangular tower to the southern defences of Crac des Chevaliers next to a rounded one commissioned by Baybars.

About 100m northeast of Burj al-Banawy is a square tower. This contains an internal level, with the remains of machicolations above.[12] The tower rises from a shallow talus, reminiscent of similar Mamluk towers at Montreal, Shayzar and elsewhere. About 150m past this tower was the eastern tunnel entrance. The pathway leading up to the entrance approached from the southwest, compelling visitors to pass below a stretch of the town wall, and perhaps also the two towers of the town beyond, before reaching the gateway. A projection in the line of the wall just east of the entrance provided further protection.

At the extreme northeast of the town is Burj al-Nasara, another square tower. According to Musil, sections of this tower and the curtain wall next to it were torn down in the 1890s to provide building stones for the new Turkish school.[13] The northern wall of the town displays no evidence of having once had any significant towers. Instead, there appear to have been a number of shallow projections, similar to those found in the castle, as well as at Montreal, all of which have traditionally been dated to the Frankish period. Another square tower, with two internal levels, can be found along the western wall of the castle, which Musil called Burj Tanas.[14]

Mosque

The site of Kerak's principal mosque has probably been the central place of worship in the town since at least the Frankish period. The current structure, however, dates to the Ottoman rebuilding efforts at the end of the nineteenth century. Bliss described the local mosque as lying in ruins in March 1895. The following year, Dowling observed that a new mosque, the only one in the town, had recently been built.[15]

The medieval mosque was in a dilapidated state by the start of the nineteenth century. Its octagonal minaret, around which ran a band of black stone, was still standing in 1818, though it had disappeared by 1866. Over the main door of the mosque was a horseshoe arch. This featured a decorative cup motif and an inscription, which dated the construction of the doorway to 782 AH [1380–81 AD], attributing credit to the *na'ib* of Kerak. Another inscription incorporated into the mosque refers to work that was carried out for al-'Adil in 1198, under the direction of Sarim al-Din Barghash al-'Adili. It remains unclear, however, whether this latter inscription corresponds with an earlier building phase, perhaps the initial conversion of the Latin church into a mosque, or if it originally belonged to a different structure altogether.[16]

During his visit in March 1899, Gautier was given a tour of the town by the local priest. Intriguingly, he noted stopping at 'the old mosque in ruins', which featured a decorative Arabic inscription. When considering the apparent rebuilding of Kerak's principal mosque a few years earlier, it is unclear which building Gautier may have viewed, or if rebuilding work was simply slower than Dowling suggests. When Deschamps visited a few decades later, he was unable to find the ruined mosque he had read about, identifying only a few column bases similar to French examples from the twelfth century.[17]

Churches

The link between the mosque and the earlier church that it replaced was established by Tristram in 1872, by which time the mosque had apparently fallen from use – its roof had collapsed and the interior space had been turned into an open cemetery. Using the pillars and arches that remained, Tristram was able to visualize the plan of the earlier building. Bliss likewise connected the two spaces a couple decades later, and Pringle has more recently collated and presented the available evidence, leaving little room to doubt this is where the Frankish cathedral was once located.[18]

Not much is known about the former Latin cathedral aside from its existence. Located so far from a significant Frankish population centre, it may have seen little ceremonial use compared to other cathedrals of the kingdom of Jerusalem. Locally, it would have functioned as the parish church for Kerak's Latin population in the twelfth century. It is quite possible that the Frankish structure rests in turn on the remains of an earlier church, though this is impossible to determine at the present time.

The great mosque, with the remains of the Catholic cathedral below it, is located in what became the Christian quarter of the city. Only slightly northeast of the mosque, the Greek church of St George can still be found.

Work on this church was underway when Lynch and his party visited Kerak in 1848. They were entertained by the Orthodox priest, who showed them into an existing church; a small, dark, vaulted structure with two granite half-columns and a central well. The new church was reportedly more than 20m long and 12m wide, accommodating three aisles, each with four bays, while a shallow apse extends from the eastern end of the central aisle. The walls were already 3m high and the bases for the six pillars had been laid by the time the Americans arrived. On the central column of the southern row, an inscription confirms that building work was carried out in 1848. According to Dowling, the new church, which was completed in 1849, had been financed by the archbishop of Petra. Like the Frankish cathedral, it is unclear what occupied the site before the church was built, though it remains a distinct possibility that the new church was built to replace an older one in the same place. Between 1848 and 1866, a monastic community developed around the new church of St George, while a priest continued to provide services for the local Christian community.[19]

About halfway between the mosque and the castle is another church. This much smaller church, which is also dedicated to St George, is covered by a single barrel vault. The structure is hard to date, though its modest size may suggest a medieval provenance. Efforts to consolidate the structure have been extensive over the years, and can be dated back as far as the mid-eighteenth century. It is tempting to suggest that this may have been the cavernous church visited by Lynch in 1848. This structure is easier to identify in Gautier's account, which mentions a smaller, much older chapel, also associated with St George, located in a different quarter of the city. According to Gautier, this smaller church benefitted from further repair work at the end of the nineteenth century.[20]

The Latin mission was also located in the northern Christian quarter, east of the mosque and down the road from the larger Greek church of St George. The site of the mission corresponds with the present Church of Our Lady of the Rosary, the town's Catholic parish church.

Other Structures

In a place like Kerak, where water can be difficult to come by at certain points in the year, management of this essential resource was always a priority. On the east side of the town, near the eastern tunnel entrance, was a large open pool, measuring about 60m by 70m. Around the northern corner of this pool, Mauss and Sauvaire observed impressive ruins that were identified to them as a bath complex. They were shown a mosaic paving inside a house, along with the bases of four columns, which were supposed to have once supported the portico of the bath structure connected to the pool. Deschamps later viewed two rooms of what he identified as a Roman (or Byzantine) bath, with fragments of marble paving.[21] Today, the site of this pool is covered by an open space that serves as a bus station. There was once a second large pool on the other side of the town. Visitors arriving by the western tunnel found this on their right; to their left, near Burj al-Zahir, was a smaller pool or enclosed cistern. Like most open spaces in the old town, these were eventually consumed by urban sprawl.[22]

Perhaps the most obvious remains from the nineteenth century are the administrative buildings erected by the Ottomans following their occupation of Kerak. Constructed at the southern end of the town, just across the ditch from the castle, most tourists pass these reasonably unimposing structures without giving them much thought. When they were originally built, however, their symbolism and representation of imperial authority would have been unmistakable.

Like the castle, the town withholds many secrets. Future archaeological excavations in this area will hopefully help improve our impression of what everyday life was like for those living in the shadow of the castle. As techniques and technologies improve, it may become possible to peer below the densely packed houses and shops. This may also yield the best indications of Kerak's earliest history; a glimpse at life before the arrival of the Franks and the construction of the great castle that has shaped the history of the town ever since.

Abbreviations

ADAJ	*Annual of the Department of Antiquities of Jordan*
Cart. Hosp.	Delaville Le Roulx (ed.), *Cartulaire général de l'ordre des Hospitaliers de S. Jean de Jérusalem*
Cart. Sep.	Bresc-Bautier (ed.), *Le cartulaire du chapitre du Saint-Sépulcre de Jérusalem*
Chartes TS	Delaville Le Roulx (ed.), 'Chartes de Terre Sainte'
EI3	*Encyclopaedia of Islam*, 3rd ed. (Brill, 2007–)
MGH	*Monumenta Germaniae Historica*
PEQ	*Palestine Exploration Fund Quarterly Statement*
RCEA	*Répertoire chronologique d'épigraphie arabe*
RHC	*Recueil des historiens des croisades*
Ar	Documents arméniens
Oc	Historiens occidentaux
Or	Historiens orientaux
PL	*Patrologiae Latinae*
ROL	*Revue de l'Orient latin*
RRH	Röhricht (ed.), *Regesta Regni Hierosolymitani*
RRHa	Röhricht (ed.), *Regesta Regni Hierosolymitani: Additamentum*
SHAJ	*Studies in the History and Archaeology of Jordan*
TOT	Strehlke (ed.), *Tabulae Ordinis Theutonici*
UKJ	Mayer (ed.), *Die Urkunden der Lateinischen Könige von Jerusalem*

Notes

Introduction

1. Lawrence, *Crusader Castles*, pp. 35–37.
2. For a list of scholarly travellers who passed through the broader region in the nineteenth century, see Brünnow and Domaszewski, *Die Provincia Arabia*, 1:481–507.

Chapter 1: Transjordan before the Crusades

1. For the water collection systems of the region, see Pace, 'Cisterns', pp. 369–74.
2. It is harder to see Kerak from the Mount of Olives; however, the castle was pointed out to MacMichael ahead of his visit in 1818, MacMichael, *Journey*, pp. 195–96.
3. Abu'l-Fida' trans. in Le Strange, *Palestine under the Moslems*, p. 479. See also Milwright, *Fortress of the Raven*, p. 88.
4. Burckhardt, *Travels in Syria*, pp. 376–79.
5. Irby and Mangles, *Travels*, pp. 361–62. Cf. Mauss and Sauvaire, 'Voyage de Jérusalem a Kerak', pp. 106, 145; Tristram, *The Land of Moab*, p. 68.
6. Miller, *Archaeological Survey*, p. 89.
7. Gubser, *Politics and Change*, pp. 12–13.
8. See also EI3, s.v. 'Karak'; Milwright, *Fortress of the Raven*, p. 29.
9. Abel, *Géographie*, 2:199–201. My thanks to Denys Pringle for this reference and for clarifying the region's early ecclesiastical structure.
10. See Bartlett, *Mapping Jordan*, p. 4; Milwright, *Fortress of the Raven*, p. 62.
11. Milwright, *Fortress of the Raven*, p. 10.
12. Schick, 'Southern Jordan', p. 76, cf. pp. 73–77.
13. Quoted in Ibn al-Furat, *Ayyubids*, 2:50–51.
14. Ibn al-Athir, *Annales*, p. 163.
15. Johns, 'Islamic Settlement', pp. 363–64; Hamarneh, et al., 'Population Dynamics', pp. 683–702. See also Schick, 'Southern Jordan', pp. 73–85.
16. Walmsley, 'Restoration or Revolution?' pp. 633–40. For a more comprehensive overview of this issue, its development and a re-evaluation of the witnessed transitions, idem, 'Fatimid, Mamluk and Ayyubid Jordan', pp. 515–59, updated as 'The Middle Islamic and Crusader Periods', pp. 495–537.

Chapter 2: Frankish Period

1. William of Tyre 15.21, pp. 703–4 (author's translation).
2. Albert of Aachen 7.16–17, pp. 506–11; RRH no. 36, pp. 5–6; Cart. Hosp. no. app. 1, 2:897–98; UKJ no. 20, pp. 124–25.
3. Fulcher of Chartres 2.4–5, pp. 370–84 (trans. pp. 143–47). See also Albert of Aachen 7.39–43, pp. 542–51.
4. Ralph of Caen 139, p. 703 (trans. p. 155); Fulcher 2.6.12, p. 390 (trans. p. 150). For an overview of the initial actions carried out by Baldwin I, see Morton, *Crusader States*, pp. 20–28.
5. Schick, 'Southern Jordan', p. 79. Schick's observation that the expedition served to keep the region beyond the control of both the Seljuks and Fatimids is less supportable; when

considering the events of 1107, this may actually have provoked Damascus to take greater interest in the area.

6. Ibn al-Qalanisi, pp. 81–82; Albert of Aachen 10.28–30, pp. 744–47. For the possible return of the expedition via the north end of the Dead Sea, cf. Schick, 'Southern Jordan', p. 79.

7. Daniel the Abbot, pp. 136, 145.

8. Albert of Aachen 10.47, pp. 760–61; Ibn al-Athir, *Chronicle*, 1:146. Duke Robert of Normandy was the eldest son of William the Conqueror, duke of Normandy and king of England. Robert had been one of the leaders of the First Crusade, and among those who returned to Europe following its conclusion.

9. Ibn al-Qalanisi, pp. 91, 113; Ibn al-Athir, *Chronicle*, 1:142.

10. Ibn al-Qalanisi, pp. 130–31; Albert of Aachen 12.8, pp. 834–37; Ibn al-Athir, *Chronicle*, 1:164; Milwright, *Fortress of the Raven*, p. 25.

11. Chalandon, 'Un diplôme inédit', pp. 12–16; RRHa no. 422a, pp. 25–26; UKJ nos. 49, 316, pp. 174, 550–53; Mayer, *Montréal*, pp. 242–45.

12. Fulcher of Chartres 2.55, pp. 592–93 (trans. p. 215).

13. William of Tyre 11.26, p. 535 (trans. 1:506–7). This description was later used by James of Vitry, *Historia* 28, pp. 180–81. Many visitors to the castle in the late nineteenth century similarly noticed the productivity of the immediate surroundings.

14. Tibble, *Monarchy and Lordships*, p. 30.

15. Albert of Aachen 12.23, pp. 856–57.

16. My thanks to Steve Tibble for sharing some of his thoughts regarding the increasing importance of Transjordan in the early twelfth century.

17. Ibn al-Qalanisi, pp. 71–72, 121; Ibn al-Athir, *Chronicle*, 1:96–97, 158. The Sawad is the region east of the Jordan, north of Jabal 'Awf, corresponding roughly with what is today known as the Golan Heights.

18. Prawer, *The Crusaders' Kingdom*, pp. 20–21.

19. Fulcher of Chartres 2.56, pp. 594–96 (trans. pp. 215–16); William of Tyre 11.29, pp. 541–42 (trans. 1:531); Mayer, 'Crusader Lordship', p. 200.

20. Albert of Aachen 12.21–22, pp. 856–59.

21. Fulcher of Chartres 3.10, 25, 50, pp. 643–45, 689–90, 784–93 (trans. pp. 234–35, 253, 288–92); Ibn al-Qalanisi, pp. 174–77, 182. Following excavations in the early twentieth century, it was concluded that the stronghold found by the Franks at Jerash in 1121 was the classical temple of Artemis, which had been fortified with large stones similar to those described by Fulcher, see Fisher and McCown, 'Jerash-Gerasa 1930', p. 4. The expedition of 1123 is described as being directed between Mount Gilead and Arabia.

22. William of Tyre 11.27, pp. 535–36 (trans. 1:507–8).

23. Cf. Mayer, 'Crusader Lordship', p. 201; Schick, 'Southern Jordan', p. 80.

24. Irby and Mangles, *Travels*, pp. 379–80; Lagrange, 'Notre exploration de Pétra', pp. 215–16; Brünnow and Domaszewski, *Die Provincia Arabia*, 1:116; Meistermann, *Guide du Nil*, p. 241. See also Mayer, *Montréal*, pp. 68–69; Pringle, *Churches*, 2:308–9 (no. 229).

25. For example, Mas Latrie, *Les Seigneurs du Crac*, pp. 5–6; Rey, 'Les seigneurs de Mont-Réal', p. 19. For an introduction to Roman and his background, see Murray, *Crusader Kingdom*, p. 228. Although Murray agrees that Roman was the first lord of Transjordan, he dates his appointment to the reign of Baldwin II, rather than that of Baldwin I. Mayer has proposed that Viscount Pisellus of Jerusalem subsequently became viscount of Transjordan, before the region passed to Roman, though Murray has expressed justifiable doubt towards this, Mayer, *Montréal*, pp. 69–73, 84–91; Murray, *Crusader Kingdom*, 220–21 n. 40. It should be noted that Roman need not have been anything more than a lord of certain lands of the Balqa' to fulfil the requirements of the charter evidence.

26. Delaborde, *Chartes* no. 5, pp. 27–28; RRH nos. 57, 79, 293, pp. 12–13, 18, 74–75; Cart. Hosp. nos. 20, 28, 225, 1:21–22, 27–28, 172–73; RRHa no. 68a, p. 4; UKJ nos. 42, 52, 58, 232, pp. 165–68, 177–79, 187–98, 424–27.

27. Delaborde, *Chartes* no. 18, pp. 45–47; RRH nos. 57, 91, 105, 121, 134, 137, 293, pp. 12–13, 21, 25, 30, 33–34, 74–75; Cart. Hosp. nos. 20, 225, 1:21–22, 172–73; UKJ nos. 42, 81, 86, 93, 105, 116, 124, 232, pp. 165–68, 215–16, 230–33, 241–47, 261–63, 276–80, 287–88, 424–27.

28. Delaborde, *Chartes* no. 14, pp. 40–41; RRH no. 115, p. 28; UKJ no. 96, pp. 250–52; William of Tyre 14.15, 15.22, pp. 651, 703 (trans. 2:70, 127).

29. Delaborde, *Chartes* no. 14, pp. 40–41; RRH nos. 91, 115, 121, pp. 21, 28, 30; UKJ nos. 86, 96, 105, pp. 230–33, 250–52, 261–63.

30. William of Tyre 15.21, 17.1, pp. 703, 761 (trans. 2:127, 185).

31. William of Tyre 14.15, p. 651 (trans. 2:70).

32. Mayer, 'Queen Melisende of Jerusalem', pp. 105–6; idem, 'The Wheel of Fortune', p. 861; Murray, 'Baldwin II and his Nobles', pp. 60–85, esp. 77–78.

33. Tibble, *Monarchy and Lordships*, pp. 31–36. For the charter of 1161, TOT no. 3, pp. 3–5; RRH no. 366, pp. 96–97; UKJ no. 263, pp. 479–86.

34. William of Tyre 14.15–18, pp. 651–56 (trans. 2:70–76). Mayer, 'Queen Melisende of Jerusalem', pp. 102–11; idem, 'Angevins *versus* Normans', esp. pp. 22–25; idem, *Montreal*, pp. 92–110; idem, 'The Wheel of Fortune', esp. pp. 862–65, 870–76; Murray, 'Baldwin II and his Nobles', esp. 79–84. Cf. Ibn al-Qalanisi, p. 215. Hugh of Jaffa was Melisende's second cousin and closest male relative in the kingdom, making him a natural figure to represent her cause.

35. William of Tyre 15.21, p. 703 (trans. 2:127).

36. For example, Müller-Wiener, *Castles of the Crusaders*, p. 12; Prawer, *The Crusaders' Kingdom*, pp. 105, 131; Kennedy, *Crusader Castles*, p. 45.

37. William of Tyre 15.21, p. 704 (trans. 2:127). For the visit of John Komnenos and his subsequent death, William of Tyre 15.19–23, pp. 700–6 (trans. 2:123–30); John Kinnamos 1.10, pp. 27–31.

38. William of Tyre 22.29(28), p. 1056 (trans. 2:499).

39. William of Tyre 15.21, 22.29(28), pp. 703–4, 1055–56 (trans. 2:127, 498–99).

40. Ibn al-Furat, *Ayyubids*, 2:50–51.

41. Cf. Milwright, *Fortress of the Raven*, p. 62.

42. Robert Crispin is identified as the royal butler in 1145, RRH no. 236, pp. 59–60; Cart. Hosp. no. 160, 1:130; UKJ no. 213, pp. 95–96.

43. RRH nos. 164, 279, pp. 40–41, 71; Cart. Hosp. no. 207, 1:160; UKJ no. 135, pp. 310–14; William of Tyre 17.1, 21, pp. 761, 790 (trans. 2:185, 218). For the rule of Maurice, see also Mayer, *Montréal*, pp. 131–34.

44. RRH no. 279, p. 71; Cart. Hosp. no. 207, 1:160. See also Mayer, *Montréal*, pp. 132–34.

45. Cart. Hosp. no. 284, 1:210; UKJ no. 123, pp. 286–87.

46. For the latter, see Mayer, 'Queen Melisende of Jerusalem', esp. p. 154.

47. William of Tyre 17.21, p. 790 (trans. 2:218).

48. For accounts of this episode, see *History of the Patriarchs* 8, 3.1:70–77; Usama ibn Munqidh, pp. 16–18, 26–34; William of Tyre 18.9, pp. 822–23 (trans. 2:251–53).

49. Ibn al-Qalanisi, pp. 323–24, 346, 348; Ibn Muyassar, pp. 470–72. See also Brett, 'Counter-Crusade', 22–23.

50. Mas Latrie, *Les Seigneurs du Crac*, pp. 6–8; Mayer, *Montréal*, pp. 135–41; *Annales of Egmond*, pp. 458–60. Cf. Benvenisti, *The Crusaders*, p. 320; Prawer, *The Crusaders' Kingdom*, p. 131, cf. p. 105.

51. *Lignages* 285, p. 59; Mayer, 'Queen Melisende of Jerusalem', p. 179; Barber, 'Philip of Nablus', p. 64.

52. Barber, 'Philip of Nablus', pp. 61–63. For Philip's lineage, see *Lignages* 285, pp. 59–60. For Guy the elder, see also Murray, *Crusader Kingdom*, 207–8. For the first mention of Guy in the Levant, see RRH no. 52, pp. 10–11; UKJ no. 32, pp. 149–51.

53. Mayer, 'Queen Melisende of Jerusalem', pp. 118–19; Barber, 'Philip of Nablus', pp. 64–68.

54. Mayer, 'Queen Melisende of Jerusalem', pp. 179–80. Cf. Barber, 'Philip of Nablus', pp. 68–71. Nablus would later become the dower lands of Maria Komnene, second wife of Amalric, Baldwin III's younger brother and successor as king of Jerusalem.

55. TOT no. 3, pp. 3–5; RRH no. 366, pp. 96–97; UKJ no. 263, pp. 479–86. For a detailed analysis of this charter, see Mayer, Montréal, pp. 145–207.

56. For events in Egypt, see Fulton, Contest for Egypt.

57. RRH nos. 368, 397, 400, pp. 97, 104–5; UKJ nos. 264, 308, 310, pp. 486–89, 533–35, 536–41; William of Tyre 22.29(28), p. 1056 (trans. 2:499).

58. For the identification of Philip by Muslim historians, see Ibn al-Athir, Chronicle, 2:184 n. 6.

59. Ibn al-Furat, in Bora, Writing History, pp. 199, 214–15.

60. RRH no. 466, p. 122; Chartes TS no. 2, pp. 183–85; UKJ nos. 314, 341, pp. 548–50, 591–95. See also Barber, 'Philip of Nablus', p. 75.

61. Barber, 'Philip of Nablus', p. 71, cf. pp. 73–74; RRH no. 308, p. 79; UKJ no. 286, pp. 514–16; Philip of Novara, Livre 64, pp. 156, 285, for the custom of eldest daughters inheriting in the absence of a son, 57, pp. 141–42, 273–74.

62. William of Tyre 20.2, pp. 913–14 (trans. 2:345–46); Lignages 296, pp. 74–75; RRH nos. 401, 454, pp. 105, 119; UKJ no. 321, pp. 558–59. For the Brisebarre lords of Beirut, see Nickerson, 'The Seigneury of Beirut', pp. 157–68; Mayer, 'The Wheel of Fortune', pp. 864–68.

63. Cf. Mayer, Montréal, pp. 215–18.

64. William of Tyre 20.22, pp. 940–42 (trans. 2:377–78); RRH nos. 308, 454, pp. 79, 119; UKJ nos. 286, 321, pp. 514–16, 558–59. For Walter, see Mayer, Montréal, pp. 215–21.

65. For this conflict, see Fulton, Contest for Egypt.

66. Fulton, 'Frankish Intervention in Egypt'.

67. William of Tyre 20.26, p. 950 (trans. 2:388); Ibn al-Athir, Chronicle, 2:184; Abu Shama, 4:153–54. Cf. Baha' al-Din, pp. 46–47; Ibn Khallikan, 4:493. See also Lyons and Jackson, Saladin, p. 38; Fulton, Contest for Egypt, pp. 124–25.

68. William of Tyre 20.18, pp. 934–36 (trans. 2:370–71); Ibn al-Athir, Chronicle, 2:185–86; Abu Shama, 4:154–55.

69. Lyons and Jackson, Saladin, pp. 42–44; Eddé, Saladin, pp. 45–46; Fulton, Contest for Egypt, pp. 127–30. See also William of Tyre 20.19, pp. 936–37 (trans. 2:371–73); Ibn al-Athir, Chronicle, 2:194; al-Maqrizi, Description, p. 533.

70. William of Tyre 20.27, pp. 950–51 (trans. 2:388–89); Ibn al-Athir, Chronicle, 2:198–200. Cf. Abu Shama, 4:155–56; Ibn Khallikan, 4:502–4; Bar Hebraeus, 1:300–1; al-Maqrizi, History, pp. 41–43. See also Fulton, Contest for Egypt, pp. 139–41.

71. Ibn al-Athir, Chronicle, 2:213–14; Abu Shama, 4:156–57; Baha' al-Din, p. 48; William of Tyre 20.28, pp. 951–52 (trans. 2:389–90). See also Fulton, Contest for Egypt, pp. 144–45. The broader sequence of events put forward by William of Tyre, building on his misdating of the 1171 siege of Montreal, suggests the attack took place in 1174. This, however, is impossible when considering that Amalric died in July 1174 and Saladin was occupied with events in Egypt that summer.

72. RRH nos. 454, 512, pp. 119, 136; UKJ nos. 321, 359, pp. 558–59, 624–26; Lignages 296, p. 75.

73. TOT no. 7, p. 8; RRH nos. 413, 504, 512, 517, pp. 107, 119, 135, 137; UKJ nos. 312, 359, 364, pp. 545–46, 624–26, 632–35.

74. For example, TOT no. 11, pp. 11–12; RRH nos. 562, 587, pp. 149–50, 156; UKJ nos. 405, 413, pp. 688–91, 706–7.

75. William of Tyre 20.3, p. 914 (trans. 2:346); John of Ibelin 226, p. 591, trans. in Edbury, John of Ibelin, p. 191; Hamilton, The Latin Church, p. 52. For the frequent confusion of Rabbath with other sites, see Pringle, Pilgrimage, p. 244 n. 12. See also Schick, 'Southern Jordan', p. 78; Edbury, John of Ibelin, pp. 181–82. For the dating of the establishment of the diocese, see Mayer, Montréal, pp. 281–83.

76. RRH no. 607, p. 161; Cart. Hosp. no. 610, 1:415–16; Roger of Howden, *Chronica*, 3:87 (trans. 2:187); Hamilton, *The Latin Church*, p. 77; Mayer, *Montréal*, pp. 211 n. 8, 221–28, 281–85.

77. James of Vitry, *Historia* 56, pp. 232–33; Brightman, *Liturgies*, p. 501; Hamilton, *The Latin Church*, pp. 182, 185; Pringle, *Churches*, 1:287, 2:50 (nos. 129, 150).

78. William of Tyre 21.4, p. 964 (trans. 2:401); RRH no. 450, pp. 117–18; UKJ no. 333, pp. 573–75.

79. William of Tyre 19.22, 20.9, pp. 893, 921–22 (trans. 2:326, 354–55); RRH nos. 449, 452, 514, pp. 117, 118, 136; Cart. Hosp. no. 402, 1:275–76; Chartes TS no. 2, pp. 183–85; UKJ nos. 314, 327, 336, 362, pp. 548–50, 564–68, 578–82, 628–29.

80. Cf. Mayer, *Montréal*, pp. 229–35.

81. William of Tyre 21.3, 4, 5, pp. 963, 964–65, 967 (trans. 2:400, 401–2, 404); *Regni Ierosolymitani brevis historia*, p. 135.

82. Hamilton, 'Miles of Plancy', pp. 135–46. See also Fulton, *Contest for Egypt*, pp. 99–100.

83. For the procedures and expectations relating to the marriage of an heiresses, see Philip of Novara, *Livre* 68, pp. 161–62, 290–93.

84. See Lyons and Jackson, *Saladin*, pp. 78–111. For a sense of Saladin's military capabilities, see Lev, *Saladin in Egypt*, pp. 143–58.

85. William of Tyre 17.21, 26, pp. 790, 795–96 (trans. 2:218, 224).

86. William of Tyre 18.1, p. 809 (trans. 2:235–36). For the dating of this, see Hamilton, 'The Elephant of Christ', p. 98 n. 9.

87. William of Tyre 18.10, 23–25, pp. 823–25, 844–49 (trans. 2:253–54, 275–81); John Kinnamos, 4.17–24, pp. 136–41. For Reynald's submission, see Buck, 'Between Byzantium and Jerusalem?', pp. 107–24.

88. William of Tyre 18.28, pp. 851–52 (trans. 2:283–85); Matthew of Edessa (Gregory the Priest), pp. 278–79.

89. Ibn al-Athir, *Chronicle*, 2:145–48; Ibn al-'Adim, *Histoire d'Alep*, pp. 30–32; Abu Shama, 4:108–9, 125–26; William of Tyre 19.9, p. 874–75 (trans. 2:306–8).

90. William of Tyre 20.28, 21.10(11), pp. 952, 976 (trans. 2:390, 414); Michael the Syrian, p. 710.

91. John Kinnamos 5.4, pp. 159–60; Niketas Choniates, pp. 96, 102; Hamilton, 'Manuel I Comnenus', pp. 359–62; idem, *The Leper King*, pp. 104–5, 111–12. Cf. Hugh Eteriano, cols. 229–30.

92. RRH no. 539, pp. 143–44; Cart. Hosp. no. 495, 1:341; UKJ no. 388, pp. 666–67.

93. Ernoul 4, p. 31.

94. For a study of the politics surrounding the reign of Baldwin IV, see Hamilton, *The Leper King*.

95. William of Tyre 21.13–14(14–15), pp. 979–81 (trans. 2:417–20). For William's opinion of Philip of Flanders, see Edbury and Rowe, *William of Tyre*, pp. 82–83 and n. 96.

96. William of Tyre 21.19–23(20–24), pp. 987–94 (trans. 2:426–33); Ernoul 7, p. 54; Baha' al-Din, p. 54. Cf. Ibn al-Athir, *Chronicle*, 2:253–54.

97. Kohler, 'Chartes' no. 45, pp. 153–54; RRHa no. 623a, p. 40; William of Tyre 22.1, 4, 5–7, pp. 1007, 1011–16 (trans. 2;446, 451–56); Ernoul 4, 7, 8, pp. 31, 60, 82–86. See also Hamilton, 'The Elephant of Christ', p. 101.

98. TOT nos. 11, 14, pp. 11–12, 13–14; RRH nos. 539, 553, 587, 593, 613, 614; pp. 143–44, 147, 156, 158, 162–63; Cart. Hosp. no. 495, 1:341; UKJ nos. 388, 413, 420, 429, 430, 493, pp. 666–67, 706–7, 714–16, 728–33, 843–45. Cf. RRH no. 562, pp. 149–50; UKJ no. 405, pp. 688–91.

99. TOT nos. 14, 15, pp. 13–15; RRH nos. 613, 614, 615, pp. 162–63; UKJ nos. 429, 430, 431, pp. 728–36; Ibn al-Athir, *Chronicle*, 2:276; Abu Shama, 4:214; al-Maqrizi, *History*, pp. 63–64, 66; William of Tyre, 22.15(14), p. 1026 (trans. 2:468–69).

100. William of Tyre 22.8, 15–16(14–15), pp. 1017, 1026–30 (trans. 2:457–58, 468–74); Ibn al-Athir, 2:281–82; Abu Shama, 4:217–18; Baha' al-Din, pp. 55–57; al-Maqrizi, *History*, p. 68.
101. Hamilton, 'The Elephant of Christ', p. 103. For mentions of a truce concluded between Saladin and Baldwin IV in 1180 or 1181, see William of Tyre 22.8, p. 1017 (trans. 2:458); Ibn al-Athir, *Chronicle*, 2:271–73. According to William of Tyre, it was Saladin who broke the truce, though he noted that Reynald was accused of seizing certain Muslims in violation of the terms of the peace, William of Tyre 22.15(14), p. 1026 (trans. 2:467–69).
102. For the relevant charters between 1182 and 1185, see TOT nos. 14, 15, 16, pp. 13–16; RRH nos. 614, 615, 617, 624, 634, pp. 162–63, 165, 168; UKJ nos. 430, 431, 432, 438, 451, pp. 730–38, 745–49, 769–71.
103. William of Tyre 22.21–23(20–22), pp. 1038–43 (trans. 2:481–86).
104. Ernoul 7, pp. 69–70, trans. in Pringle, *Pilgrimage*, p. 140. For Reynald's presence at Acre on 25 Aug 1182, see RRH no. 617, p. 163; UKJ no. 432, pp. 736–38.
105. Abu Shama, 4:230–35; Ibn al-Athir, *Chronicle*, 2:289–90; Ibn Jubayr, pp. 51–53; al-Maqrizi, *History*, p. 70. For studies of this campaign, see La Viere Leiser, 'The Crusader Raid in the Red Sea', pp. 87–100; Milwright, 'Reynald of Châtillon and the Red Sea', pp. 235–59; Mallet, 'A Trip down the Red Sea', pp. 141–53.
106. William of Tyre 22.26–28(25–27), pp. 1048–55 (trans. 2:492–98); Baha' al-Din, pp. 60–62; Abu Shama, 4:244–48; Ibn al-Athir, *Chronicle*, 2:297. For Reynald's presence in Acre on 19 March 1183, see RRH no. 624, p. 165; UKJ no. 438, pp. 745–49. He also approved a grant issued by his stepson, Humphrey, on 21 April, which was almost certainly issued in Palestine when considering the witness list, RRH no. 628, p. 166; UKJ no. 439, pp. 749–50.
107. RRH no. 551, pp. 146–47; Cart. Hosp. no. 521, 1:355–56. Theobald of Bethune seems otherwise unknown, and the granting of his lands at this time, which corresponds with the crusade of Philip of Flanders, who was accompanied by Robert V of Bethune and his sons, Robert and William, appears coincidental.
108. RRH no. 607, p. 161; Cart. Hosp. no. 610, 1:415–16.
109. For the siege of 1183, see William of Tyre 22.29–31(28–30), pp. 1055–60 (trans. 2:498–504); Ernoul 9, pp. 102–6; Abu Shama, 4:248–49; Baha' al-Din, pp. 62–63; Ibn al-Athir, *Chronicle*, 2:297–98; al-Maqrizi, *History*, pp. 71–73.
110. William of Tyre 22.29(28), p. 1056 (trans. 2:499).
111. Ernoul 9, p. 103.
112. For the development of contemporary mechanical artillery, see Fulton, *Artillery in the Era of the Crusades*.
113. Ernoul 5, 9, pp. 35–36, 103.
114. *Itinerarium* 1.3, p. 9 (trans. p. 27).
115. Baha' al-Din, p. 65.
116. Abu Shama, 4:251.
117. Al-Maqrizi, *History*, pp. 73, 76–77.
118. Ibn Jubayr, pp. 300–1. For the movement of Saladin's forces, see the following note.
119. For the siege of 1184, see Abu Shama, 4:249, 251–56; Baha' al-Din, pp. 64–65; Ibn al-Athir, *Chronicle*, 2:300–1; al-Maqrizi, *History*, pp. 73–75, 77; *History of the Patriarchs 9*, 3.2:118; Ibn al-'Adim, *Histoire d'Alep*, p. 84; Ibn al-Furat, *Ayyubids*, 2:52.
120. If this place is to be identified with Wadi al-Wala, the Franks would have arrived from the north, travelling via Jericho and the Balqa'. Wadi al-Wala joins the mouth of Wadi al-Mujib, about 30km north of Kerak, and extends away to the northeast, north of Dhiban.
121. Ibn Jubayr, pp. 313–14.
122. William of Tyre 23.1, pp. 1062–64 (trans. 2:507–9).
123. Ralph of Diceto, pp. 27–28. See also Broussillon, 'Charte d'André II', pp. 50–53; RRHa no. 637a, p. 41.

124. These assumptions appear to be informed in large part by the account of 'Imad al-Din, who often exaggerated for effect, Abu Shama, 4:254. Cf. the siege of Saone, Fulton, 'A Ridge too Far', pp. 33–53.

125. For a study of artillery during this period, see Fulton, *Artillery in the Era of the Crusades*, for Saladin's sieges of Kerak, esp. pp. 140–48.

126. For an introduction to this method of sapping, see Fulton, *Siege Warfare*, pp. 137–43.

127. Al-Maqrizi, *History*, p. 78.

128. Ibn Jubayr, p. 324; Ernoul 10, 11, pp. 115–19, 124; *Eracles* 23.4–6, 2:6–10; RRH no. 643, p. 170; UKJ no. 451, pp. 769–71. For Saladin's campaign in the Jazira from the spring of 1185 to the spring of 1186, see Baha' al-Din, pp. 66–69; Ibn al-Athir, *Chronicle*, 2:304–9.

129. William of Tyre 21.18(19), p. 986 (trans. 2:425); Ernoul 11, pp. 129–37; *Eracles* 23.17–22, 2:25–33. Cf. Ibn al-Athir, *Chronicle*, 2:315–16.

130. See Baha' al-Din, pp. 69–71; Ibn al-Athir, *Chronicle*, 2:313–15.

131. Abu Shama, 4:258–59; *Eracles* 23.23, 26, 2:34, 37. Cf. Ibn al-Athir, *Chronicle*, 2:316–17; al-Maqrizi, *History*, p. 81; *Itinerarium* 1.5, pp. 11–12 (trans. pp. 29–30). There is almost certainly no truth to the notion that Reynald captured Saladin's sister, and inconsistencies can be found in some versions of the Latin continuation of William of Tyre's history – following his capture of Jerusalem, Saladin supposedly summoned this sister and she arrived with twenty camel-loads of rose water from Damascus to help purify the city's holy places. Problematically, Kerak had not yet surrendered, and there is no mention of her being released, *Eracles*, 2:103–4 (lower text), trans. in Edbury, *The Conquest of Jerusalem*, p. 66. For more on the Ernoul and *Eracles* texts, with a discussion focusing on their presentation of the events of the 1180s, see Edbury, 'Ernoul', pp. 44–67.

132. Ernoul 12, p. 141; *Eracles* 23.24, 2:34–35; Ibn al-Athir, *Chronicle*, 2:316; al-Maqrizi, *History*, p. 81.

133. Ernoul 12, pp. 142–43; *Eracles* 23.25, 2:36; 'Imad al-Din, pp. 13–14, 93–94; Baha' al-Din, pp. 71–72; Ibn al-Athir, *Chronicle*, 2:318–19; Abu Shama, 4:261; al-Maqrizi, *History*, p. 82. Although the main army of Antioch was not sent to Palestine, a contingent was indeed dispatched.

134. TOT nos. 21, 22, 23, pp. 20–22; RRH nos. 653, 654, 655, pp. 173–74; UKJ nos. 473, 474, 475, pp. 796–803; *Eracles* 23.17, 2:25–26. Cf. RRH no. 643, p. 170; UKJ no. 451, pp. 769–71.

135. Ernoul 12, pp. 143–48; *Eracles* 23.25–27, 2:36–41; 'Imad al-Din, pp. 14–16; Ibn al-Athir, *Chronicle*, 2:319–20; Abu Shama, 4:261–62. For the location of this engagement, see Pringle, 'The Springs of Cresson', pp. 231–40.

136. Baha' al-Din, pp. 72–73; 'Imad al-Din, p. 16; Ibn al-Athir, *Chronicle*, 2:319–20; Abu Shama, 4:262; Ibn al-Furat, *Ayyubids*, 2:52.

137. *Eracles* 23.30–33, 2:47–50; Ernoul 12, pp. 157–62; Hampe, 'Reise nach England', pp. 278–80.

138. For a comprehensive look at the battle and the events leading up to it, see France, *Hattin*. For a recent assessment of the battle, which argues against certain traditional interpretations, see Morton, *Crusader States*, pp. 184–89.

139. 'Imad al-Din, pp. 27–28, 97, 104–5; Baha' al-Din, pp. 37–38, 73–75; Abu Shama, 4:275–76, 298, 299; RRH no. 664, pp. 176–77; RRHa no. 664a, pp. 45–46; Roger of Howden, *Gesta*, 2:36–38; Ernoul 15, pp. 172–74; *Eracles* 23.35, 2:52–53 and 2:68–69 (lower text); *Itinerarium* 1.5, p. 16 (trans. p. 34); *History of the Patriarchs* 9, 3.2:121–22.

140. 'Imad al-Din, pp. 105–7, 148–49; Baha' al-Din, pp. 88, 91, 247; Ibn al-Athir, *Chronicle*, 2:333, 354–55; Abu Shama, 4:332–33, 346, 381–82, 388, 391–92; al-Maqrizi, *History*, pp. 87–88.

141. Ernoul 16, p. 187; *Eracles* 2:104–5, 121–22 (lower text). Cf. *Eracles* 23.54, 2:81–82; *Itinerarium* 1.5, pp. 29–30 (trans. pp. 45–46).

142. Pringle, *Churches*, 1:286.

143. William of Tyre 15.21, p. 704. For Reynald's seal, see Schlumberger, *Renaud de Chatillon*, facing p. 400.
144. Burchard of Mount Sion, p. 22 (trans. pp. 244–45, see also n. 13). Shawbak is the Arabic name for the site, and subsequent castle, known to the Franks as Montreal. For an example of *Karak al-Shawbak*, see Ibn Sasra, 1:40. For a broader discussion of the naming, see Mayer, *Montréal*, pp. 273–75; Brown, 'Petra Deserti', pp. 716–17.
145. James of Vitry, *Historia* 50, pp. 216–17; John of Ibelin 234–37, 239, pp. 600–8, 615, trans. in Edbury, *John of Ibelin*, pp. 193–96, 199–200. See also Edbury, *John of Ibelin*, pp. 166–75; Hamilton, *The Latin Church*, p. 152. As Edbury and others have noted, Sidon, Caesarea and Bethsan were three distinct lordships.
146. Oliver of Paderborn 31, pp. 222–23 (trans. pp. 85–86). For secondary interpretations, see Deschamps, *Royaume de Jérusalem*, p. 39 n. 1; Pringle, 'Crusader Castles', pp. 678–81.
147. TOT no. 3, pp. 3–5; RRH no. 366, pp. 96–97; Chartes TS no. 2, pp. 183–85; UKJ nos. 263, 314, pp. 479–86, 548–50; Pringle, *Secular Buildings*, pp. 112–13 (no. p4); Milwright, 'Central and Southern Jordan', pp. 10–11; Northedge, 'Fortifications', pp. 437–59.
148. Abu Shama, 4:382; Ibn al-Athir, *Chronicle*, 2:354–55. Cf. 'Imad al-Din, p. 99. See also Pringle, 'Crusader Castles in Jordan', pp. 678–81; Brown, 'Petra Deserti', pp. 706–7.
149. Albert of Aachen 12.23, pp. 856–59; Ernoul 7, p. 68, trans. in Pringle, *Pilgrimage*, p. 139; Stern, *Fatimid Decrees*, pp. 46–52, 80–84.
150. Broussillon, *La maison de Craon*, no. 138, 1:101; Thietmar 20, pp. 44–45 (trans. pp. 126–27). Cf. Kohler, 'Documents inédits' no. 1, pp. 6–9; RRHa no. 265a, pp. 17–18.
151. RRH no. 897, pp. 240–41. For more on the monastery, its history and relations with the Franks, see Pringle, *Churches*, 2:49–63.
152. Pringle, 'Castles of Ayla', pp. 333–53. For the Frankish expedition to 'Aqaba in 1116, see Fulcher of Chartres 2.56, pp. 594–96 (trans. pp. 215–16).
153. For the results of excavations at 'Aqaba, see al-Shqour, *The Aqaba Khans*, pp. 235–49; al-Shqour, De Meulemeester and Herremans, 'The 'Aqaba Castle Project', pp. 641–55; De Meulemeester and Pringle, 'Al'Aqaba Castle', pp. 97–102. For a detailed description of the khan, see al-Shqour, *The Aqaba Khans*, pp. 201–34.
154. Thietmar 17, p. 40 (trans. p. 123). For accounts of the castle's capture in 1170 and the Red Sea Raid, see above. For scholarly assessments of the small castle, see Brooker and Knauf, 'Review', p. 187; Mayer, *Montréal*, pp. 52–54; Pringle, *Churches*, 1:274–75.
155. William of Tyre 16.6, pp. 721–22 (trans. 2:144–45).
156. TOT no. 3, pp. 3–5; RRH nos. 279, 366, pp. 71, 96–97; Cart. Hosp. nos. 207, 284, 1:160, 210; UKJ nos. 123, 263, pp. 286–87, 479–86. Cf. RRH no. 551, pp. 146–7; Cart. Hosp. no. 521, 1:355–56. See also Tibble, *Monarchy and Lordships*, pp. 82–84; Mayer, *Montréal*, pp. 97–99, 130; Pringle, *Churches*, 2:374. For references to Ulrich as viscount of Nablus in the charter evidence, see RRH nos. 90, 121, 134, 174, 181, pp. 21, 30, 33–34, 43–45; Kohler, 'Chartes' no. 18, p. 128; RRHa no. 137a, pp. 10–11; Hiestand, 'Zwei unbekannte Diplime', pp. 54–55; UKJ nos. 85, 105, 109, 131, 138, 139, pp. 225–30, 261–63, 268–69, 276–80, 302–4, 315–23.
157. Yaqut, trans. in Le Strange, *Palestine under the Moslems*, pp. 528, 550. For these sites and their occupation, see Hammond, *Crusader Fort*; Zayadine, 'Caravan Routes', pp. 164–67; Zayadine, 'Caravan Routes', pp. 163–70; Brown, 'A 12th Century A.D. Sequence', pp. 267–69; Brooker and Knauf, 'Review', p. 187; Marino et al., 'The Crusader Settlement in Petra', pp. 3–13; Vannini and Tonghini, 'Medieval Petra', pp. 373–78; Pringle, *Secular Buildings*, pp. 49, 95, 105–6 (nos. 97, 202, 230). For the Frankish presence in the Petra region more generally, see Sinibaldi, 'Settlement in Crusader Transjordan', pp. 110–14, 186–87.
158. Schmid, '2000 Season', p. 348; idem, '2001 Season', pp. 265–66; Schmid and Studer, '2002 Season', p. 476; Schmid, '2004 Season', pp. 74–75; idem, '200 Season', pp. 142–43; idem, '2007 Season', pp. 98–99; idem, '2009 Season', pp. 221–22, 229. See also Sinibaldi, 'Settlement in Crusader Transjordan', pp. 142–48.

159. Albert of Aachen 7.2, 5, 15, 26, 30, 45, 65, pp. 486–89, 492–93, 506–7, 522–23, 528–29, 554–55, 576–77; RRH no. 57, pp. 12–13; Cart. Hosp. no. 20, pp. 21–22; UKJ no. 42, pp. 165–68.
160. Riley-Smith, 'Motives', pp. 726 and n. 3, 735–36 and n. 1 on the latter; Mayer, 'Die Herrschaftsbildung in Hebron', pp. 66–70.
161. Albert of Aachen 9.49, 10.17, 33, pp. 706–7, 734–35, 748–49; Delaborde, *Chartes* nos. 14, 18, pp. 40–41, 45–47; RRH nos. 57, 80, 90, 91 115, 120, 121, 133, 134, pp. 12–13, 18–19, 21, 28, 30, 33–34; Cart. Hosp. no. 20, pp. 21–22; Cart. Sep. App. 1, pp. 347–48; UKJ nos. 42, 64, 85, 86, 96, 103, 105, 115, 116, pp. 165–68, 195–98, 225–33, 250–52, 257–59, 261–63, 275–80. Cf. Delaborde, *Chartes* no. 5; RRH nos. 43, 52, 79, pp. 8, 10–11, 18; Kohler, 'Chartes' no. 7, pp. 117–18; RRHa no. 76b, pp. 5–6; UKJ nos. 29, 32, 58, pp. 137–44, 149–50, 187–89. See also Murray, *Crusader Kingdom*, pp. 187, 199, 212–13.
162. RRH no. 164, pp. 40–41; UKJ no. 135, pp. 310–14.
163. RRH nos. 251, 255, p. 63; Cart. Sep. no. 110, pp. 230–31. Cf. RRH no. 169, p. 42; Cart. Sep. no. 112, pp. 232–3.
164. Mayer, 'Die Herrschaftsbildung in Hebron', pp. 70–71; Tibble, *Monarchy and Lordships*, pp. 9–11, 70–71. See also Pringle, 'Castellans', pp. 185–87.
165. William of Tyre 14.26, 17.14, pp. 665–66, 779 (trans. 2:87, 205–6).
166. Chalandon, 'Un diplôme inédit', pp. 12–16; RRHa no. 422a, pp. 25–26; UKJ no. 316, pp. 550–53.
167. William of Tyre 20.3, p. 914 (trans. 2:346). See also Hamilton, *The Latin Church*, p. 77. For the first bishop, Reynald, see Broussillon, *La maison de Craon*, no. 140, 1:102; RRH nos. 476, 480, 490, 512, pp. 125–27, 129, 135; Cart. Sep. no. 158, pp. 307–9; UKJ nos. 344, 359, pp. 599–600, 624–26.
168. RRH no. 553, p. 147; UKJ no. 493, pp. 843–45. Cf. Kohler, 'Chartes' no. 45, pp. 153–54; RRHa no. 623a, p. 40.
169. Kohler, 'Chartes', no. 45, pp. 153–54; RRHa no. 623a, p. 40.
170. Pringle, *Churches*, 1:224
171. TOT no. 3, pp. 35; RRH no. 366, pp. 96–97; UKJ no. 263, pp. 479–86. See also Mayer, 'Crusader Lordship', pp. 201–2; Milwright, *Fortress of the Raven*, pp. 60, 71–72; Sinibaldi, 'Settlement in Crusader Transjordan', pp. 198–202
172. Abu Shama, 4:155–57; Lyons and Jackson, *Saladin*, pp. 62–63; Lev, *Saladin in Egypt*, pp. 95–96.
173. Ibn al-Athir, *Chronicle*, 2:195, 230–31; al-Maqrizi, *History*, pp. 50–51; Lyons and Jackson, *Saladin*, pp. 44, 77; Lev, *Saladin in Egypt*, pp. 95, 100–1.
174. Lev, 'Saladin's Economic Policies', p. 316; idem, *Saladin in Egypt*, p. 143. Cf. al-Maqrizi, *History*, p. 40.
175. TOT no. 3, pp. 3–5; Delaborde, *Chartes* no. 14, pp. 40–41; RRH nos. 115, 164, 366, 368, 369, pp. 28, 40–41, 96–97; Cart. Sep. no. 88, pp. 201–3; UKJ nos. 96, 135, 263, 264, 265, pp. 250–52, 310–14, 479–90; William of Tyre 18.14, pp. 830–31 (trans. 2:261). Cf. Ibn al-Qalanisi, pp. 335–36. See also RRH nos. 400, 444, pp. 105, 115; UKJ no. 310, pp. 536–41.
176. RRH no. 279, p. 71; Cart. Hosp. no. 207, 1:160.
177. RRH no. 454, p. 119; UKJ no. 321, pp. 558–59.
178. TOT no. 2, pp. 2–3; RRH no. 341, p. 89; UKJ no. 253, pp. 460–62.
179. Kohler, 'Chartes', no. 6, p. 117; RRHa no. 81a, p. 6.
180. RRH no. 142, p. 36; UKJ no. 128, pp. 296–98.
181. Delaborde, *Chartes* no. 41, pp. 88–89; RRH nos. 551, 596, pp. 146–47, 159; Cart. Hosp. no. 521, 1:355–56; UKJ no. 534, p. 913. Cf. William of Tyre 22.31(30), p. 1059 (trans. 2:503)
182. RRH nos. 454, 551, 628, pp. 119, 146–47, 166; Cart. Hosp. no. 521, 1:355–56; UKJ nos. 321, 439, pp. 558–59, 749–50.
183. Delaborde *Chartes* no. 39, pp. 86–87; RRH nos. 164, 169, 542, 628, pp. 40–42, 144, 166; Kohler, 'Chartes', no. 45, pp. 153–54; RRHa no. 623a, p. 40; Cart. Sep. 112, pp. 232–33; UKJ nos. 135, 628, pp. 310–14, 749–50.

184. Delaborde *Chartes* no. 41, pp. 88–89; RRH nos. 279, 454, 551, 596, 628, pp. 71, 119, 146–47, 159, 166; Cart. Hosp. nos. 207, 521, 1:160, 355–56; RRHa no. 458b, p. 28; UKJ nos. 321, 439, 534, pp. 558–59, 749–50, 913.

185. For a collation of results and some conclusions from various previous and ongoing archaeological activities in Jordan relating to the Frankish period, see Sinibaldi, 'Settlement in Crusader Transjordan'. For the particular issues of dating 'Frankish' period sherds, see ibid., pp. 7–12.

186. Brown, 'A 12th Century A.D. Sequence', pp. 277–84; Vannini and Tonghini, 'Medieval Petra', pp. 378–82; Tonghini and Vanni Desideiri, 'Material Evidence from al-Wu'ayra', pp. 708–18; Sinibaldi, 'The Franks in Southern Transjordan', pp. 459–60.

187. Sinibaldi, 'The Franks in Southern Transjordan', pp. 451–58.

188. Pruno and Ranieri, 'HMPW in ash-Shawbak Castle', pp. 226–9; idem, 'Ceramiche da cucina', pp. 40–45; Pruno, 'Little and Great Tradition', pp. 237–39.

189. Brown and Rielly, 'Faunal Remains', pp. 182–92, for an overview of the rural economy of Montreal, see pp. 171–73; Corbino and Mazza, 'Inhabitants of Shawbak Castle', pp. 681–82. For wild boar in the region, cf. Doughty, *Travels*, 1:27.

190. Brown and Rielly, 'Faunal Assemblage from al-Wu'ayra', pp. 126–37; Corbino and Mazza, 'Faunal Remains from the Castles', pp. 160–63.

191. Schmid and Studer, '2002 Season', pp. 484–87.

192. Thietmar 14–15, pp. 36–37 (trans. pp. 120–21).

193. Abu'l-Fida', trans. in Le Strange, *Palestine under the Moslems*, p. 536. See below for demographics at the start of the Ottoman period.

194. Pringle, *Pilgrimage*, pp. 10, 44, 232–33. For Latin perceptions of, and attitudes towards, Transjordan following 1189, see Brown, 'Petra Deserti', pp. 715–27.

195. Burchard of Mount Sion, pp. 22, 58–59 (trans. pp. 244–45, 282, see also nn. 13, 299).

196. RRH no. 628, p. 166; UKJ no. 439, pp. 749–50. For a mid-thirteenth-century understanding of laws relating to the age of inheritance, marriage, and the administration of lands on behalf of minors, see John of Ibelin 153–62, pp. 377–99.

197. TOT nos. 21, 22, 23, pp. 20–22; RRH nos. 634, 653, 654, 655, pp. 168, 173–74; UKJ nos. 451, 473, 474, 475, pp. 769–71, 796–803. Cf. TOT no. 15, pp. 14–15; RRH nos. 539, 615, 617, 624, 628, pp. 143–44, 163, 165–66; Cart. Hosp. no. 495, 1:341; UKJ nos. 388, 431, 432, 438, 439, pp. 666–67, 734–38, 745–50.

198. William of Tyre 22.5, p. 1012 (trans. 2:452).

199. For the most recent study of the siege of Acre, see Hosler, *The Siege of Acre*.

200. Ernoul 24, pp. 267–68; *Eracles* 25.10–12, 2:151–54; *Itinerarium* 1.45, 46, 63, pp. 95, 97, 119–23 (trans. pp. 101, 102, 121–25). Cf. *Lignages* 291, p. 65.

201. For the enduring claim to Toron and Transjordan, see *Lignages* 291, 300, 344, pp. 66, 81, 108. See also Mas Latrie, *Les Seigneurs du Crac*, pp. 18–19.

202. Deschamps, 'Étude sur un texte latin', p. 88, trans. in Pringle, *Pilgrimage*, pp. 182–83.

203. Innocent III, 1.505, 214:466–67.

204. Gregory IX 4504, 2:1121–22; Hamilton, *The Latin Church*, pp. 215, 247, 267.

Chapter 3: Ayyubid Period

1. Adapted from Le Strange, *Palestine under the Moslems*, p. 479.

2. Baha' al-Din, p. 89.

3. For the age of Saladin's sons, see Lyons and Jackson, *Saladin*, p. 135.

4. Baha' al-Din, pp. 202, 234, 238; Abu Shama, 5:106–7.

5. *Eracles*, 2:103–4 (lower text), trans. in Edbury, *The Conquest of Jerusalem*, p. 67. Cf. Roger of Howden, *Gesta*, 2:40–41.

6. Ambroise ll. 7411–15, 1:120 (trans. 2:132); *Itinerarium* 4.31, p. 297 (trans. p. 274).

7. 'Imad al-Din, pp. 380–81; Baha' al-Din, pp. 206–8.

8. 'Imad al-Din, pp. 414–15; Ibn al-Athir, *Chronicle*, 3:7–8.

9. RCEA no. 3800A, 10:276. See also Milwright, *Fortress of the Raven*, p. 73; Pringle, *Churches*, 1:287 (no. 129).
10. *History of the Patriarchs* 9, 3.2:197; al-Maqrizi, *History*, p. 155.
11. Abu Shama, 5:166. For the division of al-'Adil's realm, see Ibn al-Athir, *Chronicle*, 3:197.
12. For a comprehensive study of the Fifth Crusade, see Powell, *Anatomy of Crusade*.
13. Ernoul 36, p. 417; Abu Shama, 5:174.
14. James of Vitry, *Letters* 6, pp. 138–41; Oliver of Paderborn 31, pp. 221–24 (trans. pp. 85–86); Roger of Wendover, 3:246–48 (trans. 2:422–23); Ernoul 37, pp. 435–36; *Eracles* 32.9, 11, 2:339, 342; Ibn al-Athir, *Chronicle*, 3:180; al-Maqrizi, *History*, p. 184.
15. Milwright, 'Central and Southern Jordan', p. 5.
16. RCEA no. 3965, 10:245–46; Mauss and Sauvaire, 'Voyage de Jérusalem a Kerak', p. 202 (no. 20).
17. Milwright, 'Central and Southern Jordan', pp. 13–17.
18. For an overview of this conflict, see al-Maqrizi, *History*, pp. 191–93, 197–98. For a closer examination, see Humphreys, *From Saladin to the Mongols*, pp. 170–85.
19. Isabella II was thus the granddaughter of Isabella I of Jerusalem, former wife of Humphrey IV of Toron. For more, see Perry, 'Isabella II or Yolanda?', pp. 73–86.
20. See Ibn al-'Amid, pp. 38–39; al-Maqrizi, *History*, pp. 198–200.
21. For a biography of al-Nasir Dawud, see Drory, 'Al-Nasir Dawud', pp. 161–87.
22. For an overview of this conflict, see Ibn al-Athir, *Chronicle*, 3:294–95; Abu Shama, 5:189–91; Ibn al-'Amid, pp. 40–43; al-Maqrizi, *History*, pp. 202–11. See also Humphreys, *From Saladin to the Mongols*, pp. 193–206.
23. See Philip of Novara, *Gestes* 135, pp. 48–49 (trans. pp. 87–89); Abu Shama, 5:186; Ibn al-'Amid, pp. 40–41; al-Maqrizi, *History*, pp. 206–7.
24. Ernoul 40, p. 464. For this agreement more generally, see Philip of Novara, *Gestes* 135, pp. 48–49 (trans. pp. 87–89); Abu Shama, 5:186; Ibn al-'Amid, pp. 40–41; al-Maqrizi, *History*, pp. 206–7.
25. Drory, 'Al-Nasir Dawud', p. 165.
26. For an overview of this episode, see al-Maqrizi, *History*, pp. 214–18; Ibn al-'Amid, pp. 44–46.
27. Ibn al-'Amid, p. 51; al-Maqrizi, *History*, p. 217.
28. Ibn al-'Amid, pp. 51–54; al-Maqrizi, *History*, pp. 218–29.
29. *History of the Patriarchs* 12, 4.2:173–74; Ibn al-'Amid, p. 56; al-Maqrizi, *History*, pp. 234, 237.
30. Ibn al-'Amid, pp. 56–61, 65–66; al-Maqrizi, *History*, pp. 238–44.
31. Ibn al-'Amid, pp. 60–61, 66–68; al-Maqrizi, *History*, pp. 240–49; *History of the Patriarchs* 12, 4.2:194–95.
32. Abu Shama, 5:193; al-Maqrizi, *History*, p. 251; *Rothelin* 28, pp. 543–46 (trans. pp. 49–50); *Eracles* 33.44, 2:123; Matthew Paris, 4:25–26 (trans. 1:272–73).
33. *Rothelin* 21, pp. 529–30 (trans. p. 40); al-Maqrizi, *History*, p. 251; Ibn al-Furat, *Ayyubids*, 2:62; al-'Ayni, p. 196; *History of the Patriarchs* 12, 4.2:197. For a comparison with Saladin's capture of the city in 1187, see Drory, 'Al-Nasir Dawud', pp. 170–71.
34. Ibn al-'Amid, pp. 61–63, 68; al-Maqrizi, *History*, pp. 252–57.
35. Matthew Paris, 4:64–65 (trans. 1:303); *Rothelin* 32, 34, pp. 551–53, 554 (trans. pp. 55–56, 57); *Eracles* 33.47–49, 2:416–20 (trans. pp. 125–27); Templar of Tyre 18 [254], p. 59 (trans. p. 20); Abu Shama, 5:193; Ibn al-'Amid, pp. 71–73; al-Maqrizi, *History*, pp. 262–64; Ibn al-Furat, *Ayyubids*, 2:6–8, 88–89, 109–10.
36. Ibn al-'Amid, pp. 70–72; al-Maqrizi, *History*, pp. 261, 263–64, 267; *History of the Patriarchs* 12, 4.2:219–20, 222, 227–33, 241–43, 294–95.
37. Abu Shama, 5:193–94; Ibn al-Furat, *Ayyubids*, 2:1–7; Ibn al-'Amid, pp. 75–78; al-Maqrizi, *History*, pp. 271–77; al-'Ayni, p. 198; *History of the Patriarchs* 12, 4.2:294–95; Matthew Paris, 4:288–91, 300–11, 337–44 (trans. 1:482–84, 491–500, 522–28); *Rothelin* 41, pp. 562–66 (trans. pp. 63–66); *Eracles* 33.56–57, 59, 2:427–31, 432–33 (trans.

pp. 133–35); Templar of Tyre 16 [252], p. 56 (trans. pp. 19–20). For the displacement of the Khwarizmians, and their early involvement in northern Syria, see al-Maqrizi, *History*, pp. 214–16, 234–37, 252, 262. This Rukn al-Din Baybars should not be confused with either of the two later Mamluk sultans of the same name: al-Zahir Rukn al-Din Baybars al-Bunduqdari (d. 1277) and al-Muzaffar Rukn al-Din Baybars al-Jashnakir al-Mansuri (d. 1310).

38. Abu Shama, 5:194; Ibn al-'Amid, pp. 79–80; al-Maqrizi, *History*, pp. 278–82.
39. Brown, 'The Middle Islamic Palace at Karak', p. 315; idem, 'Palaces in Middle Islamic Transjordan', p. 555; Drory, 'Al-Nasir Dawud', pp. 175–77.
40. Ibn Wasil, in Jackson, *The Seventh Crusade*, pp. 128–29, 132–33; Sibt ibn al-Jawzi, in Jackson, *The Seventh Crusade*, pp. 154–55; al-Maqrizi, *History*, pp. 292–93. Cf. Ibn al-'Amid, p. 84.
41. This translation of the relevant section has been adapted from that found in Milwright, *Fortress of the Raven*, p. 256. For the complete edition and French translation, see Cahen and Chabbouh, 'Le testament d'al-Malik as-Salih Ayyub', pp. 97–114.
42. For the perceived importance of retaining the castle expressed during the Third, Fifth and Sixth Crusades, see above. See also Milwright, *Fortress of the Raven*, pp. 256–57.
43. Abu Shama, 5:195–96; Ibn al-Furat, *Ayyubids*, 2:23–26; Ibn al-'Amid, pp. 86–87; al-Maqrizi, *History*, pp. 293–94.
44. For a first-hand account of the crusaders' campaign in Egypt, see John of Joinville 146–405, pp. 72–201, for the subsequent period in Palestine, 406–417, pp. 200–307.
45. Ibn Wasil, in Jackson, *The Seventh Crusade*, pp. 150–52; Abu Shama, 5:198–200; Ibn al-Furat, *Ayyubids*, 2:33–34; Ibn al-'Amid, p. 88; al-Maqrizi, *History*, pp. 311–13. For this broader episode, see Thorau, *Lion of Egypt*, pp. 33–40.
46. Ibn Wasil and Sibt ibn al-Jawzi, in Jackson, *The Seventh Crusade*, pp. 214, 217, 219; Abu Shama, 5:201; Ibn al-'Amid, p. 81.
47. Ibn 'Abd al-Zahir, *al-Malik al-Zahir*, pp. 325–37. For an excellent overview of these events, see Thorau, *Lion of Egypt*, pp. 43–57.
48. Drory, 'Al-Nasir Dawud', pp. 173–75.
49. 'Amr, 'A New Ayyubid Inscription', pp. 166–72; Milwright, 'Central and Southern Jordan', p. 15.
50. Hulagu and Mongke were both grandsons of Genghis Khan. While Hulagu would found the Ilkhanate in the Middle East, a third brother, Kublai, would succeed Mongke as great khan, and establish the line of Yuan emperors of China.
51. For these events, see Amitai, 'Mongol Raids into Palestine', pp. 236–39; Irwin, *The Middle East*, pp. 31–32; Thorau, *Lion of Egypt*, pp. 67– 69.
52. William of Rubruck, p. 114 (trans. p. 184).
53. For a detailed study of this interaction, see Amitai, 'Ayyubid Lord of Transjordan', pp. 5–16.
54. Thorau, *Lion of Egypt*, pp. 64–65, 75–79. See also Ibn 'Abd al-Zahir, *al-Malik al-Zahir*, pp. 337–40; *Eracles* 34.3, 2:444 (trans. p. 140); Bar Hebraeus, 1:437–38.

Chapter 4: Mamluk Period
1. Adapted from Le Strange, *Palestine under the Moslems*, p. 479.
2. Homs and Hama continued to be administered by members of the Ayyubid family in the aftermath of the Battle of 'Ayn Jalut, but the rulers of both served with the blessing and as the subjects of the Mamluk sultan.
3. Ibn 'Abd al-Zahir, *al-Malik al-Zahir*, pp. 411–12. See also Thorau, *Lion of Egypt*, pp. 134–37. For the arrival of the Shahrazuriyya, see Humphreys, *From Saladin to the Mongols*, p. 341; Thorau, *Lion of Egypt*, pp. 62–63.
4. Amitai, 'Ayyubid Lord of Transjordan', pp. 10–11. See also Ibn 'Abd al-Zahir, *al-Malik al-Zahir*, pp. 442–47.

5. Ibn 'Abd al-Zahir, *al-Malik al-Zahir*, pp. 463–67. For further analysis and insights into Kerak's administration, see Milwright, 'Central and Southern Jordan', pp. 8–9.

6. 'Amr, 'A New Ayyubid Inscription', p. 171.

7. RCEA nos. 4733–35, 12:222–25.

8. Ibn 'Abd al-Zahir, *al-Malik al-Zahir*, pp. 542–43, 714; Ibn al-Furat, *Ayyubids*, 2:82; al-'Ayni, p. 220.

9. Ibn 'Abd al-Zahir, *al-Malik al-Zahir*, p. 714.

10. Ibn 'Abd al-Zahir, *al-Malik al-Zahir*, pp. 611–12, 715–20, 723, 763–64, 813; Zayadine, 'Caravan Routes', pp. 162–73. See also Ibn Sasra, 1:237–38.

11. Ibn al-Furat, writing in the late fourteenth century, provided a detailed account of these events, Ibn al-Furat, *Baybars' Successors*, pp. 24–30, 36. See also Ibn Sasra, 1:237–38; Ibn Tulun, pp. 5–6; al-Maqrizi, *Histoire*, 3:7–8.

12. Baybars al-Mansuri, *Zubda*, pp. 253; idem, *Mukhtar*, p. 390; Ibn al-Furat, *Baybars' Successors*, pp. 32, 36.

13. Baybars al-Mansuri, *Zubda*, pp. 253–58; idem, *Mukhtar*, p. 390. See also Ibn al-Furat, *Baybars' Successors*, pp. 38–43.

14. Baybars al-Mansuri, *Zubda*, p. 269; idem, *al-Tuhfa al-mulukiyya*, p. 371. See also Ibn al-Furat, *Baybars' Successors*, p. 87.

15. Ibn 'Abd al-Zahir, *al-Malik al-Mansur*, pp. 71–72; Baybars al-Mansuri, *Zubda*, p. 301; idem, *al-Tuhfa al-mulukiyya*, p. 377. See also Ibn al-Furat, *Baybars' Successors*, pp. 135, 143.

16. Ibn 'Abd al-Zahir, *al-Malik al-Mansur*, pp. 141–42; Baybars al-Mansuri, *Zubda*, pp. 322–23; idem, *al-Tuhfa al-mulukiyya*, pp. 380–81; idem, *Mukhtar*, p. 394; Abu'l-Fida', p. 13. See also Ibn al-Furat, *Baybars' Successors*, pp. 177–79. For the exile and later fate of the brothers, see Baybars al-Mansuri, *Zubda*, p. 355; Abu'l-Fida', p. 49.

17. Ibn 'Abd al-Zahir, *al-Malik al-Mansur*, pp. 149–51; Baybars al-Mansuri, *Zubda*, pp. 323–24. See also Abu'l-Fida', p. 14; Ibn al-Furat, *Baybars' Successors*, pp. 180–81.

18. Baybars al-Mansuri, *Zubda*, p. 325.

19. Baybars al-Mansuri, *Zubda*, pp. 324–26; idem, *al-Tuhfa al-mulukiyya*, p. 381; idem, *Mukhtar*, p. 394.

20. See Baybars al-Mansuri, *Zubda*, pp. 334.

21. Baybars al-Mansuri, *Zubda*, p. 352; idem, *Mukhtar al-akhbar*, p. 394; Ibn al-Furat, *Baybars' Successors*, p. 238; al-Maqrizi, *Histoire*, 3:129.

22. Baybars al-Mansuri, *Zubda*, p. 360; idem, *Mukhtar al-akhbar*, p. 394; Abu'l-Fida', pp. 48, 57, 62; Ibn Sasra, 1:241. See also al-Maqrizi, *Histoire*, 4:54–55, 126, 284–85, cf. 4:184–85; Ibn Tulun, p. 8.

23. Ibn al-Furat, *Baybars' Successors*, p. 266.

24. Abu'l-Fida', p. 20; Baybars al-Mansuri, *Zubda*, p. 360; Ibn al-Furat, *Baybars' Successors*, p. 267.

25. Ibn al-Furat, *Baybars' Successors*, pp. 268–69.

26. For the political succession, see Holt, 'The Sultanate of al-Mansur Lachin', pp. 523–31; Irwin, *The Middle East*, pp. 85–86. See also Abu'l-Fida', pp. 32–33, 47–48.

27. Abu'l-Fida', p. 35. See also al-Nuwayri, pp. 260–63.

28. For this episode, see Amitai, 'Mongol Raids into Palestine', pp. 243–48.

29. Abu'l-Fida', pp. 49–51. See also Irwin, *The Middle East*, p. 86.

30. Abu'l-Fida', pp. 50–53, 56–58, 60, 69; Ibn Tulun, p. 8.

31. Abu'l-Fida', pp. 63, 69, 74, 77–78.

32. See al-Nuwayri, pp. 270–71.

33. Milwright, *Fortress of the Raven*, p. 88; Brown, 'The Middle Islamic Palace at Karak', p. 314.

34. Brown, 'Palaces in Middle Islamic Transjordan', pp. 555–56; idem, 'The Middle Islamic Palace at Karak', p. 315–16.

35. Ibn Battuta, p. 72; al-Dimashqi, trans. in Le Strange, *Palestine under the Moslems*, p. 479.

36. For the epigraphic evidence, see RCEA nos. 4278, 4735, 5048, 5049, 5050, 5051, 11:183–84, 12:224–25, 13:176–78; Mauss and Sauvaire, 'Voyage de Jérusalem a Kerak', pp. 209–13 (nos. 26, 27, 28, 29, 30, 31, 32). For further contextualization, see Milwright, *Fortress of the Raven*, pp. 88–89. For the development of Montreal's outer defences, see Faucherre, 'La forteresse de Shawbak', pp. 43–64.
37. Popper, *Egypt and Syria*, 1:13–18, 81; Milwright, *Fortress of the Raven*, pp. 78–82. See also Walker, 'Mamluk Investment in Southern Bilad Al-Sham', pp. 241–48.
38. Popper, *Egypt and Syria*, 1:86–87.
39. Milwright, *Fortress of the Raven*, pp. 43, 82–83.
40. For a closer look at this period, see Drory, 'The Prince Who Favored the Desert', pp. 19–29; Irwin, *The Middle East*, pp. 125–30. For a concise near-contemporary account, see Ibn Sasra, 1:243–44. See also Ibn Tulun, pp. 9–10.
41. See Irwin, *The Middle East*, pp. 133–44.
42. For a near-contemporary summary of Barquq's rise to power, see Ibn Taghribirdi, 1:1–4, 41. For the power struggle that brought him to power, see Irwin, *The Middle East*, pp. 144–45, 148–49.
43. Ibn Sasra, 1:8–33; Ibn Taghribirdi, 1:19–41, 60.
44. Ibn Taghribirdi, 1:60–86, 94–97; Ibn Sasra, 1:32–44, 74–77. See also Brown, 'The Middle Islamic Palace at Karak', pp. 315–16; Milwright, *Fortress of the Raven*, pp. 45–46.
45. Ibn Taghribirdi, 1:118, 122–23, 127, 150, 170, 2:100.
46. Ibn Taghribirdi, 1:13, 16–18, 21, 61, 64–67; Ibn Sasra, 1:6; Ibn Tulun, p. 15.
47. Ibn Taghribirdi, 1:13, 26, 31, 65–66, 69–76.
48. Ibn Taghribidir, 1:65–67, 81–83, 95.
49. Ibn Taghribirdi, 1:25, 97, 153, 2:103.
50. Ibn Taghribirdi, 1:114–16, 121, 178, 179–80; Ibn Sasra, 1:34.
51. Ibn Taghribridi, 1:122–23, 2:100.
52. Ibn Taghribirdi, 1:115, 139, 150, 167.
53. Ibn Taghribirdi, 1:165, 169, 170.
54. Ibn Taghribirdi, 1:164, 168.
55. Ibn Taghribirdi, 1:169–70; 2:15, 31, 74, 116. For the conflict that followed Barquq's death and the Timur's invasion of Syria in 1400–1, see Ibn Taghribirdi, 2:1–29, 35–54.
56. Ibn Taghribirdi, 2:138–39, 156, 162, 168–69, 173–74. Cf. Walker, 'Mamluk Investment in Transjordan', pp. 124, 136. For the bathhouse identified in the town, see Chapter 7.
57. Ibn Taghribirdi, 2:174–76, 180–81, 190. For the defeat, deposition, and murder of al-Nasir Faraj, see ibid, 2:193–96, 3:1–2. For the context more generally, see also Walker, 'Role of Agriculture', pp. 79, 94; Milwright, *Fortress of the Raven*, pp. 46–47, 87.
58. Al-Maqrizi, *Histoire*, 4:177–80.
59. For more on the plague and its impact, see Neustadt, 'The Plague', pp. 67–73.
60. For example, 'Ala' al-Din ibn al-Tablawi was sent there in June 1399, shortly before the death of Barquq, Ibn Taghribirdi, 1:170.
61. Pringle, *Secular Buildings*, pp. 48, 49, 93, 101 (nos. 92, 99, 193, 220, 221). For the broader context, see Jones, Levy and Najjar, 'Khirbat Nuqayb al-Asaymir', p. 92
62. Jones, Levy and Najjar, 'Khirbat Nuqayb al-Asaymir', p. 92; Burke, 'Sugar Production', pp. 109–18.
63. Francesco Balducci Pegolotti, pp. 296, 363–65.
64. This has also been concluded by Sinibaldi, 'Settlement in Crusader Transjordan', pp. 126–27. Cf. Brooker and Knauf, 'Review', p. 185.
65. For investigations around Faynan, and an introduction to copper extraction in the region, see Jones, Levy and Najjar, 'Khirbat Nuqayb al-Asaymir', pp. 67–96.
66. Milwright, 'Central and Southern Jordan', pp. 18–20.
67. Brown, 'Glazed Wares in Transjordan', esp. pp. 92–94.
68. Brown, 'Mamluk Palace at Kerak', p. 298.

69. Mason and Milwright, 'Pottery from Karak', pp. 175–76; Milwright, 'Central and Southern Jordan', p. 21; Milwright, *Fortress of the Raven*, pp. 245–46.
70. Thietmar 17, p. 40 (trans. p. 123).
71. Milwright, *Fortress of the Raven*, pp. 268, 270.
72. Little, 'The Haram Documents as Sources', pp. 68–69. See also idem, 'Rugs in the Late 14th Century', pp. 83–94; Milwright, *Fortress of the Raven*, pp. 114–15.
73. Marcotulli and Pruni, 'Teindre ou ne pas teindre', pp. 189–94.
74. Ibn Sasra, 1:37, 225. The eight *nuwwab* noted by Ibn Sasra were those of Damascus, Aleppo, Hama, Tripoli, Homs, Baalbek, Safed, and Gaza. Cf. Ibn Taghribirdi, 1:149, 153, 165, 175–77, 2:2–3, 116, 5:3, 157.
75. Ibn Taghribirdi, 4:132–33, 135, 140, 5:40, 77–78, 91, 95, 100, 102.
76. Ibn Taghribirdi, 4:150, 5:7–8, 40, 78, 173.
77. Ibn Taghribirdi, 5:148–49, 151, 157, 6:83.
78. Ibn Taghribirdi, 5:148–49, 153, 154, 245.
79. Ibn Taghribirdi, 5:107, 154, 6:85, 89, 164–65.
80. Walker, 'Role of Agriculture', pp. 91–93; idem, 'The Phenomenon', pp. 167, 168.
81. Walker, 'The Phenomenon', pp. 162–69. For an introduction to the material evidence and context, see idem,. 'Militarization to Nomadization', pp. 202–32. See also idem, 'Mamluk Investment in Transjordan', pp. 119–38.
82. Walker, 'Role of Agriculture', p. 95; idem, 'The Phenomenon', p. 169.
83. Hütteroth and Abdulfattah, *Historical Geography*, pp. 171–74.
84. Ibn Tulun, pp. 120, 124. See also Johns, 'Islamic Settlement', pp. 364–66.
85. Milwright, *Fortress of the Raven*, pp. 47–48.

Chapter 5: Ottoman Period
1. Le Strange, *Palestine under the Moslems*, p. 479.
2. Ibn Jum'a, pp. 151–59; Milwright, *Fortress of the Raven*, pp. 48–50.
3. Milwright, *Fortress of the Raven*, pp. 93–95. See also Johns, 'Islamic Settlement', pp. 365–66; Hütteroth and Abdulfattah, *Historical Geography*, pp. 17–18.
4. Ibn Battuta, pp. 72–74.
5. Gubser, *Politics and Change*, p. 14; Milwright, *Fortress of the Raven*, p. 98.
6. Ibn 'Abd al-Zahir, *al-Malik al-Zahir*, pp. 715–20, 723.
7. Milwright, *Fortress of the Raven*, pp. 50, 126, 133–34; Hütteroth and Abdulfattah, *Historical Geography*, pp. 54–63, esp. pp. 57 (fig. 7), 61.
8. Hütteroth and Abdulfattah, *Historical Geography*, pp. 18, 171–74. Additional information regarding the *mazari* was communicated to Johns, 'Islamic Settlement', p. 366.
9. See EI3, s.v. *akçe*. This apparently became equivalent to the local silver *dirham*, see al-Mubaidin, 'Economic History of Damascus', p. 150 and n. 66.
10. Hütteroth and Abdulfattah, *Historical Geography*, pp. 171–74, and maps 3, 5. See also Milwright, *Fortress of the Raven*, pp. 112, 117. For the identification of Ottoman mills around Kerak, see Schriwer, 'Water Mills', pp. 142–49, 160, 280–81. At the start of the nineteenth century, four mills were reportedly operational, Seetzen, *Reisen*, 1:417, 421.
11. Hütteroth and Abdulfattah, *Historical Geography*, pp. 85–91, 169, 171–74, and maps 3, 5. Slightly smaller markets between Kerak and Damascus included those at 'Ajlun (1,000), Irbid (2,000) and Hubras (2,000), ibid., pp. 162, 200, 203.
12. Hütteroth and Abdulfattah, *Historical Geography*, pp. 50, 171–74, and map 1.
13. See Seetzen, *Reisen*, 1:420; MacMichael, *Journey*, p. 210.
14. Milwright, *Fortress of the Raven*, p. 104.
15. Gubser, *Politics and Change*, p. 14; Johns, 'Islamic Settlement', p. 366. The Tamimiyya may have been from the Hebron area, from where a group migrated to Kerak before subsequent generations fled back to Hebron, only to see others later return to Kerak.
16. Ibn Jum'a, pp. 219, 231 Gubser, *Politics and Change*, p. 14; Milwright, *Fortress of the Raven*, pp. 49–51, 99.

17. Gubser, *Politics and Change*, pp. 14–16. See also Seetzen, *Reisen*, 1:415–16, 420; Burckhardt, *Travels in Syria*, pp. 381–82.

18. Burckhardt, *Travels in Syria*, p. 383.

19. Irby and Mangles, *Travels*, p. 366; Seetzen, *Reisen*, 1:421.

20. Layard, *Early Adventures*, 1:73–78, 94–98; Conder, *Heth and Moab*, pp. 118–19.

21. Layard, *Early Adventures*, 1:90–91; Luynes, *Voyage d'exploration*, 1:99; Gubser, *Politics and Change*, p. 16; Rogan, *Frontiers of the State*, pp. 31–32; Milwright, *Fortress of the Raven*, p. 51. Cf. Doughty, *Travels*, 1:24.

22. Klein, 'Notes on a Journey to Moab', p. 255; de Saulcy, *Voyages*, 1:356, 363; Tristram, *The Land of Moab*, p. 98; Irby and Mangles, *Travels*, p. 362; Mauss and Sauvaire, 'Voyage de Jérusalem a Kerak', p. 180.

23. Mauss and Sauvaire, 'Voyage de Jérusalem a Kerak', pp. 112–13; Tristram, *The Land of Moab*, pp. 94–95; Klein, 'Missionary Tour', p. 126.

24. Luynes, *Voyage d'exploration*, 1:109; Klein, 'Missionary Tour', p. 125; Doughty, *Travels*, 1:24–25; 'The Moabite Stone', pp. 169–83; Palmer, 'Desert of the Tíh', p. 70; Gubser, *Politics and Change*, pp. 16–17. Cf. Palmer, 'Letters [IV]', p. 321–23; Tristram, *The Land of Moab*, p. 134.

25. Klein, 'Missionary Tour', pp. 63–64, 92–93; Rogan, *Frontiers of the State*, pp. 49–52.

26. Gubser, *Politics and Change*, p. 17; Hill, *With the Beduins*, pp. 198–99.

27. Seetzen, *Reisen*, 1:414, 421; Burckhardt, *Travels in Syria*, pp. 381, 386–87; Irby and Mangles, *Travels*, p. 366; MacMichael, *Journey*, p. 209. Seetzen carried a letter from the Greek priest of Kerak to the bishop in Jerusalem, where the two men conversed through an Italian interpreter, as the bishop did not know Arabic and Seetzen knew neither Turkish nor Greek, Seetzen, 'A Brief Account', pp. 39–40; idem, *Reisen*, 1:424, 2:10–11. Cf. Dowling, 'Kerak in 1896', p. 330.

28. Layard, *Early Adventures*, 1:69–70, 89–91; Lynch, *Expedition to the River Jordan*, pp. 339, 357, 362–63; Mauss and Sauvaire, 'Voyage de Jérusalem a Kerak', pp. 113, 115. Cf. Hill, *With the Beduins*, p. 205.

29. Klein, 'Notes on a Journey to Moab', p. 255; Tristram, *The Land of Moab*, p. 81; Bliss, 'Expedition to Moab', p. 220; Meistermann, *Guide du Nil*, p. 253; Dowling, 'Kerak in 1896', pp. 329–30; Gautier, 'Autour de la mer Morte', p. 89.

30. Burckhardt, *Travels in Syria*, pp. 383; Irby and Mangles, *Travels*, p. 365; Lynch, *Expedition to the River Jordan*, pp. 339, 346; de Saulcy, *Voyages*, 1:356.

31. Gubser, *Politics and Change*, p. 18; Rogan, *Frontiers of the State*, p. 134; Abujaber, 'They Came and Stayed', pp. 401–2.

32. Conder, *Heth and Moab*, pp. 142–43; Bliss, 'Expedition to Moab', p. 205; Luynes, *Voyage d'exploration*, 1:100; Klein, 'Notes on a Journey to Moab', p. 255; Doughty, *Travels*, 1:24.

33. Musil, *Arabia Petraea*, 1:52; Dowling, 'Kerak in 1896', pp. 330–31; Gautier, 'Autour de la mer Morte', pp. 90–91; Deschamps, *Royaume de Jérusalem*, p. 93; Rogan, *Frontiers of the State*, pp. 134, 148–51; Gubser, *Politics and Change*, p. 25.

34. For example, Burckhardt, *Travels in Syria*, pp. 383–88; Klein, 'Missionary Tour', p. 64.

35. MacMichael, *Journey*, pp. 235–36; Seetzen, 'A Brief Account', p. 40; idem, *Reisen*, 1:414, 415, 417, 419; Layard, *Early Adventures*, 1:97–98; Hill, *With the Beduins*, p. 196. Close to a century later, Bliss confirmed many of these early observations, such as the seasonal exodus to the countryside during the harvest, and the presence of a few shops in the town but no regular market, Bliss, 'Expedition to Moab', p. 220.

36. Burckhardt, *Travels in Syria*, p. 388; Irby and Mangles, *Travels*, pp. 359–60; MacMichael, *Journey*, pp. 237, 239; Klein, 'Missionary Tour', p. 152; Tristram, *The Land of Moab*, p. 89.

37. Burckhardt, *Travels in Syria*, pp. 378, 380; Irby and Mangles, *Travels*, pp. 362–63; Lynch, *Expedition to the River Jordan*, pp. 356–57; Tristram, *The Land of Moab*, pp. 80–81, 83, 98; Bliss, 'Expedition to Moab', p. 220; Musil, *Arabia Petraea*, 1:52; Gautier, 'Autour de la mer Morte', pp. 89–90; Libbey and Hoskins, *The Jordan Valley*, 1:349–50.

38. Irby and Mangles, *Travels*, p. 366; MacMichael, *Journey*, p. 209; Klein, 'Missionary Tour', p. 93.
39. For discussions of the tribal networks at the time, see Luynes, *Voyage d'exploration*, 1:109; Mauss and Sauvaire, 'Voyage de Jérusalem a Kerak', pp. 116–18; Rogan, *Frontiers of the State*, pp. 30–31; Gubser, *Politics and Change*, p. 17. For another anecdote of Christian support for the Majaly, see Irby and Mangles, *Travels*, p. 368.
40. Burckhardt, *Travels in Syria*, pp. 382–83, 389.
41. Seetzen, *Reisen*, 1:414, 426; Burckhardt, *Travels in Syria*, pp. 378–79; Irby and Mangles, *Travels*, pp. 367–68. For contrasting experiences, see Burckhardt, *Travels in Syria*, pp. 377–417; MacMichael, *Journey*, pp. 196–247.
42. Layard, *Early Adventures*, 1:79–103; de Saulcy, *Voyages*, 1:358–59; Luynes, *Voyage d'exploration*, 1:94–101, 106–7, 112–14; Mauss and Sauvaire, 'Voyage de Jérusalem a Kerak', pp. 107, 126, 129; Tristram, *The Land of Moab*, pp. 83–97; Hill, *With the Beduins*, pp. 195–236.
43. Seetzen, *Reisen*, 1:412, 414, 420; Mauss and Sauvaire, 'Voyage de Jérusalem a Kerak', pp. 145–53; Hornstein, 'A Visit to Kerak', pp. 98–99.
44. Hill, *With the Beduins*, p. 202
45. See the letter composed by Mrs Lethaby to the Hills, in Hill, *With the Beduins*, pp. 319–20.
46. Gubser, *Politics and Change*, pp. 18–20; Rogan, *Frontiers of the State*, pp. 53–55; Hill, 'A Journey East of the Jordan', p. 24; Libbey and Hoskins, *The Jordan Valley*, 1:345. Cf. Bliss, 'Expedition to Moab', p. 203; Lagrange, 'Notre exploration de Pétra', p. 209. The disruption leading up to this foiled the Hills' second attempt to reach Petra, having placed themselves under the protection of Sheik Haza of the Banu Sakhr.
47. Hornstein, 'A Visit to Kerak', pp. 98–99.
48. Bliss, 'Expedition to Moab', p. 217; Hornstein, 'A Visit to Kerak', p. 95; Dowling, 'Kerak in 1896', pp. 329, 331; Musil, *Arabia Petraea*, 1:52–53; Gautier, 'Autour de la mer Morte', p. 85; Libbey and Hoskins, *The Jordan Valley*, 1:322, 345–46. Gubser specifies that 1,000 silver dollars were paid out monthly to the sheiks of Kerak, with 200 going to Sheik Salih, Gubser, *Politics and Change*, p. 20.
49. Hill, 'A Journey East of the Jordan', pp. 39–42; Bliss, 'Expedition to Moab', pp. 203, 217. On their fifth attempt, the Hills finally made it to Petra, taking the more easterly *hajj* route past Kerak. Although they felt no inclination to visit the town for a third time, they sent a request to the Ottoman official there, who duly provided a small armed escort and letters of introduction to his counterpart in Ma'an and the garrison commander at Shawbak, Hill, 'A Journey to Petra', pp. 40–41.
50. Musil, *Arabia Petraea*, 1:45–59; Libbey and Hoskins, *The Jordan Valley*, 1:345.
51. Dowling, 'Kerak in 1896', p. 332; Musil, *Arabia Petraea*, 1:54–56; Gautier, 'Autour de la mer Morte', pp. 86–88; Libbey and Hoskins, *The Jordan Valley*, 1:346. Cf. Brown, 'The Middle Islamic Palace at Karak', p. 315.
52. El-Isa, 'Earthquake Studies', p. 233; Mauss and Sauvaire, 'Voyage de Jérusalem a Kerak', pl. 3.
53. Gubser, *Politics and Change*, pp. 20, 106–10; Milwright, *Fortress of the Raven*, p. 52.
54. Abujaber, 'Cereal Production', pp. 42–43.
55. Gubser, *Politics and Change*, pp. 20–23, 98–101; Deschamps, *Royaume de Jérusalem*, p. 95.
56. MacDonald, 'Human Presence/Absence', p. 770.

Chapter 6: The Castle

1. Lynch, *Expedition to the River Jordan*, pp. 358–59.
2. Since Deschamps' early study, a range of similar yet often differing measurements have been recorded, see Deschamps, *Royaume de Jérusalem*, pp. 80, 87; Biller, Burger and Häffner, 'Neues zu den Burgen', p. 48; Pringle, *Churches*, 1:287. For the most recent explanation of the phasing, see Sinibaldi, 'Karak Castle', pp. 112–13.

3. Pringle, *Churches*, 1:287; Brown, 'Mamluk Palace at Kerak', pp. 292–98; idem, 'The Middle Islamic Palace at Karak', pp. 317–30; Milwright, *Fortress of the Raven*, pp. 137–255.
4. Biller, Burger and Häffner, 'Neues zu den Burgen', pp. 45–53; Sinibaldi, 'Karak Castle', pp. 98–113; Nucciotti and Fragai, 'Ayyubid Reception Halls'.
5. Seetzen, *Reisen*, 1:420; Burckhardt, *Travels in Syria*, p. 380; Irby and Mangles, *Travels*, p. 364; Lynch, *Expedition to the River Jordan*, p. 358; Tristram, *The Land of Moab*, pp. 71–72, 82; Bliss, 'Expedition to Moab', pp. 218–19.
6. Deschamps, *Royaume de Jérusalem*, pp. 81–82. Deschamps placed the source of the limestone at Batn Taouil, near Wadi al-Franji. Ironically, he correctly identified the Muslim masonry at Kerak, but mistakenly associated the Ayyubid work at Subayba, where later Mamluk additions are also to be found, with the Franks, having apparently failed to notice a number of Ayyubid dedicatory inscriptions, Deschamps, *Royaume de Jérusalem*, pp. 167–74. Cf. Seetzen, 'A Brief Account', p. 16; Ellenblum, 'Who Built Qal'at al-Subayba?' pp. 103–12; Amitai, 'Inscriptions at al-Subayba', pp. 113–19.
7. For example, Irby and Mangles, *Travels*, pp. 364–65.
8. See also Brooker and Knauf, 'Review', p. 186.
9. Mauss and Sauvaire, 'Voyage de Jérusalem a Kerak', pp. 106, 202 (no. 20); RCEA no. 3965, 10:245–46.
10. Deschamps, *Royaume de Jérusalem*, pp. 82, 88; Brooker and Knauf, 'Review', p. 186; Biller, Burger and Häffner, 'Neues zu den Burgen', pp. 48–49. See also Milwright, *Fortress of the Raven*, p. 63; Sinibaldi, 'Settlement in Crusader Transjordan', pp. 102, 109–11.
11. Musil, *Arabia Petraea*, 1:56.
12. Cf. Deschamps, *Royaume de Jérusalem*, pp. 84–85.
13. For nineteenth-century descriptions, see Irby and Mangles, *Travels*, p. 369; Layard, *Early Adventures*, 1:92; Mauss and Sauvaire, 'Voyage de Jérusalem a Kerak', p. 108.
14. Ibn al-Athir, *Chronicle*, 2:300; Ibn al-Furat, *Ayyubids*, 2:51; Abu'l-Fida', p. 48.
15. Deschamps, *Royaume de Jérusalem*, p. 83; Sinibaldi, 'Karak Castle', p. 104; Bliss, 'Expedition to Moab', p. 218. Cf. Sinibaldi, 'Settlement in Crusader Transjordan', p. 74. See also Biller, Burger and Häffner, 'Neues zu den Burgen', p. 49.
16. See also Deschamps, *Royaume de Jérusalem*, p. 84; Biller, Burger and Häffner, 'Neues zu den Burgen', pp. 49–50.
17. Sinibaldi, 'Settlement in Crusader Transjordan', pp. 74, 83–84; idem, 'Karak Castle', pp. 105–6. Cf. Deschamps, *Royaume de Jérusalem*, p. 84; Biller, Burger and Häffner, 'Neues zu den Burgen', pp. 49–50.
18. For assessments of contemporary artillery, see Fulton, *Artillery in the Era of the Crusades*; idem, 'A Ridge Too Far', pp. 33–53. Cf. idem, 'The Siege of Montfort', pp. 689–717.
19. William of Tyre 22.29(28), pp. 1056–57 (trans. 2:500); Abu'l-Fida', pp. 47–48.
20. Abu'l-Fida', p. 48; Ibn al-Furat, *Ayyubids*, 2:51; Ibn Battuta, p. 72; Layard, *Early Adventures*, 1:92.
21. Musil, *Arabia Petraea*, 1:53.
22. Rey, *Étude sur les monuments*, pp. 133–34. See also Bliss, 'Expedition to Moab', p. 219.
23. Oman, *A History of the Art of War*, pp. 151–52.
24. See Deschamps, *Royaume de Jérusalem*, pp. 83–84. Cf. Kennedy, *Crusader Castles*, p. 48.
25. Mayer, *Montréal*, pp. 118–19; Sinibaldi, 'Karak Castle', pp. 106–9.
26. There are also similarities with the eastern gate at Sahyun (Saone) and western gate at Belvoir, both of which are of a similar size and were accessed by bridges that could have been removed or destroyed during periods of threat. My thanks to Denys Pringle for sharing with me his thoughts on this matter.
27. Biller, Burger and Häffner, 'Neues zu den Burgen', p. 50.
28. Cart. Hosp. no. 207, 1:160; RRH no. 279, p. 71.
29. Mayer, *Montréal*, p. 227.
30. Pringle, 'Crusader Castles in Jordan', p. 678. Cf. Sinibaldi, 'Karak Castle', pp. 107–9; Pringle, 'Hospitaller Castles', pp. 157–58.

31. Deschamps, *Royaume de Jérusalem*, pp. 81–82, 90. Cf. Biller, Burger and Häffner, 'Neues zu den Burgen', p. 49.
32. Tristram, *The Land of Moab*, p. 72 (fig. 4).
33. Bliss, 'Expedition to Moab', p. 219; Deschamps, *Royaume de Jérusalem*, p. 87.
34. Deschamps, *Royaume de Jérusalem*, p. 86. Cf. Mauss and Sauvaire, 'Voyage de Jérusalem a Kerak', p. 108; Rey, *Étude sur les monuments*, p. 135.
35. Cf. Deschamps, *Royaume de Jérusalem*, pp. 85–86.
36. Cf. Deschamps, *Royaume de Jérusalem*, pp. 88–89.
37. Brown, 'The Middle Islamic Palace at Karak', p. 311.
38. Biller, Burger and Häffner, 'Neues zu den Burgen', pp. 50–52; Nucciotti and Fragai, 'Ayyubid Reception Halls'.
39. See Fulton, *Artillery in the Era of the Crusades*. Cf. Biller, Burger and Häffner, 'Neues zu den Burgen', pp. 48, 50; Pringle, 'Crusader Castles in Jordan', p. 678.
40. Cf. Deschamps, *Royaume de Jérusalem*, pp. 85, 88–89.
41. Pringle, *Churches*, 1:288–89 (no. 130). Cf. Deschamps, *Royaume de Jérusalem*, pp. 87–88.
42. Burckhardt, *Travels in Syria*, p. 380; Irby and Mangles, *Travels*, pp. 363–64; Lynch, *Expedition to the River Jordan*, p. 358; Mauss and Sauvaire, 'Voyage de Jérusalem a Kerak', p. 109; Tristram, *The Land of Moab*, pp. 76–77. Cf. Layard, *Early Adventures*, 1:92; de Saulcy, *Voyages*, 1:376.
43. Deschamps, *Royaume de Jérusalem*, pp. 81, 88; Brown, 'Mamluk Palace at Kerak', pp. 287–94; idem, 'The Middle Islamic Palace at Karak', pp. 311–32. See also Brown, 'Palaces in Middle Islamic Transjordan', pp. 543–58.
44. Brown, 'Palaces in Middle Islamic Transjordan', pp. 552–54.
45. Brown, 'Mamluk Palace at Kerak', pp. 292–98; idem, 'The Middle Islamic Palace at Karak', pp. 317–30. The initial dating was based on a damaged copper coin found in the subfloor, which was believed to be a Mamluk issue from the early fourteenth century. The coin was later judged to be a much earlier Seleucid issue from the first or second century BC, see Brown, 'The Middle Islamic Palace at Karak', p. 320 n. 2.
46. Brown, 'The Middle Islamic Palace at Karak', p. 332; idem, 'Palaces in Middle Islamic Transjordan', pp. 556. For the palace at Montreal and other parallels, see Brown, '1986 Excavations: Late Islamic Shobak', pp. 227–42; idem, 'Palaces in Middle Islamic Transjordan', pp. 543–58; Vannini and Nucciotti, 'Da Petra a Shawbak', pp. 64–68; Rugiadi, 'Il compleso di ricevimento', pp. 202–16.
47. Nucciotti and Fragai, 'Ayyubid Reception Halls'; Fragai, 'New Research', pp. 191–92.
48. Brown, 'The Middle Islamic Palace at Karak', pp. 316–17; Nucciotti and Fragai, 'Ayyubid Reception Halls'.
49. See Seetzen, *Reisen*, 1:420; Burckhardt, *Travels in Syria*, p. 380; Lynch, *Expedition to the River Jordan*, p. 358; Mauss and Sauvaire, 'Voyage de Jérusalem a Kerak', p. 108; Bliss, 'Expedition to Moab', p. 219; Deschamps, *Royaume de Jérusalem*, p. 88.
50. For a diagram of the third, see Mesqui, Goepp and Yehuda, 'Bread for all', p. 12 (fig. 23).
51. Burckhardt, *Travels in Syria*, p. 380; Lynch, *Expedition to the River Jordan*, p. 358; Mauss and Sauvaire, 'Voyage de Jérusalem a Kerak', p. 108; Bliss, 'Expedition to Moab', p. 219. Cf. Seetzen, *Reisen*, 1:414.
52. Deschamps, *Royaume de Jérusalem*, pp. 83, 87, 89–90; Pringle, *Churches*, 1:287; Milwright, *Fortress of the Raven*, pp. 63–64; Korn, *Ayyubidische Architektur*, 2:94; Biller, Burger and Häffner, 'Neues zu den Burgen', p. 48.
53. Cf. Deschamps, *Royaume de Jérusalem*, pp. 90–92.
54. Cf. Deschamps, *Royaume de Jérusalem*, p. 87.
55. Deschamps, *Royaume de Jérusalem*, p. 90.
56. Deschamps, *Royaume de Jérusalem*, p. 91; Brown, 'The Middle Islamic Palace at Karak', pp. 315–16; Fragai, 'New Research', pp. 191–98, 202–4.
57. Bliss, 'Expedition to Moab', p. 219. See also Deschamps, *Royaume de Jérusalem*, pp. 91–92.
58. Deschamps, *Royaume de Jérusalem*, pp. 87, 92–93.

Chapter 7: The Town

1. Bliss, 'Expedition to Moab', p. 218.
2. Tristram, *The Land of Moab*, p. 71
3. Mauss and Sauvaire, 'Voyage de Jérusalem a Kerak', p. 109; Bliss, 'Expedition to Moab', pp. 218–19. Cf. Deschamps, *Royaume de Jérusalem*, p. 95.
4. Irby and Mangles, *Travels*, p. 361; Lynch, *Expedition to the River Jordan*, p. 356; de Saulcy, *Voyages*, 1:364–65; Mauss and Sauvaire, 'Voyage de Jérusalem a Kerak', pp. 106, 202 (no. 20); Tristram, *The Land of Moab*, pp. 68–69; Bliss, 'Expedition to Moab', p. 219; Deschamps, *Royaume de Jérusalem*, p. 95; RCEA no. 3965, 10:245–46. Cf. Luynes, *Voyage d'exploration*, 1:100; Gautier, 'Autour de la mer Morte', p. 84.
5. For example, Ibn Battuta, p. 72.
6. Tristram, *The Land of Moab*, pp. 72–73; Gautier, 'Autour de la mer Morte', p. 95; Libbey and Hoskins, *The Jordan Valley*, 1:330; Bliss, 'Expedition to Moab', p. 219; Deschamps, *Royaume de Jérusalem*, p. 95.
7. RCEA no. 4733, 12:222–23; Mauss and Sauvaire, 'Voyage de Jérusalem a Kerak', pp. 115, 199 (no. 17); de Saulcy, *Voyages*, 1:364.
8. Deschamps, *Royaume de Jérusalem*, pp. 96–97.
9. Mauss and Sauvaire, 'Voyage de Jérusalem a Kerak', pl. 11, 12, 13; Hornstein, 'A Visit to Kerak', facing p. 96; Musil, *Arabia Petraea*, 1:49 (fig. 1), 52, 64; Gautier, 'Autour de la mer Morte', pl. 15; Libbey and Hoskins, *The Jordan Valley*, 1:339, 341–42, 347.
10. Musil, *Arabia Petraea*, 1:51–52.
11. RCEA no. 4734, 12:223–24; Mauss and Sauvaire, 'Voyage de Jérusalem a Kerak', p. 205 (no. 21); Milwright, *Fortress of the Raven*, p. 87.
12. Cf. Deschamps, *Royaume de Jérusalem*, pp. 95–96.
13. Musil, *Arabia Petraea*, 1:52.
14. Musil, *Arabia Petraea*, 1:52.
15. Bliss, 'Expedition to Moab', p. 220; Dowling, 'Kerak in 1896', p. 330. Cf. Musil, *Arabia Petraea*, 1:52.
16. Irby and Mangles, *Travels*, p. 362; MacMichael, *Journey*, p. 208; de Saulcy, *Voyages*, 1:366; Mauss and Sauvaire, 'Voyage de Jérusalem a Kerak', p. 110; RCEA no. 3800A, 10:276; Pringle, *Churches*, 1:287 (no. 129).
17. Gautier, 'Autour de la mer Morte', p. 95; Deschamps, *Royaume de Jérusalem*, p. 97.
18. Tristram, *The Land of Moab*, p. 78; Bliss, 'Expedition to Moab', p. 220; Pringle, *Churches*, 1:287 (no. 129).
19. Lynch, *Expedition to the River Jordan*, pp. 357, 358; Dowling, 'Kerak in 1896', p. 330; Pringle, *Churches*, 1:293 (no. 131). For the monastic community, see also Musil, *Arabia Petraea*, 1:52.
20. Gautier, 'Autour de la mer Morte', p. 95; Pringle, *Churches*, 1:293–95 (no. 132).
21. Mauss and Sauvaire, 'Voyage de Jérusalem a Kerak', pp. 109, 110, 122; Deschamps, *Royaume de Jérusalem*, p. 93. Cf. Bliss, 'Expedition to Moab', p. 220; Hornstein, 'A Visit to Kerak', p. 95; Dowling, 'Kerak in 1896', p. 331.
22. Cf. Musil, *Arabia Petraea*, 1:64.

Bibliography

Sources composed before *c.*1500

Chronicles and Histories
Abu'l-Fida', *al-Mukhtasar fi ta'rikh al-bashar*
   Trans. P.M. Holt. *The Memoirs of a Syrian Prince: Abu'l-Fida', Sultan of Hamah (672–732/ 1273–1331).* Wiesbaden: Steiner, 1983.
Abu Shama, *Kitab al-Raudatain*
   Ed. and trans. as *Livre des deux Jardins.* RHC Or 4–5. Paris: Imprimerie nationale, 1898–1906.
Albert of Aachen, *Historia Ierosolimitana*
   Ed. and trans. Susan B. Edgington. *Historia Ierosolimitana: History of the Journey to Jerusalem.* Oxford: Oxford University Press, 2007.
Ambroise, *Estoire de la guerre sainte*
   Ed. and trans. Marianne Ailes and Malcolm Barber. *The History of the Holy War.* 2 vols. Woodbridge: Boydell, 2003.
Annales of Egmond
   Ed. Georg Heinrich Pertz. *Annales Egmundani.* MGH Scriptores 16. Hanover: Impensis Bibliopolii Avlici Hahniani, 1859.
Al-'Ayni, *'Iqd al-Juman*
   Ed. and trans. as *Le collier de perles.* RHC Or 2a. Paris: Imprimerie nationale, 1887.
Baha' al-Din ibn Shaddad, *al-Nawadir al-sultaniyya wa al-mahasin al-Yusufiyya*
   Trans. D.S. Richards. *The Rare and Excellent History of Saladin.* Aldershot: Ashgate, 2001.
Bar Hebraeus, *Makhtebhânûth Zabhnê*
   Ed. and trans. Ernest A. Wallis Budge. *The Chronography of Gregory Abū al-Faraj.* 2 vols. London: Oxford University Press, 1932, reprinted Amsterdam: Philo Press, 1976.
Baybars al-Mansuri, *Mukhtar al-akhbar: Ta'rikh al-dawla al-ayyubiyya wa-dawlat al-mamalik*
   Trans. David Cook. In *Chronicles of Qalawun and His Son al-Ashraf Khalil.* Abingdon: Routledge, 2020.
Baybars al-Mansuri, *al-Tuhfa al-mulukiyya fi'l-dawla al-turkiyya*
   Trans. David Cook. In *Chronicles of Qalawun and His Son al-Ashraf Khalil.* Abingdon: Routledge, 2020.
Baybars al-Mansuri, *Zubdat al-fikra fi ta'rikh al-hijra*
   Trans. David Cook. In *Chronicles of Qalawun and His Son al-Ashraf Khalil.* Abingdon: Routledge, 2020.
Burchard of Mount Sion, *Descriptio Terrae Sanctae*
   Ed. J.C.M. Laurent. In *Peregrinatores medii aevi quatuor.* Leipzig: J.C. Hinrichs, 1864.
   Trans. Denys Pringle. In *Pilgrimage to Jerusalem and the Holy Land, 1187–1291.* Farnham: Ashgate, 2012.
Daniel the Abbot, *Pilgrimage*
   Trans. William F. Ryan. In *Jerusalem Pilgrimage, 1099–1185.* Ed. John Wilkinson. London: The Hakluyt Society, 1988.

Eracles Translation and Continuation of William of Tyre
  Ed. as *L'Estoire de Eracles empereur et la conqueste de la terre d'outremer*. RHC Oc 1–2, Paris: Imprimerie royale/impériale, 1844–59.
  Part. trans. Janet Shirley. In *Crusader Syria in the Thirteenth Century: The* Rothelin *Continuation of the* History *of William of Tyre with part of the* Eracles *or* Acre *text*. Aldershot: Ashgate, 1999.
Ernoul, *Chronique*
  Ed. M.L. de Mas Latrie. *Chronique d'Ernoul et de Bernard le Trésorier*. Paris: Jules Renouard, 1871.
Francesco Balducci Pegolotti, *Libro di divisamenti di paesi e di misure di mercatantie*
  Ed. Allan Evans. *La Practica della Mercatura*. Cambridge: The Medieval Academy of America, 1936.
Fulcher of Chartres, *Historia Hierosolymitana*
  Ed. Heinrich Hagenmeyer. *Historia Hierosolymitana*. Heidelberg: C. Winter, 1913.
  Trans. Frances Rita Ryan. *A History of the Expedition to Jerusalem, 1095–1127*. Ed. Harold S. Fink. Knoxville: University of Tennessee Press, 1969.
Gregory IX, *Regesta*
  Ed. Lucien Auvray. *Les Registres de Grégoire IX*. 4 vols. 1896–1955. Paris: Albert Fontemoing, 1896–1910.
History of the Patriarchs
  Pts. 1–4: ed. and trans. B.T.A. Evetts. *History of the Patriarchs of the Coptic Church of Alexandria*. In *Patrologia Orientalis* 2 [1.2] (1904), 4 [1.4] (1904), 21 [5.1] (1909), 50 [10.5] (1914).
  Pts. 5–12: ed. and trans. O.H.E. Khs-Burmester, et al. *History of the Patriarchs of the Egyptian Church: Known as the History of the Holy Church*. 3 vols. (appearing as vols. 2–4). Cairo: Société d'archéologie copte, 1943–74.
Hugh Eteriano, *Letters*
  Ed. J.-P. Migne. In *De haeresibus quas Graeci in Latinos devolvunt libri tres*. PL 202. Paris: J.-P. Migne, 1855.
Ibn 'Abd al-Zahir, *al-Rawd al-zahir fi sirat al-Malik al-Zahir*
  Ed. and trans. Abdul Aziz al-Khowayter. 'A critical edition of an unknown source for the life of al-Malik al-Zahir Baibars, with introduction, translation, and notes'. In 3 vols. Unpublished PhD thesis: S.O.A.S., 1960.
Ibn 'Abd al-Zahir, *Tashrif al-ayyam wa-l-'usur fi sirat al-Malik al-Mansur*
  Trans. David Cook. In *Chronicles of Qalawun and His Son al-Ashraf Khalil*. Abingdon: Routledge, 2020.
Ibn al-'Adim, Kamal al-Din, *Zubdat al-halab fi ta'rikh Halab*
  Ed. and trans. as *Extraits de la chronique d'Alep*. RHC Or 3. Paris: Imprimerie nationale, 1884.
  Trans. E. Blochet. 'Histoire d'Alep'. ROL 3 (1895), pp. 509–65; ROL 4 (1896), pp. 145–320; ROL 5 (1897), pp. 37–107; ROL 6 (1898), pp. 1–49, reprinted together as *Histoire d'Alep*. Paris: Ernest Leroux, 1900.
Ibn al-'Amid, al-Makin, *Kitab al-majmu' al-mubarak*
  Trans. Anne-Marie Eddé and Françoise Micheau. *Chronique des Ayyoubides (602-658 / 1205-6-1259-60)*. Paris: L'Académie des Inscriptions et Belles-Lettres, 1994.
Ibn al-Athir, *al-Kamil fi'l-ta'rikh*
  Trans. D.S. Richards. *The Annals of the Saljuq Turks*. Abingdon: Routledge, 2002.
  Trans. D.S. Richards. *The Chronicle of Ibn al-Athīr for the Crusading Period*. 3 vols. Aldershot: Ashgate, 2006–8.
Ibn Battuta, *Tuhfat al-nuzzar fi ghara'ib al-amsar wa-'aja'ib al-asfar*
  Trans. H.A.R. Gibb. *Ibn Battuta: Travels in Asia and Africa, 1325–1354*. London: Routledge, 1929.
Ibn al-Furat, *Ta'rikh al-duwal wa-l-muluk*
  Ed. and trans. U. and M.C. Lyons. *Ayyubids, Mamlukes and Crusaders: Selections from the Tarikh al-Duwal wa'l-Muluk of Ibn al-Furat*. 2 vols. Cambridge: Heffer, 1971.

Trans. David Cook. *Baybars' Successors: Ibn al-Furat on Qalawun and al-Ashraf.* Abingdon: Routledge, 2020.

Ibn Jum'a, *al-Bashat wa'l-qudat*
Trans. Henri Laoust. In *Les Gouverneurs de Damas sous les Mamlouks et les Premiers Ottomans.* Damascus: Institut française de Damas, 1952.

Ibn Jubayr, *Riḥla*
Trans. R.J.C. Broadhurst. *The Travels of Ibn Jubayr.* London, 1952, reprinted New Delhi: Goodword Books, 2001.

Ibn Khallikan, *Wafayat al-a'yan*
Trans. William Mac Guckin. *Biographical Dictionary.* 4 vols. Paris: Oriental Translation Fund of Great Britain and Ireland, 1843–71.

Ibn Muyassar, *Akhbar Misr*
Ed. and trans. as *Extraits d'Ibn Moyesser.* RHC Or 3. Paris: Imprimerie nationale, 1884.

Ibn al-Qalanisi, *Dhayl Ta'rikh Dimashq*
Trans. H.A.R. Gibb. *The Damascus Chronicle of the Crusades.* London: Luzac, 1967.

Ibn Sasra, *al-Durra al-mudi'a fi'l-dawla al-Zahiriya*
Ed. and trans. William M. Brinner. *A Chronicle of Damascus, 1389–1397.* 2 vols. Berkley: University of California Press, 1963.

Ibn Taghribirdi, *al-Nujum al-zahira fi muluk Misr wa'al-Qahira*
Trans. William Popper. *History of Egypt.* 8 vols. Berkley: University of California Press, 1954–63.

Ibn Tulun, *I'lam al-wara*
Trans. Henri Laoust. In *Les Gouverneurs de Damas sous les Mamlouks et les Premiers Ottomans.* Damascus: Institut française de Damas, 1952.

'Imad al-Din al-Isfahani, *Kitab al-fath al-qussi fi'l-fath al-qudsi*
Trans. Henri Massé. *Conquête de la Syrie et de la Palestine par Saladin.* Paris: Académie des inscriptions et belles-lettres, 1972.

Innocent III, *Regesta*
Ed. J.-P. Migne. *Regestorum sive epistolarum.* PL 214–17. Paris: Garnier, 1890–91.

Itinerarium peregrinorum et gesta regis Ricardi
Ed. William Stubbs. *Chronicles and Memorials of the Reign of Richard I, Volume I: Itinerarium Peregrinorum et Gesta Regis Ricardi.* Rolls Series. London: Longman et al., 1864.
Trans. Helen J. Nicholson. *Chronicle of the Third Crusade: A Translation of the* Itinerarium Peregrinorum et Gesta Regis Ricardi. Aldershot: Ashgate, 1997.

James of Vitry, *Historia orientalis*
Ed. and trans. Jean Donnadieu. *Histoire orientale / Historia orientalis.* Turnhout: Brepols, 2008.

James of Vitry, *Letters*
Ed. R.B.C. Huygens, trans. G. Duchet-Suchaux. *Lettres de la Cinquième Croisade.* Turnhout: Brepols, 1998.

John of Ibelin, *Assises*
Ed. Peter Edbury. *John of Ibelin: Le Livre des Assises.* Leiden: Brill, 2003.

John of Joinville, *Vie de Saint Louis*
Ed. and trans. Jacques Monfrin. *Vie de Saint Louis.* Paris: Classiques Garnier Multimédia, 1998.

John Kinnamos, *Historia*
Trans. Charles M. Brand. *Deeds of John and Manuel Comnenus.* New York: Columbia University Press, 1976.

Lignages d'outremer
Ed. Marie-Adélaïde Nielen. *Lignages d'outremer.* Paris: Académie des inscriptions et belles-lettres, 2003.

Al-Maqrizi, *Ighathat al-umma bi-kashf al-ghumma*
Trans. Adel Allouche. *Mamluk Economics: A Study and Translation of al-Maqrizi's* Ighathah. Salt Lake City: University Utah Press, 1994.

Al-Maqrizi, *Khitat*
    Trans. Urbain Bouriant and M. Paul Casanova. *Description topographique et historique de l'Égypte.* 4 vols. Paris: Libraire de la Société Asiatique, 1895–1920.
Al-Maqrizi, *al-Suluk*
    Trans. R.J.C. Broadhurst. *A History of the Ayyūbid Sultans of Egypt.* Boston: Twayne Publishers, 1980.
    Trans. Étienne Marc Quatremère. *Histoire des Sultans Mamlouks, de l'Égypte.* 4 parts, in 2 vols. Paris: Oriental Translation Fund: 1837–45.
Matthew of Edessa, *Patmowt'iwn*
    Trans. Ara Edmond Dostourian. *The Chronicle of Matthew of Edessa.* Lanham: University Press of America, 1993.
Matthew Paris, *Chronica maiora*
    Ed. Henry Richards Luard. *Chronica Majora.* 7 vols. Rolls Series. London: Longman et al., 1872–83.
    Trans. J.A. Giles. *Matthew Paris's English History: From the Year 1235 to 1273.* 3 vols. London: Bohn, 1852–54.
Michael the Syrian, *Chronique*
    Trans. Matti Moosa. *The Chronicle of Michael Rabo (The Great): A History from the Creation.* Teaneck: Beth Antioch Press, 2014.
Niketas Choniates, *Historia*
    Trans. Harry J. Magoulias. *O City of Byzantium: Annals of Niketas Choniates.* Detroit: Wayne State University Press, 1984.
Al-Nuwayri, *Nihayat al-arab fi funun al-adab*
    Trans. Elias Muhanna. *The Ultimate Ambition in the Arts of Erudition: A compendium of Knowledge from the Classical Islamic World.* New York: Penguin, 2016.
Oliver of Paderborn, *Historia Damiatina*
    Ed. Hermann Hoogeweg. In *Die Schriften des Kölner Domscholasters, späteren Bischofs von Paderborn und Kardinal-Bischofs von S. Sabina.* Tubingen: Litterarischen Verein in Stuttgart, 1894.
    Trans. John J. Gavigan. In *Christian Society and the Crusades.* Ed. Edward Peters. Philadelphia: University of Pennsylvania Press, 1971.
Philip of Novara, *Gestes des Chiprois*
    Ed. Gaston Raynaud. In *Les Gestes des Chiprois.* Recueil de Chroniques Françaises. Paris: Société de l'Orient Latin, 1887, reprinted Osnabruck: Otto Zeller, 1968.
    Trans. John L. La Monte. *The Wars of Frederick II Against the Ibelins in Syria and Cyprus.* New York: Columbia University Press, 1936.
Philip of Novara, *Livre de Forme de Plait*
    Ed. and trans. Peter Edbury. *Philip of Novara:* Le Livre de Forme de Plait. Nicosia: Cyprus Research Centre, 2009.
Ralph of Caen, *Gesta Tancredi*
    Ed. as *Gesta Tancredi.* RHC Oc. 3. Paris: Imprimerie impériale, 1866.
    Trans. Bernard S. Bachrach and David S. Bachrach. *The* Gesta Tancredi *of Ralph of Caen, A History of the Normans on the First Crusade.* Aldershot: Ashgate, 2005.
Ralph of Diceto, *Ymagines historiarum*
    Ed. William Stubbs. In *Opera Historica: The Historical Works of Ralph de Diceto, Dean of London.* 2 vols. London: Longman, 1876.
Regni Ierosolymitani brevis historia
    Ed. Luigi Tommaso Belgrano. *Annali Genovesi di Caffaro e de' suoi continuatori.* Vol. 1. *Fonti per la storia d'Italia.* Genoa: Tipografia del R. Istituto Sordo-Muti, 1890.
Roger of Howden, *Chronica*
    Ed. William Stubbs. *Chronica.* 4 vols. Rolls Series. London: Longmans et al., 1868–71.
    Trans. Henry T. Riley. *The Annals of Roger de Hoveden: Comprising the History of England and of Other Countries of Europe, from A.D. 732 to A.D. 1201.* 2 vols. London: Bohn, 1853.

Roger of Howden, *Gesta*
    Ed. William Stubbs. *Gesta regis Henrici secundi Benedicti abbatis.* 2 vols. London: Longmans et al., 1867.
Roger of Wendover, *Flores historiarum*
    Ed. Henry G. Hewlett. *Rogeri de Wendover Liber qui Dicitur Flores Historiarum ab Anno Domini MCLIV. Annoque Henrici Anglorum Regis Secundi Primo / The Flowers of History by Roger de Wendover: From the Year of Our Lord 1154, and the First Year of Henry the Second, King of the English.* 3 vols. London: Her Majesty's Stationary Office, 1886–89.
    Trans. J. A. Giles. *Roger of Wendover's Flowers of History, comprising the History of England from the descent of the Saxons to A.D. 1235.* 2 vols. London: Bohn, 1849.
Rothelin Continuation of William of Tyre
    Ed. as *La continuation de Guillaume de Tyre de 1229 a 1261, dite du manuscrit de Rothelin.* RHC Oc 2. Paris: Imprimerie impériale, 1859.
    Trans. Janet Shirley. *Crusader Syria in the Thirteenth Century: The* Rothelin *Continuation of the* History *of William of Tyre with part of the* Eracles *or* Acre *text.* Aldershot: Ashgate, 1999.
Templar of Tyre, *Gestes des Chiprois*
    Ed. and trans. Laura Minervini. *Cronaca del Templare di Tiro (1243–1314).* Naples: Liguori Editore, 2000.
    Trans. Paul Crawford. *The 'Templar of Tyre': Part III of the Deeds of the Cypriots.* Aldershot: Ashgate, 2003.
Thietmar, *Peregrinatio*
    Ed. J.C.M. Laurent. *Mag. Thitmari Peregrinatio.* Hamburg, 1857.
    Trans. Denys Pringle. In *Pilgrimage to Jerusalem and the Holy Land, 1187–1291.* Farnham: Ashgate, 2012.
Usama ibn Munqidh, *Kitab al-i'tibar*
    Trans. Paul M. Cobb. *The Book of Contemplation: Islam and the Crusades.* London: Penguin, 2008.
William of Rubruck, *Journey*
    Ed. Francisque Michel and Thomas Wright. *Relations des voyages de Guillaume de Rubruk, Bernard le sage et Saewulf.* Paris: Bourgogne et Martinet, 1839.
    Trans. Peter Jackson. *The Mission of Friar William of Rubruck.* London: The Hakluyt Society, 1990.
William of Tyre, *Chronicon*
    Ed. R.B.C. Huygens. *Cronique.* Corpus Christianorum Continuatio Mediaeualis 63. Turnhout: Brepols, 1986.
    Trans. Emily A. Babcock and A.C. Krey. *A History of Deeds Done Beyond the Sea.* 2 vols. New York: Octagon Books, 1976.

Cartularies and Collections
Barber, Malcolm and Keith Bate, eds. *Letters from the East: Crusaders, Pilgrims and Settlers in the 12th–13th Centuries.* Farnham: Ashgate, 2010.
Bora, Fozia. *Writing History in the Medieval Islamic World: The Value of Chronicles as Archives.* London: Bloomsbury, 2019.
Bresc-Bautier, Geneviève, ed. *Le cartulaire du chapitre du Saint-Sépulcre de Jérusalem.* Paris: Geuthner, 1984.
Broussillon, Bertrand de. 'La charte d'André II de Vitré et le siège de Karak en 1184'. *Bulletin Historique et Philologique* (1899), pp. 47–53.
Broussillon, Bertrand de. *La maison de Craon, 1050–1480.* 2 vols. Paris: Alphonse Picard et fils, 1893.
Brightman, F.E., ed. *Liturgies: Eastern and Western.* Vol. 1. Oxford: Oxford University Press, 1896.
Chalandon, F, ed. 'Un diplôme inédit d'Amaury I roi de Jérusalem en faveur de l'abbaye du Temple-Notre Seigneur'. ROL 8 (1900–1), pp. 311–17.

Delaborde, H.-François, ed. *Chartes de Terre Sainte provenant de l'abbaye de Notre-Dame. de Josaphat.* Paris: Ernest Thorin, 1880.

Delaville Le Roulx, J., ed. *Cartulaire général de l'ordre des Hospitaliers de S. Jean de Jérusalem.* 4 vols. Paris: Ernest Leroux, 1894–1906.

Delaville Le Roulx, J., ed. 'Chartes de Terre Sainte'. ROL 11 (1908), pp. 181–91.

Delaville Le Roulx, J., ed. 'Inventaire de pièces de Terre Sainte de l'ordre de l'Hôpital'. ROL 3 (1895), pp. 36–106.

Edbury, Peter W. *The Conquest of Jerusalem and the Third Crusade: Sources in Translation.* Aldershot: Scolar Press, 1996.

Hampe, Karl. 'Reise nach England vom Juli 1895 bis Februar 1896'. *Neues Archiv der Gesellschaft für Ältere Deutsche Geschichtskunde* 22 (1897), pp. 223–86.

Kohler, C. 'Chartes de l'abbaye de Notre-Dame de la Vallée de Josaphat en Terre Sainte'. ROL 7 (1899), pp. 108–222.

Kohler, C. 'Documents inédits concernant l'Orient latin et les croisades'. ROL 7 (1899), pp. 1–37.

Le Strange, Guy. *Palestine under the Moslems.* Boston: Houghton, Mifflin and Co., 1890.

Mayer, Hans Eberhard, ed. *Die Urkunden der Lateinischen Könige von Jerusalem.* In 4 vols. MGH Diplomata regum Latinorum Hierosolymitanorum. Hanover: Hahnsche Buchhandlung, 2010.

Répertoire chronologique d'épigraphie arabe. Ed. E. Comb, et al. 18 vols. Cairo: Institut Français d'Archéologie Orientale, 1931–1991.

Röhricht, Reinhold, ed. *Regesta Regni Hierosolymitani.* Innsbruck: Libraria Academica Wagneriana, 1893.

Röhricht, Reinhold, ed. *Regesta Regni Hierosolymitani: Additamentum.* Innsbruck: Libraria Academica Wagneriana, 1904.

Strehlke, Ernestus, ed. *Tabulae Ordinis Theutonici.* Berlin: Weidmannos, 1869.

Sources composed after *c.*1500

Abel, F.-M. 'Épigraphie Grecque'. *Revue Biblique* 39.4 (Oct. 1930), pp. 565–70.

Abel, F.-M. *Géographie de la Palestine.* 3rd ed. 3 vols. Paris: Lecoffre, 1967.

Abujaber, Raouf. 'Cereal Production During the Nineteenth Century and its Effect on Transjordanian Life: A Short Study of Multiculturalism'. SHAJ 8 (2004), pp. 41–44.

Abujaber, Raouf. '"They Came and Stayed": A Study of Population Movements into Jordan 1800–1948'. SHAJ 10 (2009), pp. 399–404.

Amitai, Reuven. 'Hülegü and the Ayyubid Lord of Transjordan'. *Archivum Eurasiae Medii Aevi* 9 (1995–97), pp. 5–16.

Amitai, Reuven. 'Mongol Raids into Palestine (A.D. 1260 and 1300)'. *Journal of the Royal Asiatic Society* 119.2 (1987), pp. 236–55.

Amitai, Reuven. *Mongols and Mamluks: The Mamluk-Ilkhanid War, 1260–1281.* Cambridge: Cambridge University Press, 1995.

Amitai, Reuven. 'Notes on the Ayyubid Inscriptions at al-Subayba (Qal'at Nimrud)'. *Dumbarton Oaks Papers* 43 (1989), pp. 113–19.

'Amr, Abdel-Jalil. 'A New Ayyubid Inscription from *al-Karak,* Jordan'. *Zeitschrift des Deutschen Palästina-Vereins.* 105 (1989), pp. 166–72.

'Amr, Khairieh, et al. 'Summary Results of the Archaeological Project at Khirbat an-Nawafla / Wadi Musa'. *Annual of Department of Antiquities of Jordan* 44 (2000), pp. 231–55.

Barber, Malcolm. 'The Career of Philip of Nablus in the kingdom of Jerusalem'. In *The Experience of Crusading: Volume II, Defining the Crusader Kingdom.* Ed. Peter Edbury and Jonathan Phillips. Cambridge: Cambridge University Press, 2003. pp. 60–75.

Bartlett, John R. *Mapping Jordan Through Two Millennia.* Maney Publishing, 2008, reprinted London: Routledge, 2017.

Benvenisti, Meron. *The Crusaders in the Holy Land.* Jerusalem: Israel Universities Press, 1970, reprinted New York: Macmillan, 1972.

Biller, Thomas, Daniel Burger and Hans-Heinrich Häffner. 'Neues zu den Burgen des Königreichs Jerusalem in Transjordanien: Montréal (Shobak), Li Vaux Moïse (Wu'eira), Kerak'. In *Architektur, Struktur, Symbol: Streifzüge durch die Architekturgeschichte von der Antike bis zur Gegenwart*. Ed. Maike Kozok. Petersberg: Michael Imhof Verlag, 1999, pp. 33–58.

Bliss, Frederick Jones. 'Narrative of an Expedition to Moab and Gilead in March, 1895'. PEQ 27.3 (1895), pp. 203–35.

Brett, Michael. *The Fatimid Empire*. Edinburgh: Edinburgh University Press, 2017.

Brett, Michael. 'The Fatimids and the Counter-Crusade'. In *Egypt and Syria in the Fatimid, Ayyubid and Mamluk Eras: V*. Ed. U. Vermeulen and K. D'hulster. Orientalia Lovaniensia Analecta 169. Leuven: Peeters, 2007, pp. 15–25.

Brooker, Colin H. and Ernst Axel Knauf. 'Review: Crusader Institutions by Joshua Prawer'. *Zeitschrift des Deutschen Palästina-Vereins* 104 (1988), pp. 184–88.

Brown, Robin M. 'A 12th Century A.D. Sequence from Southern Transjordan: Crusader and Ayyubid Occupation at el-Wu'eira'. ADAJ 31 (1987), pp. 267–88.

Brown, Robin M. 'The Distribution of Thirteenth- to Fifteenth-Century Glazed Wares in Transjordan: A Case Study from the Kerak Plateau'. In *The Archaeology of Jordan and Beyond*. Ed. Lawrence E. Stager, Joseph A. Greene and Michael D. Coogan. Winona Lake: Eisenbrauns, 2000, pp. 84–99.

Brown, Robin M. 'Excavations in the 14th Century A.D. Mamluk Palace at Kerak'. *Annual of Department of Antiquities of Jordan* 33 (1989), pp. 287–304.

Brown, Robin M. 'The Middle Islamic Palace at Karak Castle: A New Interpretation of the Grand Qā'a (Reception Hall)'. ADAJ 57 (2013), pp. 309–35.

Brown, Robin M. 'Palaces in Middle Islamic Transjordan: Reflections of the Royal Tradition of Bilad ash-Sham'. SHAJ 12 (2016), pp. 543–60.

Brown, Robin M. 'Petra Deserti (al-Karak) and the Landscape of Frankish Transjordan in European Cartography from the Twelfth through the Fifteenth Century'. SHAJ 11 (2013), pp. 703–33.

Brown, Robin M. 'Summary Report of the 1986 Excavations: Late Islamic Shobak'. ADAJ 32 (1988), pp. 225–45.

Brown, Robin M. and Kevin Rielly. 'Faunal Remains from Excavations in the Ayyubid Palace at Shawbak Castle in Southern Transjordan'. *Berytus* 51–52 (2008–2009), pp. 169–98.

Brown, Robin M. and Kevin Rielly. 'A Twelfth Century Faunal Assemblage from al-Wu'ayra in the Southern Highlands of Jordan'. ADAJ 54 (2010), pp. 121–42.

Brünnow, Rudolf-Ernst and Alfred von Domaszewski. *Die Provincia Arabia*. 3 vols. Strassburg: Verlag von Karl J. Trübner, 1904–9.

Buck, Andrew D. 'Between Byzantium and Jerusalem? The Principality of Antioch, Renaud of Châtillon, and the Penance of Mamistra in 1158'. *Mediterranean Historical Review* 30.2 (2015), pp. 107–24.

Burckhardt, John Lewis. *Travels in Syria and the Holy Land*. London: John Murray, 1822.

Burke, Katherine Strange. 'A Note on Archaeological Evidence for Sugar Production in the Middle Islamic Periods in Bilad al-Sham'. *Mamluk Studies Review* 8.2 (2004), pp. 109–18.

Cahen, Claude and Ibrahim Chabbouh. 'Le testament d'al-Malik as-Salih Ayyub'. *Bulletin d'études orientales* 29 (1977), pp. 97–114.

Conder, Claude Reignier. *Heth and Moab: Explorations in Syria in 1881 and 1882*. Palestine Exploration Fund. London: Richard Bentley and Son, 1885.

Corbino, Chiara A. and Paul Mazza. 'Faunal Remains from the Castles of Al-Wu'ayra, Petra and Shawbak (Crusader Period)'. SHAJ 11 (2013), pp. 159–64.

Corbino, Chiara A. and Paul Mazza. 'How and Where did the Inhabitants of Shawbak Castle Live? The Faunal Remains'. SHAJ 10 (2009), pp. 679–84.

De Meulemeester, Johnny and Denys Pringle. 'Al'Aqaba Castle: Jordan'. *Château Gaillard* 22 (2006), pp. 97–102.

Deschamps, Paul. *Les Château des Croisés en Terre-Sainte, II: La défense du Royaume de Jérusalem*. Paris: Librarie orientaliste Paul Gruthner, 1939.

Deschamps, Paul. 'Étude sur un texte latin énumérant les possessions musulmanes dans le royaume de Jérusalem vers l'année 1239'. *Syria* 23 (1942–43), pp. 86–104.

Dotti, Francesca. 'Qal'at al-Shawbak: An Interpretation on the Basis of the Epigraphic Data'. In *Proceedings of the 6th International Congress of the Archaeology of the Near East*. Vol. 3. Ed. Paolo Matthiae, et al. Wiesbaden: Harrassowitz Verlag, 2010, pp. 23–36.

Doughty, Charles M. *Travels in Arabia Deserta*. 2 vols. Cambridge University Press, 1888. 3rd ed. London: Philip Lee Warner, 1921.

Dowling, Theodore E. 'Kerak in 1896'. PEQ 28.4 (1896), pp. 327–32.

Drory, Joseph. 'Al-Nasir Dawud: A Much Frustrated Ayyubid Prince'. *Al-Masaq* 15.2 (2003), pp. 161–87.

Drory, Joseph. 'The Prince Who Favored the Desert: Fragmentary Biography of al-Nasir Ahmad (d. 745/1344)'. In *Mamluks and Ottomans*. Ed. David J. Wasserstein and Ami Ayalon. London: Routledge, 2006, pp. 19–33.

Edbury, Peter W. 'Ernoul, *Eracles*, and the Collapse of the Kingdom of Jerusalem'. In *The French of Outremer: Communities and Communications in the Crusading Mediterranean*. Ed. Laura K. Morreale and Nicholas L. Paul. New York: Fordham University Press, 2018, pp. 44–67.

Edbury, Peter W. *John of Ibelin and the Kingdom of Jerusalem*. Woodbridge: Boydell, 1997.

Edbury, Peter W. and John Gordon Rowe. *William of Tyre: Historian of the Latin East*. Cambridge: Cambridge University Press, 1988.

Eddé, Anne-Marie. *Saladin*. Paris: Éditions Flammarion, 2008. Trans. Jane Marie Todd, as *Saladin*. Cambridge: Harvard University Press, 2011.

El-Isa, Zuhair. 'Earthquake Studies of Some Archaeological Sites in Jordan'. SHAJ 2 (1985), pp. 229–36.

Ellenblum, Ronnie. 'Who Built Qal'at al-Subayba?' *Dumbarton Oaks Papers* 43 (1989), pp. 103–12.

Faucherre, Nicolas. 'La forteresse de Shawbak (Crac de Montréal), une des premières forteresses Franques sous son corset mamelouk'. In *La fortification au temps des croisades*. Ed. Nicolas Faucherre, Jean Mesqui and Nicolas Prouteau. Rennes: Presses Universitaires des Rennes, 2004, pp. 43–66.

Fedden, Robin and John Thomson. *Crusader Castles*. London: Art & Technics, 1950, reprinted London: John Murray, 1957.

Fisher, Clarence S. and Chester C. McCown. 'Jerash-Gerasa 1930'. *Annual of the American Schools of Oriental Research* 11 (1929–30), pp. 1–59.

Fragai, Lorenzo. 'New Research Perspectives on the Mamluk Qa'a at Kerak Castle: Building Archaeology and Historical Contextualization'. *Journal of Islamic Archaeology* 6.2 (2019), pp. 187–208.

France, John. *Hattin*. Oxford: Oxford University Press, 2015.

Fulton, Michael S. *Artillery in the Era of the Crusades*. Leiden: Brill, 2018.

Fulton, Michael S. *Contest for Egypt: The Collapse of the Fatimid Caliphate, the Ebb of Crusader Influence, and the Rise of Saladin*. Leiden: Bill, 2022.

Fulton, Michael S. 'Disaster in the Delta? Sicilian Support for the Crusades and the Siege of Alexandria, 1174'. In *Warfare in the Norman Mediterranean*. Ed. Georgios Theotokis. Woodbridge: Boydell, 2020, pp. 225–38.

Fulton, Michael S. 'Frankish Intervention in Egypt during the Reign of Amalric: Conquest or Extortion?' In *Exploring Outremer*. Ed. Rabei G. Khamisy, Rafael Y. Lewis and Vardit R. Shotten-Hallel. Routledge, forthcoming.

Fulton, Michael S. 'A Ridge Too Far: The Siege of Saone/Sahyun in 1188 and Contemporary Trebuchet Technology'. *Crusades* 16 (2017), pp. 33–53.

Fulton, Michael S. 'The Siege of Montfort and Mamluk Artillery Technology in 1271: Integrating the Archaeology and Topography with the Narrative Sources'. *Journal of Military History* 83.3 (2019), pp. 689–717.

Fulton, Michael S. *Siege Warfare during the Crusades*. Barnsley: Pen and Sword, 2019.

Gautier, Lucien. 'Autour de la mer Morte'. *Revue genevoise de géographie* 39 (1900), pp. 25–158.

Gubser, Peter. *Politics and Change in al-Karak, Jordan: A Study of a Small Arab Town and District.* London: Oxford University Press, 1973.

Hamarneh, Basema, et al., 'Population Dynamics in the al-Karak Region in the Byzantine and Islamic Periods'. SHAJ 12 (2016), pp. 683–702.

Hamilton, Bernard. 'The Elephant of Christ: Reynald of Châtillon'. *Studies in Church History* 15 (1978), pp. 97–108.

Hamilton, Bernard. *The Latin Church in the Crusader States: The Secular Church.* London: Variorum, 1980.

Hamilton, Bernard. *The Leper King and his Heirs: Baldwin IV and the Crusader Kingdom of Jerusalem.* Cambridge: Cambridge University Press, 2000.

Hamilton, Bernard. 'Manuel I Comnenus and Baldwin IV of Jerusalem'. In *Kathegetria.* Ed. J. Chrysostomides. Camberley: Porphyrogenitus, 1988, pp. 353–75.

Hamilton, Bernard. 'Miles of Plancy and the Fief of Beirut'. In *The Horns of Hattin.* Ed. Benjamin Z. Kedar. Jerusalem: Yad Izhak Ben-Zvi, 1992, pp. 136–46.

Hammond, Philip C. *The Crusader Fort on El-Habis at Petra: Its Survey and Interpretation.* Salt Lake City: Middle East Centre, University of Utah, 1970.

Hiestand, Rudolf. 'Zwei unbekannte Diplome der Lateinischen Könige von Jerusalem aus Lucca'. *Quellen und Forschungen aus italienischen Archiven und Bibliotheken* 50 (1971), pp. 1–57.

Hill, John Gray. 'A Journey East of the Jordan and the Dead Sea, 1895'. PEQ 28.1 (1896), pp. 24–46.

Hill, John Gray. 'A Journey to Petra – 1896'. PEQ 29.1 [cont. 29.2] (1897), pp. 35–44 [cont. 134–44].

Hill, John Gray. *With the Beduins.* London: T. Fisher Unwin, 1891.

Holt, Peter M. 'The Sultanate of al-Mansur Lachin (696–8/1296–9)'. *Bulleting of the School of Oriental and African Studies, University of London* 36.3 (1973), pp. 521–32.

Hornstein, Charles Alexander. 'A Visit to Kerak and Petra'. PEQ 30.2 (1898), pp. 94–103.

Hosler, John D. *The Siege of Acre, 1189–1191.* New Haven: Yale University Press, 2018.

Hull, Edward. 'Narrative of an Expedition through Arabia and Petraea, the Valley of the Arabah, and Western Palestine'. PEQ 46.2 (1884), pp. 114–36.

Humphreys, R. Stephen. *From Saladin to the Mongols: The Ayyubids of Damascus, 1193–1260.* Albany: State University of New York Press, 1977.

Hütteroth, Wolf-Dieter and Kamal Abdulfattah. *Historical Geography of Palestine, Transjordan and southern Syria in the Late 16th Century.* Erlangen: Frankischen Geographischen Gesellschaft, 1977.

Irby, Charles Leonard and James Mangles. *Travels in Egypt and Nubia, Syria and Asia Minor.* London: T. White and Co., 1823.

Irwin, Robert. *The Middle East in the Middle Ages: The Early Mamluk Sultanate 1250–1382.* Carbondale: Southern Illinois University Press, 1986.

Jackson, Peter. *The Seventh Crusade, 1244–1254: Sources and Documents.* Aldershot: Ashgate, 2007.

Johns, Jeremy. 'Islamic Settlement in Arḍ al-Karak'. SHAJ 4 (1992), pp. 363–68.

Jones, Ian W., Thomas E. Levy and Mohammad Najjar. 'Khirbat Nuqayb al-Asaymir and Middle Islamic Metallurgy in Faynan: Surveys of Wadi al-Ghuwayb and Wadi al-Jariya in Faynan, Southern Jordan'. *Bulletin of the American Schools of Oriental Research* 368 (Nov. 2012), pp. 67–102.

Kennedy, Hugh. *Crusader Castles.* Cambridge: University of Cambridge Press, 1994.

King, G.R.D, et al. 'Survey of Byzantine and Islamic Sites in Jordan: Third Season Preliminary Report (1982), the Southern Ghor'. ADAJ 31 (1987), pp. 439–59.

Klein, F.A. 'Missionary Tour into a Portion of the Trans-Jordan Countries, Jebel Ajlun, the Belka, and Kerek'. *Church Missionary Intelligencer* 5 (1869), pp. 62–64, 92–96, 123–28, 151–53.

Klein, F.A. 'Notes on a Journey to Moab'. PEQ 12.4 (1880), pp. 249–55.

Korn, Lorenz. *Ayyubidische Architektur in Ägypten und Syrien. Bautätigkeit im Kontext von Politik und Gesellschaft, 564–658/1169–1260.* 2 vols. Heidelberg: Heidelberger Orientverlag, 2004.

La Monte, John L. 'The Viscounts of Naplouse in the Twelfth Century'. *Syria* 19 (1938), pp. 272–78.

La Viere Leiser, Gary. 'The Crusader Raid in the Red Sea in 578/1182–83'. *Journal of the American Research Centre in Egypt* 14 (1997), pp. 87–100.

Lagrange, Marie-Joseph. 'Notre exploration de Pétra'. *Revue Biblique* 6 (1897), pp. 208–30.

Lawrence, T.E. *Crusader Castles.* Ed. Denys Pringle. Oxford: Oxford University Press, 1988.

Layard, A. Henry. *Early Adventures in Persia, Susiana and Babylon.* 2 vols. New York: Longman et al., 1887.

Lev, Yaacov. *Saladin in Egypt.* Leiden: Brill, 1999.

Lev, Yaacov. 'Saladin's Economic Policies and the Economy of Ayyubid Egypt'. In *Egypt and Syria in the Fatimid, Ayyubid and Mamluk Eras: V.* Ed. U. Vermeulen and K. D'hulster. Orientalia Lovaniensia Analecta 169. Leuven: Peeters, 2007, pp. 307–48.

Libbey, William and Franklin E. Hoskins. *The Jordan Valley and Petra.* 2 vols. New York: G.P. Putnam's Sons, 1905.

Linton, Gregory and Daniel Hoddman. 'Report of 1999 and 2001 Karak Resources Project Regional Survey'. ADAJ 48 (2004), pp. 267–84.

Little, Donald P. 'Data from the Haram Documents on Rugs in Late 14th Century Jerusalem'. In *Carpets of the Mediterranean Countries, 1400–1600.* Ed. Robert Pinner and Walter Denny. London: Hali, 1986, pp. 83–94.

Little, Donald P. 'The Haram Documents as Sources for the Arts and Architecture of the Mamluk Period'. *Muqarnas* 2 (1984), pp. 61–72.

Luynes, Honoré Théodoric d'Albert, duc de. *Voyage d'exploration a la Mer Morte a Petra.* 2 vols (and atlas). Paris: Arthus Bertrand [pref. 1874].

Lynch, W.F. *Narrative of the United States' Expedition to the River Jordan and the Dead Sea.* Philadelphia: Lea and Blanchard, 1849.

Lyons, Malcolm Cameron and D.E.P. Jackson. *Saladin: the Politics of the Holy War.* Cambridge: Cambridge University Press, 1982.

MacDonald, Burton. 'Human Presence/Absence in the Southern Segment of the Transjordanian Plateau'. SHAJ 10 (2009), pp. 767–86.

MacMichael, William. *Journey from Moscow to Constantinople in the Years 1817, 1818.* London: John Murray, 1819.

Majali, Rafat el and Abdul Rahim Mas'ad. 'Trade and Trade Routes in Jordan in the Mamluke Era (AD 1250–1516)'. SHAJ 3 (1987), pp. 311–16.

Mallet, Alex. 'A Trip down the Red Sea with Reynald of Châtillon'. *Journal of the Royal Asiatic Society* 18 (2008), pp. 141–53.

Marcotulli, Chiara and Elisa Pruno. 'Teindre ou ne pas teindre. Là est le problème! La cas du site de Shawbak (Jordanie)'. In *Artisanats et métiers en Méditerranée médiévale et moderné.* Ed. Sylvain Burri and Mohamed Ouerfelli. Publication Universite Provence, 2018, pp. 187–202.

Marino, Luigi, et al. 'The Crusader Settlement in Petra'. *Fortress* 7 (1990), pp. 3–13.

Mariotti Lippi, M., M. Mori Secci and C. Bini. 'Archaeobotany in the Crusader Castle of al-Wu'Aira (Petra, Jordan)'. *Webbia* 63.1 (2008), pp. 69–79.

Mas Latrie, Louis de. *Les seigneurs du Crac de Montréal, appelés d'abord seigneurs de la terre au delà du Jourdain.* Venice: Marc Visentini 1883.

Mason, Robert B. and Marcus Milwright. 'Petrography of Middle Islamic Pottery from Karak'. *Levant* 30 (1998), pp. 175–90.

Mattingly, Gerald L. 'Al-Karak resources Project 1995: A Preliminary Report on the Pilot Season'. ADAJ 40 (1996), pp. 349–68.

Mauss, Christophe and Henri Sauvaire. 'Voyage de Jérusalem a Kerak et a Chaubak'. In Luynes, Honoré Théodoric d'Albert, duc de. *Voyage d'exploration a la Mer Morte a Petra.* Vol. 2. Paris: Arthus Bertrand, n.d.

Mayer, Hans Eberhard. 'Angevins *versus* Normans: The New Men of King Fulk of Jerusalem'. *Proceedings of the American Philosophical Society* 133.1 (Mar. 1989), pp. 1–25.

Mayer, Hans Eberhard. 'The Crusader Lordship of Kerak and Shaubak: Some Preliminary Remarks'. SHAJ 3 (1987), pp. 199–203.

Mayer, Hans Eberhard. 'Die Herrschaftsbildung in Hebron'. *Zeitschrift des Deutschen Palästina-Vereins* 101.1 (1985), pp. 64–81.

Mayer, Hans Eberhard. *Die Kreuzfahrerherrschaft Montréal (Šobak): Jordanien im 12. Jahrhundert.* Wiesbaden: Otto Harrassowitz, 1990.

Mayer, Hans Eberhard. 'Studies in the History of Queen Melisende of Jerusalem'. *Dumbarton Oaks Papers* 26 (1972), pp. 93–182.

Mayer, Hans Eberhard. 'The Wheel of Fortune: Seignorial Vicissitudes under Fulk and Baldwin III of Jerusalem'. *Speculum* 65.4 (Oct. 1990), pp. 860–77.

Meistermann, Barnabé. *Guide du Nil au Jourdain par le Sinaï a Pétra.* Paris: Alphonse Picard et fils, 1909.

Meistermann, Barnabé. *Nouveau guide de Terre Sainte.* Paris: Alphonse Picard et fils, 1907.

Mesqui, Jean, Maxime Goepp and Lisa Yehuda. 'Bread for all: Double-chambered baking ovens in castles of the military orders; Le Crac des Chevaliers (Syria), Le Chastellet du gué de Jacob, Belvoir, and Arsur (Israel)'. In *Crusading and Archaeology: Some Archaeological Approaches to the Crusades.* Ed. Vardit R. Shotten-Hallel and Rosie Weetch. New York: Routledge, 2020, pp. 116–40.

Miller, J. Maxwell. *Archaeological Survey of the Kerak Plateau.* Atlanta: Scholars Press, 1991.

Milwright, Marcus. 'Central and Southern Jordan in the Ayyubid Period: Historical and Archaeological Perspectives'. *Journal of the Royal Asiatic Society* 16.1 (2006), pp. 1–27.

Milwright, Marcus. *The Fortress of the Raven: Karak in the Middle Islamic Period (1100–1650).* Leiden: Brill, 2008.

Milwright, Marcus. 'Reynald of Châtillon and the Red Sea Expedition of 1182–83'. In *Noble Ideals and Bloody Realities: Warfare in the Middle Ages.* Ed. Niall Christie and Maya Yazigi. Leiden: Brill, 2006.

'The Moabite Stone'. PEQ 2.5 (1870), pp. 169–83.

Morton, Nicholas. *The Crusader States and their Neighbours: A Military History, 1099–1187.* Oxford: Oxford University Press, 2020.

Al-Mubaidin, Mohannad. 'Aspects of the Economic History of Damascus during the First Half of the Eighteenth Century'. In *Syria and Bilad al-Sham under Ottoman Rule.* Ed. Peter Sluglett with Stefan Weber. Leiden: Brill, 2010, pp. 137–54.

Müller-Wiener, Wolfgang. *Burgen der Kreuzritter.* Munich: Deutscher Kunstverlag, 1966. Trans. J. Maxwell Brownjohn as *Castles of the Crusaders.* London: Thames and Hudson, 1966.

Murray, Alan V. 'Baldwin II and His Nobles: Baronial Factionalism and Dissent in the Kingdom of Jerusalem, 1118–1134'. *Nottingham Medieval Studies* 38 (1994), pp. 60–85.

Murray, Alan V. *Crusader Kingdom of Jerusalem: A Dynastic History, 1099–1125.* Oxford: P&G, 2000.

Musil, Alois. *Arabia Petraea.* 3 vols. Vienna: Alfred Hülder, 1907–8.

Neustadt, David. 'The Plague and Its Effects upon the Mamluk Army'. *Journal of the Royal Asiatic Society* 78.1 (1946), pp. 67–73.

Nickerson, M.E. 'The Seigneury of Beirut in the Twelfth Century and the Brisebarre Family of Beirut-Blanchegarde'. *Byzantion* 19 (1949), pp. 141–85.

Northedge, Alastair. 'The Fortifications of Qal'at 'Amman ('Amman Citadel): Preliminary Report'. ADAJ 27 (1983), pp. 437–60.

Northrup, Linda S. *From Slave to Sultan: The Career of al-Mansrur Qalawun.* Stuttgart: Steiner, 1998.

Nucciotti, Michele and Lorenzo Fragai. 'Ayyubid Reception Halls in Southern Jordan: Towards a "Light Archaeology" of Political Power'. SHAJ 13 (forthcoming).

Oman, Charles. *A History of the Art of War: The Middle Ages from the Fourth to the Fourteenth Century.* London: Methuen, 1898.

Pace, James H. 'The Cisterns of the al-Karak Plateau'. ADAJ 40 (1996), pp. 369–74.

Palmer, E.H. 'The Desert of the Tíh and the Country of Moab'. PEQ 3.1 (1871), pp. 3–76.

Palmer, E.H. 'Letters [I, II] from Mr. E.H. Palmer'. PEQ 2.5 (1870), pp. 524–59.

Palmer, E.H. 'Letters [III, IV] from Mr. E.H. Palmer'. PEQ 2.6 (1870), pp. 311–24.

Perry, Guy. 'Isabella II or Yolanda? The Name of the Queen of Jerusalem and Spouse of Frederick II'. Medieval Prosopography 30 (2015), pp. 73–86.

Petry, Carl F. The Mamluk Sultanate: A History. Cambridge: Cambridge University Press, 2022.

Popper, William. Egypt and Syria under the Circassian Sultans, 1382–1468 AD. 2 vols. Berkley: University of California Press, 1955–57.

Powell, James M. Anatomy of a Crusade, 1213–1221. Philadelphia: University of Pennsylvania Press, 1986.

Prawer, Joshua. The Crusaders' Kingdom: European Colonialism in the Middle Ages. New York: Praeger, 1972, reprinted London: Phoenix Press, 2001.

Pringle, Denys. 'The Castles of Ayla (al-'Aqaba) in the Crusader, Ayyubid and Mamluk Periods'. In Egypt and Syria in the Fatimid, Ayyubid and Mamluk Eras: 5. Ed. U. Vermeulen and J. Van Steenbergen. Orientalia Lovaniensia Analecta 140. Leuven: Peeters, 2005, pp. 333–53.

Pringle, Denys. The Churches of the Crusader Kingdom of Jerusalem. 4 vols. Cambridge: Cambridge University Press, 1993–2009.

Pringle, Denys. 'Crusader Castles in Jordan'. In The Archaeology of Jordan. Ed. Burton MacDonald, Russell Adams and Piotr Bienkowski. Sheffield: Sheffield Academic Press, 2001, pp. 677–84.

Pringle, Denys. 'Hospitaller Castles and Fortifications in the Kingdom of Jerusalem, 1136–1291'. Medievalista 33 (2023), pp. 153–97.

Pringle, Denys. Pilgrimage to Jerusalem and the Holy Land, 1187–1291. Farnham: Ashgate, 2012.

Pringle, Denys. 'The Role of Castellans in the Latin East'. In Castelos das Ordens Militares: Atas do Encontro Internacional. Ed. Isabel Cristina Ferreira Fernandes. Vol 2. Lisbon: Direção-Geral do Património Cultural, 2013, pp. 183–204.

Pringle, Denys. Secular Buildings in the Crusader Kingdom of Jerusalem. Cambridge: Cambridge University Press, 1997.

Pringle, Denys. 'The Spring of Cresson in Crusading History'. In Dei Gesta per Francos. Ed. Michel Balard, Benjamin Z. Kedar and Jonathan Riley-Smith. Aldershot: Ashgate, 2001, pp. 231–40.

Pruno, Elisa. 'Medieval Pottery in South Jordan between Little and Great Traditions: A Case-Study from Shawbak Castle'. In In & Around: Ceramiche e comunità. Ed. Margherita Ferri, Cecilia Moine and Lara Sabbionesi. Florence: All'Insegna del Giglio, 2015, pp. 237–40.

Pruno, Elisa and Raffaele Ranieri. 'Ceramiche da cucina nella Transgiordania meridionale (secc. XII-XIII): l'osservatorio stratigrafico di Shawbak'. Temporis Signa 11 (2016), pp. 37–46.

Pruno, Elisa and Raffaele Ranieri. 'Medieval Pottery in South Jordan: The Case-Study of HMPW in ash-Shawbak Castle'. SHAJ 13 (forthcoming), pp. 223–30.

Rey, Emanuel Guillaume. Étude sur les monuments de l'architecture militaire des croisés en Syrie et dans l'île de Chypres. Paris: Imprimerie nationalise, 1871.

Rey, Emanuel Guillaume. 'Les seigneurs de Mont-Réal et de la Terre d'outre le Jourdain'. ROL 4 (1896), pp. 19–24.

Riley-Smith, Jonathan. 'The Motives of the Earliest Crusaders and the Settlement of Latin Palestine, 1095–1100'. English Historical Review 98 (Oct. 1983), pp. 721–36.

Rogan, Eugene L. Frontiers of the State in the Late Ottoman Empire: Transjordan, 1850–1921. Cambridge: Cambridge University Press, 1999.

Rugiadi, Martina. 'Il complesso di ricevimento del palazzo ayyubide a Shawbak'. Vicino Oriente 16 (2002), pp. 201–25.

Saulcy, Félicien de. Voyages autour de la Mer Morte et dans les Terre Bibliques. 2 vols. (and Atlas). Paris: Gide et J. Baudry, 1853.

Schick, Robert. 'Southern Jordan in the Fatimid and Seljuq Periods'. Bulletin of the American Schools of Oriental Research 305 (Feb. 1997), pp. 73–85.

Schlumberger, Gustave. Renaud de Chatillon. Paris: E. Plon, Nourrit, etc., 1898.

Schmid, Stephan G. 'The International Wadi Farasa Project (IWFP) 2000 Season'. ADAJ 45 (2001), pp. 343–58.

Schmid, Stephan G. 'The International Wadi Farasa Project (IWFP) Preliminary Report on the 2001 Season'. ADAJ 46 (2002), pp. 257–79.

Schmid, Stephan G. 'The International Wadi Farasa Project (IWFP) Preliminary Report on the 2004 Season'. ADAJ 49 (2005), pp. 71–79.

Schmid, Stephan G. 'The International Wadi Farasa Project (IWFP): Preliminary Report on the 2006 Season'. ADAJ 51 (2007), pp. 141–50.

Schmid, Stephan G. 'The International Wadi Farasa Project (IWFP): Preliminary Report on the 2007 Season'. ADAJ 53 (2009), pp. 95–106.

Schmid, Stephan G. 'The International Wadi Farasa Project (IWFP): Preliminary Report on the 2009 Season'. ADAJ 43 (2010), pp. 221–36.

Schmid, Stephan G. and Jacqueline Studer. 'The International Wadi Farasa Project (IWFP) Preliminary Report of the 2002 Season'. ADAJ 47 (2003), pp. 473–88.

Schmid, Stephan G. and André Barmasse. 'The International Wadi Farasa Project (IWFP) Preliminary Report on the 2003 Season'. ADAJ 48 (2004), pp. 333–46.

Schmid, Stephan G. and André Barmasse. 'The International Wadi Farasa Project (IWFP) Preliminary Report on the 2005 Season'. ADAJ 50 (2006), pp. 217–27.

Schriwer, Charlotte. '"From Water Every Living Thing": Water Mills, Irrigation and Agriculture in the Bilad al-Sham: Perspectives on History, Architecture, Landscape and Society, 1100–1850 AD'. Unpublished PhD thesis: University of St Andrews, 2006.

Seetzen, Ulrich Jasper. *A Brief Account of the Countries adjoining the Lake of Tiberias, the Jordan, and the Dead Sea*. Bath: Melyer and Son, 1810.

Seetzen, Ulrich Jasper. *Reisen durch Syrien, Palästina, Phönicien, die Transjordan-Länder*, Arabia Petraea und Unter-Aegypten. Ed. F. Kruse. 4 vols. Berlin: G. Reimer, 1854–59.

Al-Shqour, Reem. *The Aqaba Khans and the Origins of Khans in Jordan: An Archaeological Approach*. Piscataway: Gorgias Press, 2019.

Al-Shqour, Reem, Johnny De Meultemeester, Davy Herremans. 'The "Aqaba Castle Project"'. SHAJ 10 (2009), pp. 641–55.

Sinibaldi, Micaela. 'The Franks in Southern Transjordan and the Contribution of Ceramic Studies: A Preliminary Report of the Pottery Assemblages of al-Bayda and Wadi Farasa'. ADAJ 53 (2009), pp. 449–64.

Sinibaldi, Micaela. 'The Crusader Lordship of Transjordan (1100–1189): Settlement Forms, Dynamics and Significance'. *Levant* (2022), https://doi.org/10.1080/00758914.2022.2033016.

Sinibaldi, Micaela. 'Karak Castle in the Lordship of Transjordan: Observations on the Chronology of the Crusader-period Fortress'. In *Bridge of Civilization: The Near East and Europe c.1100–1300*. Ed. Peter Edbury, Denys Pringle and Balázs Major. Oxford: Archaeopress, 2019, pp. 97–114.

Sinibaldi, Micaela. 'Settlement in Crusader Transjordan (1100–1189): A Historical and Archaeological Study'. Unpublished PhD thesis: Cardiff University, 2014, https://orca.cardiff.ac.uk/id/eprint/69267/.

Stern, S.M. *Fatimid Decrees*. London: Faber and Faber, 1964.

Thorau, Peter. *Sultan Baibars I. von Ägypten: Ein Beitrag zur Geschichte des Vorderen Orients im 13. Jahrhundert*. Wiesbaden: Ludwig Reichert, 1987. Trans. P.M. Holt as *The Lion of Egypt: Sultan Baybars I & the Near East in the Thirteenth Century*. Harlow: Longman, 1992.

Tibble, Steven. *Monarchy and Lordships in the Latin Kingdom of Jerusalem, 1099–1291*. Oxford: Oxford University Press, 1989.

Tonghini, Cristina and Andrea Vanni Desideiri. 'The Material Evidence from al-Wu'ayra: A Sample of Pottery'. SHAJ 7 (2001), pp. 707–19.

Tristram, H.B. *The Land of Moab*. 2nd ed. London: John Murray, 1874.

Vannini, Guido and Michele Nucciotti. 'Da Petra a Shawbak. Archeologia di una frontiera. La missione in Giordana dell'Università di Firenze'. In *La Giordania che abbiamo attraversato*.

Voci e immagini da un viaggio. Ed. Silvia Lusuardi Siena and Claudia Perassi. Scilla: Graphic e-Business, 2012, pp. 55–73.

Vannini, Guido and Cristina Tonghini. 'Medieval Petra: The Stratigraphic Evidence from Recent Archaeological Excavations at al-Wu'ayra'. SHAJ 6 (1997), pp. 371–84.

Walker, Bethany J. 'Mamluk Investment in Southern Bilad Al-Sham in the Eighth/Fourteenth Century: The Case of Hisban'. *Journal of Near Eastern Studies* 62.4 (Oct. 2003), pp. 241–61.

Walker, Bethany J. 'Mamluk Investment in Transjordan: a "Boom and Bust" Economy'. *Mamluk Studies Review* 8.2 (2004), pp. 119–47.

Walker, Bethany J. 'Militarization to Nomadization: The Middle and Late Islamic Periods'. *Near Eastern Archaeology* 62.4 (1999), pp. 202–32.

Walker, Bethany J. 'The Phenomenon of the "Disappearing" Villages of Late Medieval Jordan, as Reflected in Archaeological and Economic Sources'. *Bulletin d'études orientales* 60 (2011), pp. 161–76.

Walker, Bethany J. 'The Role of Agriculture in Mamluk-Jordanian Power Relations'. *Bulletin d'études orientales* 57 (2006–2007), pp. 79–99.

Walmsley, Alan. 'Fatimid, Ayyubid and Mamluk Jordan and the Crusader Interlude'. In *The Archaeology of Jordan*. Ed. Burton MacDonald, Russell Adams and Piotr Bienkowski. Sheffield: Sheffield Academic Press, 2001, pp. 515–59.

Walmsley Alan. 'The Middle Islamic and Crusader Periods'. In *Jordan: An Archaeological Reader*. Ed. Russell B. Adams. London: Equinox, 2008, pp. 495–537.

Walmsley, Alan. 'Restoration or Revolution? Jordan Between the Islamic Conquest and the Crusades: Impressions of Twenty-Five Years of Archaeological Research'. SHAJ 7 (2001), pp. 633–40.

Whitcomb, Donald. 'A Fatimid Residence at Aqaba, Jordan'. ADAJ 32 (1988), pp. 207–24.

Whitcomb, Donald. 'The Town and Name of 'Aqaba: An Inquiry into the Settlement History from an Archaeological Perspective'. SHAJ 6 (1997), pp. 359–63.

Zayadine, Fawzi. 'Caravan Routes Between Egypt and Nabataea and the Voyage of Sultan Baybars to Petra in 1276'. SHAJ 2 (1985), pp. 159–74.

Index